ONE MAN SHOW

The Stages of
BARRY HUMPHRIES
ANNE PENDER

ABC Books

 This research was supported under the Australian Research Council's Discovery Projects funding scheme (project DP0770554). The views expressed herein are those of the author and are not necessarily those of the Australian Research Council.

 The ABC 'Wave' device is a trademark of the Australian Broadcasting Corporation and is used under licence by HarperCollins*Publishers* Australia.

First published in Australia in 2010
by HarperCollins*Publishers* Australia Pty Limited
ABN 36 009 913 517
www.harpercollins.com.au

Copyright © Anne Pender 2010

The right of Anne Pender to be identified as the author of this work has been asserted by her in accordance with the *Copyright Amendment (Moral Rights) Act 2000*.

This work is copyright. Apart from any use as permitted under the *Copyright Act 1968*, no part may be reproduced, copied, scanned, stored in a retrieval system, recorded, or transmitted, in any form or by any means, without the prior written permission of the publisher.

HarperCollins*Publishers*
25 Ryde Road, Pymble, Sydney, NSW 2073, Australia
31 View Road, Glenfield, Auckland 0627, New Zealand
A 53, Sector 57, Noida, UP, India
77–85 Fulham Palace Road, London W6 8JB, United Kingdom
2 Bloor Street East, 20th floor, Toronto, Ontario M4W 1A8, Canada
10 East 53rd Street, New York NY 10022, USA

National Library of Australia Cataloguing-in-Publication data:

Pender, Anne.
  One man show: the stages of Barry Humphries / Anne Pender.
  ISBN 978 0 7333 2591 5 (pbk.)
  Includes index.
  Bibliography.
  Humphries, Barry, 1934–
  Comedians – Australia – Biography.
  Entertainers – Australia – Biography.
  Authors, Australian – Biography.
792.23092

Cover design: Design by Committee
Cover images: Front cover image of Barry Humphries by the Arts Centre, Performing Arts Collection, Melbourne; all other images © Lewis Morley, Lewis Morley's Flashbacks Collection, National Library of Australia.
Back cover image: © Patrick Hamilton, Newspix
Author photo: David Elkins, UNE; teapot by Suzanne Forsyth-Hatch
Typeset in 12/15pt Adobe Caslon Pro by Kirby Jones

To Peter

Introduction

Children are usually the most reliable witnesses of the activities of their parents. When Emily Humphries was just four years old and living in Little Venice in London, her father, Barry, brought home a large, white, blow-up sofa, and set it up in the living room. It was a very expensive and rather uncomfortable piece, and Emily's mother, Ros, was distinctly unimpressed. But Barry liked its novelty value, and thought it should stay. In fact, Ros was furious that Barry had bought such an item when they were short of money.

The next day, Spike Milligan appeared at the front door. He walked around the sofa, and then sat down on it, as the Humphries family waited for a reaction, a verdict. A second later he lit a cigarette, took a few puffs, stole a glance at Barry and then, a look of triumph on his face, stubbed out the cigarette on the seat of the sofa, reducing the controversial purchase to a wrinkled, stinking mess on the floor. From that day onward, Barry knew that two comedians in one room was a dangerous thing.

In an enlightening conversation, Barry's younger daughter offered insights about her father, her family and their world, insights that brought the strands of the research for this portrait of the public and the private John Barry Humphries together. Emily's stories showed that the creative spirit is alive in his children, and reinforced the idea of Humphries as a man of many masks. It is the masks that delight and intrigue an audience. And it is the masks that make Humphries such an enigmatic character, a very difficult subject for a biographer. He has given thousands of interviews and yet he remains elusive even to members of his own family.

A biographer, some say, must surrender to his or her subject.[1] The works Humphries has created over a sixty-year period, from his occasional writing as a schoolboy right through to his current projects, provide the raw material for this life story. Humphries' antics on the street and at parties, and his behaviour on and off stage over more than half a century are documented here in an account of an outlandish young man from an ordinary family, his rise to prominence as a comic actor and his attitudes to his work, to his country of origin and to his adopted country.

Manning Clark cast Humphries among the mythmakers and prophets of Australia as he witnessed the man 'enriching the culture which had been dominated by the straiteners'.[2] Peter Conrad described Humphries' adolescence as a 'one-man modern movement'.[3] Humphries' satire has been praised for exposing the 'kingdom of nothingness' and the American theatre critic John Lahr admired the art of the clown who takes the public to the 'frontiers of the marvellous'.[4] Yet Barry Humphries has also suffered from intense and vitriolic criticism of his humour throughout his career. Until recently he did not rate a mention in the work of scholars and cultural commentators.

Writing biography is an audacious act. The results are often inadequate and rarely satisfying. Yet the lives of those we admire are compelling. We want to understand and explain motivation, background, influence and art. Barry Humphries is a remarkable satirist and his life is anarchic in many respects. He has transformed Australian popular theatre and brought a distinctive Australian humour to audiences all over the world. This is the story of a provocative entertainer who is happiest alone on stage in the theatre performing his one-man show.

CONTENTS

Introduction   vii

PART ONE – DADA BOY
Chapter 1   Suburban Eden   3
Chapter 2   The Wubbos   22
Chapter 3   A Perfectly Timed Spectacle   31
Chapter 4   Orsino and the Monster   44
Chapter 5   Waiting for Barry   54
Chapter 6   Eucalypso Nights   66
Chapter 7   E-SCAPE   77

PART TWO – ACTOR
Chapter 8   A City for Performance   87
Chapter 9   The Expatriate Game   97
Chapter 10   Homecoming   108
Chapter 11   Soho Nights   116
Chapter 12   Highgate Babies   125
Chapter 13   Bazza   134
Chapter 14   My Favourite Things   140
Chapter 15   Suitor to the Devil   146
Chapter 16   On a Tightrope   152
Chapter 17   True British Spunk   162

PART THREE – DAME

Chapter 18	Sobriety	171
Chapter 19	The Mythical Australian	181
Chapter 20	Damehood	188
Chapter 21	Anarchist	201
Chapter 22	Housewife Superstar	206
Chapter 23	Hell's Kitchen	220
Chapter 24	Regeneration	227

PART FOUR – ARRIVISTE

Chapter 25	Last Night of the Poms	243
Chapter 26	Intercourse with Millions	252
Chapter 27	Chat	261
Chapter 28	Formica Lady	274
Chapter 29	Mount Edna	281
Chapter 30	Queen of the West End	299
Chapter 31	Suburbs of the Sacred	308

PART FIVE – BAWD

Chapter 32	Mauve-haired Madonna	317
Chapter 33	Suburbs of the Mind	331
Chapter 34	Flashbacks	343
Chapter 35	Banishing Edna	355

PART SIX – SATIRIST

Chapter 36	Dragging Up	363
Chapter 37	Recognition	383

Postscript: Life is Just a Show	394
Notes	397
Select Bibliography	416
Index	423
Picture Credits	449
Acknowledgements	451

PART ONE
DADA BOY

CHAPTER 1

Suburban Eden

When he was three years old, Barry's mother's help, Edna, walked him down the hill from his home to Mrs Flint's kindergarten. Barry was terrified of Mrs Flint, a stern widow dressed in an oversized apron and thick brown stockings. The mornings were interminable at kindergarten. Sometimes Mrs Flint threatened children who cried and left them outside in her backyard, riding in endless circles on their tricycles. One day she forced Barry to count to one hundred. He stood in the corner desperately trying to remember the numbers, and hoping to hear Edna's voice in the front hall, ready to take his hand and lead him away from his tormentor. Hot tears of rage and frustration ran down his face.

Another day, after he committed some minor naughtiness, Mrs Flint seized Barry by the forearm and marched him down the corridor. She opened a cupboard and forced him into it, closing the door with a loud bang. Alone in the darkness he howled, and when his tears subsided he listened to the muffled sound of the other children playing outside. At last he heard the chimes of the doorbell, and Mrs Flint greeting mothers and nannies who had come to collect their children at the end of the session. 'Please come Edna,' he whispered to himself. 'Please hurry.' Another few minutes passed and Barry heard footsteps. Mrs Flint opened the door and silently ushered him out of the closet, and back along the corridor. On the porch, bathed in sunshine, stood the smiling figure of Edna. He ran towards her without looking back.

When Louisa Agnes Brown married John Albert Eric Humphries (always called Eric by family and friends) at the small Holy Trinity Church in the lower middle-class suburb of Thornbury, Melbourne, on 31 October 1931, most of the guests already knew one another. Both families had lived in Thornbury for many years. The eldest son, Eric had followed his father, Jack, into the building trade. He had met Louisa at church and had enjoyed her performances in concerts in the church hall. His bride-to-be had a fine singing voice and long slender legs.

Both families were poor and had struggled like so many others during the Depression years. But by the time of his marriage at the age of twenty-six, Eric had established a building business, and would soon take his bride to live in a new housing enclave in Camberwell, the Golf Links Estate. This was not just a move across Melbourne, but a leap into a new social sphere.

Louisa, or 'Lou', Brown was the fourth of six children, five girls and one boy. The Browns were staunch churchgoers, sometimes attending services three times a day. Louisa's mother had died of a stroke in 1928, leaving the unmarried daughters, Elsie and Lou, and their brother Breckston to look after their father and bring up their younger sister, Dorothy, fondly called Billie by family and friends. It was not easy.

Lou became a professional dressmaker, and before she married Eric she worked at the Myer Emporium in the city, managing a team of seamstresses who altered dresses, jackets and ballgowns for the ladies of Melbourne. She would watch as each customer paraded from the dressing room in her new garment, and then give instructions to the young women in the back room who would undertake the alterations. A shy woman with a dry wit, Lou was a perfectionist and a worrier; she only occasionally showed her more theatrical side.

Eric Humphries was a confident, happy and generous man. Gregarious and jovial in social situations, he was also hard-working and had an instinct for business. When blocks became available in the Golf Links Estate in the early 1930s at very reasonable prices, he immediately set about building the first of several substantial houses there, in Christowel Street. The estate offered a 'new Eden' in civic design. It was completely different to the suburb of Thornbury where Eric and Lou had grown up. There was no weatherboard or corrugated iron in this suburban idyll. Only brick, stone or concrete construction was allowed and roofs had to be made of tile or slate. Everything was highly regulated, with a minimum size of ten squares (93 m^2) for all the dwellings. The streets and footpaths of the estate were paved in smooth white cement, their names set into the paving. Each house boasted a 36-foot (11-metre) setback, grassy islands graced the intersections of the streets, and the public gardens offered a sense of 'old world order and quality'.[1]

Ignoring the flowering gums dotted sparsely around the estate, the new residents set about creating a leafy avenue of European trees for the garden suburb, planting pin oaks, cypress, prunus, silver birch and magnolias in the rich soil. When Eric began building there were only a few houses in Christowel Street, each on a large, cleared block of land. The first house Mr and Mrs Humphries occupied, at number 38, was a Tudor-inspired cottage with gables, a red tiled roof and two arched entrances. There were no limits on building style; as a result English cottages shared fences with mock Tudor, Georgian, Mediterranean and jazz moderne constructions. Eventually, Eric Humphries would be responsible for designing and building some eighteen houses of varying provenance on the estate.[2]

The area was special in another way as well: the district had been designated as 'dry' in 1920, which meant there were no pubs allowed. To this day Melbourne's Camberwell is still subject to the temperance laws established between the wars. Typically, residents of the estate were members of the professions, business people or civil servants. In addition to banning hotels they prohibited advertising in the area.

After she married, Lou still enjoyed trips into the city to meet her sisters for lunch. She was a keen decorator, and selected fashionable lamps and carpets for her house, even as Eric busied himself with the plans and construction of a new residence down the road.

On 17 February 1934 Louisa gave birth to John Barry Humphries (known as Barry) at St George's Hospital in Kew. While the birth itself was uncomplicated, her fair-haired baby was diagnosed as a 'lazy breather' and placed in an oxygen tent. When she brought him home she quickly adopted the then fashionable routine prescribed by Dr Truby King, leaving Barry in a pram to breathe in the fresh summer breezes for several hours a day, feeding him at regular intervals, and rationing cuddles and body contact. He was a delightfully easy baby who slept, fed and gurgled. When the new house at number 30 was ready, the family moved in. Eric sold number 38 and set about building yet another house in the street. Before Barry's third birthday they moved again, this time into an imposing neo-Georgian two-storey house at number 36. Constructed of red brick, it offered a sweeping view down the steep hill of Marlborough Avenue across the railway lines to Frog Hollow Reserve.

The new house was larger than the Humphries' previous homes, with four bedrooms and an office for Eric. There was even a tradesmen's entrance, and a hatch for bread and milk deliveries. The backyard was bare, but Eric immediately installed a sprinkler system and planted grass, and on a hot afternoon there was nothing the toddler Barry liked better than dashing between the showers of silvery spray from the sprinklers.

Another of his favourite pastimes was to dress up as a sailor, and to try on hats. He played with his wheelbarrow in the garden and relished trips to the beach with his parents. His father would gather him in his arms and hoist him onto his shoulders shouting joyfully, 'It's Sunny Sam!' As a little boy Barry accompanied Eric to the Camberwell market to buy oysters, and to the barber, where he and his father would take turns to have Mr McGrath cut their hair.[3] Sometimes Eric took Barry with him in the car to his building sites to check on the progress of the solid suburban villas he had been commissioned to construct for a whole generation of young, middle-class couples.

A few months before Barry celebrated his third birthday, Louisa gave birth to her second child, a dark-haired baby girl named Barbara Helen. Although it was quite unusual for children to go to kindergarten in the 1930s, when Barry's sister arrived, he was sent to Mrs Flint's establishment a few minutes walk from Christowel Street. Edna, whom he was fond of, walked Barry to and from kindergarten. Barry hated being sent away from the house, and felt rejected. He would tell awful tales about things that happened at kindergarten, and after the cupboard incident, Louisa decided not to continue her son's daily torture at the hands of Mrs Flint.

Barry was also distinctly unimpressed with his local primary school, Camberwell South State School, or, as the family referred to it, Peate Avenue school. Unlike the other children who ate their sandwiches in a noisy shed, Barry was collected by Eric each day in the Oldsmobile and driven home, where he enjoyed a relaxed lunch either in the back garden at a small picnic table or chatting to his parents inside. Lousia and Eric may not have been aware that they were setting their boy up as different, and perhaps superior, to other children.

Barry's early experience of school was not happy. The other children and his teacher seemed to dislike him. One day Barry took a toy submarine to school. A group of boys formed a circle around him in the treeless playground, and demanded that he hand over his prized toy. Barry picked up a handful of gravel in case he needed it to fend off the menacing boys who quickly backed off. When they returned to the classroom, Barry's teacher, Mrs Jensen, pulled him up in front of the class and reprimanded him. She sent him to a corner for the rest of the day as a punishment for throwing stones. Even worse, she hung a sign around his neck that read 'I AM A BULLY'. Barry was mortified at being chastised for something he had not done. It left a scar on the small boy who was not an aggressive child, but one who felt slights keenly.

Regardless of his schoolyard unpopularity, Barry was generally a cheerful boy who engaged in ordinary boyish activities. Once he took off at speed down the street on his bicycle and fell off beside an open manhole. Lou dashed after him, but when she caught up with him he had completely forgotten his injuries and was happily chatting to two workmen.

He didn't suffer Mrs Jensen's tyranny for long. The following year Barry's parents enrolled him at Camberwell Grammar School. It was a bracing bicycle ride away from home, and gave Barry a new sense of independence and freedom. Before long his teachers noticed his prodigious vocabulary and originality of expression. But Barry struggled with arithmetic. Eric worried about his son's inability to comprehend figures, but his attempts to help only made Barry's frustration worse.

Nor did Barry take to games. A cruel Scottish sportsmaster noticed his awkwardness in the gym, and belittled him with the nickname 'Granny' Humphries. The boys in his class yelled out 'Come on Granny' whenever Barry reluctantly participated in the hateful sports carnivals organised regularly for the boys. But Barry's skill with language and his ability to sketch were clear to all of his teachers. One teacher counselled another not to display Barry's extraordinary prose offerings because they made the other children's work look so poor.[4] His school reports were excellent and he flourished academically.

Performing in front of an audience was a regular expectation in the Humphries family. Afternoon tea gatherings featured performances by each child. Barbara would play something from Mozart on the piano, cousin Margaret would recite a poem and Barry took his turn, usually performing a magic trick. One of his ambitions was to be a magician, and at his request Eric bought him a sparkling cape to wear as he performed for the assembled family members. As well as performing, he assumed the role of master of ceremonies, and would usher the younger children into the living room when their turn came. He did not particularly enjoy singing, but at his mother's request he agreed to perform Purcell's 'Nymphs and Shepherds' at a gathering. When he was six an adult visitor to the house put the question beloved by adults: 'What would you like to be when you grow up?' Barry replied without hesitation — 'Famous'.

The cape was just one of many costumes and toys purchased by Barry's parents; he was an indulged eldest child. When he was five he pleaded with his father to build him a shop. Dutifully Eric set about constructing a small timber make-believe shop at the back of the house, with two shelves and a sign, 'Barry's Shoppe', in elegant script on a panel that hung above the counter. There Barry sold all sorts of 'knick-knacks' gathered from showbags he had acquired at the Royal Melbourne Show. At Barbara's third birthday party he 'sold' ice cream to a group of little girls in frilly dresses and ribbons.

Unusually for the time, Eric Humphries had been taught by his mother to cook. When Louisa went into hospital to have her third child, Christopher Charles, in October 1943, Eric competently took over the cooking. He continued to cook for his family and was as enthusiastic about it as everything else, delighting the children with his energy and good humour. He would say, 'I'll rustle you up a batch of scones while you're thinking about it'; within minutes the kitchen would fill with the aroma of steaming fresh scones and the sound of beaters whipping thick yellow cream. Louisa was also a skilled cook who impressed visitors to the house with her delicious and nutritious meals. The children looked forward to returning home from church on Sundays when Louisa would serve them freshly baked cakes.

Eric had nicknames for everyone. Sometimes he called Louisa 'Beauty'. He would often whistle, and he loved to sing. He was uninhibited and sang loudly and sometimes off-key, something that irritated the more musically inclined Louisa. When he took the children out in the car without their mother, perhaps for a drive around the new suburbs, he would sing lustily. One of his favourite tunes was 'Home to Beauty', which he would launch into as they made their way back towards Camberwell. Once inside the house, he would gather Louisa in his arms and say, 'Isn't she lovely, children?' The children would answer in chorus 'Yes!' Then Eric would kiss Lou dramatically, as though they were movie stars, and Lou would groan, 'Oh Eric,' in laughing exasperation.

Eric adored Louisa, and arrived home with bunches of carnations, and sometimes roses, almost every week.

Growing up, Barry was close to his sister, Barbara, and they played happily together. When Barbara invited her friends over, he took on his master of ceremonies role and would orchestrate their games. Sometimes he would direct them in re-enactments of Bible stories and invent dance-like sequences for them, herding the girls around the back garden in circles, waving hydrangea leaves and calling out 'Hosanna'. Barry also enjoyed adult company; he loved dressing up and accompanying his mother on trips to the city or out for lunch with other ladies. However, he was essentially a self-contained child and many of his activities were solitary.

By the time Barry was five, the world was at war. Two years later, in 1941, news of the Warsaw Ghetto reached horrified citizens of other countries, including Australia. But the full horror of World War II would not be revealed for three more years. In 1945, when Barry was eleven, the world learned that six million Jews had been executed in Europe. But in his comfortable home in Camberwell, with his father safe in Melbourne contributing to the home front, Barry was cushioned from hardship and horror. His immediate world was safe and prosperous; the Humphries family was largely unaffected by the trauma of war, with all the serving relatives, including Eric's brother, Uncle Dick, engaged in non-active roles.

Louisa's eldest sister, Violet, was married to Wilfred Gatliff, a great mate to Eric. Together they built a shack near Healesville on a bush block, an hour's drive from Camberwell. This holiday shack became Barry and Barbara's favourite place. To reach it they drove past Box Hill, crossed a low rickety wooden bridge over a billabong, then took a winding, rutted track through the bush. On weekend visits Barbara and Barry picked mushrooms and played with their cousin John, Wilf and Vi's son who had cerebral palsy. In the evenings the families sat in the kitchen around a kerosene lamp and played Belisha, an English motoring-card game. Eric constructed a log fort and a bark treehouse for the children in one of the silver-leaved stringy-bark trees on the block. It had a battery phone rigged up to it, to connect the children to the main house. Barry and John, who was a willing accomplice in Barry's enterprises, made their own radio programs, and typed out a newspaper they called the *Arbiter Monthly*. Eric even supplied Barry and his cousin with a real microphone for their journalistic activities. While some of the adults, including Auntie Billie, found the Healesville shack, with its cardboard-lined walls, spiders and its outdoor can toilet rather primitive, for Barry and his sister it was an idyllic place.

When Barry was ten years old, Uncle Wilf died of a brain tumour. Barry and Barbara were distressed, but were not allowed to attend the funeral, a decision Barry found harsh and unjust. Eric later arranged to sell the shack and the surrounding acres of eucalypt forest. Barry has never forgotten the sadness of their last visit to the Arcadia of his childhood, when he and his sister wandered around silently. They stopped on the way home in a windy paddock and watched mournfully as Eric did battle with a small fire on which he cooked lamb chops for the three of them.[5]

The Humphries were connected to their local community in many ways. They were active in the church; Barry taught Sunday school for a short while as an adolescent. Every week, Louisa and Eric played tennis at the Camberwell club, and Barry looked forward to the afternoon tea break, when one of the ladies would slice a vast cake for all the players, who would sit idly in the shade with their cups of tea, chatting. Ever curious about the adult world, Barry listened to the grown-ups' conversations intently. Once a week, while the children slept, his parents held a cards night at home for their friends. The next day Lou would report to the children on how the evening had gone. She would describe funny moments, and detail the guests' behaviour: 'Why did you play that card, Margaret?' she would say, replaying the dramas of the evening and the conversations between couples. Louisa had an eye for human foibles and her sharp observations always amused the children. She could be very direct and sometimes sarcastic, preferring to tell the truth than spare a person's feelings. Louisa perhaps did not appreciate how hurtful her barbs could be, and she could never have predicted that her innocent mimicry of ordinary conversation would be indelibly imprinted on her son's imagination.

Barry's introduction to the theatre began when he was young. Louisa enjoyed live theatre, and frequently took the children to musicals, pantomime and comedies. They saw *Oklahoma!*, *South Pacific* and Laurence Olivier in the Old Vic tour of *Richard III*, but only Barry was permitted to attend the production of *The School for Scandal*. Their aunties also took the children to town and to the theatre. Auntie Elsie, who was more liberal minded than her younger sister, frequently treated the children to the movies. Lou would say, 'I don't think that film is quite suitable for Barbara.' Elsie would reply firmly, 'It is quite suitable,' and move on to another topic.[6]

Louisa suffered what was then called a nervous breakdown when Barry was thirteen, a year after giving birth to another boy, Michael Eric. One day Barbara arrived home from school to find Louisa prostrate on the couch, shaking all over. When she finally spoke she confessed that she had driven through Camberwell Junction, a busy intersection, without looking. She was painfully aware of the implications of this dangerous act, but unable to regain control of herself. It was not the first time she had suffered from depression and anxiety. For months she did not leave the house, something that was very difficult for the children to understand, and her illness created stress for everyone in the family. Barry found it confusing and disturbing. Along with an earlier episode when Barry was six, and the unexplained departure of Edna from the house, this was a very traumatic time for Barry. Lou gradually recovered but relied heavily on her sisters for support and help with the younger children.

Lou also grew more dependent on her helpers 'Shores' and 'Fergie'. Mrs Shores was a chatty woman who seemed to get on well with Louisa, laughing loudly as she did the washing and ironing. Mrs Ferguson did the housekeeping and was a trusted, hardworking member of the household.

After the war, in 1946, Barry's father built a prefabricated timber and fibro holiday house on Beleura Hill Road in Mornington. The family would retreat to their beachside cottage with aunts, uncles and cousins during the long summer holidays. Here Eric could play tennis and golf. Barry and Barbara and the two younger boys swam in the calm waters of Port Phillip Bay. Barry particularly liked to sit in the garden reading, or set up his easel on a cliff top to paint the pretty coves, shimmering blue and gold, or the boats bobbing on the cobalt Southern Ocean. He had a naïve style and found the focus of painting relaxed and refreshed him.

Barry was an avid reader and convinced his parents to buy him scores of novels, a set of Kingsway Histories and lavishly illustrated art books. They obligingly obtained the Phaidon books on Cezanne, Van Gogh and Gauguin for his twelfth birthday at his request. Barry was also fussy about food and started various campaigns to improve the gastronomic range and experience of the household. He advised his mother to buy the brands he considered superior for all sorts of household items; for instance, he insisted Lou should not buy Kolynos toothpaste but should switch to Macleans. Barry also recommended that his mother only purchase Heinz tomato sauce. Seated at the table at Mornington one lunchtime, he reached for the bowl of tomato sauce in the middle of the table. He raised the bowl towards his nose and sniffed it like a connoisseur, in an effort to determine whether it was the preferred Heinz. Infuriated with this display, Lou pushed his head into the bowl. When he looked up at Barbara and the other children, his nose was coated in thick red sauce. The other children were laughing hysterically, but Barry's eyes smarted in humiliation. He felt small and ridiculous. Although the absurdity of the situation was not lost on him, he did not see the humour in it.

As he grew older Barry spent more and more time on his own reading, mystifying his parents who were not readers themselves. This gulf in interests was increasingly pronounced, and Barry became introspective, cheeky and argumentative. He felt his parents were overly critical of him, and he began to be angry and defensive. He found his mother mysterious and distant, especially since her illness, and as he approached adolescence he and his father were often embattled. When Barry was confronted by a group of local toughs, Eric, appalled, bought him some boxing gloves so he could learn to defend himself. Although Barry felt ashamed of his fears and physical weakness, and anxious about what his parents thought of him, he had no interest in learning to box. But he longed to please his parents, and began to feel that in some inexplicable way he didn't belong to his family.

Louisa repeatedly and hurtfully expressed her own sense of alienation from her son. Barry recalls her rather quizzical and exasperated joking remark: 'Your father and I don't know where you came from.'[7] Barry felt unworthy of his parents; he felt that he did not and could not measure up. At times he suffered from debilitating shame and resultant narcissistic rage. His feelings were exacerbated by his parents' ever-growing worry about what people would think of him.

Throughout this period of Barry's early adolescence, Eric and Louisa were reassured somewhat by Barry's scholarly aptitude and enthusiasm for learning. Canon Robinson at St Mark's in Camberwell commented to Eric that Barry was a clever boy and should be taken out of Camberwell Grammar and sent to the much larger, highly regarded Melbourne Grammar School. Coming from large families with few educational opportunities, Eric and Lou were keen to give all of their children the best.

Eric accompanied Barry to an interview with the headmaster, Mr Sutcliffe, at the school in South Yarra. Barry recalls sitting opposite this cold and formal man in his gloomy office, and sensing that his father was nervous.[8] Eric was usually a friendly and relaxed character, and Barry was unsettled by his father's obvious lack of confidence. Regardless of the way Mr Sutcliffe affected him, he was also a decisive parent and felt that Barry needed a firm hand. With somewhat naïve optimism he also harboured a hope that Barry might enjoy the sports at Melbourne Grammar.

Barry's life changed. No longer could he pedal at leisure to school dressed in short pants. Now he was compelled to wear an uncomfortable blue serge suit, and make his way by train into Flinders Street with the commuter crowds, boarding a tram for the last part of the trip, hoping to make it through the imposing iron gates for the morning chapel service. Strangely, the boarders were exempted from wearing the suit; they wore grey trousers and khaki shirts. They were noisy and oafish, and they seemed to the newcomer to be more like pack animals than young gentlemen. He was shocked by the crude comments they made about the maids in the dining hall and listened with horror to the tales of the boxing tournaments held in Memorial Hall, when roaring boarders on the balcony would urge one of their number to flatten his opponent. Initially Barry was placed in 'Shell', a holding class for new boys whose abilities were untested.

Mr Sutcliffe presided over a staff that included many teachers brought back from retirement when younger ones had left to serve in the war. To Barry these reluctant teachers seemed ancient and dull. The boys who excelled in football, cricket and rowing at Melbourne Grammar were rewarded and praised for their achievements. Everyone else was a second-class citizen. An interest in art or music was considered by the headmaster to be suspicious, a disappointment for Barry who was passionate about art. His first year seemed interminable; he was lonely and miserable. As he recalled years later, nobody recognised him, or seemed to care enough to get to know him.

In Barry's second year at Melbourne Grammar, when he was fourteen, he chose subjects that appealed to him and in these classes he met some like-minded boys. His German classes were conducted in a small house called the Lodge near the school gates. On the long walks to and from the Lodge, Barry chatted to his new friends, John Levi and John Perry, who had known each other since primary school. Like Barry, Perry was talented at drawing, and was known for his ability to write witty scripts. Levi was a keen scholar and affable companion. In these two boys, the increasingly learned young Humphries found a ready audience for his appreciation of art and literature. In fact the boys found Barry more interesting and more knowledgeable than most of the teachers. They also admired his spirit and wit, and his flamboyant personality.

The burgeoning friendships partly made up for the crushing regime of house and school sport, the thing Barry detested above all. He was so awkward when he attempted to run or catch a ball that the cruellest boarders jeered at him, referring to him derisively as 'Queenie Humphries'. There was no escape. Day-boys were expected to turn out for sport twice a week. Orders were barked for laps of the oval, push-ups or kicking practice, and in the warmer months the boys would be made to catch cricket balls off the shots of the first XI's best batsmen. Barry simply refused to co-operate. Instead he devised a plan: on sports days he would appear for the roll call, then slip out the gates unnoticed into the throng of St Kilda Road. He would head into town and visit Mrs Bird's second-hand bookshop at the top of Bourke Street. When his truancy was discovered he was caned viciously by one of the prefects, a humiliating and distressing experience. It wasn't simply the brutality of the punishment that Barry resented. He found the routine bullying carried out by prefects and masters terrifying. For a teenager with a fragile self-image and a complex about his physical weakness, the school environment was crippling.

In time Barry found a way to survive Melbourne Grammar — through provocation. When he was called to the headmaster's office and reprimanded for failing to cut his hair to regulation length, he stared coolly and said, 'There's one man in the chapel with hair that is longer than mine. His name is Jesus.'[9] Barry's comment was not punished, and before long everyone had heard of his audacious retort.

Barry loathed the compulsory attendance at inter-school football matches: Grammar versus Xavier; Grammar versus Wesley; Grammar versus Geelong Grammar. The games seemed endless. When Grammar played Scotch the bloodlust in the boys for victory reached its peak. Old boys, parents, teachers and students would gather to barrack. Forced to walk to the MCG on icy winter afternoons to watch the titans of the school wrestle in the mud, Barry found an ingenious way of expressing his view of proceedings. On more than one occasion he positioned himself in a chair with his back to the football field, facing the spectators. Slowly he drew out of his specially made Gladstone bag a set of large knitting needles and a ball of wool, and would sit for the duration of the match calmly knitting a cardigan. Everyone in those days was taught to knit, so he could not be punished for his bizarre activity. Many of the boys found his behaviour disconcerting and strange, but at last everyone knew who he was.

He was not alone in causing disruption at the school. There were other boys who enjoyed pranks. At a Friday night dance a group of seniors let off crackers on the dance floor, setting some of the Merton Hall girls' dresses alight. When Sutcliffe expelled the boys responsible for the prank, a group of parents objected to the punishment and forced the headmaster to resign.[10] It was a dizzying lesson in power politics for the entire school.

Barry joined the small debating society, dazzling teachers and students with his piercing wit, extraordinary intellect and grandiose gestures.[11] He also enjoyed the opportunities of the mini-parliament that was established at school. Each boy was able to name his own seat. Barry claimed that he was the member for Detroit, borrowing the name of John Perry's family business, Detroit Motors, in the bayside suburb of Sandringham. Robert Maclellan and Race Mathews, both of whom went on to become real politicians on opposite sides of the fence, were among the apprentice parliamentarians.

As well as securing a reputation for verbal prowess, Barry also found solace and stimulation in his studies of art. He painted in watercolour and sketched in ink and charcoal. A few drawings that survive from this period depict strange creatures, monster figures with large hooked noses and craggy hands. His interest in theatre inspired him to invent musicals and he designed posters for imaginary Hollywood films.

In his final years of secondary school, he joined other enthusiasts in a church hall not far from the school, eager to listen to contemporary music, such as that of Paul Hindemith, that some might have regarded as provocative and risque. Alex Berry from the ABC would introduce the tunes as Barry and his friends sat enraptured by the new 78s the radio guru brought in from America. People brought cushions to the hall and there was a slightly clandestine feeling to the meetings.

Despite his father's best efforts and the assistance of a succession of tutors employed to help him, Barry still could not comprehend mathematics. He failed the subject in every examination. Eric was extremely concerned: 'You must get your Intermediate,' he implored. But his eldest son gave up trying, ashamed of himself and bitterly aware of his father's frustration. While most of the teachers were unsympathetic, there were a couple who offered Barry a lifeline. One of them was Albert Greed, the music teacher — moon-faced, pigeon-toed and friendly. Greed's classes were refreshing. He played the piano enthusiastically, and although he failed to keep order in the room he somehow taught the boys to sing a variety of popular tunes, including 'Annie Laurie' and the 'Marseillaise', in addition to the traditional Anglican hymns 'Jerusalem' and 'Jesu, Joy of Man's Desiring'.

There was also the popular 'Whizzer Grant', as the boys called him, who taught both art and sport. He had been a great runner in his day, hence the nickname. Grant allowed the boys to establish an Art Club. Barry leaped at the opportunity to invite the controversial local artists Max Meldrum and Noel Counihan to address the club. Barry particularly relished the idea of Counihan visiting the school because he was a member of the Communist Party and drew caricatures of Menzies that had been published in the party's newspaper.

Barry was particularly drawn to Dadaist painting and ideas — to Duchamp, Picabia and Schwitters.[12] He experimented with the style, and longed to exhibit his own work. Whizzer Grant agreed to hold an exhibition at school. John Perry and Barry revelled in their preparations. They created a couple of 'rubbishscapes' that included meat and other rotting items of garbage, and dragooned others to help them create several 'exquisite corpses', large collaborative drawings of human bodies on folded paper. Perry created a work made entirely of broken glass but it was considered too dangerous to display.

The shock value of the exhibits thrilled Barry and his friends. The exhibition allowed him to demonstrate his keen understanding of Dadaist ideas. He loved to be able to surprise people with his mastery, and understanding of books and art, and had also begun to enjoy being looked at. He took to wearing expensive jackets and outlandish hats, and wrote his school essays in purple ink. He was lean and lanky and began to wear his hair longer in the front, in the style of one of his heroes, the fin-de-siècle artist Aubrey Beardsley. He cultivated an interest in obscure works of literature, and on the weekends he would lead John Levi through the streets of Fitzroy to one of his favourite second-hand bookshops where he would browse until he found a tome nobody else would recognise, and buy it.

At the time Fitzroy was a very poor area of Melbourne. The pages of *Truth* carried stories of shootings in Gore Street, one of the most infamous streets in the city. Barry's sartorial elegance was conspicuous and he spoke to shopkeepers with an exaggerated English accent, making it as clear as possible that he was of a superior class to all those around him. His sense of entitlement, honed at Melbourne Grammar, turned into a cheeky performance of snobbery. Barry's perambulations around Fitzroy created a disguise and an aura. He perfected his protective wit, and felt strong and indomitable.

Barry experienced a similar thrill when he adopted a role on stage. He played several female parts in school plays, entranced by his new-found talent to transform himself, and to delight an audience. As Mrs Brash, the distressed wife of a trapped miner in *A Safety Match*, Mrs Pengard in *Ambrose Applejohn's Adventure* and as the obsessive Julia Price in *The Ghost Train*, he impressed his peers and their parents. There was a sensual pleasure in the velvet jackets and the long satin dresses, and the freedom they allowed him on stage. Eric, Louisa, Barbara and the younger boys came to every show. They were surprised and impressed by his performances.

Barry was a child at heart and still loved Luna Park, with its twisting roller coaster and tawdry sideshow amusements. He was particularly drawn to the recording booths where he recited poetry and recorded his own monologues. He befriended a boy whose father owned the Princess Theatre and possessed a large tape recorder. Barry experimented with the borrowed machine, a coveted piece of equipment in the eyes of all the boys. Barry, John Perry and a few others recorded skits, poems and musical pieces. One of John and Barry's recordings was a parody of a back-fence conversation between two housewives discussing their Christmas shopping and the quality of vegetables.

During Barry's senior years of secondary school, Eric built his son a new room upstairs at the back of the house. Encouraged by his father to order furniture for his salon, Barry bought a grey smoky glass table, a hammock chair, a modern lamp and two Miro prints. A birdlike sculpture made by Barry out of old stove parts and umbrella fronds called 'Phoenix Resurrected' provided the centrepiece. The room quickly filled with piles of books and records, and Barry's friends were frequent visitors. John Perry, John Levi and Robert Nathan enjoyed the entertainment Barry provided. On one occasion they listened to a recording of Edith Sitwell reading *Façade*. On other evenings he would play and critique works by composers he admired: Stravinksy's *Histoire du soldat*, works by Vaughan Williams, Delius and Benjamin Britten. He also introduced his friends to one of his favourite books, *The Secret Life of Salvador Dali*.

The idea of a secret life fascinated and haunted Barry, who already had a sophisticated secret life of his own: the naked lady models at his Saturday morning art classes in George Bell's Malvern home, for instance, were not mentioned to his parents. His doubts about his own worth remained the biggest secret of all. He spent more and more time alone in his room, cultivating his private, artistic interests and developing a persona that he believed would be attractive and enigmatic, impressive and charming, like one of the aristocratic Sitwell brothers. Sometimes though, when he was alone, he would stare into the mirror in his bathroom and try to see who he really was. He felt strangely insubstantial and flimsy, reckless and cold. He did not like what he saw.[13]

Shame was an emotion that he knew well. The slights he had suffered at school wounded him, but he kept his anger to himself and found a way to retaliate. He satirised school bullies and the aggressive school spirit. If he had learned anything at Melbourne

Grammar it was that wit could defuse attack, and laughter was a most potent and attractive weapon.

By the time Barry was ready to leave school, he had achieved his desire for recognition through painting and performance. But he spent countless hours worrying about what would become of him, and he feared that he was a terrible disappointment to his father. The new headmaster had expressed his own concerns about Barry: 'I hope you're not turning pansy,' said the large and rather ungainly Mr Hone, looking at him quizzically. It was impossible for Barry to answer him. He knew that Eric and Louisa were extremely anxious about his future, but his profound self-doubt was not something he could ever discuss with anyone. He could not express any of his worries. Like other artistic prodigies, Barry poured his energies into his aesthetic interests and buried his doubts. His feelings of uncertainty faded to nothing in the exhilarating moments of a performance, on or off the stage. The more extravagant the performance the safer he felt.

CHAPTER 2

The Wubbos

After Christmas, 1951, when the exam results were published, Barry finally relaxed. His marks were excellent and he was awarded a scholarship to Melbourne University. A few of the boys from his year moved into Trinity College and carried on as before, holding Saturday night parties in Darling Street, South Yarra, dining with their parents at the Windsor and joining in pub crawls. Some even wore their old school ties to golf days at Healesville. Not Barry.

By the time Humphries began his studies in 1952, his taste for the bizarre and the strange was well developed. He attempted to throw off the arrogant hauteur of his Grammar contemporaries. Imaginatively he was still captivated by Dadaism and obsessed with grotesque parodies of art, and with forms that challenged the idea of art itself. It was as if he had been seduced by the savage aesthetic critique of the period after World War I. Barry studied the demonstrations of the French and German Dadaists of the 1920s, and he was particularly intrigued by Man Ray and Picabia. Later when photographed, Humphries would stare straight at the camera and make 'wild eyes', just as Dali and Man Ray had done for Carl Van Vechten. Dadaism was largely experimental and was based on freedom to play and to take chances. It was risky and confrontational; sometimes it was downright cruel.

Humphries started to practise Dadaist tricks and pranks around the city. He recalls in his own memoir offering lifts to strangers on Melbourne streets and taking them on long car rides in which he sat in the front passenger seat playing a crazed psychopath, shouting at his friend Robert Nathan, and imploring him to gun the accelerator harder and harder. After a few minutes in the speeding vehicle with a screaming lunatic in the front, the terrified victims would plead for release, or would leap from the car at the first red light.[1] It was pure pleasure for Humphries.

He still relished evenings at Luna Park in St Kilda. His favourite ride was a rotating platform called the Rotor. As it whirled faster and faster, the platform dropped away, leaving the riders spread like insects against the wall due to its powerful centrifugal force. His friends have memories of Barry shrieking with delight as he spun around.[2] Barry remembers his glee at donning a ghoulish mask with fake blood dripping from the eye sockets; just as the Big Dipper made its stomach-turning plunge, he would tap the shoulders of the couple seated in front of him and give them a terrifying leer.[3] All of his pranks were carried out with dramatic flair and precision. He invented a character called Dr Aaron Azimuth who embodied menace and insanity in the figure of a demented scientist who enjoyed tinkering with the personalities of his hapless victims, and who, as Barry recalls vividly in his memoir, resembled one of his favourite film characters, Dr Caligari.[4] Barry also enjoyed playing an Edwardian toff and dandy. Once he had taken on a persona he was both unreachable and unpredictable. When he drank red wine in the ceramic coffee cups of the cafés in Carlton, Barry became even more flamboyant.

Gradually students around the campus began to recognise Humphries' outlandish appearance and strange behaviour. He was wraith-like, with unfashionably long hair, and draped himself in scarves and large overcoats. He always looked mysterious, as though he was escaping something. He often wore a pair of rust-coloured woollen gloves, with elongated fingers like long prongs hanging off them. He entertained readers in the library by dashing through the front doors clad in a billowing opera cloak and cavalier's hat with a peacock plume in it. He mimed admiring a painting or a bunch of flowers, or mischievously piled up towers of books to the ceiling.

In his first year Humphries launched an exhibition, 'Piescapes'. It was his first organised Dadaist assault on the university. His friend Keith Dunstan remembers that in one performance piece the eighteen-year-old placed his elbow into a tub of tomato sauce to check its temperature and then proceeded to drink it.[5] After that he tipped the sauce on his head. Humphries gleefully described this act as a tribute to the Australian national drink. Another of his exhibits was called 'I was eating a pie and I coughed'. One of the features of this kind of modern art, he said, was that it only lasts two days.[6]

Humphries gradually became even bolder and made a name for himself around the university. He and John Perry, also a student at Melbourne University, called themselves the Wubbos, in deference to the Dadaists they attempted to imitate. Perry's two-year-old nephew coined the name as he watched a horse-drawn cart back up the lane behind his house to collect the rubbish. Little Alex Bernard Smith would rush up to the carter shouting, 'Hello Mr Wubbo'. His mispronunciation of the word 'rubbish' inspired the undergraduates. Barry wrote a brief manifesto for Wubbo and tried to articulate its metaphysical propositions. He declared that it was not a movement but a quasi-religious view of the world, explaining that Buddhism 'could best be described as proto-Wubbo in its endeavour to smooth the contours of experience ... I am merely a kind of Wubbo John the Baptist'.[7]

Barry and a number of his friends formed another group that they called the Wubbophonic Chamber Ensemble, and recorded several pieces of music. One of them was called 'The Malouf Concerto', in recognition of an infamous incident in Mr Malouf's shop in Carlton. Barry had walked into the shop and bought a cake of Lux soap, and then walked out of the shop, leaving the soap on the counter. When Malouf ran outside to give him the item, Barry turned to him and said, 'I don't want it. I just wanted to purchase it.' The ensemble played a strange, cacophonous kind of music together called 'Wubbo Music'. It featured a series of loud flourishes on the piano, some tuneless violin and an accelerating banging of a boot on the floor, with occasional whistles, harmonica and other sound effects.[8] Although the young musicians recorded their efforts, they otherwise kept their musical endeavours private.

But Humphries' own tricks had to be performed in public. The sites varied but the tricks were always controversial and reckless. He often had helpers. John Perry, Graeme Hughes and Colin Munro were the chief enthusiasts. He placed bread in an electric toaster until plumes of smoke drifted through the small women's lounge of the Union building, the smell of burning toast acrid and overpowering. Then one of his acolytes ran in carrying fire hoses. One day Humphries stood in front of a portrait of the Queen on the wall in the same lounge, and gravely announced his intention to execute a painting. He pulled out an axe and chopped up the portrait of the monarch. On another occasion, he appeared on a tram dressed as an old fat man, sidled up — as pre-arranged — to a young girl clad in prim school uniform, and began to make up to her lecherously. Several stops later Barry and his accomplice got off the tram together and walked off hand in hand, outraging the other passengers.

Humphries and John Perry staged two further exhibitions in the Union building. They offered a kind of visual satirical spectacle and included various found objects. A beer bottle with the Old Melburnian tie draped around its neck was called 'Old Fool's Tie'. There was a 'cakescape', consisting of two framed glass sheets with squashed lamingtons, swiss roll and cream cake smeared between them, and a 'shoescape', featuring two battered and worn old shoes salvaged from the dump that were nailed to panels of wood — it was called 'My Foetus Killing Me'. Humphries piled up a whole lot of university texts, covered them with yellow globs of custard and captioned the exhibit 'I was reading these books and I felt sick'. Another piece, 'Pus in Boots', showed a pair of filthy leather workman's boots retrieved from the rubbish and filled to overflowing with bright yellow custard with flies floating in it. The works were childish and rebellious, and revealed Barry's urge to shock, provoke and to break free from institutionalised learning. Another exhibit showed a gold-painted jockstrap resting on a jewel-studded velvet cushion. Barry called it 'The Support of Kings'.

Barry's parents and his sister, Barbara, traipsed around the Dada art exhibitions. While Barbara found the exhibits intriguing, Eric and Louisa were not impressed. Eric was particularly concerned, furious according to his daughter, when he saw a photograph of 'Old Fool's Tie' in *Truth* magazine. Rodney Davidson, who had been a few years ahead of Barry at school, issued a statement declaring that Humphries would be expelled from the Old Melburnians. Barry lapped up the attention. It was exactly the kind of reaction he hoped to arouse.

But Louisa Humphries was worried about her son's future and this public escapade only reinforced her anxieties. She disapproved of his appearance and his behaviour. His steadfast refusal to have his hair cut enraged his mother, and irritated his father. Despite their growing concern about Barry, his parents sometimes found themselves unwitting accomplices in his activities. When Colin Munro and Barry made a strange, expressionist-style film called *Le Bain Vorace* that involved a lot of dashing across the campus and climbing up the drainpipes at home in Christowel Street, Louisa and Barbara cooked sausages for the cast and crew. The film bore the subtitle 'He who bathes last bathes longest' and its male lead, played by Barry, vanished down the plughole of a bath that had 'acid' tipped into it.

Humphries was the most daring student prankster Melbourne University had ever known. He was unafraid of outraging bystanders no matter who they were. He had a kind of brazenness that he put on like a costume when he began to perform one of his Dadaist pranks. He summoned up all his courage, assuming absolute confidence in order to pull off some outlandish stunt. His ruses seemed to assuage some of his doubts and anxieties about himself; he gradually created a kind of bravado, an impenetrable persona. It was instinctive and compulsive. The more improbable and disturbing the pranks, the more pleasure Humphries seemed to derive.

His provocation aroused strong reactions. Humphries had grown up in a household in which emotions and passions were not readily expressed. He had spent a decade or so taming his own passions through his painting, music, reading and meticulous attention to the details of his apparel. He was obsessive about his appearance and the impression his unusual physical presence had on others.

Humphries' Dada-inspired works and his street performances foreshadowed performance art in Australia. At the time he was not taken seriously as an artist, but his activities had a greater impact on those who saw them than his early theatrical ventures. His pranks on campus and around the streets of the city are now both celebrated and renowned.

All the while the young aesthete was still living at home in Camberwell, where he spent hours listening to music on his own. In spite of his unusual antics Barry was fond of his family and a part of him loved the orderliness and industry of the household. Barbara was busily preparing to take her final examinations. Barry gave her a Jane Austen novel for her fifteenth birthday and another for every birthday after that. The younger boys kept out of Barry's way. Humphries worried about his future but never let on to his parents that he felt anxious. Well schooled in the art of reserve he did not let his guard slip. Nor did he ever consciously consider becoming an actor. His interest was primarily in art. But when Barry began staying out late his parents became furious. Barbara would hear the shouting from her bedroom upstairs.

Due to the success of Humphries' art exhibitions, the ALP Club (even though Barry was not a member) confidently hired the Union Theatre to stage a Barry Humphries revue in September 1953. This was to live on as his most shocking and notorious Dadaist event, entitled *Call Me Madman!*. It was a chaotic, crazed and anarchic revue, just like the early Dada shows of the Cabaret Voltaire in Zurich several decades earlier.

The fact that the proceeds of the day were to be donated to a charity, World Student Relief, made the material in Barry's raucous performance even more potent. The title parodied a popular musical by Irving Berlin, *Call Me Madam*, starring Ethel Merman. *Call Me Madman!* opened with a single musical phrase played on a violin over and over again, then a pianist sitting out of view of the audience sounded the same chords and notes in repetition. Nothing happened on stage, just the sounding of these same notes over and over, infuriating the audience.

A provocative skit then incensed some of the loyalists in the audience. It included the line 'Why are you kicking that rotten old football about like that?'. 'Because it reminds me of Her Royal Maggoty Queen Lizard' came the daring answer.[9] In another sketch Humphries exclaimed, 'I hated my mother because she untied her navel in the tram.'[10] Barry and John Perry performed one of the more sedate sketches called 'Hello Jim', in which two men, both called Jim, conversed about their wives, the football and their children. It satirised the inane, clichéd and colloquial conversational style of many Australians. The sketch was one of the first performances on stage to be presented in the Australian accent since the premiere of the play *Rusty Bugles* in 1948.[11]

Jim B: How's Marj these days?
Jim A: Well, to tell you the truth she's only just so-so …
Jim B: Will I see you at the footy nex' Sat'dy?
Jim A: Too right. You wouldn't catch me missing an
     important semi.
Jim B: Okay. Well I'll see you then. Hooroo.[12]

In an interminable mime, Barry played a priest and Perry a nun. For what seemed like hours the two actors 'dug' a tunnel towards each other. There was complete silence in the auditorium as they crawled on their hands and knees at a snail's pace across the stage, miming a shovelling action, and inching closer to a union. As they came nearer and nearer, they suddenly veered off, so that they passed one another, but did not meet, and then disappeared into the wings. It was excruciating to watch but the audience laughed.

By far the most provocative sketch in the show featured Dada Australian-style. It was called 'The Indian Famine'. In this sketch Humphries, dressed in a wig and a floor-length evening gown, hastily put on over his suit, played the wife of a missionary. Barry's friend Graeme Hughes played the missionary. In a grey suit and grey silk tie and tiepin, he looked and sounded like the then foreign minister, Richard Casey, who had recently given a speech about the tragic Indian famine. When the sketch began, the two actors were sitting at a table. The missionary stood up and announced: 'We Australians are a most fortunate country, we have enough to eat; those poor little yellow people have not got enough to eat.' In front of the pair was a pile of food: a pyramid of raw meat, vegetables and cakes. There were blood-oozing rump steaks and lamb chops, cauliflower heads, slimy fish and creamy pastries — all scavenged especially for this performance.

The missionary continued with a series of shocking statistics detailing the current famine as his wife (Barry) shrieked in falsetto: 'I don't care ... don't be boring, I've got plenty of food ... lots of food ... and they've got nothing ... wogs, nigs, yids!' She bit into a chop, immediately discarding it as she chewed. Disgusted by her husband's endless litany, she proceeded to pelt him with half-eaten cakes and rotting vegetables. Her husband retaliated. A few seconds later she started throwing plate loads of food at the audience, shouting, 'You little yellow person, have a chop.' Incensed audience members began flinging food back at the actors and all around the theatre while the voice of the missionary continued with the grim statistics over the amplifiers. Humphries had trapped his audience in an ugly food fight.

Appalled at the scene in front of them, some Indian students started to rush at the stage as Humphries appeared again, this time dressed as a nun singing jauntily, 'I wish I could shimmy like my sister Kate ...' Then the 'nun' flung her grubby black bra and pair of black stockings into the audience. Various members of the Newman Society seated in the auditorium were horrified and loud protests filled the 500-seat theatre. The mass of students then stormed the stage as 'God Save the Queen' blared out over a gramophone at various speeds over and over again, daring the students to stand still in their places as was the custom. As the strains of the anthem rang out, however, food was flung around the theatre and students ran in every direction. Barry took refuge in a cupboard in the dressing room.

As a result of the damage caused by the flying food and the complaints of many in the audience, the ALP Club was banned from the Union Theatre for the next three years. However, for Humphries, *Call Me Madman!* was a success. In his recollections he revels in the memory of the 'irrational frenzy of retaliation' that the sketch provoked. The biting parody of the controversial famine sketch had taught him how to provoke his audience, securing their complicit and violent participation in his act. It also gave him his first taste of the power of an audience to determine what happens in the theatre. It was both risky and intoxicating. Barry had made his mark.

CHAPTER 3

A Perfectly Timed Spectacle

It was the complaints of a group of young women on campus that landed Humphries his first paid acting role. The man responsible for the job offer was John Sumner, a dedicated young professional fresh from the West End, who had worked with the prestigious HM Tennent group under the entrepreneur Hugh Beaumont. Sumner had impulsively taken a job as manager of the Union Theatre in Melbourne. The decision to leave England was a brave one for someone used to working with luminaries such as Laurence Olivier, Vivien Leigh, Terence Rattigan, John Gielgud, Peter Brook and Noel Coward. Most of the theatrical traffic travelled in the opposite direction, with dozens of actors leaving Australia for Britain each year.

After a very short period in his new post, Sumner persuaded the Vice-Chancellor at the University of Melbourne, George Paton, to fund a professional repertory company using the Union Theatre on a trial basis, with an annual budget of £1500. At the time there was no professional repertory company in Melbourne. Sumner set up the Union Theatre Repertory Company (UTRC) along the lines of English repertory theatre, and began to present fortnightly shows on a minuscule budget. Under Sumner this new venture in repertory theatre later became the Melbourne Theatre Company.

John Sumner was a towering, dark-haired man with a ramrod bearing; he had spent the war years in the British Navy and was determined to succeed in theatre. He commanded respect because he would involve himself in every aspect of production: collecting props, cleaning, set construction, as well as directing, marketing, running the front of house and managing the purse strings. Sumner fully understood the stress of the work, the late nights and the exhaustion of rehearsing and performing night after night. For many of the actors working around the few small theatres in Melbourne in the early 1950s, the opportunity offered by Sumner meant a chance to gain some rigorous training, as long as they could survive the discipline. Sumner ran his company with an authoritarian seriousness. Zoe Caldwell recalls that an actor who arrived late for rehearsals would risk a lambasting in front of the cast and crew. Once she was the culprit and the entire troupe was forced to sit in silence for ten excruciating minutes before Sumner permitted the rehearsal to begin.[1]

Sitting in his office one day at the theatre, Sumner opened the door to a 'deputation of ladies complaining about Humphries' act in a student revue'.[2] After watching Humphries perform, Sumner promptly offered him a job in the new company. In the act that had offended the young women, Humphries played a skinny politician standing on a soapbox, waiting to be introduced to an audience; he was wearing a long coat, with straw sticking out from under his battered hat, and spent the whole sketch trying to pull off his gloves, clasping his hat and 'chasing the elusive sheets of his speech'. It was more mime than anything else, and was at times suggestive. Sumner was impressed by the sharpness of Humphries' observations embodied in the sketch.[3]

Sometimes Barry went on so long in this sketch that he had to be carried off the stage. The show was called *Terra Australis*; it was the annual university students' revue, presented at the end of the first term in 1954. Barry also performed a strange solo sketch he had written himself. He sat under a ghoulish green spotlight spitting and drooling as he slowly intoned the monologue of a matricidal madman:

I'm just a boy who killed his mother
I was always up to tricks
I took a gun and shot her
In her chronic appendix.[4]

The sketch was based on a party turn by F. Scott Fitzgerald. Barry recalls that it was always 'startling and enjoyable, and I made it go on a long time'.[5]

With two other students, Brian Westmore and Eve Strasser, Barry was supposed to sing a rousing finale. The three of them appeared on stage as the triplets from *Bandwagon*, dressed in gingham skirts with large bows. But Barry let the others do the singing while he walked to the front of the stage and pelted the orchestra with carnations.

Humphries was pleased with the opportunity of paid work in the fledgling university theatre company. His first role was a courtier in a play called *The Young Elizabeth*, chosen to coincide with the new Queen's visit to Australia in 1954, the first time a reigning British monarch had visited the nation. The royal visit was both a grand and somewhat folksy event. A guard of honour at Government House included fifty Welsh corgis on leashes. Myer's city store was festooned with flowing fabric bunting, and a massive coat of arms with a banner exultantly declaring the message of all Melburnians: 'Hail to Elizabeth Our Queen'. The city came to a standstill as the Queen made her progress along the royal route from the airport at Essendon to the city.[6]

The dark-haired leading lady in *The Young Elizabeth* was Zoe Caldwell, who earned ten pounds a week; her male counterparts were paid eleven. For his debut performance as a professional actor in a supporting role, Humphries received five pounds a week. The conditions were tough: there were no understudies and when Caldwell developed an abscess on a tooth just before opening night and her face was swollen and sore, she had no choice but to play the part. It was the thirteenth play presented by the new company which performed fifteen plays over a thirty-one week season. Sumner's UTRC produced a new play every fortnight with the total rehearsal period for each play lasting only two weeks. This meant that the play opened on a Monday, and on the Tuesday morning the cast would read the next play. The actors would perform one play at night and rehearse another by day for a fortnight, until dress rehearsal on the Sunday night. It was an exhausting schedule for everyone and may explain Sumner's fanatical emphasis on punctuality.

The dizzying rehearsal program meant that there was time for only one dress rehearsal. To Sumner's horror, in the dress rehearsal for *The Young Elizabeth*, Humphries, who was clad in Elizabethan hose, altered his moves and seemed to be playing upstage of the furniture, contrary to the blocking that had been agreed. When Sumner asked him what he thought he was doing, he said he was anxious about the appearance of his skinny legs in tights. The cast broke into uncontrollable laughter as Humphries appeared, the crotch in his tights dropping almost to his knees, his thin, long, spider-like legs making him look ridiculous.[7]

Humphries met Peter O'Shaughnessy during the rehearsals for *The Young Elizabeth*. O'Shaughnessy, who also had a part in the play, had recently returned to Melbourne after spending four years in English repertory theatre. O'Shaughnessy and Humphries shared a dressing room, and finding they had a great deal in common, became very close over the following months.[8] Peter was ten years older than Barry, and like Barry had been educated at an exclusive private school in Melbourne. O'Shaughnessy, a Roman Catholic by birth, had attended Xavier College. Like Barry, he had loathed school sport and school spirit. He had travelled throughout Europe and regaled Humphries with vivid descriptions of concerts at the Royal Albert Hall conducted by the likes of Furtwängler, Koussevitzky and Vaughan Williams. The two men shared a passion for Mozart and Mahler.[9]

With his talent for collecting already quite established and his insatiable appetite for art, Humphries thrilled to O'Shaughnessy's tales of his visits to the great palaces of Europe. O'Shaughnessy found the young actor highly amusing, and his unco-ordinated movements, skinny legs and eccentric appearance endearing. Barry also seemed to him to be a tender-hearted and generous character. O'Shaughnessy also quickly observed Humphries' eagle eye for human weakness, his razor-sharp wit and unusual sense of humour.[10] Occasionally he noticed another side of Humphries' personality: the way his predilection for the black and surreal would sometimes find expression in extraordinary cruelty.[11]

Though ambitious as an actor, O'Shaughnessy also liked to direct. Working alongside Barry, he began to imagine the younger actor in various roles. O'Shaughnessy found himself more and more impressed by the nineteen year old who, he recalled, groomed himself to look like the young Brahms: his hair hanging to his collar and combed across the top of his head.[12] Humphries' extensive knowledge of literature also interested him. But most of all Peter found Barry's peculiarly childlike imagination refreshing: his friend had confessed that he had believed in Father Christmas until he was twelve.[13]

Humphries initially studied Law at the University of Melbourne because he was not qualified to undertake Arts subjects, despite his remarkable aptitude for English. He had not studied another language at the required level. In order to gain admission he took up German again at night school. He was then admitted to the Arts faculty. He enrolled in English I three times during his stint as a student but failed each exam, an outcome that seems absurd given his prodigious talent for writing. In one of his examination papers he answered only two of the five required questions on the paper, and wrote an essay making an odd but ingenious comparison between Gerard Manley Hopkins and Baron Corvo, an English writer and would-be priest who was a popular figure in the 1950s. In refusing to write to the guidelines, Humphries ruined his chances of passing, following in the footsteps of other renowned academic failures such as Christopher Isherwood, who deliberately botched his Cambridge tripos by answering the questions in verse and limericks.[14]

Humphries also played in another of Sumner's Union Theatre productions, this time as a corrupt chief of police in *His Excellency* by Dorothy and Campbell Christie. Barry transformed his role into a comic centrepiece: he made his entrance at the dress rehearsal wearing a very noisy and distracting row of jangling medals, and once the play opened, embellished his role by making all sorts of strange gestures that drew wild laughter from the audience. He frequently seemed to be reaching for his forgotten lines, but received an enthusiastic round of applause when he made his exit from the stage, to the chagrin of Sumner and his cast.[15]

In his second year at university, Humphries found less and less to interest him in his subjects, and began to wonder what he was doing there. He was by this stage a student of art, film, poetry and costume, but his curriculum was self-devised. He attended at least one lecture that he particularly enjoyed, given by the visiting English poet Stephen Spender, who had founded a literary magazine called *Encounter*. (Spender's daughter, Lizzie, would become Barry's fourth wife.) Humphries vividly recalls the way in which the urbane and seasoned speaker dealt with the interjections of a group of student communists.[16] Predictably, at the end of the year he received a letter informing him that his undergraduate scholarship had been withdrawn. Eric and Louisa were extremely disappointed.

Eric was particularly concerned at his son's lack of focus, and suggested he take a job as a trainee executive at EMI Records in the city. Barry went along with the plan reluctantly, only to find that his main task turned out to be smashing hundreds of discontinued 78 rpm records in the basement of the Flinders Lane offices, to make way for the new microgroove records. He told his friend Freddy Parslow disdainfully that the new discs would 'serve up Melocrino for the masses'.[17] Humphries spent his days sitting in a tiny and stuffy basement room endlessly pulverising recorded music. The absurdity of this activity struck him but he missed his more carefree life at university and felt a sense of futility and failure in his new occupation.[18]

Humphries still found time for acting. In his lunch breaks he dashed across the road to the Assembly Hall in Collins Street to play in an abridged version of Molière's *Le Malade Imaginaire*, as part of O'Shaughnessy's newly established lunch-hour theatre. The hall was a sandstone Gothic revival building next to the Scots' Church. It was dark, with stained-glass windows, and smelled of wood polish. O'Shaughnessy had been encouraged by the energetic actor Noel Ferrier to start these accessible lunchtime productions. Barry played Thomas Diafoirus, or Thomas Purgit, as O'Shaughnessy liked to call the character.[19]

While Barry was working at EMI, he heard that Peter O'Shaughnessy's friend Ian Garrett was looking for someone to rent his studio-loft in East Melbourne. Barry leaped at the chance to escape staid Camberwell and to cultivate his bohemian persona with a new life in the city. For a few short weeks Humphries enjoyed some late nights in the company of his theatre friends. But his freedom wasn't to last. Eric Humphries appeared one day and ordered his son to pack up the loft and return to the family home. Eric was not impressed with Peter O'Shaughnessy, and was certain he was a bad influence on Barry. Peter looked on helplessly as Barry's father backed his car into the cobbled laneway, collected Barry's belongings and drove off with his son. As they sped away, Peter noticed a strange, long, prong-fingered glove trailing out of the car window in a last whimsical gesture of thwarted independence.[20]

Barry moved back into his comfortable upstairs room in Christowel Street and continued to entertain his friends in the evenings, playing records of Bartok, Hindemith and Kurt Weill's *Threepenny Opera*. He recalls the way he meticulously sharpened the fibre needle of the gramophone to play the Weill recordings, and how he lectured his guests about the music they were about to hear. He delighted in teaching his friends about music, literature and art, and read the fiction of the 1920s obsessively.

In 1955, Peter O'Shaughnessy cast Humphries as Holofernes, the pedantic schoolmaster in *Love's Labour's Lost*. In this and in his role as Thomas in the Molière play, Humphries seemed to find his voice. It was apparent to Peter that Humphries excelled at portraying grotesque and monstrous characters, and that he seemed to grasp instinctively the way in which timidity can so easily become 'monstrous arrogance'.[21]

The transformation was a blueprint for the later development of his signature character, Edna Everage. Humphries' Edna drew on the traits of the Molière character, becoming pompous, domineering and full of false, self-devised notions of her own authority. Mrs Norm Everage, the shy housewife from Moonee Ponds, would evolve into a monstrous caricature of a celebrity. In these early roles Humphries rediscovered the potency of the actor's mask that he first savoured in high school, and the way it offered him escape and freedom from himself.

Prior to this Humphries had been somewhat tentative and uneasy in his straight roles. At times he experienced difficulties projecting his voice; it would sometimes sound thin, weak, too high, even quavering. Like many actors in Melbourne at the time, Humphries had not received any vocal training. In fact Humphries had not had any acting training either. He was a novice, with a flair for the bizarre. His physical appearance presented problems as well: his movements were awkward and he was self-conscious about his legs. In a world where the willingness to take direction and to remain focused was essential, he seemed to lack discipline. These shortcomings did not make him an obvious choice for straight roles. Regardless of the character he played, he always managed to get a laugh, sometimes at the expense of other cast members. The humour he exploited in playing straight roles usually arose from his novel deviations from the script and eccentric interpretation of the characters.

Off stage, too, Humphries affected eccentric ways and had not given up his street performances. He frequently adopted a strange persona in public, perhaps in a pub or on a tram. The more outrageous the act, the more satisfaction Humphries gained. With a heavily disguised friend, Humphries put on a performance on a suburban train. Dressed in a garish outfit with large rings on every finger, he smoked a foul-smelling Turkish cigarette and read a large German newspaper, while the friend hobbled to a seat with a plaster cast on his leg, a neck brace and dark glasses. All the other passengers fixed their eyes on the ostentatious 'foreigner' or the 'cripple'. When the train drew into a station Barry gave the 'blind', 'crippled' man a brutal kick, snatched at his glasses and tore his Braille reading sheet in half, before escaping out the door and onto the platform. It was an outrageous stunt that left the others on the train gasping in horror.

More than once Barry surreptitiously placed a bottle of chilled champagne and a cooked platter of chicken in the bottom of a garbage bin near the tram stop in Swanston Street at rush hour. When a sufficient number of people had gathered, he would appear dressed as a tramp and scavenge the planted food and drink from the bin, sit down in the gutter and have his meal. Anxious onlookers were amazed to see what he had found in the rubbish. Some would curiously look inside the bin. Others feigned unawareness. No one ever said anything.

John Brack portrayed the crowds of grim-faced commuters in his famous painting of Collins Street at rush hour, entitled *Collins St. 5 p.m.*, in the same year that Barry played the tramp. It was 1955 and Brack showed rows of office workers trudging through the streets, all of them looking straight ahead. He captured the grim intensity and isolation of each individual and the regimentation of their lives in his painting. The young actor tried to amuse and shock those same frowning commuters out of their torpor with his strange stunts.

Even worse than this stunt was Humphries' other tramp impersonation: he would stoop on the pavement, pulling a spoon from his pocket, and eat the spilled contents of a jar of Heinz Russian Salad, a concoction of coarsely chopped carrots, peas and potatoes floating in a greying soup of mayonnaise. Smeared over the pavement it resembled greasy vomit. In these strange street spectacles Humphries secured the desired response from his audience of onlookers. People were visibly disgusted, disturbed and confused. He would always tell a friend about his planned prank in advance, so that someone would see the act, someone would be able to report on his performance, someone would remember the horror on the faces of the onlookers.

One day Humphries boarded a tram at Lonsdale Street with the actress Joan Parslow. He had his arms full, manoeuvring a huge man-size box, resembling a coffin, onto the crowded tram. He insisted on paying three adult fares, one for Joan, one for himself and one for the box, and argued the point with the conductress, until she relented and accepted three fares. After all this fuss, he insisted on getting off just moments later, at Flinders Street.

Most of the stunts involved only momentary excitement, though occasionally Humphries did something that would have more lasting impact. He would loiter in the menswear department of Myer, and when no one was looking he sprinkled rice between the folded pullovers, hoping to frighten the shoppers who would later lift up the garments and fear that maggots had got into the clothes. Sometimes he scampered through the lonely rows of shelves in the university library, placing rashers of bacon inside the books, leaving them to rot, only to be discovered by horrified future readers.

Humphries started to introduce himself at parties as 'Des Esseintes', thereby proudly proclaiming his status as an aesthete and announcing his esoteric knowledge of Huysmans, his character Jean des Esseintes, and other fin-de-siècle figures. He rather enjoyed imagining himself as a reclusive, decadent and improbable anti-hero. Barry had a number of café tricks too. Zoe Caldwell sometimes accompanied him on jaunts into the city for tea. On one occasion he was seated quietly with her one minute, then suddenly he upended the milk jug over his head, to the horror of those around him. A kindly waitress replaced the jug and mopped up the mess. He relied on the sympathy and forgiveness of those around him, and although he loved to torment his friends and his audiences he was also charming and funny. He relished watching the reactions to his offences; he observed the barriers and screens people put up in public, and the lengths they go to in order to avoid acknowledging behaviour that is provocative. Like the figures in Brack's painting, people tended to shut each other out. Barry always wanted to puncture the screens and arouse emotions.

Before his departure from the university, Humphries had reported for compulsory national service, during the holidays, as a member of the student regiment. He dreaded his three-month incarceration in a desolate army camp in central Victoria. It was like going back to school, with the tough professional soldiers replaying the role of prefects at Melbourne Grammar. But Barry's experience of army life proved to be slightly less oppressive than his school days.

On the first day he was delighted when an immaculately groomed colonel took charge of some eight hundred young men. He appeared to have had his batman starch his trousers until they almost stood up on their own, and his dog wandered onto the parade ground every now and then. He bellowed, 'We'll make men of you. There'll be none of this poofter university business here.' It was an absurdist paradise: some of the officers even wore Bombay bloomers, and almost every day there were laughable breaches of security and military form. Once, the anti-tank artillery inadvertently destroyed a brand new tank that had been recklessly abandoned in a paddock. And all the new soldiers had to do bayonet practice in the blazing midsummer heat. Each soldier ran through a paddock, wielding his bayonet and stabbing at a straw figure suspended from a tree, screaming out and then waiting and watching as every other private performed the macabre exercise.

More pleasant were the concert parties and productions of Gilbert and Sullivan. Barry didn't bother to audition but painted several large sets, and because of the work involved he managed to avoid some of the more gruelling training activities.

Barry noticed that several of the university men could not make beds and refused to learn. The larrikins among them sneaked off base, and drank beer illegally. Barry took up smoking. Some of the men even collected unexploded shells as mementos. Like them, Barry prowled around the shooting range picking up the deformed bullet-riddled canisters to add to his collection of Dada sculptural objects.

Humphries' military training took place during the Cold War. The Americans had detonated their first thermonuclear weapon. The Soviets had also shown their capabilities with a fission bomb nicknamed Joe 4. Barry listened incredulously as the recruits were instructed on what to do in the event of a nuclear bomb blast.

'Anyone within eight hundred yards of the bomb will perish instantly,' barked the dapper colonel. 'Soldiers who are positioned between eight hundred and sixteen hundred yards are under strict orders to fight on.' He hastened to inform them that they would certainly die within twenty-four hours.

The officers in charge of training the student recruits were Korean War veterans, including some British servicemen. Although they were hardened soldiers, Humphries delighted in mocking them. At the end of the first week the new soldiers were instructed to write a 500-word essay on army life. Humphries wrote 'Left Right Left Right' over and over again, until he had five hundred words.

Humphries boasted to the others about his particularly poor marksmanship when he was a member of the university rifle club. So plausible were his fabricated tales that the other recruits lived in terror of having to practise alongside Private Humphries.[22] To make matters worse Barry deliberately dropped his rifle on parade.

One evening as darkness fell over the camp, Humphries marched into a tent where soldiers were polishing their boots. They could not see whether the unannounced visitor had stripes on his uniform or not. When the young soldiers failed to salute him, Barry bellowed, 'What's the matter with your right hand, Private!' The officers considered Barry incorrigible and uncontrollable. He ended up on permanent latrine duty for his many breaches of army regulations. Barry and his friend Peter Batey put honey around the toilet seats, then hid in the cubicles waiting to hear the officers swearing as they realised their predicament.

Early one morning Barry opened the grease pits behind the kitchen and fished out the effluent on a long pole. At breakfast time, as the troops lined up with their tin plates for their ration of scrambled eggs, he entered the mess hall toting his long pole with its putrid mess hanging off it, offering the soldiers a whiff of the foul matter and leering as he walked among the bewildered young soldiers.

After the first ninety-eight days of training, the troops were sent home, but had to return in mid January for refresher training. Assembled for parade in the scorching heat on the first day back at

Puckapunyal, the troops watched as an army truck juddered to a halt. Two military police lifted the khaki awning, whereupon a lanky Private Humphries fell from the truck to the ground, his rifle clanking noisily onto the hot bitumen. He was wearing a heavy winter coat and immediately started haranguing the assembled troops while the bemused corporal warned the others, 'Eyes front.' It was a perfectly timed spectacle; Humphries had planned it, knowing that if he was late he'd be picked up by the military police. He succeeded in bringing the first parade to a grinding halt.

CHAPTER 4

Orsino and the Monster

John Sumner left the Union Theatre Repertory Company to join the newly established Elizabethan Theatre Trust in Sydney in 1955. Before he handed over the reins, he cast the last play for the season, Shakespeare's comedy *Twelfth Night*. Ray Lawler directed the production and played Feste; Zoe Caldwell played Viola. When the actor playing Orsino for the Melbourne run turned down a nine-week country tour of the play, Humphries was offered the role at six pounds a week. Sumner had arranged the tour in partnership with the Council of Adult Education. This last-minute offer was just what Humphries needed to escape from his record-crushing drudgery in Flinders Lane.

Barry was a complete mystery to Ray Lawler. He had not met him before they set out on the tour. Lawler had never seen Barry perform either. Although Humphries was perhaps an odd choice for Orsino, he played the part well in a very 'poetic, far-away, in love with love way'.[1] But he looked ridiculous. The gawky young actor came onto the stage like a big black spider in a too-small black velvet suit, his hat's silk tassels hanging around his lank bobbed hair. He felt completely out of place as the duke and was certain that the audience was laughing at his absurd performance and ridiculous legs, once more clad in tights and breeches.[2] With his large Gainsborough-style bonnet, he looked to his fellow cast member Peter Batey like a 'strange Restoration transvestite'.[3]

Although he acted well, even children in the audience found him ludicrous and hurled their Jaffas at him soon after his entrance. Embarrassed by the response, Barry asked Lawler time and time again in a bewildered and plaintive voice: 'Why does everyone hate me?'[4] He kept the cast alert with his frequent and deliberate misreadings of the famous lines. After the celebrated opening: 'If music be the food of love, play on,' he would pause so that the stage manager stopped the music, only for Humphries to keep going 'Enough, No. *More!*' The record was hastily put back on with a loud scratch of the needle. Barry would then say, 'It's not as sweet as before,' making the scene uproarious rather than wistful and romantic.[5]

Lawler found Barry infuriating. A dedicated, no-nonsense director, he came from a large family and began his working life in a foundry at the age of thirteen. He was meticulous and highly disciplined. In his spare time on the tour he worked on revisions to his newest play script, destined to become an Australian classic, which he had decided to call *Summer of the Seventeenth Doll*. He had developed an intriguing narrative about two canecutters who return each year to Melbourne from north Queensland to enjoy a break with their girlfriends. As the tour progressed from town to town, Lawler gradually came to regard Humphries as strange and irritatingly undisciplined. His boyish pranks and wicked sense of humour marked him out from the other cast members, who thought he was weird, funny and certain to fail as an actor.

The company toured Victoria in the winter of 1955 in a bus affectionately known as 'the monster'. Nine weeks of one and two-night stands with two shows a day made an exhausting routine for the actors. Some of the smaller places did not even have a church hall and one small town had to build a stage for the play. The troupe would arrive in a town, unload all the props and costumes, iron the crushed garments and then drop their belongings at their assigned hotel or pub. Barry had a habit of abandoning the cast after the carry-in of props and sets, in order to explore the town. In spite of Lawler's protests, he simply refused to carry his own bags into his room, and did not seem concerned about what the others thought of him.

When all the jobs were done, the cast members would head to the main street in search of a café. On one occasion Barry sat quietly sipping his tea, then all of a sudden he convulsed and gasped as if he was asphyxiating. He then fell to the floor. When everyone around him had rushed off in search of an ambulance, Barry just as suddenly stood up and said calmly, 'Right, let's go,' and walked out of the café.

Barry had a lank pageboy hairstyle during the season and trailed a very long scarf. He went to extremes to shock people. He loved to pretend to have cerebral palsy, and would walk down the streets of those country towns as if he was afflicted, arousing pitying looks from the locals. He also made a habit of carrying a long tube of cardboard and would shriek into it, 'Look at the old man's shoes!' over and over again, in a high-pitched madman's voice.[6]

Sometimes he would go into a country chemist shop and buy something, then walk out without the purchase, just as he had done to Mr Malouf in Carlton. On one occasion Barry and his friend Stanley Page, who played Andrew Aguecheek, were taken into police custody in Ararat after a local assumed they were escapees from the nearby mental asylum and reported them to the police. A furious Ray Lawler had to extract his two cast members from the police station, and apologise to the unamused sergeant for wasting police time.

One evening a few members of the company were relaxing over a drink and exchanging horrified tales of the cold-water showers in their digs. Only hotel guests could drink on after the infamous six o'clock swill, but many of the locals ignored the rule and were sitting around enjoying each other's company. Without introduction Barry stood up and addressed the whole room: 'I would like to take you to the top end of Collins Street, to a psychiatrist,' he began, impervious to the reactions around him. There were loud protests of 'Shut up mate! We don't want to listen to you.' Ray Lawler, sensing danger, interrupted with a pleading remonstration. But there was no stopping Humphries: his performance was lengthy and entrancing. Incredibly, by the time Barry got to the end of the solo sketch in which the mute patient, Tid, became a suave gentleman and the urbane psychiatrist turned into a blithering idiot, the locals were roaring with laughter. They took Barry to a party and the next morning came to farewell him at the bus.

With his bold interventions Humphries established a pattern of shocking a potential audience, facing initial resistance and achieving enchantment and success. It was to become the pattern of his career over the next half-century, in which he would first bewilder and then delight audiences across three continents with his monologues and improvised banter.

Humphries also enjoyed entertaining and annoying the cast on the long, dusty bus rides, with falsetto speeches in cruel but hilarious parody of the predictable words of thanks given in every town by ladies of the Country Women's Association (CWA) or Arts Society over tea. Barry has never forgotten these 'bun fights', held in dreary church halls with everyone in their best clothes and tables of food 'groaning with asparagus rolls, party pies and lamingtons'.[7] Humphries' high-pitched mimicry of the speeches nearly drove the other cast members mad. It also revealed the way his satirical impulse was often directed at those who admired and appreciated him. It marked the beginning of a talent for barbed parody and a penchant for a tormenting humour that Humphries would cultivate and hone until teasing of his adoring audience became a hallmark.

After the *Twelfth Night* country tour Barry stayed with the company. It was back to the dizzying fortnightly rehearsal schedule. He was always late for rehearsals, a habit that everyone in the company found infuriating. Lawler rehearsed the cast all day and they performed at night; the actors were always tired. In *The Time of Your Life* by William Saroyan, set in a bar in San Francisco, Barry played a philosophically inclined prospector who had just come into the city from the desert. Lawler suggested that Barry wear a sombrero and get a little bit of Fuller's earth and sprinkle it on his clothes to give the impression of dust. When Barry made his entrance on the opening night and touched his hat, the entire stage seemed to disappear in fine white dust. It covered everyone and everything. Lawler was speechless. He had also instructed Barry to stand each evening in the wings in case a stage-effect gunshot didn't come off; in that event he was to give a leather cushion a whack with a crop to mimic the sound. The one night the gun didn't go off, there was no crack of the crop on leather. Barry had forgotten all about it.

During the rehearsals for a production of *Love's Labour's Lost*, Humphries had met Brenda Wright, a petite, dark-haired comedienne and dancer who played Maria. Although Barry had confided to Peter O'Shaughnessy that he was timid with girls, his romance with Brenda progressed quickly.[8] When he announced later to his friends that he was going to marry her many of them were flabbergasted. As she was only eighteen, and they had known each other a very short time, many of them assumed that Brenda was pregnant. Eric and Louisa Humphries were not happy about the marriage, believing that both Barry and Brenda were too young; they sensed also that Barry was simply using marriage as an opportunity to escape from home.

Although anxious about making such a binding commitment at just twenty-one years of age, Barry was besotted with the young dancer. He arranged for the wedding to take place at the Wesley Church in Lonsdale Street, Melbourne, with Peter O'Shaughnessy as his best man, and Peter's wife, Shirley, as an attendant. Barry failed to appear at the church at the appointed hour. He had forgotten the ring, and had to retrace his steps. As a consequence he was running late. But eventually he materialised sporting a new haircut and neatly turned out in a dapper, well-tailored suit. Brenda wore a white ballerina dress and a delicate tulle veil. She stood just five feet tall (150 cm), and beside the spindly Humphries looked like a pretty doll. Eric, Barbara and Michael Humphries attended the ceremony. Auntie Elsie also attended, but Louisa Humphries did not witness her son's marriage. On the day she complained of a severe headache. In fact she was a nervous wreck, and had hoped

Barry would change his mind. Barry's Uncle Dick held a wedding breakfast for the couple and their friends.

There was no honeymoon for the newlyweds. The morning after the wedding Barry arrived for rehearsal and announced the news of his marriage to Ray Lawler. 'Take the day off,' Lawler shouted gruffly, realising there was no point trying to conduct rehearsals with Barry the morning after his wedding. Throughout the season Lawler had continued to struggle with Barry who was exasperatingly difficult. Sometimes he felt he virtually had to push Barry onto the stage, especially if his role involved singing.[9]

There was very little revue theatre in Melbourne at the time, and Lawler was keen to produce as much new Australian material as possible for his Christmas revue of 1955, entitled *Return Fare*. Lawler asked for sketch suggestions from the company. With the grand new world of television just about to transform entertainment, Noel Ferrier offered a sketch called 'The TV Showman', written by John Cargher, in which he lampooned the actor–director Frank Thring, by having the protagonist sound off at various members of the theatre fraternity in Melbourne.[10] Humphries came forward with a sketch about a woman called Edna Everage who was offering her home to billet athletes visiting for the Olympic Games. Peter Batey, one of the other cast members who had been on the *Twelfth Night* tour, helped Barry work up the sketch. They got on very well together and slowly the details of a new character emerged. Edna's voice was like the one he had adopted to terrorise the others on the long bus tour, imitating the hospitable ladies of regional Victoria.

The Olympic Games were to be staged in Melbourne the following year and the organisers were fixated on the problem of housing the expected influx of visitors. The athletes village at Ivanhoe was not yet finished. In a twist on the pronunciation of 'average', Barry called his plain and timid character Mrs Norm Everage, or Edna, after the kind lady who had helped look after him when he was a small child. Edna Everage offered to open her home in Humouresque Street, Moonee Ponds to a visiting athlete, and asked the most preposterous questions about the visitors. In the sketch a government official listed the nationalities of the potential guests and Edna responded with bigoted comments about all of them. The sketch was called 'The Olympic Hostess' and Noel Ferrier played Mr Hopechest, the official interviewing Mrs Everage. Barry had suggested that Zoe Caldwell play Edna, but Lawler insisted that Barry do it himself.

The character invented to pass the time on the bus on the *Twelfth Night* country tour made her debut in Lawler's Christmas revue on 19 December 1955. 'Excuse I,' said Edna timidly as she entered. Although Humphries used phrases he'd heard his mother's helpers use, as well as those copied from the matrons of the CWA, Edna was a composite portrait of various women whose mannerisms had imprinted themselves in his brain. With his new character, Barry seemed to summon a whole new world to the stage, and create a comedy of ordinariness that had never been presented before.

Edna Everage represented Australian suburbia, and Humphries understood the suburbs perfectly. His father had constructed hundreds of houses in the sprawling new estates of Melbourne, and Barry had experienced first-hand the smugness of those who lived in them. The knowledge of what the architect Robin Boyd diagnosed as the 'aesthetic calamity' of Australian 'material triumph' gave Humphries his subject matter. Unlike Boyd, who bemoaned the choices of this race of 'cheerful agoraphobes', Humphries found in the suburbs a human comedy.[11]

The Mrs Everage of 1955 was shy in comparison to her later incarnations. She described her bedroom with its newly painted duck-egg blue walls and chenille bedspread. 'But you surely don't wish to share your bedroom with the athletes?' the official exclaimed. 'Oh, goodness, no. Norm isn't as sporting as all that,' she replied. She stated that she would prefer to host someone from the Commonwealth, and that she didn't mind if they were 'a little tinted', 'perhaps from Ceylon'. She felt sure that meeting an athlete would be good for her son, Kenny, and broaden his horizons.

The fact that Mrs Everage nominated her home to billet an athlete demonstrated the authority women had in Australian families, something not lost on Humphries who had been surrounded by strong, capable and opinioned women throughout his childhood. Humphries had become an expert on the Australian 'matriduxy', as Craig McGregor called it some ten years later.[12]

Barry borrowed a yellow felt hat belonging to his mother, one she had intended to wear to the races. Edna wore a twinset underneath a light beige coat, the kind of garment women wore into the city on the tram to cover their bare arms. The tall, spindly-legged Humphries spoke to the audience in their own vernacular about their own homes. It was an important moment for Australian theatre, but the audience was slightly stunned, and the sketch was regarded as only moderately successful. The reviewer for the *Listener-In* said that Ferrier's impression of Thring was the best item in the revue.[13]

Just before the company staged the revue, Lawler's *Summer of the Seventeenth Doll* made its premiere. It was to become the most significant play in Australian theatre history. June Jago played Olive, Roma Johnston played Pearl, Noel Ferrier played Roo and Lawler himself played Barney. The contrast between Humphries' Mrs Everage sketch and the *Doll* (as Lawler's play was fondly nicknamed) was extreme. But in both works, Australians were portrayed as conservative, comfortable, sometimes childlike city dwellers forced to confront changes in their society. Together, Barry's playful experiment with Edna and Ray Lawler's poignant play sounded the death knell for bush realism in the Australian theatre.

One night during the *Return Fare* run, Barry asked Lawler if he could cut a segment of the sketch. It was the part when Edna insisted on telephoning her mother to ask her some questions about having someone stay at the house during the Olympics. Edna's son, Kenny, answered. Edna was shrill and ridiculous: 'Oh it's you, Kenny? What does the dicky bird say, Kenny? "Birdie? Birdie".'

Lawler objected to the cut because the segment needed to be a certain length to allow for the set-up of the next sketch. Barry then had to explain why he'd made the request and told Lawler nervously: 'You see, the trouble is I've got my landlady coming in tonight and this birdie thing is what she does when she talks to her grandson on the telephone.'[14]

Barry enjoyed playing Edna but never imagined that he would perform the character again. Little did he realise that this 1950s 'Mrs Average' would take on a life of her own. When the season finished he wondered what the future held. All of the actors were now technically out of work, except the lucky few who were invited to play in a Sydney season of the *Doll*. Humphries and Ferrier were not among the chosen ones.

John Sumner, Peter O'Shaughnessy and Ray Lawler had glimpsed Barry's talent for the eccentric, the melodramatic and the comic. But almost everyone questioned his commitment to acting. Barry recalls the Czech actor, George Pravda, putting the case more forcefully than anyone else. 'You see, Barry, to be an actor, you must have it here, [pointing to the head] … here [pointing to the heart] … and here! [pointing to his genital region]. You, Barry, have it here [gesture to the head].' He then made a dramatic shrug of his shoulders, as if to say: 'You certainly don't have it anywhere else.'[15]

Humphries infuriated other cast members, who endured a nightmare performance of Noel Coward's *Design for Living* one night during his last season at the UTRC. Barry forgot his lines and slumped into a chair in frozen desperation, until a semblance of the script came back to him. He has never forgotten the humiliation of those silent pauses and the tone of the leading lady, June Brunell, as they took their bows to muted applause: 'I'm never going to speak to you again.'[16]

Another time Barry had a solo sketch in a revue directed by Peter Batey. The other cast members had gone downstairs for a quick costume change and grew nervous when they realised the theatre had turned silent. Nobody was performing. Batey raced up to the wings to find Barry standing in the middle of the stage, stock-still and mute, staring out at the audience. It was just one more of his tricks, to see how long the audience would last. Batey was furious and reprimanded Barry for his experiment. The others were left to try and pick up the pace after the rupture. Barry was unrepentant.

It was clear to Lawler that Humphries did not fit well into a small repertory company. His flair was for the bizarre and eccentric, whereas the demands of straight roles often eluded him. But he recognised the opportunity for Barry in revue theatre. Sydney producer Bill Orr had asked Lawler to recommend actors for the popular and glamorous Phillip Street Theatre. Orr particularly wanted married couples for his next show. With a flicker of hesitation, Barry's subversive pranks dancing through his brain, Lawler recommended Barry and Brenda. Before long the newlyweds were invited to perform in the next production, entitled *Mr and Mrs*. When the other cast members heard that Barry had been invited to join the popular group in Sydney, they were amazed at his good fortune. Each one of them had been certain that Humphries would never make a success of himself as an actor.

CHAPTER 5

Waiting for Barry

Phillip Street Theatre, under the direction of the Scotsman Bill Orr and his partner, Eric Duckworth, was one of the first Australian theatres to present intimate revue, and the move to Sydney promised Humphries the chance to experiment with cabaret and to work with some of the best-known comic actors in Australia. Phillip Street was one of the most successful theatres in Australia, attracting a fashionable and elegant crowd, and one of only a few fully professional theatres operating in Sydney.

Ruth Cracknell, Max Oldaker, Bud Tingwell and June Salter all graced the stage during the first few years. Hopeful audience members queued around the corner down to Castlereagh Street for tickets to the shows. The humour was irreverent but it was never vulgar.[1] Sydney society queen Nola Dekyvere, novelist Morris West and journalist Elizabeth Best were on the board, as was John Kerr, then a specialist in industrial law and recent member of the Australian Labor Party. The sketches and songs for the revues were written by John McKellar and Gerry Donovan and the music was composed by Lance Mulcahy. They produced a number of hit songs, among them a version of Cole Porter's 'Begin the Beguine'.

The theatre seated three hundred, and had a small stage and a narrow gallery — called the dress circle — of only three rows, running around three of the walls. It was full almost every night.[2] It had originally been a church hall belonging to the handsome St James' Church, designed by Francis Greenway in the 1820s. Bill Orr attended every show and stood in the foyer greeting the audience members as they arrived. Afterwards he mingled and chatted, asking people what they thought of the performance. The custom was to strike a chord with Humphries, who continued the tradition in his own way.

In his first appearance at Phillip Street in *Mr and Mrs*, Barry impressed the other cast members. When the young English actor Gordon Chater first saw Humphries perform he marvelled at his ability to submerge himself in the character, leaving no trace of his 'off-stage persona'.[3] Humphries developed this ability even further at Phillip Street, but very occasionally his own personality intruded into the act. In one of his early appearances Humphries sang a duet with the petite, good-looking comedienne, Wendy Blacklock, who had trained as an actress in Sydney but had limited experience of revue. In the middle of their song Barry started to sing different words, ad-libbing outrageously, and making Wendy's part almost impossible and very frustrating.

Off stage he continued his subversive behaviour, and shocked some of the cast with his black sense of humour. But nothing seemed to faze the pianist Dot Mendoza, whom the cast called Dottie. Mendoza, who was tiny, feisty and walked with a limp, had endured more than thirty hip operations before she was twelve. In spite of her size, she seemed to Gordon Chater to play the piano 'with the attack of a man'.[4] As she struggled to walk up the front steps beside Barry one day (there was no stage door), Humphries shouted, 'Race you to the pit, Dot.' Dot roared with laughter.[5]

But Barry was unimpressed with the material at Phillip Street, and declared in a letter to Peter O'Shaughnessy that the revue, like *Return Fare*, failed because of a 'complete absence of real satire'.[6] The closest thing to political satire during Barry's period at Phillip Street was a short sketch about the Petrov Affair performed by Gordon Chater, Bud Tingwell and Margo Lee who sang 'Three Bright Reds' to the tune of 'Three Blind Mice'.[7]

In 1956 Humphries appeared in *Around the Loop*, a revue that played eight shows a week for fourteen months. (The title of the show referred to the tram loop at the top of King Street in Sydney.) Eventually the show was forced to close due to the exhaustion of the cast, which included the luminaries Max Oldaker, June Salter and Gordon Chater, as well as Humphries and Blacklock. Oldaker was a legendary performer who had sung with Gladys Moncrieff, had starred in opera and musical comedy in London and was regarded as a matinee idol. He was a tall, good-looking actor who was adored by audiences, and by those who worked with him on stage.[8] As a child, Humphries had been taken to see Oldaker star in several wartime presentations at Her Majesty's Theatre in Melbourne, including a famous production of *The Desert Song* in which Max, in disguise as the Red Shadow, and astride a white charger, dazzled hundreds of female admirers in every performance.

Oldaker was charming, witty, kind and generous.[9] He even lent money to desperate fans. Humphries borrowed the name of one of these supplicants for a new character called Basil Clissold. The pitiful and socially ineffectual Clissold of Humphries' imagination haunted his frequent letters to Peter O'Shaughnessy.

Humphries shared an underground dressing room with Oldaker and Gordon Chater. In those days Chater became anxious if the pattern of laughter changed for his performance, and if he didn't get a laugh for a particular line one night when he'd got one the night before.[10] He was obsessively tidy in the dressing room and backstage as well. Humphries' instinct was to upset the equilibrium and goad his colleagues. One night as they all applied their make-up, and Max blacked in his bald patch, Barry stared into the mirror and exclaimed, 'I wonder where we'll all be in ten years? I'll be almost thirty-five. You'll be forty-five, Gordon.' After a short pause he said: 'Max'll be dead.'[11] It was the kind of remark the future Dame Edna would later hurl at her hapless guests on her television show.

Despite his teasing attempts to unsettle Oldaker, Humphries genuinely admired the older actor and his ability to satirise his own artistic career. To Humphries, Max was most 'piquant' in a send-up of himself called 'I'm Just a Shadow of My Former Self'. The song was ostensibly about Tasmania, but also alluded to his role in *The Desert Song*.[12]

Once again Barry entertained the cast off stage. At the end of the show, before they all headed home, he would perform for them, often presenting them with the character of a ghoulish psychiatrist. One night after he finished one of these acts, he shocked the others when he said with a sigh, 'Oh well, that's all. Gotta go home and make love to the midget.'[13] They found him a very strange character, somebody who did not make an effort to be liked. But they all believed in his talent, in contrast to many of the actors with whom he had worked in Melbourne.

Initially Barry and Brenda lived at the Rembrandt Private Hotel in Kings Cross, then for a short time in a flat on Lang Road, Centennial Park, before moving to a house within earshot of the rumbling Pacific Ocean in Fletcher Street, Bondi. Humphries was particularly alarmed by the cockroaches that seemed to invade every household in Sydney, filling his letters to Peter O'Shaughnessy with suggested uses for them in culinary delights such as 'Roached Egg' and a drink he called 'Black Cocky'. He also learned that a previous resident had committed suicide by placing his head in the oven of the Fletcher Street flat. Barry found this disturbing and hated to be alone in the place. In letters to Peter, he complained that he didn't much like Sydney, that the pubs and beer were hideous, and that everyone in the city hated art. His one pleasure, he told his friend, consisted in looking around old churches.[14]

Humphries complained to Peter that he found the sketch material at Phillip Street tedious and tepid, and longed to convince the management to stage his own more robust, even shocking material. But the management was cautious and had rejected one of his sketches, in which he expressed his rage at the Goossens affair, and pilloried the attitude of the popular press to artists. The celebrated English composer and conductor Sir Eugene Goossens, Director of the New South Wales Conservatorium of Music, had become public enemy number one. He was suspected of engaging in a lurid affair, and 'perverse practices' such as bondage, with the notorious 'witch of Kings Cross', Rosaleen Norton. Goossens was detained by police at Mascot Airport on 9 March 1956 after a trip to Europe, and later pleaded guilty to having pornographic items in his possession. He had some prints, books and a few sticks of incense in his bags, and was fined one hundred pounds. But Goossens' reputation and career were destroyed by the scandal, just as he was at the peak of his powers. Humphries was appalled at the way in which the talented musician was portrayed in the newspapers, and the heavy price he paid for his interest in erotic literature. He loathed the way artists seemed to be despised by ordinary Australians. His attempt to satirise this attitude was considered to be in bad taste and unsuitable for Phillip Street audiences.

During the long season of *Around the Loop*, Barry was surprised one night when John Cargher strode into a pub around the corner from the theatre. Barry had been sitting by himself, desperately trying to create a solo sketch. He confessed to Cargher that he was short of ideas. Cargher noticed immediately that Barry was recycling his own *Return Fare* gags. Barry was caught red-handed, but to his relief Cargher laughed out loud, then convinced Barry to come over to the Hotel Australia so that they could go over the script in comfort. The resulting sketch offered a version of 'The TV Showman' sketch that had so pleased Melbourne audiences in 1955. It was accepted by the management and was a success.[15]

Humphries was lonely and unsettled in Sydney. He missed his friends, especially Peter and Shirley O'Shaughnessy. At Christmas Barry and Brenda were invited to dinner at Dulcie Gray's home. The English actress was starring in *Tea and Sympathy* at the Theatre Royal. Barry was very pleased to be invited but anxious about what to take the leading lady. Gordon Chater suggested that he purchase a bottle of Chanel No 5, and offered to lend him the money. Barry duly obtained the tiny bottle, alarmed at having to pay four pounds for the gift, which was a good portion of his week's wages. The company at Christmas dinner was lively, the present a success, and the food and drink were excellent. As Barry opened the door for Brenda on their way out, however, a functionary pulled him aside and said, 'That'll be ten pounds for the two of youse.'[16]

Humphries realised for the first time that he missed 'Gothick' Melbourne, as he called it in his letters to O'Shaughnessy. He denounced Sydney as the 'centre of the Great Australian Decadence'.[17] His melancholy state of mind inspired him to write a couple of short stories about a fey, timid, almost mute character called Tid. He was an alter ego for Barry's childhood self, whom Humphries was now trying to leave behind. He enclosed the stories in his letters to Peter, and also included his first story about Sandy Stone. Barry's correspondence also featured a gossipy and acerbic commentary on Sydney events, people and places. In one letter he described a party he had attended, vividly recounting the guitar music, Virginian cigarettes, improvised jazz and a girl in a long angora jumper dancing frenetically: 'If you can, imagine the plump face of a widgie suffused with the carnal ecstasy of Bernini's St Teresa,' he wrote, thrilled with the bohemian decadence of the party and his description of the participants.[18]

Barry was scathing about the revised version of *Summer of the Seventeenth Doll* playing in Sydney. He described the text as marginally improved from the original but the production as 'flagrantly dishonest', yet adored by the fashionable audience.[19] However, he later noted with genuine interest the reports of the success of the *Doll* on its provincial tour of England. Such was the sense of inferiority about Australian theatre in the 1950s that even after Lawler's play received acclaim in London, there were expressions of doubt all over Australia about the truth of its success.[20] In spite of the sceptics, the triumph of the *Doll* on the London stage heralded a change in the status of Australian drama within and beyond the country's borders.

Australians were still sceptical, however, about their capacity to make dramatic dialogue in the vernacular interesting. Patrick White wrote to the actor Keith Michell at this time, despairing of the sound of Australians talking. He said 'we are undramatic, too boring. The average Australian can't tell one anything without making it sound pointless. Such a chronic shapelessness can build novels, but the drama will hardly flourish in it.'[21] But it was exactly this kind of banal, shapeless chat that Humphries would later transform into searing satirical monologues.

If he found the Sydney sketch material unadventurous, Humphries capitalised on the opportunity to hone his cabaret skills. Phillip Street taught him how to please a crowd, and how to affect a suave and sophisticated persona on stage. It gave him new confidence in himself as a performer. In one of the revues Barry played Tarzan. He looked ridiculous but carried it off. He learned to control his physical awkwardness, and increased his confidence performing in front of children; he played the Mad Hatter in a marvellous production of *Alice in Wonderland* with the dancer Kathleen Gorham.

Phillip Street opened Barry's eyes to the ways in which he could hold the audience, and how to communicate with them intimately. It also gave him a feeling for professional musical revue and the crowd-pleasing techniques of music hall. The lessons he learned have stayed with him since those difficult yet heady months in the harbour city. Humphries had never been shy of taking liberties with an audience, but he experimented at Phillip Street with longer and longer pauses, holding a pause mid-monologue for longer than is usually safe — just to see if he could.

While Humphries could at times admire John McKellar's solid original writing, he found the scripts he adapted from English revue particularly irritating and banal. However, the technique of updating, adapting and tossing in the names of local socialites stuck with him, and he mastered the art of name-dropping in revue. This technique, borrowed from music hall, was to become a central element of his satirical repertoire later in his career. Socialites, celebrities and politicians from the city in which he performs are always incorporated into Humphries' scripts.

On 4 November 1956, Edna Everage appeared in the inaugural broadcast of HSV7 in Melbourne, in a live telecast from the newly refurbished Tivoli Theatre. The variety show was called *The Olympic Follies*. Humphries and Gordon Chater were flown to Melbourne especially to appear.

During this period relations with Brenda were strained. Barry reported almost glumly in one letter to Peter that Brenda was still very much in love with him, and confessed to bouts of late-night brandy drinking without her.[22] On a number of occasions Brenda was woken in the early hours of the morning by a taxi driver who needed help lifting her husband from the back of the cab to the living-room floor.

After a few drinks Barry sometimes reverted to his old trick of terrifying the weak and gullible. At one party, he singled out a young man who had pustules on his skin. He put him in a chair in the middle of the room and began to taunt him. Humphries did not receive much sympathy after this incident. Max Oldaker even told him quietly that none of this would have happened if he had done something about his unsuitably long hair, which continued to provoke.[23] When Alan Riddell pointed out Kenneth Slessor late one night in a pub, Barry was thrilled to meet the great Australian poet. He vividly recalls introducing himself just as Slessor was about to shoot a billiard ball. The poet took a long look at Humphries, sipped his drink and exclaimed, 'Why don't you get your fucking hair cut!'[24] Once, a man even appeared at the stage door and threatened Barry with a knife.

At another party Humphries was knocked to the floor by someone he had offended. He lay on his back with his long, skinny legs in the air and cried out, 'Don't hit me, I'm a coward,' forcing everyone into fits of laughter.[25] Physical aggression for the adult Barry was as terrifying as it had been when he was a schoolboy. Once Brenda tried to pull someone off Barry and ended up with a black eye herself.

Humphries affected a brash, confident and urbane exterior in his Phillip Street days, but found the daily reality of earning his living difficult and sometimes demoralising. He complained to Peter about working in a dreary commercial (for the 'Skintite container'), but boasted about an invitation to appear in an ABC Saturday night variety program on radio, performing his own material. But nothing came of this invitation. He kept Peter up to date with his indefatigable reading, offering his contrary interpretations of various influential writers. He described *Lucky Jim* as a study in 'Anglo Saxon Attitudes', and felt that TS Eliot's conviction that April 'is the cruellest month' would have been better expressed 'less melodramatically'.[26] He despaired of any real artistic opportunity in Sydney, however, and rather melodramatically himself decreed that 'the time seems ripe for some heroic act of espionage'. He did not give any indication of what this act might entail, but noted that to be hated and disturbed was akin to living in a state of grace in Australia.[27]

Humphries felt his creative impulse was stymied, but his social life made up for it. Although he didn't feel he truly fitted in with the acting fraternity who frequented the pubs around Phillip Street, he would occasionally drink there in the evenings before the show, and frequently afterwards. At the Assembly Hotel near the theatre, he recalls watching radio actresses smoking Garricks and drinking gin, and listening to the conversations about SP betting, abortion and shoplifting by members of the Push.[28] Although he longed to return to Melbourne, the glamorous live theatre scene at the Tivoli and Phillip Street provided some excitement and intrigue.

One night Humphries turned up at a Sydney Push party at the family home of the glamorous Roelof Smilde in Mosman. Humphries always turned heads with his long hair. He was good-looking in a strange way, with penetrating brown eyes and shapely, sensual lips. He noticed a dark-haired, strikingly attractive young woman, Margaret Elliott. Margaret, who was twenty-four, earned her living teaching art. She seemed to know everyone, and was romantically involved with one of the key members of the Push, the idealistic, anarchist poet Harry Hooton, who was twenty-five years older than her. There was an instant attraction between Barry and Margaret. He cornered her in the bathroom and tried to kiss her. They arranged to meet the next day.

Margaret lived with Hooton in Potts Point; she was devoted to him. Overnight she thought better of getting involved with Barry. After she finished teaching at Strathfield the next day, she dropped a note into the Phillip Street Theatre for Barry, explaining that she would not meet him, and hurried off to catch her tram home. Barry rushed out of the theatre after her, boarded the tram and implored her to reconsider as the tram made its way to the top of William Street. She agreed to have a drink with him, and then arranged another meeting at a pub in Circular Quay the next day. Within a few days their clandestine affair was in full swing. Barry was smitten.

For Margaret the affair was agonising because she knew that her heart belonged to Harry. But Barry was charming, witty, handsome and young. She found his urbane glamour and comical self-regard appealing. The intrigue appealed to both of them. They went to parties and pretended not to know one another, and met late at night in the smoky darkness of Pakie's nightclub in Elizabeth Street, where very few people recognised them.

Humphries admired the defiant, anti-elitist, egalitarian elements of Push ideology, but found the political intensity too didactic and some of the members rather too desperate. For him the talk was aridly political, with few of the core Push characters genuinely interested in art. As well as the anarchists, atheists and revolutionaries there were also some right-wingers, such as David Armstrong and Peter Coleman, with whom Barry became friends. In general he found others in the Push unappealing and referred to Harry Hooton as one of 'Sydney's most prominent labourer-poets — a typical Australian inverted aesthete'.[29]

When they first met Barry asked Margaret her age, and when she answered that she was twenty-four he said he was twenty-five, not wanting to admit to being a year younger than her. Many years later, he described her — by then well known as the film producer Margaret Fink — as an 'exciting older woman'.[30] In a letter to Peter at the time he portrayed her as 'twenty-four and sensitive in a blunt and carnal way'.[31] Margaret was a sultry beauty, with dark eyes and glossy hair. Like Barry she was quick-witted, well-read and sharp-tongued. Barry found himself utterly enchanted by her, captivated in particular by her fine wrists, slender neck and high cheekbones as well as her arty ways. He confessed to Peter that the passion they felt for one another was 'instant and powerful and mutual', but predicted an uncertain time ahead. 'Back on the verge of the crater, I am recklessly without a thought of the morrow,' he wrote.[32] In reporting his tumultuous emotions, Humphries seemed to have found the situation both funny and dangerous. 'So far it has been difficult to know whether one is involved in an affair or a caprice as the thing has been conducted with lewd stealth. Lately I have felt quite cold and mad.' He urged Peter to burn the letter, terrified that Brenda would find out about the affair. He relished the danger, and felt at last that he was 'in touch with the total reality of Sydney', and its corrupt essence.

In the early months of 1957 Peter O'Shaughnessy moved to Sydney, to work temporarily as assistant director to Doris Fitton at the Independent Theatre, leaving his wife, Shirley, and their new baby daughter Caitlin, in Melbourne. He sometimes stayed with the Humphries at Bondi where Peter, Barry and Brenda drank and played music on a borrowed gramophone. They played Schubert's *Die Winterreise* with Hans Hotter and Gerald Moore over and over again, before collapsing at dawn — but only after drinking a gallon of water. This was Humphries' trusted cure for excessive alcohol intake.[33]

Despite his obsession with Margaret, Barry could not forget the Goossens affair. It was in his view emblematic of Australian attitudes to art and artists. He wrote a new script in which a philistinish male character railed at the waste of public money lavished on the new opera house designed by Joern Utzon. The disgraced conductor Goossens had himself lobbied hard for a new venue for opera and drama to be built in Sydney. As Humphries considered the type of person who would have the gall to speak out against the plans for an opera house, he made the character a woman. Ultimately Edna was brought back for the job of complaining about the 'poor' design of the Opera House, featuring its now iconic cement shells, to be built at Bennelong Point.

Edna focused on the unsuitability of the building for young families. 'Now,' she began, 'I'd like to offer a few little suggestions for what they're worth as regards the amenities and general facilities of this new building. Unless these amenities are provided, I see very little likelihood of any mother dragging herself from the comfort of her own home all the way out to Bennelong Point when she could go to a local picture show, and for a fraction of the price.' Peter O'Shaughnessy made some suggestions for the sketch for this rather bossy Mrs Everage, and Humphries tried it out at Phillip Street.[34] The newly confident Edna prefigured the brazen and highly opinionated Edna of the future. But the sketch did not find a ready audience and only lasted a few performances.

Disappointed with its lukewarm reception and fed up both with Sydney, and *Around the Loop*, Barry determined to extricate himself from Phillip Street. He knew he wanted to return to Melbourne, and ultimately make his way to London. Unable to secure his release from Phillip Street in time to play the Fool to O'Shaughnessy's Lear in Melbourne, Humphries put his mind to tackling the management anew in order to get away.

Around this time Humphries started reading Beckett and was ecstatic to see the dramatist's directions that read 'Pause', 'Long pause' and 'Pause again'. He enjoyed Beckett's extraordinary short-story collection *More Pricks than Kicks*, but it was the strange rhythms of his plays that struck Humphries powerfully. They seemed to be made for him. He did not hesitate when Peter O'Shaughnessy wrote to ask him if he would come back to his hometown to play Estragon to Peter's Vladimir in Beckett's *Waiting for Godot*. He was ecstatic at the thought of performing in a Beckett play.

It suited Barry to return to Melbourne when *Around the Loop* finally closed in August. His affair with Margaret and his neglect of Brenda made him feel decadent, dangerous and wicked; and he was exhausted by the long season at Phillip Street. In one of his last letters to Peter from Sydney he described his recurring nightmares about forgetting lines, and promised faithfully not to 'bugger up the play'.[35]

CHAPTER 6

Eucalypso Nights

As soon as he was free of Phillip Street, Humphries left Sydney to begin rehearsing *Waiting for Godot* in Melbourne at the Arrow Theatre in Middle Park. It was a small theatre owned by Frank Thring and inexpensive to rent. Brenda stayed in Sydney and Margaret Elliott accompanied Barry for the season, as it was school holidays. They shared a flat in St Kilda with the corpulent English actor Philip Stainton and his partner, Betsy. Stainton, who had performed in various Ealing comedies, was to play Pozzo.

Barry and Peter were excited at the prospect of presenting *Waiting for Godot*. It was the first production of the play in Australia, and its expressionist texture and absurdist lyricism enthralled the two actors. O'Shaughnessy found the 'fractured syntax' and 'ping-pong monosyllabic dialogue' bleak and beautiful. The two of them threw themselves into rehearsing the challenging play; neither of them had ever before encountered lines like Beckett's.[1]

O'Shaughnessy and Humphries strapped themselves to sandwich boards and tramped around Melbourne in their ragged clothes to advertise the play. Humphries had made the set himself, raiding backyards for old tin cans, bicycle wheels and prams to create a kind of aerial 'rubbishscape' that was suspended over the stage.[2]

Audience reaction varied. As in the London production, some members of the audience walked out, finding the dialogue strange and the pace excruciating. Several audience members found the play dreary, far too slow and rather self-indulgent. One or two even asked whether Humphries had written the script himself. Others enjoyed Barry's funny, improvised moments and his asides. At one point Estragon's trousers fell down and he muttered insults to the other characters, such as, 'Kick him in the crutch, kick him in the crutch.'[3] But most of the audience, stunned by the unusual nature of the play, seemed unsure whether or not to laugh, and found Humphries' attempt at comedy disconcerting. Barry's parents took the family to the play; Michael was very impressed with the performance of his elder brother, and the play itself.

Only one photograph survives of Peter and Barry dressed as the tramps. Taken by Philip Stainton, it shows a seated Peter, as Vladimir, staring straight ahead, his right arm protectively round Estragon's (Barry's) shoulders. Estragon looks downcast and forlorn. This image captures the intense emotion each man brought to his role, and something of their own relationship, revealing Peter's tender and almost proprietorial feeling for Barry. It also captures the existential dilemma, the pain and suffering that the play dramatises.

O'Shaughnessy understood the play as an 'inquest' on Western, or Christian, civilisation. For him, Beckett's agnostic searching offered a pessimistic judgment on that civilisation and each of the characters represented regions of the European imagination.[4] His performance was enigmatic and intensely serious, reflecting his sense of the larger meaning of the play. He was to become a devotee of the work of the Irish playwright, and played Krapp in the Australian premiere of *Krapp's Last Tape* in Melbourne in 1959. In contrast, Humphries brought comic energy to the play's exploration of profound questions. He revelled in the long pauses that infuse the work with its pathos.

In the second week, the houses filled up, and the play became a topic of conversation among Melbourne's artists and writers. The critical reception for this first production of Beckett in Australia was mixed. The Melbourne *Sun* critic proclaimed it an 'extraordinary adventure', 'engrossing' and 'well done'. HA Standish in the *Herald* was less enthusiastic, but declared that Humphries' acting was 'brilliant' and that the play 'would give intellectuals and pseudo-intellectuals plenty to talk about'. He added, however, that many would agree with these lines from the play that 'Nothing happens. Nobody comes, nobody goes. It's awful.'[5] Bruce Grant of *The Age* declared the play to be 'the weirdest play of the decade, (perhaps, ever?)', and described O'Shaughnessy as 'the stronger of the two tramps'.[6] He found Barry's performance lacking in 'dramatic power'.

At the end of the two-week season and the school holidays, Margaret returned to Sydney for work, and to her partner, Harry Hooton. She cried all the way home on the plane. The next day Barry followed her. By this stage Harry Hooton was determined to prevent Margaret seeing Barry and insisted that she refuse all contact with him. In spite of the intensity of their feelings for one another they were very different. Margaret baulked at Barry's assumption that she would cook his breakfast, though she was not particularly surprised by the unthinking sexism because it was all around her in the Push.[7] But she was incensed by his snobbery and found his lack of interest in politics incomprehensible. As far as she could see, Barry had no inkling of the implications of human inequality and was spectacularly self-centred. Margaret had fallen in love with him but the short and passionate relationship was over.

Humphries returned to Melbourne and was relieved to be mixing with a more congenial crowd. *Waiting for Godot* gave him a sense of achievement, and might be seen as his first real break as an actor. Peter O'Shaughnessy, too, was pleased with the success of *Waiting for Godot*, and began preparing to present *Pygmalion* and a children's pantomime. Barry and Peter met regularly at the Swanston Family Hotel; it was one of the pubs frequented by various artists, and through Peter and his brother Brian, Barry met Clifton Pugh, Charles Blackman, John Perceval, Matcham Skipper, Leonard French, Arthur and David Boyd, and David's wife, Hermia. Arthur Boyd had been chosen to represent Australia at the Venice Biennale, and was shortly to leave Melbourne for London. In fact everyone talked about going to Europe.

During their long drinking sessions, Barry and Peter also mixed with poets Glen Tomasetti and Chris Wallace-Crabbe, historian Brian Fitzpatrick, the young and rambunctious film maker Tim Burstall and his partner, Betty, the activist Beatrice Faust and a young English literature student, Germaine Greer. Greer was one of the youngest members of this group of Melbourne bohemians, sometimes called the Drift. The name was a response to the Push in Sydney, but the group in Melbourne was more Marxist than the libertarian Andersonians to the north, with the exception of Humphries and the philosopher David Armstrong. The oddly assorted artists and writers 'drifted' around Italian restaurants in Lygon Street, Carlton and the pubs, and after the pubs closed they drifted out to various houses in the village of Eltham on a Friday or Saturday evening, or to Clifton Pugh's small city abode, enjoying long discussions on art, philosophy and politics.

Encouraged by his recent success as Estragon, Barry put on an occasional turn or an improvised sketch that impressed the men and enchanted the women at noisy parties after the pub. But not everyone warmed to him. Some people found his improvisations annoyingly immature. Clifton Pugh recalled that at a party at the home of David and Hermia Boyd one of the children urinated into a wine glass and handed it to Barry, who drank it. The children told everyone the story, delighted that they had evened up the score with the guest who had a tendency to order them around, and to demand drinks from them as if they were servants.[8]

Like the Push members in Sydney, the Drift believed in free love but were not bound by any unifying ideology. Members of the Push were united in following their highly influential mentor, the Scottish-born Sydney University philosopher, John Anderson, who espoused free love, free thought and free association well before these values became the catchcry of the 1960s counterculture. Alternatively Push members embraced the Utopian anarchist ideals of Margaret Elliott's partner, Harry Hooton, who believed that humans were perfect and that technology would eventually liberate mankind. The Drift was much more floating and fluid, as the name implied. Humphries had been largely unimpressed with the Push;

he found them down-at-heel and fixated on ideology. But the Drift artists, particularly the painters, captured his attention and admiration.

When *Pygmalion* opened at the Eastern Hill Theatre, Humphries' portrayal of Colonel Pickering was said to be 'highly convincing', though the reviewer questioned his casting in the role because of his youth. But with 'a prim mouth, an open suntanned face, an astonishing white wig,' he smiled his way through the performance. O'Shaughnessy's performance as Higgins received almost universal praise, but *The Age* reviewer argued that his interpretation of the character was wrong.[9] For Humphries it was an enjoyable opportunity to perform in the popular play.

At a 1957 New Year's Eve party in a flat in Millswyn Street, South Yarra, Barry met Rosalind Tong, a ballet dancer from New Zealand, who was visiting Melbourne with a friend en route to Paris where she hoped to develop her career with the Paris Opera Ballet. At twenty, Rosalind had danced already with the renowned Danish dancer Poul Gnatt, performed in the Auckland Light Opera Company, the New Zealand Ballet Company and managed her own successful ballet school. She was a sweet-natured, elegant young woman who found Barry charming and very funny. He was enchanted by her fine blonde hair, serene expression and graceful movements. He thought she looked like Flora, the goddess of spring in Botticelli's *Primavera*, and fell in love with her immediately. Shortly after they met, Ros danced in the musical *Lola Montez*, partnered with one of Barry's old revue friends, Brian Westmore.

By day, Rosalind worked in a clothing emporium to help pay for her ballet classes. Several times soon after they met, Barry asked her out for dinner. Every time she would arrive accompanied by a female friend, which frustrated Barry. One day he appeared unannounced at the clothing shop, looking for Ros. He cast his eyes over the team of middle-aged shop assistants and remarked in a loud voice, 'What a lot of old bags!' Turning to Ros he said, 'Get your coat, we're going out for lunch.' He drove her to her lodgings in South Yarra, explaining, 'I want to see where you live.' Rosalind took him inside the grand house where she boarded, the landlady looking askance as they walked to her room. Pointing at her small suitcase in the corner, Barry said commandingly, 'Pack! I'm going to take you somewhere amazing.' He drove through the suburbs of Melbourne, finally pulling up outside a place beyond bushy rural Eltham. It was 'Dunmoochin', home to Cliff Pugh and his wife, Marlene. Breaking down a rather flimsy bamboo door, Barry told Ros not to worry, reassuring her that Cliff had said he could stay there. For the next few days Barry and Ros talked about music, painting, books and, of course, themselves in the idyllic surrounds of the painter's bush retreat. Ros was also a fan of the Sitwells, admired the music of Satie and was delighted with Barry's outlandish stories and whimsical humour. Barry was happier than he had ever been. He felt that he had found a soulmate and someone with a '"real" sense of humour'.[10]

One of the Pughs' neighbours, the artist Frank Werther, was shocked to see the two lovers on the balcony one day and shouted at Barry, demanding to know why they were in the house. Humphries looked down at Werther and replied in his poshest accent, 'I'm Barry Humphries.' When Frank said, 'I don't give a stuff who you are, just get out of here,' Barry retaliated, 'You're just a pathetic, illiterate little German peasant with no seat to your pants and what's more you haven't an artistic bone in your body.' Clifton Pugh was amused to hear of the exchange when he returned from the coast, and the indignant expression 'I'm Barry Humphries' brought a smile to his friends in Eltham for months afterwards.[11]

In December 1957, Barry had worked with Peter O'Shaughnessy. Peter had invited two radio script writers, Jeffrey Underhill and Don Whitelock, to script a children's pantomime he had devised that he hoped would allow Barry to celebrate his comic spirit and play a bush clown, someone Peter believed was 'close to his secret heart'.[12] The new play was called *The Bunyip and the Satellite*, and was inspired by Frank Dalby Davison's *The Children of the Dark People*.

Even though the pantomime was at the opposite end of the theatrical spectrum to *Waiting for Godot*, O'Shaughnessy felt confident that the role of Bunyip was perfect for Barry. Both productions drew on Humphries' strange, dreamy and tender alter ego. Barry's triumphant Bunyip character was a spirit of the bush, a clown-like Papageno. There was a lost boy in the play, assorted bush creatures and a swaggie played by Peter himself. The first earth-orbiting satellite, *Sputnik*, had been launched in October, and Peter included a satellite in the story, which dealt with the problem of how to fight a bush fire when the Spirit of the Bush Fire had teamed up with the dreaded north winds of Melbourne. Enchanted by the characters in the play, Barry wrote the lyrics for three songs. He dubbed one of them a 'Eucalypso', because of its combination of calypso rhythm and Australian bush themes. He sang another of his songs during the climax of the play from the top of a tree, as he spied the bush fire, now transformed into a satellite.

The play was a success and warmly praised throughout Melbourne. Bruce Grant, writing in *The Age*, praised Humphries' tenderness and wit, describing him as a 'legend with gum leaves in his hair'. He celebrated the character as a 'true relation of the greatest fools and clowns of the stage', and recognised Barry's 'innocent gaiety'.[13]

Soon afterwards Humphries was invited to appear in a regular Monday evening spot on *The Magic Forest*, a children's television program. He played Mr Bunyip from Ferntree Gully, and sat on a log telling stories to a group of a dozen seven year olds, for which he was delighted to receive nine pounds per appearance.[14] During the week Rosalind helped Barry devise the storyline for each show.[15]

A good-looking, unfailingly polite young man called Don Bennetts briefed Barry each week about who else was scheduled to appear on the show. There were magicians, jugglers and Weg the cartoonist ahead of the Bunyip segment. Then Barry would appear in his hessian outfit adorned with gum leaves and enthral the children with bush lore. He talked seriously to the enraptured audience about the right gum leaves for a koala to eat, the need to be gentle with bush creatures, what to do if you want to watch a lyrebird, how to avoid causing a bush fire and the meaning of the dawn chorus. Humphries described the way in which birds call out each morning to let one another know 'I'm all right, day is breaking'.[16]

In these lyrical interludes Humphries recalled the magic of his own childhood holidays at the family shack near Healesville and picnics with his parents at Warrandyte. All of his Bunyip stories were unscripted and revealed his love of the Australian bush and his ingenious talent for improvisation. Only once Mr Bunyip lost his cool, and became a little too grumpy for the children. After a spattering of something unpleasant from a tall gum tree, he gruffly expostulated, 'I hate Mr Koala!' When he explained why, the children laughed with glee.[17]

Barry Humphries as Mr Bunyip was a natural on television. The audiences for the new broadcasting medium were still small. Only a fraction of Melbourne's citizens owned a television, although hundreds had invested in the new technology when the Olympic Games were broadcast in 1956.[18] Many people considered it a rather lowbrow form of entertainment. Barry had appeared on television just twice before, once when a friend from his university days, Anton Bowler, invited him to perform a mime sequence. Bowler was a flamboyant character, and very sympathetic to Barry's whims and affectations. Bowler played the roué with aplomb and boasted of becoming a Spanish bullfighter. In real life he worked for Channel 7. Bowler convinced Barry to appear on live television clad in a dark cloak and his elongated Dada gloves to perform a ghostly mime to the tune of the hit parade favourite 'The Purple People Eater'. In the segment, Barry surveyed a number of empty artwork frames, then stopped at his own 'forkscape' — dozens of twisted forks welded together — and played it as though it was a harp. It was a perfect appearance for the *BP Hit Parade* which was the most popular television show in Australia, and regularly created rather surreal sketches.

It was the colourful Anton Bowler who had first introduced Barry to Don Bennetts, the creative young man who was to become a life-long friend. Already Barry had his sights set on London, and urged Don to make a break from his hometown.

'There's nothing for you here,' Barry said with conviction, as he looked out across the city from Don's South Yarra apartment. Bennetts realised that it was Humphries' feeling about his own life that he articulated. For Humphries, Melbourne was too safe and too small. He seemed to need risk and constant change in his life to feel that he was living.[19]

Rosalind and Barry both played in Peter O'Shaughnessy's lunch-hour revues, and Ros tried her hardest to teach the others how to warm up properly before they performed. She worried about Barry's heavy drinking. In the autumn of 1958, Peter O'Shaughnessy and Barry appeared at the Wangaratta Festival. As soon as Peter finished a dramatic reading of Henry Lawson, Edna swept onto the stage. 'Excuse I!' she exclaimed, and began a spirited fulmination against the Sydney Opera House, but with higher energy than in her earlier renditions. A local newspaper remarked that Humphries demonstrated 'a highly developed talent for caricature' and pronounced him to be 'an actor of quality'.[20]

A couple of weeks later Peter presented *Waiting for Godot* and the Bunyip pantomime in a short season at the Independent Theatre in North Sydney. Peter and Barry executed an 'action painting' for the Godot set, tossing dirty rags and muddy objects at the back wall of the stage. In front they hung a tangled mat of fishermen's nets. Ros was very impressed with the production and thought Peter's direction of the play brilliant. She sat in the prompt corner for *Godot*, and performed the role of the dancing Spirit of the Bush Fire in the pantomime.[21] For this play, they resurrected a rich and magical forest backdrop painted by Arthur Boyd for *Love's Labour's Lost* a few years earlier in Melbourne.

The reviews of *Godot* in Sydney were excellent, with the *Sydney Morning Herald* critic praising the 'well-played' tramps and their 'brilliant theatrical shocks'.[22] The *Bulletin* declared the play to be 'outrageously offensive', 'intellectually fascinating' and 'superbly acted'.[23] Another reviewer judged the directing and acting to be highly effective, observing that both actors 'do splendid work as a couple of human derelicts'.[24] But the nightly attendance was poor, and theatre-goers found the play hard to understand.

More surprisingly the Sydney audiences did not take to the *Bunyip* as Melbourne audiences had. Unfazed by the poor box-office returns, Barry and Rosalind, who had been staying in shabby, cockroach-infested rooms in Crows Nest, joined Peter and Shirley and other cast members for a weekend at Palm Beach. They sat listening to grunting koalas in the tall scribbly-gums, and eating lobster in the cliff-top garden. In the evening Barry gave a halting impromptu speech in a wispy, crackly old man's voice, reminiscing about Melbourne. His nostalgic ramblings belonged to an emerging character called Sandy Stone.

If Phillip Street had offered Humphries a chance to hone his skills in revue and pantomime, his passionate new interest in Beckett provided the inspiration for his stage character Alexander, or 'Sandy', Horace Stone. The character originated in a short story he wrote in 1956, based on one of his parents' neighbours in Camberwell, a Mr Whittle, who would greet him every morning as he ran for the train. There were traces of Barry's Uncle Lewis in Sandy too. He also adopted the 'vocal mannerisms' of an elderly man he met on Bondi Beach. The man spoke in a 'cracked falsetto voice', had 'thin, sandy hair and rosy finely capillaried cheeks, two-toned cardigan and a pair of marsupial freckled paws'.[25] With pauses reminiscent of Beckett, Sandy's speech was excruciatingly slow, and his banal descriptions of his day revealed someone preoccupied with the mundane domestic details of life in the respectable suburbs — a kindly bore whose monologues are both pitiful and poignant.

Before long O'Shaughnessy persuaded Barry to accompany him to the Glen Iris living room of an emerging producer, Peter Mann, to ad-lib some Sandy material into a microphone. He had not yet committed Sandy's monologue to paper, but Barry decided to give him a home at 36 Gallipoli Crescent, Glen Iris. The 's' at the end of 'Iris' allowed Humphries to make the most of the whistling sibilants produced by Sandy's dentures. Mann liked what he heard, and Barry recorded Sandy's recollections under the glorious title 'Wild Life in Suburbia', with Sandy Stone on one side and a revised and updated version of his original Edna sketch called 'The Migrant

Hostess' on the reverse, with Colin Munro playing the part of the official.

With the characters Sandy and Edna, Humphries created a new vision of Australian suburbia and a comic appreciation of its small-minded, bigoted, childlike and materialistic denizens. The communist historian Russel Ward argued in his book *The Australian Legend*, published in the same year that Barry recorded Sandy's musings, that Australians shared a distinctive bush ethos. Ward identified the outlines of a national character, centred around the typical Australian and his independence of spirit, ability to improvise, practical skills, rough manners and irritation with affectation. It was squarely based on perceptions of men of the bush and the bush ballads Ward had studied. The legend was just that — a legend — but it rested on historical fact, and as Peter Conrad observes, 'myths are consciously contrived to serve a social need'.[26] Humphries also began to dramatise his sense of a typical Australian, though he did not imagine his project to be a study of national character in the way Ward had. And Humphries' Australian legend was set in suburbia. In the case of Sandy Stone, though, the legend was almost as nostalgic as Ward's. Over the next decade Humphries' legend grew to embody the musings of a married woman from Moonee Ponds and articulated a passionate attack on philistinism and ignorance in Australian society. It would ultimately make Ward's legend look out of touch and out of date.

CHAPTER 7

E-SCAPE

With a great deal of help from Rosalind and Clifton Pugh, Humphries mounted an art exhibition of forty-eight pieces in August 1958 at the Victorian Artists' Society gallery at Eastern Hill. The exhibition was put together under false pretences, with Pugh promising the Artists' Society a 'serious exhibition': its Dadaist content was kept a secret until it opened.[1]

Humphries did his own advertising for the exhibition which was planned to coincide with a new show called *Rock 'n' Reel Revue*. In his ads for the exhibition, he boldly promised art by 'Tom Roberts, Dargie, Meldrum and Arthur Boyd'. Germaine Greer enthusiastically helped Barry and Ros install some of the bizarre works in the cavernous gallery.

At the opening Humphries locked all the guests out on the pavement and opened the show inside to an empty gallery. During the course of the exhibition, he opened the show over and over again, whenever the mood seized him. The cluttered pages of the black-and-white catalogue announced a new award for critics to be called 'The Barry'. Humphries remade some of his earlier Dadaist works from the 1952 university exhibition he had staged with his friend John Perry. The rust-coloured gloves Barbara knitted made a comeback. Their twenty-inch (51-cm) forefingers were designed, according to Humphries, for 'extra flexibility', and were draped over the side of a small table looking like elongated condoms in a piece called 'Dress Reform for the Australian Male'. The exhibit also had a 'single breasted' hat with a zip sewn into the crown as an 'exit opening' and two shoes joined together at the toes entitled 'Siamese Shoe'.[2] Ros cooked a massive vat of custard and Germaine Greer helped her lift and pour it into some boots for a revival of the spectacularly gross 'Pus in Boots' installation. A new sculpture made of a purée of mixed vegetables, a blow-up wading pool and various books appeared under the title 'I was reading these books and felt sick'. An electric toaster on butchers' plastic grass and a strange butterfly formed another sculpture entitled 'Design for Proposed Cultural Centre (Humphries, Humphries & Humphries)'.

A large headshot of Barry appeared in a feature on the exhibition in the *Australian Women's Weekly* under the headline 'The Year's Zaniest Art Show'. A bespectacled Humphries, wearing a black felt hat, stared menacingly from the page. He was described grandly as an 'actor and playwright', and declared another of his exhibits entitled 'E-SCAPE' — a mass of cut-out printed Es — as 'having no point ... except that "E" is just another unused art form'. In this installation Humphries was simultaneously celebrating and mocking the 'cut up' technique of the provocative American author William Burroughs. Another exhibit was a 'forkscape'; Barry and Ros had collected the steel forks at a pig farm, along with other rubbish that had been sent to the farm from hospitals.

Clifton Pugh painted his first portrait of Barry at this time, capturing his thin and haughty face, large eyes and strange hands, his long fingers twisted together as though carrying all his anxieties in them. For Cliff the fingers caught a personality that seemed intelligent, uncertain and sad.[3]

In a back room at the dreary New Theatre hall in Flinders Street, Barry and Peter O'Shaughnessy rehearsed their next show. O'Shaughnessy produced and underwrote *Rock 'n' Reel Revue* in a clear reference to the style of music that had transformed popular culture in the 1950s. Humphries and O'Shaughnessy continued to work as a tight unit, and even Barry's new love, Rosalind, felt excluded by the two of them at times. To make matters worse, O'Shaughnessy paid Humphries his wages with Rosalind's portion included in the one cheque. Ros objected and insisted that she should be paid independently.

In the next room a young communist called Phillip Adams was preparing for his realist film association evenings, spending hours trying to synchronise the music of Shostakovich with scenes from *The Battleship Potemkin*. Every so often Adams caught a glimpse of Barry dressed as Mrs Everage, looking like a stick insect in 'flatties, yellow sockettes and a strange conical hat', singing songs for the show.[4]

Rock 'n' Reel Revue gave Melbourne a taste of Phillip Street and featured Sandy Stone in his stage debut, clad in slippers and dressing gown, in addition to Edna Everage and a host of other characters in fifteen sketches. O'Shaughnessy and Humphries devised a format for the sketch called 'Days of the Week', in which each day of Sandy's week was introduced with a tune such as 'When I Grow Too Old to Dream', 'Smoke Gets in Your Eyes', 'Look for the Silver Lining' and 'Goodnight Sweetheart', to evoke the man's youth.

In this early monologue, Humphries satirised the idiom of his parents' generation using phrases he remembered from his childhood: 'Well, not much that I can say about Tuesday, except that it was a very nice night's entertainment,' Stone mused. 'We're not one for the pictures as a rule, but when we do go we like to see a good, bright show. After all, there's enough unhappiness in the world ...' Then, 'Had a bit of strife parking the vehicle,' reported Sandy as he described his late arrival at the MCG for a 'semi'. 'Beryl had packed me a lovely hot thermos of Milo, and I was very glad of it ... it's very cold and blowy in the Outer.'[5] As she stood in the wings waiting to perform Rosalind felt a surge of joy and relief that the Sandy Stone sketch had succeeded.[6]

In another sketch, Ron Pinnell played a scientist keen to give his new nuclear weapons a try-out. Then the 'Voice of the Traveller' parodied a popular Melbourne radio program called 'Voice of the Voyager'. The sketch denounced the relentless demolition of the city's grand nineteenth-century buildings by Whelan the Wrecker. They even joked about Whelan planning to wreck the Shrine of Remembrance. In addition to Barry, Peter and Ron Pinnell, the cast included Peter's wife, Shirley, Rosalind, Dorothy Bradley and Bettine Kauffmann.

O'Shaughnessy was shocked to observe that over the course of the short season the show grew by about-one third with Barry's incessant ad-libs, but was very pleased with the packed houses. Here was the proof that seemingly boring, small-minded characters such as Edna and Sandy were not only provocative, they were entertaining. Ros stood off stage listening to the laughter of the audience as she marvelled at Humphries' power to control them as Edna. One night the show went on until midnight as Barry kept adding more and more funny asides. He was delighted with the success of the revue.

In the program notes for the show Humphries was described as 'the most gifted clown in Australia', who 'first came into theatrical prominence when he started a sensational "Dada" revue at Melbourne University under the title *Call Me Madman!*'. The comment was both audacious and prophetic. This description of Humphries' rise to 'theatrical prominence', penned by one of the cast members, was at once whimsical and accurate, if a little grandiose.[7]

Not long afterwards, Barry once more performed as Edna at a fundraising event in the future prime minister Harold Holt's elegant drawing room in St Georges Road, Toorak, organised by the art patron John Reed, who was setting up a Museum of Modern Art in Tavistock Place, and was an admirer of Humphries. He and his partner, Sunday, had seen Barry perform and they had also purchased one of Barry's Dadaist forkscapes. Humphries was thrilled at the invitation to perform at the Holt residence, and to have an opportunity to impress the influential figures of the arts establishment.

Early in the New Year, buoyed by the success of *Rock 'n' Reel Revue*, Rosalind and Barry and Peter and Shirley decided the time was right to make the move to England. Many of their artist friends were planning to leave Australia. Ros never doubted that she needed to go to Europe if she wanted to continue her career as a dancer; Barry was more ambivalent about leaving. He still harboured a hope of becoming a painter. His sister, Barbara, had already left for Europe and was living in London.

Peter O'Shaughnessy appeared in court as a witness in Barry's divorce hearing, 'tying himself up in knots', as he attempted to answer a series of detailed questions about 'the intimacy' between Barry and his named co-respondent, Margaret Elliott.[8] Rosalind was not mentioned in the hearing as Barry's marriage to Brenda had broken up well before she met him. The judge, however, insisted on all the details of the adultery with Margaret being recounted. At the time fault had to be established in divorce cases, and adultery was a common means of doing so. But it had to be proven. In keeping with her status as a Push radical, Margaret was not even aware that her name was being published in a divorce case. There was also the problem for Barry and Ros of paying Brenda maintenance, a responsibility that caused them financial strain for years to come.

Barry and Rosalind married in April 1959, in a short and very romantic ceremony at Dora McClellan's garden studio in Brighton. Ros altered a *Les Sylphides* ballet dress she had danced in, and wore wildflowers in her hair. Matcham Skipper fashioned a ring for her made of delicate entwined gold strands. Louisa Humphries brought a wedding cake, and she and Eric gave the couple a gift of six acres of land. Rosalind's parents did not attend the wedding but sent a cheque to help with various expenses. Clifton Pugh painted a second portrait of Barry, which he presented to the couple as a gift. Ros and Barry spent the first night of their marriage in an apricot-coloured farm cottage at Greenhill, north-east of Melbourne.

Despite the fact this was his second marriage, Barry still seemed to many people 'too hectically bohemian' to be married.[9] Dora McClellan warned Rosalind against the marriage. Ros mentioned the comment to Barry and he said dismissively: 'She's just saying that because she's a lesbian.'[10]

Barry and Rosalind had earlier travelled to New Zealand in order for Barry to meet Rosalind's parents in Takapuna. Barry enjoyed the trip. He was relaxed, carefree and happy. Jim and Angela Tong's house, 'Ildewilde', stood on an acre of land with towering eucalypts, a fernery and a wild orchard. In a letter to Peter, Barry confessed to having written very little because of his preference for sightseeing; he reported that the country was full of Sandy Stones (he borrowed Jim Tong's dressing gown for the character), the beer was 'dark, sweet and warm', and that the houses rather spoiled the landscape. 'I haven't seen any volcanoes yet; nor have Mr and Mrs Tong erupted …' he joked.

Barry took a strong liking to Rosalind's parents, and they found him to be excellent company. Barry thought Mr Tong a 'decent stick' and described his mother-in-law as a 'plump good-looking cooker of chickens, fishes and puddings'.[11] He was delighted to be welcomed by such warm, knowledgable, good-humoured people. 'This is my idea of heaven,' said Barry to Ros, as they rambled together on a mountain walk outside Auckland.[12]

With very little money to their names, Peter and Barry set about writing some sketches for a new revue to fund their passage to England, referring to the show conspiratorially as 'the Benefit'. Barry got on with the job of drafting a monologue for Sandy Stone called 'Dear Beryl', in which Sandy, alone at home in Glen Iris, writes to his wife who has gone on a trip to the 'Old Country'. The monologue was never performed on stage but was recorded by Peter Mann in 1959.

The grandly named *Testimonial Performance* ran for three nights at the Assembly Hall in Melbourne's CBD, and offered an odd assortment of O'Shaughnessy and Humphries' favourite pieces, among them the opening scene of *Waiting for Godot* and a scene from Ionesco's *The Chairs*. Peter presented some selected speeches from Shakespeare, two Henry Lawson character sketches and several Judith Wright poems. Barry played Sandy Stone, using a different script.

The program notes again included a slightly overblown description of the young actor's standing. Clearly after working closely with Humphries over the previous few years, O'Shaughnessy had the measure of his talent, identifying Humphries' 'microscopically accurate eye for pretentiousness'. O'Shaughnessy described the sketches as having the sort of 'authenticity in rendering the life of the suburbs that Henry Lawson's stories have in showing us life "on the track"'.[13]

A small group of family members and friends appeared at Port Melbourne to farewell Barry and Rosalind on 12 May 1959, as the couple boarded the *Toscana* bound for Venice. Tom Sanders, Marlene Pugh and Eric and Louisa Humphries were there. Peter O'Shaughnessy and his wife had decided to postpone their travel plans until later. Uncle Lewis also came to say goodbye to Barry and his wife. Confused to see Rosalind standing beside Barry, Lewis asked Eric: 'Where's Brenda?' Eric had been too ashamed to mention that Barry's first marriage had broken up and that he was off to England with his second wife.

Unbeknown to Barry, the ship was not due to sail until the next day. Eric insisted that Barry and Rosalind come back to Christowel Street for the night. The boisterous group of well-wishers trooped off to Camberwell for tea at the Humphries' family home in a strange anticlimax to the noisy farewell gathering at the port. The next day, Louisa Humphries held a pink streamer which snapped right near her hand, as she watched her eldest son grow smaller and smaller on the receding ship. For Barry the scene was both beautiful and surreal. He watched the city sail 'backwards into a Turner sunset'.[14]

Barry and Rosalind were ecstatic to be travelling, and pleased to have a four-berth cabin to themselves. They ate the huge meals provided on the ship with gusto, and revelled in the lively banter of the Italian sailors. The voyage was a carefree period for the young couple. In Rome they slept on the floor of Lawrence Daws' studio and met Martin Boyd. Ros sat quietly and listened to the men talk, mainly about Boyd's nephew, Arthur, and Martin's most recent novel, *Outbreak of Love*. Barry was disappointed when Boyd said that he would be out of the city for the next few days. He felt that Boyd was 'palming them off'.[15]

When Barry and Rosalind arrived in London in June 1959, Humphries was delighted to hear that his talent for satire had been celebrated in the Australian magazine *Australian Letters*. Denison Deasey, the unconventional scion of a well-to-do Melbourne family, had published a mordant account of Humphries' activities, pointing to his witty, sometimes 'merciless' critique of suburbia. Alongside the article was a reproduction of Clifton Pugh's portrait of a bird-like and youthful Barry Humphries. Deasey reported that Humphries as Mrs Everage had gone to England where she will 'appear as an Australian housewife in search of culture'.[16]

PART TWO
ACTOR

CHAPTER 8

A City for Performance

Barry and Ros arrived in London in June 1959 with enough money between them to make a phone call to Barbara Humphries. Barbara cooked a meal for them and lent them twenty pounds. On his first full day in London, Humphries met up with an Australian actor from Brisbane, Charles Osborne. The star of Phillip Street Theatre, Max Oldaker, had written to Osborne, introducing Humphries and describing him as 'inexperienced, but [he] has a devastating sense of quiet comedy and, I think, a touch of genius'.[1] Osborne was an amiable and softly spoken actor who had been working in repertory theatre for the previous couple of years and had recently taken up a job as editor of the *London Magazine*. He also worked as director of literature for the Arts Council of Great Britain, immediately warmed to Barry and did his best to help him with introductions.

The Humphries quickly realised that life in London would be hard. Fortunately, just two days after they arrived, Ros began working at a delicatessen near Portobello Market, and they found digs in Ladbroke Grove. Until Ros was paid they could barely afford groceries. The new arrivals visited Barbara one night unannounced at her tiny flat in Lancaster Gate. Barbara and a friend were about to tuck into sausages and mashed potatoes but generously split the meal four ways.

Like many young Australians Barry was enraptured with the city that he had imagined since boyhood. For centuries the English capital has attracted artists, writers and musicians. The Australian expatriate poet Peter Porter described London as 'a city for performance. You go there to do things, to write, to compose, to act, to find your way into your own creativity'.² Over the next ten years Humphries found his way into his creative self, gaining sufficient physical and mental distance from his homeland, which remained nonetheless the inspiration for his satire.

Soon after Barry and Rosalind arrived in London, a sour note was struck when Barry received a bitter letter from Peter O'Shaughnessy in Melbourne, admonishing Humphries for snubbing him after the *Testimonial* performance, and chastising him for his selfishness. Peter reminded Barry that he had allowed himself to be whisked off to a South Yarra party by some admirers, leaving his old friends for dead. In August 1959 Humphries wrote a long, anguished reply, stating that Peter's anger had caused 'a dense shadow ... across my first months in London'. He melodramatically told Peter he had been paralysed by the letter, unable to pursue work, and horrified by the implication that he was an 'unscrupulous success sucker'. Barry had not taken the reprimand from Peter lightly; he was hurt and provoked enough to tell Peter that his reproaches were 'aggressive, curdled and self-indulgent', and that they amounted to a 'deliberate attempt to smash my morale'. But Barry also held out an olive branch with the words Peter wanted to hear: 'Did you imagine that I am unconscious of your role in shaping my wayward talents?'³ The matter was laid to rest and a flow of letters recommenced.

Barry's letters to Peter mirrored the pattern of all his close relationships. He instinctively did his best to entertain Peter, as he did with all his friends and lovers in person, and if not in person, in writing. He only occasionally showed his true feelings. During the first few months in London Barry had a lot of time to think about his friendship with Peter and came face to face with its troubling elements. He realised that Peter could be overbearing and controlling. From this point, Barry's letters to Peter, while newsy and affectionate, suggest there were new reservations on his part, after the dressing down. With striking honesty and a note of challenge, he quipped, when signing off one letter, 'Please write to me soon … it's so easy since we don't have to labour a rapport.'[4]

Lawrence Daws, meanwhile, had arrived in London a few days after Barry and Ros, and he helped Humphries find work at Wall's ice cream factory in Acton, where the two of them toiled at night. Humphries hoped that working night shifts would allow him time to attend auditions by day. Barry confessed to Peter O'Shaughnessy that his 'ridiculous labour' of ensuring the smooth passage of packets of raspberry ripple ice cream along a conveyor belt made him 'absurdly cheerful'.[5] It was perhaps a step up from crushing old records.

If he found his situation depressing, and a far cry from what he had envisaged for himself in London, he certainly did not let on. His letters to Peter continued to be jaunty and expansive, and included a number of acerbic vignettes depicting his exchanges with various mutual friends in pubs, tube stations and on the street. As the months passed, his encounters with the scores of Australian expatriates in London became the focus for a new, as yet unformed, satiric project. It was all grist for the mill.

Like so many actors before him who fled their Antipodean homes for the bright lights of the West End, Humphries searched tirelessly for work, following every lead. Since the war the path from agent to agent had been well trodden by Australian actors. Some of them returned to Australia, but many stayed away.[6]

Humphries had his heart set on working in the West End and vowed not to settle for roles in repertory theatre. He gave his agent, Myrette Morven, the telephone number of the pub around the corner, and waited there hopefully between long walks around Covent Garden and Fleet Street. He also dropped in to see Myrette at least once a week.

In a letter to Peter's wife, Shirley, after eight months in London, Rosalind listed her succession of jobs: delicatessen assistant, barmaid, Wimpy Bar attendant and 'for the last seven months in the hateful fruitshop'. Of Barry's ice cream factory stint, Ros wrote: 'Can you imagine anything sadder for him?'[7] Rosalind longed to work in the theatre again, but found it hard to attend dance classes given her demanding work schedule. She also suffered from some unspecific ailments and spent some time in hospital. The city was smoggy and dirty and bitterly cold, which made the couple's circumstances seem more desperate. Barry and Ros even talked about going to Germany for a few months to work if theatre roles did not turn up.

Humphries auditioned for BBC television drama and for the director Joan Littlewood, and managed to get a voice-over piece for ITV, using the tones he had cultivated in his 'Voice of the Traveller' sketch in Melbourne. By the end of the year he had won a part in *The Demon Barber*, an early musical version of the story of Sweeney Todd at the Lyric, Hammersmith. In his audition Barry drew on his ghoulish psychiatrist character, and was given the role of Jonas Fogg, the madhouse keeper. It was a good part, 'if conventionally "zany", "off-beat", "whacky" — what's the latest vile term?', as he described it to Peter O'Shaughnessy.[8]

Although it was a small role, Humphries found the show pleasantly camp and the singing training with a first-rate musical director, Colin Graham, very welcome.[9] One of Barry's old school friends, Ian Donaldson, had left Melbourne in 1958 and was studying English at Oxford. He took the train down to London to see the show, and waited for Barry afterwards. Barry did not bother to change out of his costume and walked beside Ian through the streets of Notting Hill, terrifying passers-by, his hair plastered down with white paste and his eyes ringed with black.

In spite of a couple of television engagements, Humphries decided he would steer clear of television in order to pursue the 'right' stage roles. He could see no point in reviving Sandy Stone or Edna Everage because of the need for so much explanation of the characters in England: 'Better to plough them in, don't you think,' he wrote to Peter. Although he envisaged Sandy as a central character for a novel or play, he confessed that Mrs Everage no longer excited his imagination. Humphries thought that Edna had 'achieved her moment of maximum expressiveness' and now 'she dwindles, poor woman!'.[10]

By the end of that first year in London, however, Barry had made several five-minute episodes of 'Edna's Travel Diary' for the ABC Saturday night radio program *Roundabout*. Delighted with them, Humphries told Peter they were not 'too hysterically chaotic' but more like the Opera House sketches, or Edna's 'classic' style, as he liked to call it.

In December, as the days shortened, Barry and Rosalind found a basement flat in Pembridge Gardens, Notting Hill, close to a ballet studio and not far from the Lyric Theatre where Barry was performing in *The Demon Barber*. Barry was upbeat in his description of their new home, but to Rosalind it was 'pleasant but shabby'. Rosalind took another job at a café near the British Museum, and evening work as a barmaid at a cricketers club in Knightsbridge. Eventually she saved enough money to drop one of her three jobs and enrol in morning classes at the studio near the flat, where she met dancers from the Sadler's Wells and Royal Ballet.

The rather introverted Australian painter Francis Lymburner shared the flat with Barry and Ros for some months. Lymburner had been living in England for seven months but had yet to hold an exhibition. Humphries, with his usual cutting candour, described the strain of living with a 'pathological failure' to Peter in a letter, blaming Lymburner's 'enervated romanticism' and delusions of grandeur for the painter's troubles. In spite of this he added cheerfully, 'We quite like him.'[11]

Most of Barry's Australian friends were trying to make headway as painters, writers or actors. They were all short of money and many seemed to be prone to mawkish nostalgia for Melbourne. Humphries found their reluctance to mix with the English pathetic and annoying. The tired reminiscences about Eltham personages, stale gossip and Drift folklore made him cringe. In fact they knew 'so many gloomy people', he told Peter, that 'our lives positively scintillate in comparison'. He declared that they knew enough dull people in London that they could easily hold a 'classic bores' party'. He even supplied a list of those guests he considered to be 'thunderous bores'. 'We will play a *South Pacific* record in the background and heat the room to a slumberous temperature,' Barry wrote.[12]

Barry still played tricks on people. When the mercurial potter, Tom Sanders, arrived from Melbourne, he came knocking on Humphries' door. Barry hid. Rosalind stood at the door wondering what excuse she could make. 'Barry's been taken to hospital with appendicitis,' she found herself saying to the persistent Sanders. When he pressed her for the name of the hospital she said she couldn't quite remember. Tom Sanders spent the next few hours telephoning hospitals in London looking for Barry.

Humphries' first season on the London stage had been disappointingly short. The reviews of *The Demon Barber* were not favourable and the musical closed a few days before Christmas. During that first bleak winter in London, Humphries worked up a long monologue for Sandy that had been conceived in Melbourne with Ros. He called it 'Sandy Agonistes', in parody of the Milton poem. It is an agonisingly slow recitation, and a poetic meditation on the Melbourne of Humphries' boyhood. Barry recorded the haunting voice of Sandy reciting names using a borrowed tape recorder. He listed railway stations and street names, brands of chewing gum, tomato sauce and breakfast cereal. Stone also catalogued matinee idols, Hollywood stars, Melbourne theatres and cinemas; he even hummed fragments of his favourite tunes such as 'Somewhere Over the Rainbow' and 'I'm Forever Blowing Bubbles'. Barry proudly took the tape to Earls Court to play to his old friends Brian Westmore and Joy Grissold, who found it very funny if rather too long. It was unlike anything Barry had done before. Sibilant and halting, the voice of Sandy and his banal list are strangely captivating and soothing. With its Beckett-like futility and pausing, almost floating quality, the recording remains one of Humphries' most lyrical, yet excruciating dramatic pieces.

The extremes of Barry's artistic personality were now in constant tension. On the one hand he was determined to live up to his ideal of the 'uncorrupted actor'; his impulse was towards satire, but only if it was 'pure'. For him so much of the theatre he saw was corrupt and dishonest. For example he found Joan Littlewood's productions to be uneven, praising *The Hostage* but disliking *A Taste of Honey* and considering *Fings Ain't Wot They*

Used T'Be utterly lacking in ideas and patently sentimental. On the other hand he realised that to succeed he would have to secure conventional roles in commercial theatre, yet he was still very uncertain about his worth. He was only too aware of the difficulty of getting a foot in the door of the London theatre scene, and of the need to earn a living.

Humphries was still drawn to satirical expression in art but even in London he found little to excite him. It wasn't just theatre that frustrated him at this time. He longed to be able to paint but feared that he lacked genuine talent. He despised paintings that lacked a satirical agenda, and was as keen an observer of pretence and caprice in art, at this time, as in drama or in real life.[13]

Apart from the daily struggle to find employment, the main irritation for Barry in London was the jealousy and competitiveness among his friends, which led to constant sniping between the artists, actors and writers who had fled Australia, all hoping to make a living and achieve some recognition in Britain. Even the sometimes inscrutable artist Arthur Boyd was fiercely competitive. But several of the painters had a head start and already had an income that had allowed them to travel to London in relative comfort. Although not immune to the expatriate pettiness, they were not forced to find menial jobs to support their artistic work. Charles Blackman had won a Helena Rubinstein scholarship and Boyd had twenty pounds per week from the Australian Galleries for his first five months in London.[14]

It was an exciting time for the Australian artists. Australian painting was the talk of London, thanks to Bryan Robertson, curator of the Whitechapel Gallery in the East End, who launched Lawrence Daws, Clifton Pugh and Brett Whiteley, and championed Boyd, Blackman and Sidney Nolan. Robertson described Australians as a 'paradoxical people from a paradoxical land', 'new settlers in an ancient place' and 'unconventional, anti-authoritarian', but also aggressively 'puritanical'.[15] The words impressed the English art world and struck a chord with Humphries.

* * *

But London was not ready to look afresh at Australian actors. They had no special funding or patronage; for them there was nothing but snobbery and indifference. Humphries found it hard to make a living. In the West End and even on the repertory circuit, it was best to disguise one's accent. Theatrical agents seemed to be of little help. Competitive and independent by nature, Barry hated to be out of work and unnoticed. He was flabbergasted that the New Zealand-born actor Walter Brown kept a filing system of important London producers and one or two others took agents to dinner at the Ivy. The feverish ill will and envy he observed in his friends — and in himself — became a pet hate and then a satiric target for him. They also came to represent for Humphries a peculiarly Australian syndrome, and one that he took on with the full force of his imaginative genius.

Desperate for both work and money, Humphries applied to the Commonwealth Literary Fund in Australia for a fellowship. Using his parents' address in Camberwell, he submitted a last-minute application, pleading to be considered after the closing date. His application was received, but he was disappointed to learn just before Christmas that he was not listed alongside Alan Marshall and Thea Astley as a winner.

It wasn't all misery though. Humphries enjoyed the company of Arthur and Yvonne Boyd, Charles and Barbara Blackman, the dancer Ruth Bergner and her artist brother Yosl, and Peter's brother, Brian O'Shaughnessy, with whom he found initially a genuine rather than a conscientious friendship. Humphries sought out friends during these first few years in London much more openly and enthusiastically than when he lived in Sydney. Barry and Ros became popular guests at parties and gatherings. The new environment had awakened a new maturity and interest in people in Barry. Barbara Blackman recalls him moving around the room at parties eager 'to know and be known'.[16]

In spite of the hardships of London Barry was happier than he had ever been. His letters to Peter from this period are lengthy, disarmingly candid and amusing. His razor-sharp observations of the ups and downs of his own relationships and those between others are worked into the letters in addition to his reports on all his activities and moods. His eye for human folly and his acute understanding of people and group behaviour complemented his inherently satirical cast of mind.[17] The descriptions in his letters prefigure the biting portraits that would emerge on stage over the next two decades.

Humphries relished the opportunity to explore London. He marvelled at the city skyline, the Wren churches and the dark wood-panelled pubs in back lanes and alleys. On weekdays he wandered the cobbled lanes of the West End, Fleet Street and the Inns of Court. On Sundays when Ros had free time, the two of them would walk for miles. Barry enjoyed the sound of cockney English with its glottal stops and rhyming slang, while Ros loved London 'with a passion' and felt at home among the English.[18] Although he continued to worry about finding work in the theatre, cursed his indolent agent and felt downcast for long periods of time, nothing dampened Humphries' enthusiasm for the foggy city he had dreamed about for years.

Both Barry and Rosalind made the most of the offerings of the West End. They were impressed by Ibsen's *Rosmersholm*, in which Peggy Ashcroft played an older woman desperate to hold on to the shreds of sexual allure. They saw Joan Sutherland in *La Sonnambula* at Covent Garden, and Barry saw Olivier in Ionesco's *Rhinoceros*, but found the play somewhat empty and maddening in its pretentious apocalyptic effect, nothing like Beckett's vision, which he felt was unfairly maligned. Barry found Pinter's *The Caretaker* both compelling and baffling; he could not work out what it was saying, and thought it, in the end, vacuous. But he recommended it to Peter in a letter, and mischievously pointed out that there was a part as a 'c--t' for Peter himself.[19] His passion for art was nourished; he attended a large exhibition of German Expressionist paintings at a Bond Street gallery just before Christmas, featuring everything he particularly admired: several Kokoschka portraits and paintings by Klee, Nolde, Beckmann and Kirchner.

By February 1960 things were still grim and Barry went on 'the national assistance'. He spent his time walking around London and writing at home. He found it hard going at first but gradually began to work productively, drafting sketch material he hoped to record professionally. When spring came he felt a rush of energy and relief, and particularly loved the long, soft, light evenings. He vowed to be a perfectionist with his new writing venture, and told Peter that aside from acting 'the only route to clear thinking is through writing'.[20] It was a poignant admission for Barry who was beginning to drink more than was good for clear thinking.

On a trip to Snowdonia Barry revelled in the beauty of the Welsh countryside. With Ros, the rather melancholy Colin Munro, the urbane and genial Ian Donaldson and Alan Froome, they toured in a hired car, devouring the local ale and reciting Housman. During the summer Rosalind and Barry drove to Cornwall via Salisbury and Stonehenge, sleeping in the moonlight under a haystack near Exeter. The wild and windblown countryside and austere granite cottages of Cornwall particularly appealed to Barry.

Across the miles Barry and Peter had begun planning a London version of the Bunyip play. Barry was confident that there was a market for children's theatre, but no matter how hard he pushed, he was unable to get an appointment with Joan Littlewood to try and secure a commitment to produce the pantomime for Christmas. However, he promised to draft a few lyrics for the new show if Peter succeeded in producing it again in Melbourne.

CHAPTER 9

The Expatriate Game

In May 1960 after an agonising wait following several auditions, Humphries was offered the role of Mr Sowerberry in a new musical based on Charles Dickens' *Oliver Twist*. He was disappointed because the part was small and he had his heart set on playing Fagin, or possibly the Artful Dodger. Ron Moody would play Dickens' 'very old, shrivelled Jew', as Dickens describes him early in the novel, while Martin Horsey landed the part of the Dodger.[1] But for Humphries there was a sweetener: for an additional five pounds a week he would understudy Moody.

The music was written by Lionel Bart, a young composer whose *Fings Ain't Wot They Used T"Be* had recently concluded a two-year run in London. His spectacular success gave the English musical a new lease of life, after a long period of domination by American shows. Regardless of its popularity, Barry found *Fings* rather fragmented, chaotic and insubstantial.

Bart, the son of an East End tailor, had a particular understanding of the characters that fill Dickens' novels, and was determined to put them on the stage. He also understood what would appeal to audiences, and appreciated the place of the vernacular in the stage musical, with its music hall heritage. He was not afraid to use cockney English in his shows, determined as he was to differentiate them from the Broadway style.

Humphries somewhat cynically regarded Bart's new show as a 'particularly far-fetched attempt at THE English musical'.[2] At the outset even the producer, Donald Albery, expressed reservations about it. He thought it might not even live to see the West End. The mere mention of an adaptation of a Dickens novel aroused contemptuous laughter from most of the people Barry talked to about it.[3] With only six songs written, the company began three weeks of rehearsals at the Donmar rooms in Covent Garden. It wasn't until right at the end of this period that Bart wrote the other tunes for the show, including a song for Sowerberry the undertaker, called 'That's Your Funeral'. Bart recalled many years later that he thought Barry looked more like a grave snatcher than an undertaker, with his long skinny legs, lank hair and melancholy eyes.[4]

Humphries was very pleased to feel like an actor again when the rehearsals for *Oliver!* commenced. He admitted to feeling 'blank and somehow delinquent' during the period without work.[5] During his long lunch breaks he spent the warm spring afternoons wandering the grimy streets behind St Pancras Station and up the hill towards Finsbury. He filled his letters to Peter O'Shaughnessy with descriptions of his discoveries. The area reminded him a little of the slums of Surry Hills and Paddington in Sydney, except that he would suddenly stumble upon perfectly arranged squares of pedimented Regency houses, all facing a fenced garden.

Humphries was extremely nervous on the first night of *Oliver!*. Ros couldn't help thinking that he hammed his part a bit. But nobody else noticed. *Oliver!* was a huge hit, beyond all expectations. Moody was perfect as Fagin, Georgia Brown was an appealing Nancy and the extravagant revolving sets made for an extraordinary spectacle. The part of the 'tall, gaunt' Sowerberry turned out to be right for Humphries.[6] He had an uncanny ability as a young man to play an older person, and to embody the gait, posture and actions of his character. When he sang his number, 'That's Your Funeral', he hit the high notes, his diction was perfect and every line carried the sinister, macabre humour of the character.

The satirist in Humphries could not help noticing that the musical emasculated Dickens, but he admired the production and was pleased to be earning his twenty pounds each week in this new and successful West End venture. At last he seemed comfortable singing on stage, and promised himself some lessons in dancing and singing. The *Record Mirror* reviewer lamented the fact that Humphries, whom he described as a 'fine actor', was 'offered no further opportunity than his splendidly performed song and dialogue sequence in the first act'.

Humphries now took to smoking Woodbines, wearing velvet trousers, polo-neck sweaters and sporting a Campaign for Nuclear Disarmament badge. Like his earlier fin-de-siècle dandy persona, this South Kensington look was one he enjoyed immensely and performed with the full strength of his talent for mimicry. And like the earlier incarnation this persona was partly real. It was his London actor look, and reflected his new life as a West End professional. But this time Barry was more relaxed in the role and did not stand out from the crowd. It was 1960 and his outfit did not mark him out from his contemporaries in modish London as his Aubrey Beardsley costume and long hair had in Camberwell.

At Easter, Barry and Rosalind joined thousands of protestors who walked from Aldermaston to London to express their horror at the build-up of nuclear weapons and their solidarity with the Campaign for Nuclear Disarmament. Together with Tom Sanders, Brian O'Shaughnessy and Arthur Boyd, they marched in the spring sunshine. Boyd was a pacifist, but did not involve himself in politics. Like Barry he didn't like aligning himself with one group or another. But this was different. Standing in Trafalgar Square among the 100,000-strong crowd, Humphries felt it was worth the 'nervous hangover' afterwards to experience the power of such a massive protest. He also felt there was something slightly unpleasant about being in such a huge mass of people.[7] Barry had a performer's dual fear of and fascination with crowds, finding the power of the throng both exciting and terrifying.

With the repayment of forty pounds he had lent Alan Riddell in Sydney, Barry bought a painting on silk by the Australian impressionist Charles Conder. In October he and Ros moved to a flat in a Georgian house in Grove Terrace, Highgate. Ros agreed to help with three children who lived in the house, and to undertake some cleaning duties, and as a result there was no rent to pay. After living in a small basement, the apartment near Parliament Hill was liberating. With a real shower, the flat seemed luxurious, and from the windows the majestic heath beckoned, with its wide green spaces, massive trees and brooding ponds. Constable's house was only a few streets away; the elegant spire of St Michael's, the undulating and immense Highgate cemetery, Waterlow Park and Keats' house were all at their doorstep. DH Lawrence had wandered across the heath with the poet Anna Wickham. It was a romantic idyll high above London.

If Ros hoped the change of scene would help steer Barry away from the Soho pubs she was to be disappointed. Barry had recently developed a taste for a strong beer with a creamy froth called Underberg. He had also started drinking in the Colony Club in Soho, because it was open in the afternoons when the pubs were closed, and late into the night after the show finished. More productively, Barry started working up a cabaret act, hoping he might perform in late-night sessions at the Royal Court Theatre Club.

Rosalind was ecstatic at the offer of a role in the Festival Ballet. When she told Barry his response was odd: 'Why would they want you?', Ros answered, 'Because I can dance.' Humphries implored her not to take up the offer, insisting that he would not cope on his own in London when she went on tour. Reluctantly, Ros turned down the role.[8] She was disappointed by Barry's reaction because she desperately wanted to dance. The thought of Ros touring with the Festival Ballet aroused feelings of envy and insecurity in Barry. His lack of confidence and direction made him somewhat controlling of Ros.

Humphries rehearsed some of his own performance ideas in letters to Peter, and as in his earlier correspondence vented his spleen, offering tantalising short satirical fragments about real and imaginary people. He was blunt about his loathing for aggressive Australian boorishness. He recoiled when, in the company of Peter's brother Brian and others, they would all of a sudden become stridently Australian; Barry found himself adopting quieter, more reserved English ways. After hearing the voices of Londoners for nearly a year he found the Australian accent hilarious. When he met up with the actress Zoe Caldwell, he cringed when she shouted across the room to her friend Martin: 'Morteen!'[9] Whenever he described people, Barry exaggerated their traits and foibles to the point of caricature. It was an instinctive and venomous talent.

Devastating for Barry was an impromptu visit to an Earls Court pub, smack in the middle of Kangaroo Valley, as it was sometimes called. He felt physically ill and frightened by what he saw. The packs of loutish Australian youths swilling beer and swearing revived painful memories of the bullies at Melbourne Grammar. But occasionally, when he read the ads on the back of his mother's newspaper cuttings from Melbourne, he felt a twinge of homesickness. One freezing January day, he noticed a photograph of a student production of *Waiting for Godot* in the *Sunday Times*. It brought on a wave of nostalgia for the play; Barry recalled the reverence and purity of his feelings for Beckett during O'Shaughnessy's production at the Arrow Theatre in Melbourne three years earlier. He wrote to Peter confessing to the extraordinary power of the play: 'I don't think our lives can ever be the same after the second entrance of the Boy. I like to try and relive that extraordinary *Godot* existence in the same way in which one tries to conjure back childhood.'[10]

Humphries relished Peter's frequent postcards from such places as Wagga Wagga and Tumbarumba, and the irony of this delight in Australiana was not lost on him, as he recalled his obsessive passion for English music and English writers as a young man in Melbourne. In spite of his delight in the English countryside, he loved to parody himself. In his 'love of field and coppice' and his zeal for uncovering the treasures of London, he knew that there was a limit to his appreciation of all things English, and was all too aware that 'you can be too intensely expatriate'.[11] But he was in no danger of that.

The expatriate game was one he loved playing, however, and it became a lively preoccupation. The longer he was away from Australia the more piquant his observations, and the more acutely he felt his Australianness. He wrote a few short pieces, mostly unpublished, about London, including a humorous one about the need to keep your eyes on the pavement lest you slip on the dog dirt that littered the pathways and streets.[12] But he hit his stride in an article on what was becoming his favourite topic: 'Australians in London'. He described the Sandys and Beryls, the older folk 'doing the trip', the pilgrimage of the retired to Anne Hathaway's cottage, the Devon lanes and Trafalgar Square, and the antics of the youngsters, the 'Keiths, Jeffs and Janices, the Barrys and Barbaras … whizzing from city to city' on the continent, or 'sharing in the flatlets and bedsitters of Earls Court'. Humphries' observations and extraordinary gift for description are most poignant in his vivid account of the older, fatherly male Australians: 'The men have little red veins like spidery road maps printed on their shiny expectant cheeks.' Like his Sandy Stone monologues, the article is both satirical and compassionate. There is no contempt in this piece, just wry amusement. Aware of the specificities of class in these touring 'classless' Australians, with the wealthier women 'who totter, frizzed and frangipanied, to receptions at Australia House', 'that tubby-grey building' on the Strand, Humphries revealed what struck him so powerfully. It was the sense of inferiority these people felt that kept them huddled in their 'anglophobic ghetto'.[13]

In another intriguing piece, a macabre short story called 'The Stranger in the Princess Louise', Humphries wrote of a man lured from a pub in High Holborn into the attic of another man who speaks of reincarnation and his need for spare body parts. Barry had always enjoyed the strange and the grotesque and took a keen interest in grisly crime and funerary customs. It was natural that he attempt a ghost story of his own.

Humphries also tried drafting a few autobiographical sketches and a travel piece for *Vogue* but found it difficult to break into journalism. His candid letters to his friends make more amusing reading than most of his magazine drafts of the time.

Barry had given Charles and Barbara Blackman some tapes of his planned recordings of single voice sketches about young Australians in England, with their endless discussions of who is arriving and leaving on which boat and who is hitchhiking or bunking with whom, and what country they plan to 'do' next. He also played his monologue of Sandy Stone listing place names and products to Barbara, who was reminded of Charles's early paintings, in which he covered the whole canvas with hoardings 'all patchworked together with a lone figure small in the foreground'.[14] Charles and Barry became close friends at this time; Barbara Blackman thought 'they were like brothers'.[15] They competed at outdoing one other in playing cruel jokes on others: Charles would answer the phone and bark 'Auschwitz'.[16]

Barry and Charles travelled to Vienna together to look at paintings. In a drawing of Barry's face in profile produced during this period, Blackman captured Barry's almost feminine whimsicality, his dreamy eyes, long dark hair and haunted beauty. But both Humphries and Blackman were drinking too much, and at times were unreachable. Ros worried and hoped for reform; her instinctive response to Barry's drinking was to nurse him and prop him up, and try to help him get over his problems. A more aggressive attitude might have forced the issue, or it might have made things worse. But aggression was not in her nature.

In July 1961 Peter O'Shaughnessy at last moved to London with Shirley and their two little girls, Caitlin and Sally. Peter owed money in Melbourne for several failed shows, and as a result he was keen to find work as an actor as quickly as possible.

Barry and Peter set about reworking some of the *Bunyip* material, and planned a new project searching for forgotten nineteenth-century plays set in Australia. However, neither of them seemed to know how to go about this time-consuming research. And both of them were primarily focused on earning a living. They drank on Sunday nights at the Duke of Wellington in Highgate with members of the London Drift, as Barry called it: Arthur and Yvonne Boyd, Len French, Charles and Barbara Blackman, Brian O'Shaughnessy and Brian's partner, Red. John and Mary Perceval were also among the regulars. They would frequently finish up at the Boyds' place for bowls of soup or spaghetti provided by the ever-generous and rather long-suffering Yvonne. Occasionally

Arthur would simply leave the group and resume work.[17] Sometimes Rosalind, too, would tire of all the shouting between the men, and their relentless griping and competitive sparring. At one party she settled down in a corner and read a book.[18]

Barry hadn't quite given up his pranks. He still loved to perform them in public, altering the social script in order to shock onlookers. Barbara Blackman, at least, found him very amusing. 'Everywhere was stage and backstage for him,' she observed.[19] One evening Barry led Ros and the Blackmans to an unfamiliar and rather rough pub. He said to the barman: 'A few drinks and one for yourself.' 'And what shall it be?' replied the solid fellow behind the bar. 'Straight waters,' said Barry without flinching. They drank their water sheepishly before leaving for the next pub where Barry ordered a pint of Guinness apiece, to the immense relief of everyone in his small party.[20]

Humphries frequently offered a cockney song to the assembled drinkers on a Sunday evening, accompanied by the Duke of Wellington's resident pianist, Denzil. Yet he was preoccupied with problems. *Oliver!* was still pulling in the crowds, but Barry was tiring of his small part as Sowerberry; he had yet to play Fagin as Ron Moody had not missed a single night. Humphries was starting to feel anxious about how to get out of the show. He felt he deserved better than his minor role.

Humphries pondered his chances of breaking into straight theatre. If he was ever to make the break, now was the time to try. For one thing he had his friend Peter O'Shaughnessy beside him in the same situation. He and Peter set about working up an audition together for Sir Peter Hall at the Royal Shakespeare Company (RSC) in Stratford-upon-Avon. They settled on a short piece from *King Lear* with Peter as the king and Barry as his Fool. This was the role Barry had wanted to play when he was unable to break his harness from Phillip Street. Hall offered O'Shaughnessy a role in *Cymbeline*, but there was nothing for Barry. It was an important moment for both actors. Like the photo of the two of them in *Godot*, the scene they rehearsed from *King Lear* reproduced some of the strange currents of their friendship. Peter played the fiery and ambitious purist who had at times conducted himself as though he was king and master of Barry's revels, with Barry the dependent all-seeing clown. As a result of Barry's disappointment, they went their separate ways. Ultimately Peter turned down the RSC offer for something more permanent with the Bristol Old Vic. Humphries was free to pursue his own acting career, away from his mentor. But he was unsure of his own mode, and did not know what to try next.

Rosalind suggested to Barry that he devise a one-man show of his own. He was very low and fulminated against his country and its people, and also raged against the British, with their love of royalty and their hideous class system. He did not think he could mount a show of his own, and felt anxious about his future.[21]

Then came the turning point. Cliff Hocking, a young, ambitious and intelligent Australian entrepreneur, approached Humphries to do a one-man show featuring Edna and Sandy Stone, to premiere in Melbourne. It was a huge risk for both Hocking and Humphries. Initially Barry was reluctant. Ros spent hours over the next weeks trying to persuade him to give it a shot. But Barry was not sure he could do it. Eventually he came around to the idea, feeling more optimistic when he heard of praise for his work from none other than John Betjeman who had been given a recording of *Wild Life in Suburbia* while touring Australia. Betjeman was so enthralled with the ramblings of Sandy Stone, in particular his quavering musings on Beryl's 'lovely sponge fingers' and his 'strife parking the vehicle', that he made mention of Humphries at one of his Australian press conferences. The famed English poet could see the everyman in Sandy and the poetry in his utterances. He recognised the pathos and humour in this 'prototype' of the older suburban male.[22]

Delighted to read a newspaper clipping reporting Betjeman's comments, Barry wrote to the poet and received an invitation to lunch in Smithfield at Betjeman's bachelor flat. Over roast beef, Brussels sprouts and champagne, the poet regaled the astonished Humphries with tales of his recent visit to Melbourne, 'Brizzie' and Sydney, the splendid Victorian churches he had seen and the marvellous place names he'd heard. Betjeman laughed out loud at some of the names, especially Moonee Ponds.[23]

Humphries was intrigued by the middle-aged aesthete's quintessentially English life, with his entanglements, coteries, enthusiasms and penchant for practical jokes. Betjeman had even been known to feign epileptic fits on the street. His life seemed to mirror Humphries' own in so many ways, and yet to be vastly different. Betjeman had been brought up in Highgate, an indulged only child. He was thought of as snobby and affected at Oxford where he failed to complete his degree. By the time Humphries met him he had been knighted and was involved with two women: Penelope Chetwode, his wife, and Lady Elizabeth Cavendish, his mistress. He shuttled between residences. Over the next few years Barry and Betjeman became firm friends.

It still seemed that *Oliver!* would go on forever and that Barry would never get a chance to play Fagin. The long West End run had 'worn out' at least one child actor and Barry was beginning to think he would never get out of it. He began to project his anger onto Lionel Bart. Barry told Barbara Blackman rather poetically that the musical was a kind of swirling 'Sargasso Sea' in which one may easily drown.[24] He had signed his contract privately and so could not prevail on his agent to extricate him from the musical. It was agonising to hear that the management would not release him when the young comedian Peter Cook offered him a stint at his new club in Soho. Barry also reluctantly turned down a part in a masked version of *The Caucasian Chalk Circle*.

Desperate to escape *Oliver!*, he convinced a doctor that he was at the point of breakdown. The management agreed to give him a few weeks leave on medical grounds, and in a frenzy of excitement Barry planned a two-week holiday from London to begin working on the sketches for his Australian show. He and Ros travelled to a cottage near Zennor in Cornwall. It was a rather eerie place but offered beautiful walks and healthy ocean breezes. Huddled next to a wood stove, Barry spent his days catching up on his *Australian Women's Weekly* reading and devouring the envelopes full of newspaper clippings sent to him by his mother. He always enjoyed the advertisements, and found the illustrated column 'What people are Wearing Overseas', particularly diverting.

Walking along the cliffs near Zennor one morning beside an icy cold stream, Ros slipped and fell into a cascading torrent of freezing water. At the edge of the cliff Ros hung on, desperately managing to prevent herself going over. Barry reached down to haul her out, slipped and went crashing down on top of her. They both went backwards over the cliff, coming to rest on a ledge, suspended hundreds of feet above the sea. Humphries seemed to have broken bones and dislocated his shoulder, and could barely move.[25] If not for Rosalind's agility and strength, built up over the years as a professional dancer, both of them may have perished that day. Ros carefully took off her gumboots and scrambled up the cliff face, before stumbling barefoot across paddocks in search of help, eventually arriving at a cottage and summoning assistance. Barry, by this stage, was fading in and out of consciousness. Hours later he was winched to safety and taken to hospital by helicopter.

Barry's dramatic cliff-top rescue made headlines in London, and the television news in Australia. A cameraman knocked Ros over in his attempt to secure a close-up of the stricken Barry. Auntie Billie wrote to her nephew stating, 'Barry dear, you are now world famous on the tellie.' Humphries was ordered to take six weeks break. Rosalind suffered from concussion and cut feet. Both of them were traumatised. Barry had a pin inserted in his arm and his recovery in a London hospital was slow. When a doctor told Humphries, in a false alarm, that his arm would most likely never be the same he felt desperate. The night after Barry's accident, Ron Moody fell ill, but there was no question of Barry stepping in as Fagin; he was now genuinely not fit to return to *Oliver!*.

CHAPTER 10

Homecoming

Once Humphries was well enough to travel, he and Rosalind boarded a Norwegian cargo ship in Rotterdam bound for Auckland. They were determined to complete the script for Humphries' first one-man show during the voyage. The captain offered to vacate his quarters so that the two of them could work in peace. Delighted with their luck, they spent hours working on the show in the comfort of a large cabin. On the long sea voyage, they wrote and talked and laughed.[1] With her musical talent, her ear for the vernacular and her understanding of revue theatre, Ros was a more than able assistant for Barry as he drafted his monologues and song lyrics. She had a knack for rhyme that was uncanny and also helped him learn his lines. They were a perfect creative match for one another.

When the ship docked at Portofino, and the passengers discovered the bars, Ros demonstrated her talent for modern dance with an expert rendition of the twist. Barry sat watching her; he rarely danced. The couple were relaxed, excited and happy, as they often were when they were together, away from the everyday humdrum and the distractions of London. Humphries wrote three new sketches and several songs, including a ditty called 'Drop the Bomb', to be sung by a teenager doing the twist. It was a frenzied parody of the perilous situation between the Soviet bloc and the

Western world, a world divided into two: 'They're like two teenagers petting in a car/And they are afraid to go too far …'[2]

Humphries also wrote a rousing, nostalgic music hall number called the 'War Saving Street Song'. It recalled the patriotic efforts of Melbourne communities whose valiant contributions to the war effort were recognised in the yellow tin plaques attached to telegraph poles, bearing the words 'This is a War Saving Certificate Street'. Concerned citizens had purchased bonds for the war effort and proudly hung up their gold signs.

Eric Humphries bought tickets for the show at the Assembly Hall in Melbourne for all the family, and went back to purchase more tickets later on, anxious at the thought that nobody else would. When *A Nice Night's Entertainment* opened on 30 July 1962, on a gusty winter evening in Melbourne, Edna Everage strode onto the stage in a green pillbox hat with a net à la Jacqueline Kennedy, a crimson coat, gloves, pearls and butterfly-style glasses with diamante details. Edna had thrown off her dowdy look of the earlier Melbourne shows for a more gaudy, fashionable outfit. She wore a slash of bright lipstick, but at this stage no other make-up. She told the audience all about her visit to the old country and reassured them that they had nothing to fear from overseas fashions: 'I visited all the big cities, and though I was from Australia, quite a few heads turned, I can tell you!'

She launched into a jaunty song about trends overseas, about 'a persisting Oz Malaise', and the Australian obsession with not falling behind the fashions from abroad:

> *Now I'm back from Europe in the bosom of my home*
> *Far from dear old London and New York, Paris, Rome,*
> *Far from the fashion houses which decree the latest styles*
> *The latest shade of lipstick has to come twelve thousand miles*
> *But the fastest jet you can possibly get is still to no avail*
> *For when the fashions reach us they're the teeniest bit stale;*
> *Oh there's no place like Australia, but still I can't pretend*
> *That our womenfolk aren't keen to know the very latest trend.*

It was Edna's first homecoming and Humphries was physically ill with anxiety. He worried about whether the skits were sharp enough, whether the sketches were varied enough, whether there was sufficient music, if the show was too long, whether his ad-libs would go down well with the audience, and whether there was a theme to unite the seven sketches. For the first time Edna cast judgment on all things Australian, as one who knows, because she had been 'OVERSEAS'.

Edna congratulated Prime Minister Robert Menzies on his statement that Australia may now be regarded as a 'melting-pot'. 'It's just a question of who's going to melt first ...' she exclaimed. There was a short pause for gales of laughter before she trilled, 'It won't be me!' Edna set about showing her 'one million' colour slides of her trip, including various shots of garbage tips in Aden, the deck of the ocean liner and 'yours truly' clasping her hat and grinning in front of Tower Bridge, Whitehall, Buckingham Palace and numerous other tourist sites of significance.

Sandy Stone appeared in a long sketch in the second act in his pyjamas and dressing gown. He sat in his armchair and recounted a rather sad tale about how he and his wife, Beryl, had looked after their neighbours' children, Marilyn and Wayne, over the Easter holidays. It was a poignant monologue as Sandy and Beryl had no children of their own, and when the children left, Sandy reported that Beryl 'got quite weepy'. Barry had tried out the sketch in Auckland in front of friends at a party given by his old drinking buddy Murray Groves and was very pleased with it.

Barry appeared in a program photograph in Sandy's dressing gown over his trousers and shirt, drinking from an upended bottle of tomato sauce in front of a Humphries 'action painting'. A selection of Edna's recipes was included, with instructions for making 'Australia's preferred beverage', tomato sauce; banana trifle, 'a treat for older members of the family'; and snowball and apple sandwiches — 'a lunch-hour thrill for kiddies and senior citizens alike'. The notes on the performer mentioned that Barry had been educated at 'a well-known St Kilda branch of the Junior Chamber of Commerce, whose motto was *Crines Longi Crines Foetidi*', glossed at the bottom of the page as 'long hair is dirty hair'. A quick quiz from Dr Humphries included questions that would reveal 'just how up to date you really are'. The questions satirised pseudo-intellectual pretensions and mocked the fads of the moment and the facile quizzes of women's magazines. 'When chatting about books, what two modern British authors should you disparage? Answer: DH Lawrence and Dylan Thomas.' 'If you enjoyed the play, what adjectives of approbation should you use: Stylish, pacey, well-produced, audible, moving, elegant, poignant, handsome. Answer: Well-produced.'

The back cover of the program offered a black-and-white photograph of a benign-looking young man in coat and tie. Barry, who was looking straight at the camera with a faint smile on his lips, seemed wide-eyed, innocent and almost whimsical. He also included in the program a quote from John Betjeman who called Sandy 'a sort of verbal and Australian Charlie Chaplin ... decent, honest, kind-hearted but deeply conventional'. Betjeman had immediately recognised that Barry's inspiration derived from his childhood in Melbourne, and Barry knew that theatre-goers would be impressed by a quote from the esteemed English poet.

In a short sketch called 'Witchetty Grub Street', included at the last minute, Humphries lampooned Australian journalists and critics. He modelled his journalist character on a composite of Bert Tucker, Peter Coleman and Max Harris. Dressed in a suit the journalist began, 'You probably know me as a poet or painter ... For my sins I bash out a regular feature article ... on matters artistic ...' Then he read from his own 'article', an open letter to Joan Sutherland, published under the headline 'Sorry Joan, You've Lost Your Touch!'

> Heard your latest disc the other night, Joan, and you didn't fool anyone ... What's happened to that voice we knew and loved before you got on that boat and went for the big time, and the bouquets and Covent Garden and all that jazz? Was it really worth it, Joan?
>
> I'm not just getting at you, Joan. The same goes for all your ex-Australian mates ... I hope you're having a ball ...

it cost you enough to get there, didn't it … a little item called talent, remember? The sad fact is, you're all on the skids, and have been since you turned your back on Australia and went after the bright lights and the facile acclamation of a bunch of snobs. You might fool them in England, but you can't pull the wool over our eyes back in Australia.

We don't want people who've spent the last few years of their lives at plushy Chelsea parties knocking their mates back home and ratting on Australia. Don't think we've forgotten you! — Dick Bentley, Sidney Nolan, Ray Lawler, Elsie Morison, Arthur Boyd, Ray Matthew, Peter Finch, Shirley Abicair, Charles Blackman, Joy Nichols, Kenneth Rowell, Wilfred Thomas!

The sketch offered a heartfelt jibe at Max Harris, the critic from Adelaide, who had reviewed Humphries' record *Sandy Agonistes*, claiming with disdain that, 'It had always been an open question whether Barry Humphrey [sic] would see the distance', and that it was apparent now that his satires were 'thin', 'profitless' and that he was in fact a 'flash in the pan'.[3] Barry was terrified that his sketch would be recognised and dismissed as a personal grievance.

But the sketch disarmed the critics and aroused speculation about who was being pilloried. Some thought it was Harris, but Harris said it was Coleman. Coleman said Graeme Hughes and Hughes said Cyril Pearl.[4] It was the first of many brilliant masterstrokes included in Humphries' performances designed to deflect criticism and deflate critics without naming them. Humphries returned the sting of their wounding remarks, and made everyone laugh.

In Melbourne, Sydney and Adelaide the show was well received. Hocking had only booked very short seasons in small halls and so a return season was arranged for Melbourne at the unappealing barn-like Melba Hall, with unraked seating for five hundred. Geoff Hutton described Humphries in *The Age* as a deadly humorist; Roger Covell wrote in the *Sydney Morning Herald* that he 'was the most original entertainer at large in Australia', and although he found the critic sketch less focused, he predicted that Humphries would be the envy of any of our playwrights.[5] The *Sun Herald* reviewer described Humphries as 'probably Australia's most original wit and outrageous social observer'.[6] But the *Daily Telegraph* critic was less effusive and wrote that the jokes were likely to appeal to a coterie and that the humour was 'too private for mass Sydney'.[7]

Humphries appeared on *Startime*, the Friday night variety show hosted by a rather gaunt, if urbane, John Laws dressed in a white suit and pencil-thin black tie. Taking his bow as himself at the beginning of the show, Humphries looked nervous as the other stars filed rather stiffly onto the set. Tommy Tycho and his Orchestra played 'I'm Getting Sentimental Over You', there were song and dance routines by the Taylor Sisters and the Joy Boys, and a ballet solo by Meryl Hughes. Laws then introduced Barry encouragingly as 'the star of a one-man show, *A Nice Night's Entertainment*'.[8] Standing erect in his striped three-piece suit, Humphries faced the camera earnestly and began his sketch: 'Good evening, I'd like to introduce you to a very close friend of mine, Mrs Norm Everage, a housewife from 36 Humouresque Street, Moonee Ponds.' There was a rather long pause before Edna, in a coat with a large corsage and a small hat, emerged from behind a curtain into a timber-panelled room.

'Excuse I,' she ventured and straight away retreated out of sight. Another long silence followed then she returned clutching her handbag: 'Oh dear,' she said, biting her lip, 'isn't this mad? Look, I'm that nervous. I've only addressed branch meetings of the housewives association before. Mind you, isn't television marvellous? Such a lovely piece of furniture.' The camera hovered on a vase of gladioli on the far side of the room. 'Oh there's no doubt about it, there's nothing like it, is there? A flesh-pink gladdie to make you feel at home. And they're plastic too, so hygienic. If only all nature was so easy to wipe down with a Wettex.'

Next Edna looked straight at the camera and smiled. 'You haven't changed a bit. It's wonderful to be back in Australia,' she said in a cultivated, rather pretentious accent. 'I expect in a week or so I'll have my Australian accent back again,' she went on. 'But there's one thing we've got that they haven't got anywhere else in the world — our wonderful Australian smile ... I suppose you'll notice a few changes in me — a few more crow's feet. But what are they but the dried up beds of old smiles.' Edna then launched into a long explanation of her trip overseas. 'Norm couldn't come,' she confided. 'We'd sold this block of land in the Melbourne suburb of Sunshine ... he has a new Holden ... I think they're marvellous, General Motors ... letting us call it Australia's own car — they didn't have to.'

After giving the audience news about her children Kenny, Brucie and Valmai, and then Joylene, her new daughter-in-law — at this Edna's mouth contorted downwards, in clear disapproval of the young woman — she proceeded to offer hints from her recipe book. The studio audience laughed loudly at the familiar but suddenly hilarious concoctions. At the end Edna shuffled out backwards with a little curtsey. 'Bye bye,' she shouted, as the strains of 'God Save the Queen' played. Encouraged by the applause she returned, took off her hat and glasses, and bowed again.

Edna Everage was supposed to be an average suburban housewife from Melbourne. But Barry's hair hung limp and long around his shoulders, and in a still photograph from the show his legs are visible, complete with a mat of thick black hair.[9] Even so, Edna's commentary on Australian manners and mores would become the centrepiece of an ongoing drama devised by Barry Humphries on the subject of his homeland over the next fifty years.

Humphries was ecstatic with his reception and exhausted by the end of three months performing in Australia. He barely made any time to spend with his family in Melbourne, in part because of the hectic tour schedule. Anxious to get back to London, he told Peter O'Shaughnessy that he found 'Australia nice enough, but somehow desperate'.[10] Ros and Barry managed a visit for a few days at 'Dunmoochin' with Clifton and Marlene Pugh. The artist admired Barry enormously and also had great affection and respect for Ros. He wanted to paint a double portrait of the couple, and hoped to submit it for the Archibald Prize. Pugh began painting Barry standing with his hand resting on Ros's shoulder; she was seated on a high-backed Victorian-style chair and both of them looked straight out at the viewer. Pugh recalled years later that before the painting was finished Humphries inexplicably changed his mind about the project, urged Pugh not to include Ros in the work, and insisted they must leave 'Dunmoochin' before the portrait could be finished. Without the two of them in front of him, Pugh felt he could not complete the double portrait; he was bitterly disappointed.[11] Humphries recalls the events of that day very differently, and always felt enthusiastic about the idea of a double portrait.[12]

Barry and Rosalind took a 'silver bird' back to London in November. It only took a week but was not nearly as romantic as the long sea voyage they had experienced on the way out to Australia. They hoped to put a deposit on a house in England with the proceeds of the tour. Back in London Peter O'Shaughnessy tried to convince Barry to put some money into a new production of the Bunyip play for a London audience. But Barry was reluctant. He told his friend that he dare not put money into a pantomime even though he believed it would be a great success. For Barry the strain of playing the Bunyip while worrying about the box office would be too terrifying. He had good reason to be cautious: Rosalind was expecting a baby in the spring.

CHAPTER 11

Soho Nights

In the New Year Humphries signed up for a North American tour of *Oliver!*. Ros was unable to fly out with him because she had been refused a visa for the United States. Before she met Barry she had taught ballet to the daughter of a well-known communist in New Zealand, and feared it was this association that had crippled her chances of meeting up with him in New York.

As soon as Humphries stepped off the aircraft into the snowbound, frigid city of Toronto he was told that he was to play Fagin for the first time. In a panic he quickly re-learned the lines he had always wanted to perform. Remarkably, he carried the role well though he hammed it due to his nervousness. Barry instantly loathed Canada. He found the cold so severe that he felt he was 'walking naked' into a blizzard whenever he ventured outside.[1] He was aghast at the arrangements for buying wine at government liquor stores where he had to sign for the bottles, wait around in a draughty warehouse, and then fight off aggressive drunken tramps outside, begging for his loot. Relieved to discover the Toronto Art Gallery, he looked at paintings by Rembrandt, Monticelli, Chardin and Fantin-Latour. But he was horrified by the amplified kitschy Christmas music playing everywhere he went, including the art gallery.

Oliver! soon transferred to New York where it was a commercial success, despite the very expensive tickets and lukewarm reviews.

For Humphries it was an eye-opener to be playing at the Imperial Theater on West 45th Street. Once again he was playing Sowerberry the undertaker, and understudied Clive Revill as Fagin. Although David Merrick, the producer, had wanted the original cast to play in the Broadway launch of the show, they were forced by union rules to employ many local actors. Barry was fascinated by the attitude of the American actors and astonished that they would miss performances because they were suffering from depression. The cast was well remunerated in New York, but to Barry's irritation Actors' Equity rules meant that foreign actors paid a 5 per cent alien tax.[2]

Eventually representations made on behalf of Rosalind Humphries to the American embassy in London were successful, she was granted a visa, and reunited with Barry in New York. At first the Humphries stayed in a squalid hotel. Barry complained and soon they were offered an apartment at 69 West 10th Street. There was no hot water and no lift, but in spite of their spartan existence, Greenwich Village restored Barry's equilibrium after Toronto. It reminded him of Soho without prostitutes, or a blend of Kings Cross and Chelsea. There were artists everywhere, second-hand bookshops galore, cheap wine and bars that stayed open until dawn. Barry was at once shocked by the shabbiness of New York and mesmerised by the magnificent shops. Rosalind was enchanted by the vibrant street life and the energy of the people. As a keen cook she delighted in the range of items sold in the grocery stores, as well as the fact that everything stayed open so late. She bought an elegant white dinner set at midnight and spent her days walking through the city and browsing in the bookshops.

But it was the people and their speech that impressed Humphries the most. 'The rudeness of shopkeepers is so fabulous you can hardly believe your ears,' he wrote to Peter O'Shaughnessy. 'The subways are filthy and poverty stricken and much chundered in. The people are either tarty or gaudy or threadbare and ill-looking ... No one says please or thank you, everyone says sonuvvabitch and crap and screw.'[3] He was impressed and horrified all at once by the vitality of the city and the extreme language of its citizens. He loved the tawdry, ramshackle buildings of the Village and the aggressively arty people on the streets.

In New York Barry and Rosalind occasionally went out with Peter and Wendy Cook. Cook was in New York performing in the London phenomenon *Beyond the Fringe*. Barry had first met Peter in a Covent Garden pub in 1961 when he was playing in the first production of *Oliver!* and they had become friends, spending a lot of time at the Colony Room and the other drinking clubs of Soho. Cook found Barry's flamboyant practical jokes extraordinary, but he told the critic John Lahr years later that he thought Barry a rather mysterious character.[4] Both men were tall, outwardly self-possessed creatures who loved to show off their wit and had a knack for transforming the trivial experiences of everyday life into startling satire.

It was in vibrant New York that Humphries met two of his Dada heroes. First he encountered the artist Marcel Duchamp early in 1963 at the launch of one of his art exhibitions. Barry was photographed with Duchamp and his wife who was quite taken with Barry. Even more heady was a chance sighting in the Gotham Book Mart of the surrealist artist Salvador Dali with whom he chatted. Afterwards, the two went back to Dali's lodgings at the St Regis Hotel for afternoon tea. But not all of New York's buzz was positive. After the show, Barry would drink at his favourite bar, the Ninth Circle, not far from the apartment, while Rosalind, who was rather unwell in her pregnancy, sat at home watching television. One night some local Haitian louts burst into the apartment. Ros was terrified because they simply refused to leave. They started following her around the streets. At least once, Peter Cook came over to see that she was all right, when she was alone and Barry was drinking.

One of the regulars at the Ninth Circle bar was the Beat poet Jack Kerouac, who referred to Barry amiably as the 'English poet'.[5] One freezing night the drinkers were ushered out of the bar by Kerouac onto the back of a truck lit by flickering candles. While the truck negotiated the icy streets of Manhattan, the revellers sprawled in the back drinking and smoking. Feeling guilty about leaving Rosalind alone after her troubles with the drug-crazed local youths, Humphries asked Kerouac to let him out in 10th Street. When the truck deposited him outside his apartment block, he was half-annoyed and half-relieved to be escaping Kerouac's magical mystery tour.

Rosalind and Barry took advantage of the magnificent shops and spent Barry's relatively generous earnings on baby clothes, toys, records, books and linen. Barry found himself an elegantly cut suit. When they finally sailed for Liverpool on the *Sylvania* in March 1963, their bags bulged with the spoils of the New York *Oliver!* season. On arrival in England they hired a car for the drive home to London. Delighted to be back in the familiar surrounds of Highgate, they parked the car outside Charles and Barbara Blackman's Georgian house and headed off to the Rose and Crown with Charles and a gang of others. Thieves helped themselves to the contents of the car in their absence. Barbara had stayed home with the children and had heard a noise outside. But with her near-blindness, she could not be sure what was going on. Everything in the car was stolen, including Barry's draft scripts, scrapbook and portfolio of professional photographs. Humphries rang the police and an officer appeared many hours later. Barry opened the glove box, which he had thought to lock, and extracted two items missed by the thieves. 'Take these,' he said mischievously, 'as a token of my appreciation for your prompt response.' He handed the policeman two volumes: *The Kama Sutra* and *The Naked Lunch*, both of them banned in England. It was all they had left, and both Ros and Barry were deeply upset by the loss of their possessions. Charles Blackman felt sorry for his friend and bought Barry a duffel coat from a disposal shop to help get him through the chilly spring nights.

While in New York, Humphries had played Peter Cook his gramophone recordings of his characters Sandy and Edna. Peter found them remarkable. It was no small thing for Barry to receive interest in his solo work from such a successful young comedian. *Beyond the Fringe* had transformed the Edinburgh Fringe Festival of 1960, and played to sell-out crowds in London for some months.

With his friend from Cambridge, Jonathan Miller, and two other Oxford revue actors, Alan Bennett and Dudley Moore, Cook had created a work of comic theatre that brought a new explicitly political, anti-authoritarian focus to English satire. With minimalist staging the sketches of *Beyond the Fringe* represented a bold assault on the elite classes in the United Kingdom. The young gentlemen of Oxbridge sent up British ineptitude and ineffectiveness, as well as the decline of Britain as a world power.[6] In one of Cook's routines he played Harold Macmillan, then the British prime minister, and stood beside a globe pointing incorrectly at all the places in the world he had visited. More than any other comedian over the previous twenty years, Cook had transformed British comedy.

Cook's parody of establishment figures also revealed a paradoxical nostalgia for Britain's glorious imperial past. It was no surprise that Cook found Humphries' nostalgic satirical portrait of a returned serviceman, Sandy Stone, so amusing. When Barry and Ros returned to London, Cook offered Barry a second chance to perform at the Establishment at 18 Greek Street, Soho. The Establishment Club was a former strip joint that Cook had bought in partnership with Nick Luard, who had been the treasurer of the Footlights Revue in Cambridge and had a reputation for being a tough character. He and Cook had convinced ten thousand people to pay a two-guinea membership fee before the club even opened its doors. Four young Cambridge actors — Eleanor Bron, John Bird, John Fortune and Jeremy Geidt — made up the resident cast, and the club quickly became known as the satire club, the first of its kind in London. Frankie Howerd and Lenny Bruce also made successful appearances on the minute stage, all of them invited by Peter Cook.

Cook made Humphries a very generous offer: a three-week season at the Establishment performing some of the characters from his one-man show for a salary of £100 a week. Even though it was a princely sum for a little-known Australian actor in a try-out season in 1963, it was a risky venture for Humphries. However, with nothing else on the horizon except the prospect of returning to *Oliver!* at £20 a week, he could not resist the opportunity. But he was very anxious about performing a one-man comedy show at the fashionable venue. He was particularly worried about what the audience would make of Edna Everage. For one thing his comedy was nothing like that of the stalwarts of the club who satirised the pretensions of the English middle and upper classes, often mimicking politicians of the day. His routines were not politically motivated or topical; they were completely different to the satire that had made the club such a success.

Humphries was so nervous about the Establishment show that he wondered whether to ask Peter O'Shaughnessy to look over the Edna sketch material. Ros thought he should not perform Edna at all. Barry was in two minds about approaching O'Shaughnessy, but eventually requested his older friend's advice. With a gnawing sense of the potential for disaster he prepared for the opening night of *A Nice Night's Entertainment* at the Establishment Club.

On Cook's instruction he appeared one day at the studio on the first floor of the club building for publicity shots. Lewis Morley, who had taken the first photos for *Beyond the Fringe*, set about capturing Barry in his corduroy jacket and desert boots. Morley had grown up in Hong Kong, and visited Australia as a teenager. He was ten years older than Barry, had been imprisoned during the war, and had a kindly, philosophical disposition. He felt some sympathy for the rather dishevelled, lank-haired Humphries. They chatted and laughed as Morley suggested Barry sit with his arms around his knees on the floor and look up at the camera. The amiable Morley was used to dealing with a parade of over-confident ex-public-school-boys who took their turn performing at the Establishment, and found Barry refreshingly innocent and charming.

Humphries' fears were well founded. No one in the cramped, uncomfortable Establishment knew what to make of the skinny, rather nervous young man with long hair, dressed up as a housewife in a drab brown skirt and jacket, talking about a distant suburb of Melbourne called Moonee Ponds. In one sketch Humphries appeared in his stolen suit — it had been recovered at a garbage tip outside London with one arm cut out of it. He made a joke of the dismembered outfit, parading across the stage in the crumpled garment: 'a suit direct from New York', not mentioning the missing arm.

The audiences were polite but perplexed. Edna's attempts to address them as intimates fell flat. Humphries' ad-libs were greeted with indifferent silence. His comedy seemed disconnected from the world of the club. Just a few weeks earlier a stolen copy of Morley's now infamous studio photograph of Christine Keeler had been published in the *Sunday Mirror*, adding fuel to the fire that was raging around John Profumo, the Tory Secretary of State for War, and providing a wealth of salacious subject matter for the regulars at the club. But Humphries' act did not once refer to the goings-on in Westminster nor the Profumo affair.

The muted reception of his act was humiliating. Humphries went backstage to find Nick Luard waiting for him with a look of ill-concealed disdain. Luard didn't wait long before offering gratuitous advice about cutting bits of the show. Humphries felt sick. In the corner of the dressing room, listening to this glib and condescending assessment of his act was Peter O'Shaughnessy, who chimed in with his own comments on what had gone awry. O'Shaughnessy's presence in the dressing room was hard enough to bear but his contribution to the discussion of all that was wrong with his performance left Humphries seething.

The reviews were wounding but not surprising. Julian Holland in the *Daily Mail* lamented that Humphries' performance 'lacked anger', while Bamber Gascoigne remarked in the *Spectator* that the skits were 'distinctly soporific'. Nick Luard advised Barry that the show would close before the end of the run.[7]

Barry was extremely disappointed with the failure of his act at the Establishment and found himself depressed and directionless. If not for Rosalind's constant reassurances that his act was clever and funny, he might never have performed again. She believed in the power of his comedy and reminded him of her strong faith in his talent regularly. Barry always listened to Rosalind's comments and valued her opinions about his performance.

This period of despondency allowed some time for reflection. Though he had no desire to return to live in Australia, he found himself thinking more and more about life at home in Melbourne. The contrast between the two cities made him aware of the intrinsic comic potential of his homeland, and especially of the streetscapes of his youth: Melbourne's 'Anzac-coloured' river and the 'beautiful cream and Rexona-green' trams. Even the names of the suburbs were comical: Rosanna, Keon Park, Niddrie, Syndal, Research and, of course, Moonee Ponds.[8]

While Barry lamented his failure to impress the audiences in the Soho nightclub, back in Australia he was gaining a following as Mrs Norm Everage. Edna appeared again on John Laws' show *Startime '63* in short sketches filmed during his visit in 1962. The sketches, screened between modern dance numbers by troupes of women sporting beehive hairdos, drew on the success of the Australian run of *A Nice Night's Entertainment* to offer an incisive parody of the new middle-class phenomenon: the slide evening.

Seated at home in front of her heater Edna got straight to the point. 'I want to ask you an intimate question,' she said, staring down the lens of the camera. 'I wonder if any of you have been to a slide evening before?' Edna then proceeded with her slide presentation entitled 'My Trip'. 'That's me in Piccadilly,' she informed the viewers, 'standing underneath the statue of Ethos' and outside Australia House. 'Inside it's just like your own home,' she reassured the audience, hastening to add, 'I made a point of meeting the people. So many Australians don't, so I bowled up to people and said, "I've come 13,000 miles to meet you."' In a glorious reversal of the standard scenario Edna emerged as the opinionated and rather guileless but forthright colonial, treating the locals as native specimens. In one of the slides she was shown apprehending a man in a bowler hat and coat — 'a London city type', she explained. She towered over him and seemed to be almost cuddling him: 'Isn't he gorgeous?' she demanded of the audience. 'I just had to touch him. It was then that I encountered English reserve,' she concluded. As a slide flashed up of Edna outside the tiny Old Curiosity Shop in Portsmouth Street, she informed the audience that the shop was 'immobilised by Charles Dickens. You'll notice they've got the Tudor idea over there too,' she added, to howls of laughter in the audience.[9]

Humphries had captured the gauche behaviour of Australians abroad, as well as their obsessive domestic routines, and television audiences responded enthusiastically. He was not the only writer to satirise the banality of Australian speech and preoccupations. Patrick White's exploration of Australian suburbia offered a similar kind of satire. There was even a touch of Mrs Norm Everage in White's Miss Docker, the protagonist of his expressionistic play *A Cheery Soul*. White had written the play the previous winter while Barry had been touring with his own show. Both men shared a profound frustration with Australian mediocrity and an even greater antagonism towards Australians in London.

CHAPTER 12

Highgate Babies

In the spring, Barry and Rosalind moved to a rented house at 27A Jacksons Lane, vacated by the Blackmans, who moved up the hill to Highgate village. On 14 May 1963 Rosalind gave birth to a baby girl, Tessa Louise, at Charing Cross Hospital. When she came home Ros and Barry took the baby for long walks in her pram across the heath and up and down to the Blackmans' house. Humphries was delighted with his baby daughter and instantly his mood lifted. He was enchanted by Tessa's tiny fingers and loved to hold her as she gazed up at him. Barbara gave birth to her third child, Barnaby, in July, strengthening the bond between the two families.

During their residence at the Jacksons Lane house, the Blackmans had a lodger, Edith Tighe, from Brisbane. When Barry and Ros were preparing to take over the lease, Barry said, 'I don't want any Edith living here. I'll let the room to a stranger.' Barbara replied wittily, 'You won't find anyone stranger than Edith.' Edith was a big-boned ungainly woman with large spectacles. She had an ordinary office job but was somewhat eccentric. Edith went to Mass early every day and loved to visit graveyards, museums and zoos. Perhaps Humphries appreciated her interests; Edith stayed. She enjoyed a sherry each evening with Ros and adored baby Tessa. She listened to the BBC in bed every night. Barry would sneak in late after his show and snatch Edith's radio from beside her bed so he could listen to music as he ate his supper alone downstairs. Edith would scold him loudly the next morning. She had an argot of her own, and Barry sometimes borrowed her expressions — like 'woebegone character' and 'they live way out to hell and gone' — to use in his scripts. Edith could also be drily funny. Humphries would say to her challengingly, 'Edith, who is the comedian in this house?' She would give him a demure smile and say sweetly: 'You are, Barry.'[1]

On the day Tessa was born, Barry received a telegram from Spike Milligan asking him to play the lead role in a play called *The Bedsitting Room*, a farce he had written with John Antrobus. Milligan had seen Humphries' show in Melbourne the previous year, and asked him to replace the lead actor, Graham Stark, with whom Milligan had quarrelled, when the play transferred from the Mermaid Theatre to the Comedy in Whitehall. It was an irresistible offer for Barry who was delighted to be given his own understudy, an actor called Michael Gambon.

Spike Milligan also made an appearance in the play in Act II, as Barry and the rather baby-faced female lead, Jacqueline Ellis, lay in bed together on stage. The black-and-white photo of Barry in the program is a head and shoulders portrait; an odd, slightly quizzical smile plays about his face and his hair is parted at the side and combed over into a foppish bob. He wears a three-piece suit and, as usual, looks straight at the camera. The notes for each actor parodied conventional theatre notes, with Milligan 'seen here' in this 'heavily posed portrait at the end of World War II' and Humphries 'born at the turn of the century in Van Diemen's Land', recently having 'completed a highly successful five-minute season at the Establishment'. The joke on Barry belonged to Spike. Humphries still could not laugh about his disappointing effort at Peter Cook's club. But his performance drew considerable laughter and the success of the play restored Barry's confidence.

On a visit to Paris Charles and Barbara Blackman picked up an intriguing magazine and passed it on to Barry. It was called *Bizarre*, and displayed on its cover a photo of a man peeling a banana at crotch level. Indulging his long-held fascination with the lurid and the grotesque, Barry borrowed the title of the magazine and began work on a book for the publisher Paul Elek. Barry asked Barbara Blackman to write some poems for this new illustrated anthology of poetry and prose. The two of them were always trying out limericks and ditties together. They were also fond of a curious book filled with photographs of strange physiological phenomena called *Anatomical Anomalies and Medical Freaks*, that Barbara's friends John and Alannah Newell had found in a public library in Melbourne.

Bizarre offers a road map to Humphries' psyche as a young man. It reproduces quotations from de Sade and Ronald Firbank, and weird stories by Lafcadio Hearn, MP Shiel, Arthur Machen, Baron Corvo, Joris-Karl Huysmans and other writers whose work he had admired for the previous ten years. It was also an attack on niceness with Dadaist 'household hints for the mutilation of the *Mona Lisa*', expressionist photomontages and notes on genital circumcision. There are drawings by Beardsley, Humphries' favourite poem by Stephen Phillips, 'The Blow', and a couple of blasphemous illustrations by Barbey d'Aurevilly. One of these depicts a naked woman nailed to a cross. The publication of this image was guaranteed to shock readers and makes Madonna's much more recent and much criticised luminous images of herself against a silver cross look rather tame.[2] The book also features images of people afflicted by cretinism, conjoined twins, a man without legs appearing as if served up on a plate and other human deformities. The benign, almost sweet, poetry and illustrations contributed by Barbara and Charles Blackman offer a stark contrast to the rest of the book.

Humphries revealed his knowledge of the recherché aspects of the Edwardian and Victorian periods, but also his belief that nothing is taboo. He clearly delighted in the gruesome, but also demonstrated an appreciation of language. Most of the literary matter is drawn from French and German writers. Humphries included selections from *The Torture Garden* by Octave Mirbeau, recommended by Oscar Wilde to Frank Harris in 1899 because 'a sadique joy in pain pulses in it …'.[3] Humphries also featured Ben Jonson's marvellous 'Witches' Song' with its final line from the Dame: 'And now our orgies let's begin.'

Now a collector's item, *Bizarre* captured Humphries' fascination with the grotesque, but also an unresolved strand of his personality at that time: his capacity for misanthropic, cruel attacks on unfortunate people, or people he seized on to victimise. Like his ridicule of the young man at the Sydney Push party, the book draws attention to aberrant physical types and curious physical anomalies. It is a literary encapsulation of Humphries' merciless teasing of an individual in public. Later, Barry would work mildly cruel pranks into his shows, with audience members as fully consenting, enthusiastic victims. This element of his act has come to signify an important dimension of the revelry of a Humphries show, and has largely buried his instinct for real cruelty. If comedy is socialised aggression then Humphries learned that art over the twenty years following the publication of *Bizarre*.[4] But he has never entirely let go of the manic teasing spirit of his younger days.

When Barry sent an inscribed copy to his friend Carl Stead in New Zealand, with the motto, 'Life is a melody if only you'll hum the tune', Stead was staggered that his 'charming and inventive companion' had published such material. He was shocked by the images in it and hid the book.[5] Barbara Blackman implored Barry not to let her mother, who was living in London, discover the volume. But for Humphries and his friends the images were intriguing rather than shocking. He didn't quite understand the reaction to *Bizarre*, but he was disappointed with its reception. His reaction resembled Arthur Boyd's when the director of the Royal Ballet, Dame Ninette de Valois, requested that Boyd paint out the generous quantities of pubic hair from his backdrop for *Elektra*. Boyd couldn't really understand the need — he was certain that the Queen would not mind — but complied.[6] It was too late for Humphries to make alterations by the time his book was published. Booksellers throughout the land simply refused to stock *Bizarre*.

In Australia an article about the controversial book appeared in the Melbourne *Truth*. Eric Humphries was mortified when he found out about the volume that booksellers were refusing to sell, and bought multiple copies of *Truth* in the forlorn hope that others would not read about his son's strange and shameful publication.

He could not believe that 'a son of his could write such a book'.[7] Thirty years later the book still aroused criticism and contempt: in 1997 the journalist Craig McGregor described it as a 'masturbator's handbook'.[8]

Depressed by the lack of interest in *Bizarre*, envious of the success of his friends and with few prospects of his own, Humphries continued to drink heavily. He cut a forlorn and raffish figure wandering alone and spending long hours in pubs. There were, however, one or two offers of work. Lionel Bart, who had spotted Barry trudging down Earls Court Road in a large hat and long, tatty raincoat, his hair trailing down his back in ratty tendrils, offered him a part in his new musical, *Maggie May*. Humphries would perform the role of the balladeer, a one-man band with bass drum, harmonica and cymbals. It was only a small role, but Barry was desperate for work. He appeared at the beginning and the end of the show.

In spite of the change in his daily routine that the musical demanded, Barry continued to spend long periods drinking. In fact the extended break between his appearances on stage left plenty of time for him to slip out the stage door and into the pub next to the theatre. He drank excessively: once he took a chance and attended a party in Putney and only just made it back to the theatre on time for his last appearance at the end of the show. Afterwards the company manager warned him that he was never to leave the theatre again between his appearances.

Ros found herself alone for long stretches of time. When *Maggie May* opened in Manchester at its out-of-town try-out, Humphries telephoned her and encouraged her to come up from London to see the show. Bill Walker, whom Barry and Ros had met through Cliff Hocking, was then sharing the flat with the Humphries and Edith, and offered to drive Ros and Tessa to Manchester. When they arrived at the address Barry had given Ros for his lodgings, there was no sign of him. Ros was appalled to find a gang of squatters on the ground floor and upstairs a squalid flat with very little in it save for a dirty, stained mattress and a few aluminium saucepans. The condemned flat overlooked rows of tenements and vacant land overgrown with thistles, still scarred from the bombing of the war. Ros went to the theatre in search of Barry, and still there was no sign of him. Someone muttered to her that he was off in London with his 'fancy girl'. When she found Rex Harrison in the bar and described the state of the digs, he said, 'I know.' Harrison continued: 'He asked all of us to look for something really awful for you.' Ros replied, 'You mean that's not where he lives?' Rex nodded. The whole thing was one of Barry's elaborate and cruel jokes.[9]

On a bitterly cold day in January 1965 thousands of Britons lined the streets of central London to pay their respects to Winston Churchill. They stood for hours to watch as the funeral procession passed by, to hear the guns cracking in the winter silence and to observe all the cranes dipping in unison down by the Thames. Among the crowds at Whitehall was John Sumner, back from Melbourne for a visit. Like so many Britons, he felt compelled to pay his respects to the great wartime leader.

The following day Sumner dropped into the Adelphi Theatre to see *Maggie May*. He was delighted by Humphries' portrayal of the narrator. At the end of the show Sumner looked for Barry backstage. He was a little unsure of how Humphries would receive him. But Humphries was warm and effusive. Egged on by the rather manic young actor, the two of them toured around the bars of Soho. In the small hours of the morning Barry took John back to the house, waking Ros up to see the visitor, seemingly unaware of the hour or her need for sleep. Alcohol fuelled his already expansive natural reserves of energy, but made him oblivious to the needs of even those who were closest to him.

At a party Barry met the Australian historian Manning Clark who was staying in Twickenham. The two men were drawn to one another and talked for a long time. Clark recognised Humphries' vulnerability, creativity and daring. The historian observed in Barry something of his own anxiety and determination to express his own ideas, to 'uncover' himself and 'hold up the coat so that others may see one's view, but afraid of the pain when the mockers laugh'.[10]

He also recognised alcoholic tendencies and the selfish neglect of others that they cause.

Humphries remained bewildered by the failure of *Bizarre*. He had hoped that the new-found liberalism of 'swinging London' would guarantee interest and acceptance of the strange anthology. He began to cultivate his more benign instinct for the humour of the ordinary and to bury his intense interest in the grotesque, but privately he retained his fascination with the outlandish and macabre. He felt compelled to publish, but realised he needed to change tack. With his appetite for resurrecting literature from earlier periods undampened, Barry began collecting material in earnest for another anthology that he eventually called *Barry Humphries' Book of Innocent Austral Verse*.

Inspired by the English anthology *The Stuffed Owl*, the volume demonstrated Humphries' passion for conserving strange artefacts of culture and his bowerbird mentality for exhuming the obscure and ridiculous. In this slim paperback, dedicated to John Betjeman, Barry paraded his taste for the whimsical, the perverse and the absurd in Australian poetry. His anthology consisted of poetic oddments and oddities penned between the 1890s and the 1960s. The volume includes innocent ditties such as 'A Bunch of Gum Leaves' and the shocking doggerel of 'A Plea for the Niggers' by JE Liddle. There are heartfelt, awkward bush laments with long titles such as Elizabeth Hardwicke's 'On Removing the Remains of a Pioneer Gold Digger from the Old Bush Grave where his Comrades had Laid Him', amusing short rhymes such as 'Birth Control' and 'Instant Potato' by Elsie Carew, and poignant poems such as 'The Old Actors', written by Joan Torrance for a benefit in 1900. Its evocative lines sent a shiver down the young actor's spine:

> *That trembling form, now knitting, once played the Fairy Queen —*
> *In evening's shade is dreaming of glad days that have been;*
> *In fairyland she's soaring, with airy host again,*
> *Showering on all kind blessings, with wand dispersing pain;*
> *On a silver barge sailing into the golden West,*
> *Through clouds of changing colour, to where the fairies rest.*[11]

Barry's faun-like figure graced the painted front cover, amid brightly coloured childlike images of an Australian idyll with galahs, a kangaroo, a koala and a windmill. His face is youthfully sensual, rounded and benign, as he crouches into the painted scene. On the back cover Humphries appeared in the slightly more menacing form of a black-and-white portrait by Cecil Beaton. His eyes are piercing, his face is pinched and his long hair is draped across his face, revealing one sideburn, a somewhat manic expression and a strong hint of his earlier Dadaist hero Tristan Tzara. The front and back cover images captured two sides of the man: the innocent, fey dreamer and the haunted, freakish eccentric in Edwardian dress. Indeed the blurb on the back cover began with the words, 'Who is Barry Humphries?' If his career as an actor was faltering, Barry remained fully engaged in keeping his name before the public while cultivating an aura of mystery. He dreamed of packing up and moving to Portugal or Greece to write full time, away from the temptations and pressures of London.

In the Highgate years Humphries drove a bright blue Mini Minor from home to the West End each day. His driving, like his personality, exhibited anarchic impulses. Once he was stopped by a policeman for driving with one foot on the steering wheel. In the afternoons he now played Heinrich, 'a scientist', in the matinee of *The Merry Roosters Panto* at Wyndham's Theatre at the top of Charing Cross Road, before dashing across Leicester Square to the Comedy and *The Bedsitting Room* in Panton Street. He would invariably stop for a drink in one of the bars of Soho before driving home. When the pubs closed there was always the Colony Room upstairs in Dean Street, a cramped and stuffy private club where Barry remembers catching glimpses of the artist Francis Bacon, leather clad, 'ordering champagne for everybody' with a set of camp businessmen encircling him.[12] The drinks were expensive, but Colony regulars were permitted to keep a tab and pay later.

One of the regulars at the Colony Room, Frank Norman, had written a new play called *A Kayf Up West*, and Barry was pleased when Joan Littlewood invited him to join her company, the Theatre Workshop, in the heart of the East End, to perform in it.

It was a much needed opportunity for Barry. Littlewood was a celebrated producer and writer who had stunned audiences with *Oh, What a Lovely War!* just months earlier. Norman had set his play in a café and in the streets of Soho in 1949. Humphries played five roles, including one called Lord Sexkilling. It was a chaotic production and the play did not make it to the West End.

CHAPTER 13

Bazza

By 1965, the good-looking, hard-drinking Peter Cook had become a kind of satire king, complete with empire, and he was always on the look-out for new material for his recently acquired magazine, *Private Eye*. Cook had bought into it when it ran into financial difficulties in 1964, and one of his friends, Nicholas Garland, a tall, affable New Zealander, occasionally drew illustrations for the small comic ads that appeared at the back of the magazine. Garland also worked at the BBC, but was tired of television and longed to make his living as a cartoonist. He had recently had some luck publishing cartoons in the *Spectator*, and avidly read the American comic strips of *Mad* magazine. Over a few weeks in the summer of 1964, he and Cook tossed around ideas for a new comic strip. They were keen to use some of the Australian slang they had heard Humphries toss off in his impromptu impersonations of a young traveller recently arrived in London from Sydney, and in permanent search of a Foster's and a good time.

Cook told Garland he would be delighted to publish a strip capturing this character in the *Eye*. Garland played around with various drawings, intent on creating a suitable cartoon figure; when he was happy with some mocked-up episodes he presented them to Cook and asked if he would write the script. Cook was adamant that he could not do it; the right person for the job was Barry

Humphries. Over a coffee at Barry's place in Highgate, the two expatriates, Garland and Humphries, discussed the cartoon strip and the infamous figure of Bazza McKenzie was born.

The Adventures of Barry McKenzie documented a fresh-faced young Australian's encounters with the English. Garland took Bazza's prominent chin from the comic strip character Desperate Dan and his double-breasted suit and wide-brimmed hat from the middle-aged Anzacs he had seen walking down Whitehall on Remembrance Day. Barry McKenzie looked to Barry Humphries like someone from the country visiting the city for the Royal Agricultural Show.[1]

Barry and Nick met every week to discuss the strip. Garland was in awe of Humphries, yet found him charming and preposterously funny. After the meetings Barry would send copious, wordy script blocks to Nick, who would then draw the comic figures. Nick always had to cut Barry's lengthy dialogue in order to meet the very tight demands of the short fortnightly strip. Barry wrote the dialogue as if it were a film script, with instructions for Garland such as 'close up' or 'long shot', but he had no idea about narrative sequence or how to introduce characters. When he thought of a joke, the storyline meant nothing to him. He simply bent the character or the plot around in order to highlight the joke, so that a particular character could say the funny line, even if it was inconceivable for that character to speak or act that way. For example, Humphries revealed out of the blue that Bazza had a twin brother, a minister of the church called 'the Rev Kev'. Humphries wanted Kevin to appear without any introduction in a toilet cubicle next to Bazza in London.[2]

In fact Humphries scorned most of the conventions of comic strip narratives, and scolded Nick if the drawings weren't just as he wanted them. He had broken rules on stage and was unrepentant about breaking the rules of writing cartoon stories. Sometimes he would reprimand Nick, and tell him that his cartoon figures were hopeless. Garland never complained but would simply re-do the drawings and edit the material so that it all made sense. Sometimes Nick and Ros wrote segments of the script in order to make the cartoon work, or when they could not find Barry who occasionally disappeared for days at a time.

He would always pop up again full of apologies and outlandish stories, charming Nick with his jokes and kind gestures. For Ros the absences were hellish. After one disappearance Barry returned home and gave Ros an etching by Ryland entitled *Faith*. He begged her to hold on to her faith in him. For the time being, she continued to do so.[3]

Not long after they had begun working together on the Bazza McKenzie strip, Nick drew Barry in pen and ink. It was not a cartoon but a whimsical caricature. Inside a black frame he sketched Barry's face with shading across one side, obscuring the left eye. The right eye is large and bulging, the nose hooked and the mouth turned down at the corners. There is a haunted but innocent look about Humphries, and an almost other-worldly presence. In the top left corner, partly hidden by swirling clouds, a bat flaps about Barry's head. The caption in Nick's rather boyish handwriting reads: 'Barry Humphries: the Famous Loony'. The image captured Nick's bewildered admiration for his friend, and offers a glimpse of Barry's odd behaviour and quirky private self. It also presents a rather dark picture of a man embattled and lost.

Private Eye was a daring, sometimes shocking publication dedicated to satirising British pretension and corruption in public life, and the Barry McKenzie comic strip was firmly in the mode of the magazine. Spike Milligan published cartoons and short pieces in it, calling himself the Reverend Spike, as well as penning regular features such as the 'Grovel Column', 'Pseuds' Corner' and a spoof on the royal family called 'Love in the Saddle'. There was an editorial penned by a fictitious press baron called Lord Gnome, in parody of Lords Beaverbrook and Thomson. Another column by 'Glenda Slagg' lampooned a Fleet Street columnist by the name of Jean Rook, who would either savage or lionise a different public figure every week with unprecedented ferocity. The editor, Richard Ingrams, knew it was a raw and dangerous game. People used the magazine to launch scathing stories about politicians and to exact revenge on others. *Private Eye* feasted on several political scandals including the Profumo affair. It was an extraordinary publishing venture that gave journalism in the UK a new tone and licence.

Humphries and Garland originally intended their cartoon to poke fun at English pomposity, but it took off in a different direction. Although they both admired English satire and understood its targets, at times Humphries found it nauseatingly self-congratulatory and he knew also that he could not create material like that of Cook, Milligan and the other *Eye* regulars.[4] So although it started as a cartoon about English types, Bazza himself soon took over and the English found themselves 'relegated to supporting roles'; they were mere pantomime figures as observed by the young man in Earls Court.[5] The picaresque tales of Bazza in London portrayed England as an impoverished country of would-be migrants to Australia. It was not popular at first, but picked up a following as Humphries persisted in initiating English readers into the mysterious world of Australian slang. The real target of the strip then became the crude parochialism of Australians in London, a favourite satiric target of Barry's for some time.

Some of the language in the strip was invented, but much of the slang was real. Humphries revelled in the vulgarity of this highly exaggerated idiom. If Lionel Bart could do it with cockney slang, Humphries could do it with Strine. Peter Cook, John Wells, William Rushton, Christopher Booker, Barry Fantoni and Gerald Scarfe, all of whom contributed to *Private Eye*, found the material hilarious. Cook encouraged Barry to use as many obscure Australian expressions as possible. For the editor Richard Ingrams, a rather unkempt, schoolboyish and strangely puritanical figure, the strip was worth nurturing. Within a short period people were talking about 'chundering' and 'pointing Percy at the porcelain'. Every woman was now a 'sheila'. Around the Establishment Club, people picked up the slang and spoke it to one another as a running joke. Readers loved the language of Barry McKenzie and the gormless, gentle figure of Bazza himself. As Cook had hoped, the cartoon eventually helped to boost circulation and rescue the magazine from the doldrums.[6]

For Barry the strip offered a regular income as he persevered with his acting career. He and Nick were paid £7 10s each for every episode. It was a relief to Humphries that Bazza McKenzie thrilled English audiences whereas Edna and Sandy had failed to raise a laugh. He enjoyed the success of the cartoon. He particularly liked the fact that as long as the cartoon strip featured every fortnight in *Private Eye*, nobody would forget him. He also relished the slightly conspiratorial nature of the partnership between Garland and himself. Everyone thought of it as Humphries' cartoon strip, and in a real sense it was Barry's creation. Humphries wrote the brilliantly witty and daring text that taught its ever-widening English audience a hilarious new Australian idiom. Barry was both the boss and the facilitator of the cartoon strip. But the actual figure of Barry McKenzie, as imagined by Garland, with his huge chin, broad-brimmed hat and suit, was critical to the success of the comic strip and the enduring career of the character. Garland's figure would soon provide the essential visual cues for the film character that brought Barry Humphries international acclaim and the opprobrium of many influential Australians.

The last few months of 1964 and the first few weeks of 1965 were a time of tumult for Barry and Rosalind. Ros was pregnant and Barry kept disappearing for longer and longer stretches. Bill Walker was a support to Ros, helping her with Tessa and attempting to calm her rising anxiety about the next Australian tour, planned to commence in October 1965. After another series of binges Barry was at last medically diagnosed as an alcoholic. Ros wrote to Cliff Hocking in Melbourne to inform him of Barry's condition. Hocking's faith in Humphries was almost as unshakable as that of Rosalind. In spite of the news of Humphries' very poor state of health, Hocking organised an extended tour of Australia for the new show, entitled *Excuse I: Another Nice Night's Entertainment* in JC Williamson theatres in Sydney, Melbourne and Adelaide.

With the tour dates firmly in view the tension caused by Barry's drinking eased for a while in the months leading up to the tour. Desmond Fennessy, the Humphries' witty and intelligent journalist friend, stayed with them and helped maintain Barry's focus on and enthusiasm for developing the show. He reported on Australian expressions and made suggestions for the script. Fennessy brought a sense of calm and humour to the household at a time of desperation for Barry and Ros. It was a bit like the old times before they left Melbourne when they had sat around joking and playing as they devised the sketches for *Rock 'n' Reel Revue* with Peter O'Shaughnessy. Humphries relished the prospect of leaving his messy life in London behind and began to feel at home with the new sketches and his new one-man show.

CHAPTER 14

My Favourite Things

On 25 January 1965 Rosalind gave birth to a second daughter, Emily Sarah. Shortly after the baby's arrival, Barry and Ros moved their young family to a spacious flat in a Regency house at 25 Maida Ave, Maida Vale near Regent's Canal in Little Venice. It had a pretty outlook over the treetops and the canal but the flat had been unoccupied since the war, when it was used as a brothel, and was in a very bad state. Ros spent days cleaning and whitewashing the walls with paint donated from the set department at the Palladium. The Humphries filled their new abode with assorted objets d'art, including Victorian silk flowers under glass domes, a massive statue of Ariadne, pieces of Gallé glass, their prized collection of Conder paintings, two works by Arthur Boyd and various obscure Symbolist works, some of them bizarre and some erotic. Even at this time, the Humphries owned so many paintings they couldn't hang them all.

Leaving Highgate had been very stressful. Barry was increasingly absent from home, and Ros had suffered from a perforated duodenal ulcer before Emily was born. At Charing Cross Hospital she was told that she had lost the baby, but the next day the foetal heartbeat was audible once more.

The next six months seemed to pass in a flash as the Humphries prepared for the long Australian tour of *Excuse I: Another Nice*

Night's Entertainment. Not only was the script to be written and the characters honed, but all the arrangements for leaving the flat for an extended period had to be made.

With baby Emily and little Tessa, the Humphries set out on a journey from London to Sydney, via the Qantas 'Fiesta Route'. They let the flat to a friend, filled with the anticipation of stopovers in Bermuda, Nassau, Mexico City, Acapulco, Tahiti and Nandi before finally landing in Sydney. In Mexico City they visited Cliff and Marlene Pugh at their hotel room. Marlene was stricken with a bout of diarrhoea. Barry screeched with laughter: 'You've got Montezuma's Revenge', shocking his friends with his callous humour. From Mexico City they travelled to the mountains where they stayed for an extended period to work on their scripts. Ros developed mastitis, but they were miles from help and she had to endure the misery and excruciating pain of the condition without treatment. The preparations for the new show, *Excuse I*, had been exhausting, and the tour had not even begun. Barry had spent hours in the London office of the *Herald and Weekly Times*, absorbing the details of the 'Miranda' column in which advice was dispensed to readers from all around the nation on diverse subjects. He and Ros read piles of the *Australian Women's Weekly*, borrowed from friends and sent from home, as he wrote his scripts.

Ros's diverse theatrical skills and organisational abilities were increasingly put to use by Barry. Her gentleness and ability to deal calmly with all sorts of people also made her an asset to Barry's enterprise. Clifton Pugh had been impressed with Rosalind's dedication and talent from early on. He had dropped into a rehearsal at Melba Hall on the first Australian tour, and was struck by the way Ros directed Barry. She had also helped perfect the fast costume changes wherein Humphries transformed from 'man to woman and character to character in a matter of seconds'.[1]

A French au pair accompanied the Humphries on this second trip to Australia. Dominique had moved into the Little Venice flat a few months before they departed to look after Tessa and Emily three mornings a week, so that Ros could begin her preparatory work managing the new show. On top of her research for *Excuse I*, Ros remained practical and well organised in the house. The girls were easy to manage and Ros was an adoring and capable mother. Barry, on the other hand, was erratic with the children: at times playful and solicitous, but at other times he was childlike himself.

Those childlike qualities were displayed in a simple yet effective adaptation of the song 'My Favourite Things', from the popular musical *The Sound of Music*, that Barry and Ros wrote for the show as a celebration of Edna's homecoming from cosmopolitan London. It was a hymn of praise to Melbourne, a jaunty parody of popular music and a quirky catalogue of the things Barry genuinely missed about his hometown.

> *The beautiful music bowl given by Myer*
> *Bernard Heinz, the Beatles, the Luton Girls Choir …*
> *White cabbage moths round tomato plants flitting*
> *The swish of a sprinkler, the smell of new knitting*
> *Tea leaves in the gully trap, silver fish in the bath*
> *A sugar ant's trail up my front cement path.*
>
> *A spin in the Bendix, a spin in the car*
> *While our newspapers tell us what nice folk we are*
> *And all of these wonderful speeches of Ming's*[2]
> *These are a few of my favourite things.*

Excuse I opened at the Theatre Royal in Sydney for a two-week season in October before moving to Melbourne, and then back to Sydney for a return season after Christmas. The notices quoted the English playwright John Osborne, declaring Humphries to be a 'marvellous humorist and marvellous poet', and Spike Milligan proclaiming Humphries to be the first Australian satirist, 'one of the funniest men in the world. If you don't think so, then it's your loss. Signed by Spike (being of sound mind).'[3]

These endorsements reflected an emerging affection on the part of the English for things Australian. Partly through Humphries and partly through their own encounters, they tuned in to the more gentle satire of Australian humour. Betjeman, of course, had fallen in love with the country on his visit, and Humphries' idol Dame Edith Sitwell, visiting in 1963, exclaimed, 'I am struck by something indisputably gentle about Australia.' When the Queen's sixteen-year-old son, Prince Charles, arrived in Australia to spend two terms at Geelong Grammar's Timbertop campus in 1966, a new relationship between the countries was no longer simply imagined.

Humphries opened the show with Edna Everage trilling 'Excuse I,' and talking about her new-found interest in yoga and also in making pasta, an activity made simple by drying it on her backyard rotary clothesline. Edna's eyebrows were drawn sharp and black, and were set off powerfully by spectacles and a hat with a 'fascinator'. Dressed in a bright pink coat and wearing diamante earrings, two bracelets and matching black patent shoes and handbag, Humphries presented a new, more glamorous Edna.

A Sandy Stone sketch opened the second act. He sat clutching his hot-water bottle and described the tedious details of his Christmas Day. His monologue, 'Sandy Claus', revealed that the day was a 'real scorcher', and that the 'very go-ahead young chappie' at Holy Trinity told the 'menfolk they could take their coats off if they were so desirous of so doing'. Beryl gave the 'home a good going over with the Flytox so we wouldn't have to race the blowies to our dinner'. They watched 'the Queen's speech and the bush-fire warnings', and when the hot north wind blew up later on, Sandy could 'hear people laughing way up at the Jeffries' place. It rattled the venetians and blew the majority of the cards off the mantelpiece.' Sandy's relentlessly dull commentary provided a foil for the vibrant and provocative Edna Everage.

Humphries' other characters included a repulsive public relations man and a young playboy on skis, exclaiming about his assignations with various snow bunnies at Mt Buller. In a sketch called 'Neskafka or Neil Singleton's Wake', Barry played the pretentious host of a party desperately parading his knowledge of all things fashionable and intellectual. Neil Singleton, based in part on the film director Tim Burstall, was a trendy, pseudo-bohemian, Sydney try-hard, who listened to Miles Davis and fondly recalled the watering holes of the Push in the 'days of the Lincoln and the Tudor'. Singleton had an obligatory Breughel print and a rubber tree in the corner of the room, near the exposed-brick wall. He smoked Chesterfields and talked about 'the early Ellington' as 'moving and meaningful', and some of the other jazz greats as 'downright elegiac'.[4]

As part of the sketch, Neil would open a door to let some guests in. They were named after a series of deadbeat characters he had known in London. One of them was Tony Austen. The real Tony Austen would hang about, beg for handouts of cash and stay for hours on end. He would say, 'I've got a brother in television. Barry, I can get you on television.' Austen was such a nuisance that in the end Barry would refuse to open the door to him, but would pass him out a sandwich, a ripped fiver or a sponge soaked with beer through the letterbox slot. One night during the Melbourne run, Humphries had given Charles and Barbara Blackman tickets for seats in the front row of the theatre. When Barry, dressed as Neil, opened the door to Tony Austen, Barbara began to hoot and screech with laughter, recalling the real Austen. She was the only one in the auditorium laughing. Suddenly Humphries walked to the edge of the stage and said, 'Sometimes you get a freak in here and it's better to humour them and then you will hear no more from them.' It was the first time Humphries had offered a comment on the behaviour of the audience in the middle of a sketch, but he frequently inserted the name of a real person if an audience member was in the 'know' and would get it.[5]

The reviewers in each city were impressed, with the *Sydney Morning Herald* critic remarking on the sophistication of Humphries' characters, his 'astonishing versatility' and 'exceptionally hilarious' material, with Mrs Everage 'fairly dripping with essence of suburbia flavoured with just a pinch of malice'. However, he found Sandy Stone's monologue simply too long.[6] The *Sun-Herald*'s Jock Veitch described Sandy's 'high-pitched voice and low-pitched clichés' as dreary, but identified Humphries' portrayal of the new characters in the show as 'nigh on perfect'.[7] The show was a huge success.

Before the show closed in Adelaide, Barry, as Edna, handed a bunch of gladioli to a woman in the first row during the finale.

With only a few days until Christmas and so many glorious gladdies in full bloom in a vase on the piano, Barry passed them to the woman spontaneously because he thought they would otherwise be wasted. The woman who took the blooms passed them one by one along the row so that everyone had a stem. Seeing a whole row of audience members sitting with their glads upright, Edna instructed them to hold up their flowers, wave and 'quiver' them to the music, and then to join in the singing of 'Home Sweet Home'. He had decided on Nellie Melba's favourite ending for the show because the Australian diva, Joan Sutherland, had recently concluded one of her recitals with the crowd-pleaser. He knew how audiences loved sentimental songs, and feeling that they were part of the show.

For his next few performances Humphries printed song sheets and distributed them among the audience, inviting the crowd to sing. It was a nostalgic re-enactment of a community singing session, just like the ones he had attended with his aunts as a child in Melbourne. At one of the events the young Humphries had even witnessed women shelling peas as they sang along. But it was the gladdie-waving that really caught on. This ingenious activity quickly became Edna's signature device for audience engagement at the end of every show. It allows Edna the last laugh as she croons scornfully: 'You don't know how silly you look doing that!' Gladdie-waving was so successful that Barry wrote a song soon after the Adelaide season to accompany this new ritual, to the popular tune 'If You Wore a Tulip'.

> *If you wave a gladdie and they wave a gladdie*
> *And I wave a big pink glad.*
> *Then we all, holus bolus, wave our gladiolus*
> *'Twould be a sight to cheer the sad.*
> *There's no vision more holy than massed gladioli*
> *They're Australian through and through*
> *So keep your courage and trust up*
> *Give your gladdies a thrust up*
> *And all of your dreams will come true.*

CHAPTER 15

Suitor to the Devil

The Humphries took a leisurely trip back home to London, travelling through Turkey by bus and back to England via Prague and Amsterdam. It was gruelling but enjoyable. As always, the break from theatre life meant Barry was relaxed and happy.

Back in London Humphries was at last offered the coveted role of Fagin for a new production of *Oliver!*. He was delighted. A young singer called Marti Webb played Nancy and Philip Collins, who later achieved fame with Genesis and as a solo performer, played the undertaker's apprentice, Noah Claypole. Hippies with floppy hats and flowers emblazoned on every garment filled the streets of London and sat in the parks on the long summer evenings playing guitars and smoking. A gaunt and gangly Humphries gave a somewhat camp portrayal of Fagin. He recalls in his memoir ad-libbing provocatively at least once during the run. Just after the Six Day War in Israel, a loud explosive sound shook the theatre. It was balloons popping in the wings. Barry piped up mischievously, 'Arabs?' and then in a stage whisper, 'Bloody Arabs at it again!'[1]

Shortly afterwards, following a disappointing rejection at his audition for the role of the MC in *Cabaret*, Humphries played Long John Silver in a stage adaptation of *Treasure Island*. Spike Milligan played Ben Gunn and John Antrobus produced the show, which featured Humphries with a parrot on one shoulder in a rather chaotic performance. But his sessions with a Harley Street hypnotist meant he had no trouble learning all his lines.

Humphries energetically kept his name in print in Australia. He penned a regular column for the *Australian* on Saturdays, in which he reflected on ghastly trips to the dentist, forlorn encounters with airport officials, late night sorties in Chelsea discotheques and inefficient English tradesmen. There was even a column devoted to holding a 'bores' party', the subject that had so amused Peter O'Shaughnessy when Barry first arrived in London. In another column Barry discoursed on the subject of 'our native land' and some recent Australian publications. He parodied the titles, listing Robin Boyd's *The Australian Ugliness* as 'Robin Boyd's Ugliness' and added new titles of his own devising, such as 'The Australian Stupidity', 'Chunder with Humphries' and 'Australia is Mad'. He explained that the plethora of such books was forcing 'our countrymen ... to accept their intrinsic worthlessness'. He claimed that he had recently found a volume entitled *The Wit of Sir Robert Menzies*, declaring 'I look forward to its sequel, *The Kindness of Adolf Hitler*.[2] Barry's drinking meant that once or twice he missed his deadline, forcing the editor to make a joke of his disappearance, announcing that he could not find his London-based columnist. Once he concluded his explanation with this exhortation: 'You try looking for a man, who, like as not, is dressed up as Mrs Everage, queuing to get through the Berlin Wall.'[3]

Humphries' drinking was certainly out of control. He had been abusing alcohol for at least ten years. At times his behaviour was frightening for those around him. Once Ros discovered her husband prostrate on the bed; he was stone cold and his eyes were wide open. She yelled out in horror to Peter O'Shaughnessy, 'He's dead.' But he was not dead, just in a catatonic state. On another occasion Humphries was rushed to hospital where he had his stomach pumped. Ros was frustrated by his reluctance to seek help. He listened to her on matters theatrical, and always respected her views and suggestions. Also, at her urging, he had tried hypnotism to help him overcome his problems learning lines. The treatment was a success. But he would not admit to his drinking problem, let alone try to overcome it. His friends were powerless. Humphries would not listen to medical advice and seemed to have an impulse for self-destruction that was bound up with deep psychological rage and struggles with depression.

Although Humphries had marched against the bomb in London, he did not share the outrage of many of his countrymen about Australia's involvement in the Vietnam War. Unlike Arthur Boyd, Barry did not sign the petition demanding that the Australian prime minister withdraw Australian soldiers from Vietnam. But he didn't support the war either. In a letter to Max Oldaker, Humphries included the slogan, 'Fight Thrip not the Vietcong/ They don't kill our Gladdies'.[4] As was his way, Humphries put politics to the side. He did not wish to be aligned with any specific group, reserving his energy for satirising corrupt behaviour of all kinds on both sides of politics.

Humphries' political affiliations were always difficult to pin down. During the 1960s, as he struggled to make a living in London, Humphries painted large pop caricatures of various Australian political figures. He painted Arthur Fadden in a pinstriped suit, John Curtin with a glass eye, and Arthur Calwell, Ben Chifley and John Gorton in various fashionable poses. His arresting portrait of Billy Hughes, with his serious expression and craggy face, stares out at the viewer with a compelling realistic gaze. The image of Hughes is humane and intense, and suggests Humphries' genuine interest in attempting to portray something of the personality of the man. In a reference to the pig-iron controversy in 1939, Robert Gordon Menzies' portrait is composed of dozens of little red pigs. The paintings were exhibited under the title 'Ten Little Australians' in the Myer Mural Hall, Melbourne, and at the Bonython Art Gallery in Sydney to coincide with the tour of *Just A Show* in July–August 1968.

Humphries posed for a newspaper photographer in a plaid jacket and stovepipe trousers, next to the Calwell portrait, his paintbrush held up to Calwell's right ear. The exhibition revealed Humphries to be a keen caricaturist and a cutting satirist, who was genuinely apolitical.

He had developed, however, a taste for entertaining and mixing with the smart set — whatever their political allegiance. He seemed to possess a radar for tracking the influential, and a talent for charming the famous, and his wit and humour drew people to him. On his elegant Maida Avenue letterhead, Humphries wrote to the Australian prime minister, Harold Holt, who was visiting London in 1967. With his characteristic mix of insouciance and grandiosity, Barry addressed the leader as 'My dear Harold', and invited him to 'make a peace time visit … and have dinner with one admiring expatriate'. Humphries signed his name in large letters in blue ink.[5] Holt replied the next day, regretting that he had not sufficient time 'for such welcome diversion'.[6]

One morning during the *Treasure Island* run in the winter of 1967, Humphries received a phone call from a young Australian film maker, Bruce Beresford. Their mutual acquaintance Patrick White had suggested that Beresford and Humphries should meet. Barry and Bruce became friends, and found that they shared tastes in music, poetry and art. Beresford was astonished to see Barry's collection of Conder paintings. Conder was not then a collectable artist, and not even considered worth anything much at the time, but Barry had a significant number of his works. He bought art he admired; paintings and sculptures were to be enjoyed, not for their resale value.

The two men got on well, but Bruce found that Barry's heavy drinking made him unpredictable and sometimes remote. Some days Barry would start drinking as early as eight o'clock in the morning. Remarkably, he still made it onto the stage every night, but for Ros the drinking and long absences from home were becoming a nightmare, especially as she had the welfare of their two small girls to consider.

Beresford, who, like Nick Garland, was affable, loyal, reliable and talented, was working at the British Film Institute in London, producing low-budget art films. He entertained Barry with detailed descriptions of his conversations with the more lugubrious and pretentious of the would-be directors with whom he worked. This was music to Barry's ears and he began to cultivate a sketch based on a denizen of the 'Underground Cinema'. The curly-haired and laconic young Beresford was a great fan of the *Private Eye* Bazza McKenzie strip, and suggested to Barry it would make a terrific film. Barry had been experimenting with the idea of a musical based on Bazza's adventures and showed Bruce the material. He had written several scripts for the show under titles such as 'Barry McKenzie — A Picaresque Puritan's Progress in a Permissive Society' and 'Kangaroo Valley'. Stanley Myers, whom Barry knew from the BBC and from *A Kayf Up West,* had composed music for songs such as 'I've Got a Sheila Called Sheila'. Barry and Stanley envisaged the lead, Bazza, as twenty-seven, large of chin, fixated on beer and both lovable and foul-mouthed.[7] A small orchestra and a choir on stage would provide a continuous commentary on the action just like a Greek chorus. But Humphries never finished the script, and the musical did not come to anything.

Bruce Beresford immediately began work adapting the draft as a screenplay. Fed up with union pressure in the British film industry and disenchanted with the lack of encouragement for young film makers, he was planning to return to the more hopeful fledgling Australian scene. For years Beresford had dreamed of making a film of his favourite Australian novel, Henry Handel Richardson's *The Getting of Wisdom*. He had been enchanted with the book since his boyhood in Parramatta. When he met Barry Humphries, and thought about making a film about Bazza, Beresford could see the commercial possibilities, and the freedom that success would offer him as a director. Instinctively, he knew that a film version of Richardson's story of a Melbourne schoolgirl in the 1890s would not attract backing until he had proven himself capable of making a commercial film.

Barry, also, was trying his hand in films. On the recommendation of Peter Cook he had been invited to audition for a minor role as one of the seven deadly sins in a film eventually called *Bedazzled*, to be directed by Stanley Donen. It was Barry's first professional appearance in a feature film; he was ecstatic to be earning £150 a week for the job, though he knew his role would only last a couple of weeks at the most. He played an alluring and convincing 'Envy', alongside Peter Cook, Dudley Moore and Eleanor Bron in the star roles. It was a particularly enticing, if small, part for Barry. The film is clever, witty and very English, presenting a modern-day version of the Faust story, with Dudley Moore playing a downcast short-order chef, Stanley Moon, who is offered seven wishes by the 'devil incarnate', a spiv called George Spiggott, played by Cook. In receiving his wishes Moon encounters each of the seven deadly sins. A guest appearance by Raquel Welch as Lilian Lust in a hot-pink mini-dress that she quickly peeled off to reveal a fire-engine red bra, brought a kind of crass eroticism and American glamour to the otherwise very English cast. When the hapless Moon meets Envy, Humphries' querulous character is reclining in a sumptuous bed, puffing on a cigarette, decorous in a pale green blouse and cravat. In perfectly rendered aristocratic tones, Envy complains of neglect by Spiggott who tended to favour the ladies, Lust and Gluttony. Humphries played Envy as a slightly creepy, camp, disaffected and lonely gentleman, a green-eyed suitor to the devil. The character of Envy was, according to Barry, 'perfect' for an Australian actor.[8] He knew from his own experience that Australians in London specialised in the sin.

With a new Australian tour planned for 1968 Humphries promised to accept medical treatment in London prior to departing for Sydney. In the presence of Rosalind and his doctor, Barry affirmed that he wanted to stay with Ros and that he would co-operate with her and the doctor, and that he would take his counselling seriously. In spite of his promises and his good intentions, Humphries deeply resented what he thought was unfair pressure and ultimatums from those around him.

He settled down to devise a new show but inwardly simmered, nursing suspicions, anger and paranoid fantasies towards everyone who was trying to help him and ensure his very survival. The targets included Cliff Hocking whom Humphries thought was spying on him and cheating him of money. During the roller-coaster months ahead Humphries' behaviour created so much trouble that those who were closest to him were pushed away and the goodwill in some of his relationships was stretched beyond repair.

CHAPTER 16

On a Tightrope

Barry and Ros packed up their family and belongings in June 1968 and headed once more for Australia, with a nanny and Edith Tighe, their lodger, who now worked for them as a secretary, in tow. Ros had invited Donald Harris to take over from her as stage manager. She had known him in the New Zealand Ballet Company, and was confident that he was reliable and robust. She could relax a little, knowing that Donald could cope with anything. During a stopover in a small mountain village in Mexico, away from the chaos of their London lives, Barry and Ros wrote the scripts for *Just A Show*.

Soon after arriving in Australia, Humphries appeared on ABC Television as himself, wearing a long coat, an odd hat and neatly combed long hair. In fact the long dark hair was a wig he would wear when he played Edna Everage. Under the wig his own hair was short, cropped and blond. It was the hairstyle for a new character called Brian Graham.

In Sydney, where the show would open, the Humphries rented a sprawling house in Randwick, a short drive from both Coogee Beach and Centennial Park. Barry set about preparing for his five-week season at the palatial Tivoli Theatre in Castlereagh Street. It was the first time he had played in an auditorium that seated 1800, and he was very nervous.

Edna entered from the stalls, chatting with the audience and searching desperately for Sue Becker, known to all at that time as the television exercise guru. Barry had taken the title of his show from the throwaway comments of his aunts, when he asked them about a musical they had seen in Melbourne. 'Oh, it was just a show,' they would reply nonchalantly. Unlike his well-dressed aunts, however, Edna was brash and gaudy in a red coat of Thai silk, a green dress and blue floral hat. She pointed to her pom-pom shoes and asked her 'possums', as she had began to call members of the audience: 'Am I overdressed?' Edna won over the crowd with her rendition of 'All Things Bright and Beautiful', renamed 'Edna's Hymn'. It was a witty and rousing anthem to Humphries' homeland.

All things bright and beautiful
All creatures great and small
All things wise and wonderful
Australia has them all.

All things bright and beautiful
Pavlovas that we bake
All things wise and wonderful
Australia takes the cake.

Australia is a Saturday
With races on the trannie
Australia is the talcy smell
Of someone else's Granny.

Australia is a kiddie with zinc cream on its nose
Australia's voice is Melba's voice
It's also Normie Rowe's.[1]

The hymn built to a dramatic crescendo and finished with the lines:

Australia is a sunburnt land
Of drought and rain and snow
Oh ye who doth not love her
Ye know where ye can go.

Sandy, recovering from an 'op' in the Blamey ward of the 'Repat', appeared beside his bed in a wheelchair, reminiscing about his courting days with Beryl at Lake Wendouree. He recalled his excitement at one picnic.

> I let my hand slide along the grass till my little finger was just touching Beryl's and she didn't move it and we stayed for what seemed like donkey's years till it got dark and I could feel me old ticker going ninety to the dozen and I knew it was the real thing. Then Beryl jumped up laughing ... and I could still feel the burning of her little finger, and I looked and saw my hand was touching the blessed Thermos. I didn't mess around much after that.

Barry's new character, Brian Graham, appeared in an office wearing blue linen shorts, a white shirt and a tie, a thick, gold chain bracelet, signet ring and black square-framed glasses. Graham, loosely based on Barry's manager, Cliff Hocking, with whom he was feuding, was a smart, young and obviously homosexual superphosphate salesman working for his father's company. Barry had written the script quickly in just one night. Ros was not keen for Barry to perform the sketch and thought it was a vengeful and not particularly funny caricature. Fortunately, Cliff did not recognise himself.

The sketch began with the young man on the phone talking to customers. He said confidently, 'Can do ... will do ... I appreciate that ... no probs ... getting a bit cheesed,' in rapid-fire conversations about prices and delivery. In his next call with his father he was defensive, and protested about having to work late again. Although the audience could only hear Brian's side of the conversation, his father had clearly accused him of laziness and too much socialising. Brian was sweet to an older woman in another phone call, and in another conversation, he gossiped bitchily to a friend. Finally, at the end of the sketch, Brian collapsed under the strain of his multiple roles and exclaimed pathetically to his father 'I am alone'.

This portrayal of a queer man was a landmark on the Australian stage, as it wasn't until the 1970s that Australian playwrights began to portray explicitly the concerns of homosexual characters. Brian Graham may have been a prototype for the nameless elocution teacher in Steven J Spear's tragicomedy, *The Elocution of Benjamin Franklin*, staged nearly a decade later. Graham was clearly a lonely and conflicted person who tried to please everyone around him. The character demonstrated Humphries' ability to show both malice and sympathy towards his satiric victims, and the sketch offered a poignant exploration of a man caught between masks.

Humphries introduced another new character in *Just A Show*, the pretentious underground film maker Martin Agrippa, based on Albie Thoms. Agrippa appeared fresh from Helsinki where he had 'carried away the big prize for the finest Australian entry in the experimental film section' — the prestigious Bronzed Scrotum award. Dressed in a beige corduroy jacket, wearing a huge moustache, the egomaniac sat hunched over, legs crossed and puffing on his Discque Bleu cigarettes, raving about life scenarios, collage and 'film as film'. He boasted that his approach to film-making was just like the 'finest modern jazz ... I just took myself down to remote Nungar Beach with a tape recorder and I talked ... It isn't a nice cosy motion picture made by nice, cosy, sold-out professionals. But is the universe cosy? Is God a professional? It is a voyage into the buried contents of the self.'

Agrippa's monologue was fuelled by the pretentious jargon passed on to Barry by Bruce Beresford, and the sketch included a short, scratchy film Beresford had made at home in Brixton, featuring a Nigerian man as an Aboriginal character, and a girl streaking through a Highgate park.

There was also a hippy character called Lionel Stephen Donald Hunter in the show. He began his monologue with the earnest line, 'I'm worried about my parents ... man, they seem to be drifting away from me.' More powerful, however, was Humphries' father-of-the-bride character, Rex Lear, who gave a booze-drenched speech about his daughter, Gillian Sandra, at her wedding in the Regency Rooms in Toorak Road. The cigar-smoking Lear, in full morning suit and topper, insulted his guests and berated the Italian waiter before declaring, 'All I can say is that as far as I'm concerned I've lost a daughter and gained a dependant.' The audience relished the portrayal of the new characters.

Back in Humphries' hometown, where *Just A Show* would transfer next, the theatre scene was changing. Betty Burstall had leased an old shirt factory in Carlton as a performance space, and in July 1967 her theatre collective, La Mama, had put on its first play, *Three Old Friends*, written by a young, newly qualified doctor, Jack Hibberd. Rather than working under a conventional model, La Mama was a collective of like-minded individuals, who dedicated themselves to performing new Australian plays.

In 1969 La Mama would present an uproarious play called *Dimboola*, also written by Jack Hibberd. It featured a chaotic and drunken wedding reception, in which tensions over the union of the Protestant Morrie McAdam and the Catholic Reen Delaney erupt into chaos. *Dimboola* went on to become one of the most popular and most performed works in Australian theatre history, running for two-and-a-half years in Sydney. Humphries' Rex Lear sketch had undoubtedly provided vital inspiration for the play. Indeed by the end of the decade it was clear that Humphries' work was salient and powerful, offering audiences touchstones for the changing mores and attitudes around them, and giving playwrights a new sense of licence for their own satirical impulses.[2]

During the tour of *Just A Show*, Humphries re-encountered Barry Crocker, a young Australian singer–actor, and immediately telephoned Bruce Beresford in London. 'I've found Bazza,' he said excitedly, 'and he has a great big chin.'[3] Crocker was already well known to Australian audiences; he had featured in *66 and All That*, an imitation of *The Mavis Bramston Show* with more music and dancing, and had gone on to host his own successful television variety program, *The Barry Crocker Show*, for Channel 10. He was shocked to read in the

TV Listener one morning that he was to play the lead in a 'hilarious comedy about the adventures of a young Aussie thrown into the chaos of swinging London': it was the first he had heard of it.[4]

Crocker had met Humphries on three previous occasions, and remembered with gratitude Barry's praise for his act with David Clark at the Embers Supper Club in Toorak. Crocker had always dreamed of a film opportunity, and so the *TV Listener*'s news, though surprising, was welcome. He telephoned Humphries and invited him to lunch at his home in Wahroonga. Humphries apologised about the early release of the story, drank half a bottle of Johnnie Walker and promised to send the script to Crocker. When he still had not received the script a year later, Crocker gave up hope of a new career in cinema.

The reviews of *Just A Show* were generally positive, with the *Sun-Herald* proclaiming Humphries the 'high priest of high camp ... undoubtedly Australia's most original wit'.[5] HG Kippax was tepid about Edna and Sandy, whose humour he found 'outdated and mechanical', but he praised the Rex Lear character as original and savagely satirical, the pretentious auteur as 'wonderfully funny', and Brian Graham as the 'cleverest piece in the show'.[6]

However, in the *Sydney Morning Herald*, Cyril Pearl expressed sanctimonious dissatisfaction with *Just A Show* and articulated a critical viewpoint that was gradually to become commonplace among critics as Humphries' career progressed. Pearl suggested that those who enjoy jokes about 'burgundy wall-to-wall, the vehicle, and flights of china ducks' are people who have recently escaped this kind of milieu with the 'glossy pages of women's magazines ... as mentor'. Going one step further, he remarked that 'both Mr Humphries and Mr Patrick White ... have a contempt for people who do not share their elegant cultural — ie, public school, University, Grand Tour — background and have little knowledge of the lesser breeds they deride'.[7] The criticism missed the pathos and the celebratory dimension of Humphries' satire altogether as well as the permission he offered to an audience to laugh at themselves. Pearl also misread Humphries' class origins. He seemed to be oblivious to the compassion in White's fiction too. Humphries' characters are not 'lesser breeds'. He makes little people of all of his characters, whether they are rich and egotistical businessmen with ungrateful children like those of his Lear character, pretentious art-house film makers, or self-satisfied, yet desperate, academics such as Neil Singleton.

Barry and Rosalind stayed for a few days at Clifton and Marlene Pugh's bush retreat near Eltham, where they had spent their first idyllic days together as lovers, ten years earlier. Clifton felt Barry had changed. He had been shocked when he first laid eyes on his friend backstage in Melbourne: 'The booze was everywhere and he looked bloated with success,' he recalled. Humphries asked Pugh to paint another portrait of him. As he sat facing Barry in the studio, brush in his hand, Pugh sensed an 'emptiness' in his old friend, and the finished work reflected Pugh's reaction to the changes he observed.[8] Humphries was very unhappy with the portrait, which showed him with a rounded stomach and his shirt unbuttoned, looking dissolute and lost. Perhaps Humphries mentioned the portrait to his father as Eric Humphries arrived at 'Dunmoochin' a few days later. Eric first suggested that Pugh destroy the painting, and then told Pugh he would buy it at any price. But Pugh would not sell the work to Eric Humphries. Barry did not speak to the artist for years afterwards.[9]

Around this time Humphries also approached John Brack to paint Edna's portrait. 'You've got to paint Edna. You're the perfect artist,' he said to Brack encouragingly. Brack allegedly 'let out a long, low groan'.[10] But the finished portrait is mesmerising in its portrayal of the housewife character who is obsessed with display and utterly obedient to the dictates of fashion. John Brack's painting of Edna in her lollipop-pink coat and iridescent green dress captured a new, shark-like quality in the character that contrasted with her earlier timidity, as well as Humphries' fascination with artifice and kitsch. In the portrait Edna bares her teeth and rests her long, pink-gloved, cadaverous hands on the edge of her chair. This grinning figure in pearls and a garish aqua pillbox hat covered in fake roses had come a long way from the frumpy housewife of Humphries' early performances.

Humphries was right to approach Brack, as both the artist and the actor shared a fascination for watching people, and attempted to satirise the public face of the people they portrayed. Later in his life, Brack grew tired of his constant association with his painting of Collins Street at the end of the work day, and came to hate the painting. He came to regret his attitude to the people he depicted.[11] Humphries would show no weariness of Edna as his career developed, and has never revised his attitude or shown regret about his portrayal of dull lives. Edna Everage personified the Australian ugliness that Robin Boyd had observed in the suburbs and Humphries found the mask of Mrs Everage electrifying.

It was during the *Just A Show* tour that Humphries' drinking reached dangerous levels. He sometimes drank throughout the day even when he had to perform at night. Remarkably he managed to cope well most of the time, and it was not usually obvious to the audience that he had been drinking. But the crew worried about him; they added extra planks to the edge of the stage to prevent him from falling. It was especially risky in venues with deep orchestra pits, such as the Canberra Theatre.

One night during the Canberra run, Barry did not appear in his dressing room at the usual hour to dress and make up for the show. Ros was extremely anxious about him. He was not at the hotel, and nobody knew where he had been during the day. Various members of the press had gathered to speak to him and they were becoming restless and snide. With only five minutes until curtain-up, Ros urged Cliff to announce that the show had been cancelled, but he refused to make the decision that he thought properly belonged to the performer. At 8.05 pm, five minutes after the show should have started, Barry arrived in a taxi, and staggered into the theatre. He could barely speak, let alone perform, but he insisted on carrying on with the show. As he lurched around the stage, Ros hissed lines at him from the wings, wondering how long he could continue, and when the nightmare would end. Audience members began to walk out after a few minutes. As they left the theatre they were offered a refund. A small number remained, curious to witness the spectacle of an actor sabotaging his own one-man show.

Humphries launched his anthology of 'neglected' verse during the tour. He received a letter from the art collector John Reed thanking him for the volume, and complimenting Barry on his latest stage offering. Reed told Barry that he admired all of his work, but added that he imagined the performer 'as someone balancing dangerously on a tightrope ... risking all the time a slip that will plunge you to disaster. You disturb us — and we rejoice and love you when you soar into the air.'[12] Underneath the praise was perhaps a diplomatic but pointed warning that Barry's friends feared for his life.

Reed was right about Humphries. In his live shows he soared and his ingenious comic talent delighted his audiences. His balancing acts were part of his personality, and his hunger to excel. These knife-edge moments were built into his performances. As a comedian he relished risk. As a man he flourished under pressure, knowing he might fall or crash at any time. Once he even mortgaged his flat in South Kensington in order to purchase a painting by the English Pre-Raphaelite artist John Everett Millais. The metaphor of the tightrope signalled the perilous levels of Humphries' drinking. It was becoming obvious to people who knew him that Barry's very life was in danger.

Humphries occasionally visited his old flame Margaret Elliott, who had married a wealthy businessman, Leon Fink. One day she returned to the capacious foyer of her grand apartment building in Toorak to find the dishevelled form of Humphries asleep on the floor. Her extremely polite neighbours simply walked past him until Margaret helped him upstairs to sleep off his delirium.

The pattern continued. When Margaret moved to her Sydney residence in Woollahra, Humphries visited her whenever he was in town. One morning, she had just waved her children off to school when the phone rang. Her neighbour several houses away announced nervously, 'I think I have a friend of yours here.' Margaret rushed down to the house to find Barry, slumped in the living room. He had just vomited on the neighbour's ice-blue damask chair covers, having arrived by taxi from the airport in an alcoholic stupor and mistaken the address. Margaret took him home and put him in her daughter's bed for the rest of the day.[13]

Humphries was an incorrigible alcoholic, and stopped at nothing to satisfy his addiction. He looked ragged and sick. Once, while with his family, he flagged down Margot Braybrook, whom he'd known years earlier, as she was driving down Punt Road in Melbourne. She stopped and Barry jumped in, instructing her to drive him to the Phoenix Pub in Flinders Street. She was flabbergasted that Barry thought nothing of leaving Ros and his two small children standing on the side of the road.

After the tour finished Ros made the agonising decision to stay in Australia rather than return to London with Barry. To add to her troubles she had contracted the Hong Kong flu, and the exertions of assisting with stage direction, prop keeping and dressing Barry left her ragged and exhausted. An earthquake in Perth had showered the entire wardrobe with plaster dust and made the departure from the west coast a nightmare. More than this, Rosalind could not bear the anxiety, narcissism and betrayals of living with an alcoholic any longer. Her life of nursing Humphries and trying to mother the two girls was not sustainable. She decided to stay in Australia without Barry. It wasn't just the alcohol that made Barry a difficult husband. She no longer held out any hope for his recovery because he did not seek treatment after the tour.

The ultimate relationship for Humphries was always going to be expressed across the footlights rather than with another person. Like many other performers, seeking and gaining the approval of the beloved audience was the only constant for Barry at this time.[14]

Barry and Ros had been together for ten years. For at least half of those years Barry had left Ros at home alone, night after night after the theatre, while he drank at pubs, clubs and parties, and sometimes chased other women. It became so bad towards the end that he confessed later that he didn't even look at his watch or give Ros and his children a second thought. In spite of everything her decision to stay in Melbourne wounded him. He was deeply unhappy for a long time afterwards.[15] Yet he could not find a way out of the darkness.

CHAPTER 17

True British Spunk

Depressed and angry, Humphries returned to London without Rosalind and the children. Although his personal life was falling apart, he threw himself into his work once more. He had broken off all dealings with Cliff Hocking and began preparing to open *Just A Show* at the tiny Fortune Theatre in Russell Street, in London's West End for the English producer Peter Bridge. He offered sketches from his last two Australian shows and included two of his newest characters: Rex Lear and Martin Agrippa. But the English critics were generally unimpressed with everything but the gladdie-waving finale and the show only lasted two weeks.

Sheridan Morley described Humphries' show as 'a sustained hymn of hatred of his native Australia' and remarked that in spite of slides urging the audience to 'Emigrate Now', 'nothing I have ever seen about Australia makes me feel less inclined to do so'. Robert Waterhouse said the show would only appeal to the obsessively anti-Australian or excruciatingly homesick'.[1] Irving Wardle in *The Times* denounced Humphries as a version of the 'unlovable type of Commonwealth entertainer who specialises in flattering the metropolitan public by sneering at the habits of his own country'.[2] It was a devastating reception.

The disappointing response to his second attempt to win over a London audience strengthened Humphries in his resolve to transform his Barry McKenzie comic strip figure into a screen character. Humphries travelled to Cyprus for a break, and to consider his future. In Salamis he ran into Lewis Morley in a hotel bar. Barry was dressed in a white suit, brown-and-white brogues and a gleaming white fedora. 'Jeezus Chroist Loo-us, whadda' ya doin' 'ere?' shouted Barry in his most exaggerated Australian drawl. When Lewis returned the question Barry replied mischievously, 'I'm on my honeymoon.'[3] Barry found out that Lewis was shooting photos for a travel brochure. 'You could take some of me with the local wildlife,' suggested Barry. Morley took a few shots of the dapper Humphries. In one photograph he knelt in rough sand next to a scruffy camel, looking whimsically into the distance. He managed to look serene, despite the fact that his life was in turmoil. In another he lounged inside a proscenium sculpted into a rock. It was clear to Morley that Humphries missed Rosalind and his two little daughters and desperately needed help to release him from the vice-like grip of alcohol.

Back in London, Humphries joined the cast of the *The Late Show* on BBC Television, singing and performing monologues with John Wells and John Bird. Barry met the comedy writer Ian Davidson on the show. After he finished recording Humphries simply disappeared in the evenings. Davidson often fielded questions from people looking for him, and in desperation would telephone taxi companies to find out where the wayward actor had last been seen. During this very difficult period, Humphries and Davidson created a BBC program of six episodes called *The Barry Humphries Scandals*. Although Barry was not yet ready to accept help for his drinking, he did have some insight into his condition, and used it to inspire a comic song.

I'm too drunk to dance
Too drunk to dance
I'm always so plastered I miss the main chance
I've tried marijuana, I've tried LSD

> *But old fashioned liquor's the best thing for me*
> *I'm attractive God knows, I've had girls by the score*
> *But as soon as I get near a discotheque floor*
> *I seem to forget what we've both come there for*
> *Which makes me too drunk to dance.*

Together Ian and Barry wrote a polished script satirising the 'Ten Pound Pom' emigration scheme. Edna made an appearance from Stratford-upon-Avon, 'one of the loveliest shrines in the British Isles', explaining why Anne Hathaway 'kept her maiden name to avoid publicity — like Elizabeth Taylor doesn't call herself Elizabeth Burton'.

There were also some revolting cooking sketches with Edna parading her peanut and prawn flan and curried rabbit spaghetti. She even invited a reluctant audience member to eat the food on camera. It was a taste of things to come on stage and screen.

The show was produced in front of a live audience at the Television Centre in West London, and ultimately created a massive scandal. It wasn't Humphries' jibes at the Irish, or his gentle mockery of homosexual men in sketches about Oscar Wilde, whom he portrayed in conversation with Lord Alfred Douglas before breaking into the hit song 'What's It All About, Alfie?' Nor did the less than enticing close-ups of Edna in her role as the 'Garrulous Gourmet' — satirising another Antipodean export, Graham Kerr, 'Galloping Gourmet' — create a stir.

It was one song called 'True British Spunk', written for the final episode by Barry, that caused the trouble at the BBC. The producer of the show, Dennis Main Wilson, who had produced *The Goon Show* in the late 1950s enthusiastically and expensively engaged an orchestra, a men's choir and a chorus of thirty-six extras dressed up as figures from British history for the sketch. Billowing Union Jacks festooned the set. The three-minute spectacular cost £5000 to produce, and featured Barry dressed as Edna, impersonating Vera Lynn, and singing a rather provocative song under a veil of patriotic fervour:

The English have a quality I'd like to sing about
It's not the sort of quality bestowed on Wog or Kraut
When things are on the sticky side
You never throw a tizz
A special something sees you through
I'll tell you what it is

Spunk, Spunk, Spunk
You're so full of British Spunk[4]

The jaunty song gleefully parodied the celebrated British *sang froid* that made the Empire great, as it mischievously reminded the listener of major experiences of crisis for the nation and Empire at various stages in history. Humphries began the song with an account of the dissolution of the monasteries, crooning about the poor, besieged monks, the assault on their splendid stained glass and their indomitable spirits and spunk. Next he celebrated the pluck of the British in India in spite of the squalor of the country and the nastiness of unfamiliar food. In the third verse the satire came closer to home with Humphries praising 'a handful of ex-public-schoolboys' who through their fine spirits and manful handling of the Spitfires won the Battle of Britain. Humphries also sang about Churchill's rousing good cheer and spirited reassurances of the 'poor little Poms' during the worst of the wartime ravages, the coolness and bravery of the English in spite of the drop in the value of the pound and the influx of immigrants to the nation. He warbled in a high-pitched falsetto and the chorus of deep men's voices provided the harmonies.

The BBC management deemed the song to be obscene because of the double entendre in the word 'spunk' (schoolboy slang for semen) and its use in connection with British soldiers, members of the Church, the Raj and, indeed, the entire population. But the performance of the song in the studio was one of Barry's great television moments. 'True British Spunk' was to remain an unheard anthem for his adopted home, a country he loved and loathed almost as passionately as Australia.

In this song, he proved that he was willing and able to outdo the best of British satirists at their own game, lampooning the ideals of British spirit and fortitude. Humphries parodied British pretension and patriotic fervour more vividly and yet more gently than many of the local satirists. When he sang 'True British Spunk' privately to John Betjeman, the poet laughed so much that he wept.[5] The song was utterly subversive, and yet without the double entendre the lyrics were almost benign. The only problem was that the sketch was axed.

Humphries was furious. He complained in an interview that the BBC was insufferably prim, and repeatedly protested his innocence of the double meaning of the word 'spunk'.[6] But it was not surprising that the BBC clamped down on Humphries. The song was crude. Humphries had pushed too far.

Humphries thought perhaps it was time to return to Australia. But when he heard that several Australian newspapers had reported almost gleefully that his sketch had been dropped, under the banner headline 'BARRY AXED', he felt sick, even embattled. In his finest appearance, with a potential audience of millions, he had been censored. The Australian press seemed to be gloating over his humiliation. And because he had refused to assign overseas rights to the BBC, specifically to prevent it selling the show to the ABC cheaply, *The Barry Humphries Scandals* did not make it to Australia. Subsequently, the BBC destroyed all the tapes of the program.

Barry wrestled with his disappointment and his sense of failure. To add to his woes, he was more isolated than he had ever been in London. Many of his friends had re-settled in the 'paradoxical' land down under. The Blackmans had gone; Len French and Tom Sanders had gone. But Barry knew he could not settle permanently in Australia. He still loved living in London and was determined to succeed in the United Kingdom.

Humphries secretly hoped for a reconciliation with Rosalind, and asked her to come to London to see him. Hoping to convince him to come back to Australia with her for treatment, Ros travelled to London in April 1970. She knew that Barry wanted to work in earnest on a new pantomime he was writing for an Australian audience, under the magnificent title 'The Lizard of Oz'. Barry would play the lizard, and he hoped the show would open at the Princess Theatre in Melbourne. He did return to Melbourne with Rosalind. But there was no reconciliation and no pantomime.

PART THREE
DAME

CHAPTER 18

Sobriety

If you want to put your feet up,
Relax and just unbend,
There's a peaceful Richmond gutter
That I highly recommend ...

Barry Humphries recited these self-mocking lines at the opening of an exhibition of Balinese paintings in Melbourne the day after he was robbed and bashed by two men at a Richmond pub in June 1970. Earlier that week he had been charged with drunk and disorderly behaviour for insulting and resisting a policeman on his home turf in Camberwell. A few months later Humphries was photographed in bed with a blonde woman pouring beer into his mouth. Barry was posing as a swinger and he performed this stunt live at Sutton's Music Store in Melbourne.

With assistance from Rosalind, who was alarmed by his disintegration, Barry had returned to Melbourne after the BBC debacle. He was thirty-six years old, dangerously alcoholic, and feared for his future. Eric and Louisa Humphries were extremely concerned about their son and even his good friends found him unapproachable at this time.

That summer, in an attempt to deal with his difficulties, Barry had spent several weeks in the psychiatric wing of St Vincent's

Hospital, Fitzroy. Even in the ward, Barry furtively consumed alcohol. A recovered alcoholic and AA member, Tony Bourke, read about the attack on Barry in the newspaper and decided to visit the comedian in hospital. He convinced Barry to attend an AA meeting in Sandringham. Humphries agreed but only in order to get Bourke off his back. At the meeting an old-timer nicknamed 'Antique Harry' addressed the group. Barry could not contain himself and shouted, 'Tell us something we don't know already.' Quick as a flash Antique Harry replied, 'I'll tell you something; you're pissed and we're all sober.'[1] Barry hated to be outwitted. Antique Harry had humiliated him.

Once again Barry was admitted to hospital, this time to the Delmont Private Hospital in Glen Iris, where he was treated by a psychiatrist, Dr John Moon. Barry was so ill that Ros feared he might not survive; she brought the girls in to see him and to say goodbye. In the care of Dr Moon, Barry realised he was suffering from a severe illness, and not a lack of willpower or a moral weakness. The gentle Dr Moon spent hours listening to Barry talk and taught him to move beyond his crippling feelings of shame.

At Delmont, Barry encountered Ross Fitzgerald, with whom he used to drink and who was recovering from an attempted suicide and years of alcohol abuse. Fitzgerald had been drinking heavily since he was fourteen. The two men realised that unless they found release from drinking they would both be dead within a very short period. Dr Moon warned them that their battered bodies would not recover quickly. 'The most important thing in your life,' he urged them, 'is not to pick up that first drink,' and to 'take your life one day at a time'.[2] Moon managed to break down Barry's egotistical defences to prepare him for recovery. Fitzgerald, ten years younger than Humphries, was given shock treatment. Dr Moon's treatment was successful: both Barry and Ross overcame their addictions, Fitzgerald going on to a distinguished career as a university scholar and author.[3]

During the long days in Delmont, Barry and Ross talked about their lives and futures; they had a lot in common. Initially they had drawn energy from alcohol but after years of excessive drinking both men were seriously ill and their lives were a mess. The previous two years had been the hardest for Barry. He had been stripped of dignity, literally fallen in the gutter, and read about his ordeals in the newspaper. He had offended many people who tried to help him. But at last he was ready to face up to the crippling effects of his addiction.

Barry helped Ross with his plans to resume studying for his doctorate; Ross was a good sounding-board for Barry's jokes. They laughed conspiratorially when they overheard Eric Humphries telling Ross's father, Bill, about his anxiety: 'I was so worried about Barry that I couldn't play golf on Tuesday,' confessed Eric. It was worthy of Sandy Stone.[4]

By the end of the summer of 1971, Humphries had broken free of his addiction and had become a regular at AA. Phillip Adams was relieved at the change in his friend but saw the irony in his situation, declaring that 'the least anonymous person on Earth' had found an anonymous group to help him stay sober.[5] Humphries took the pledge and meant it, recognising that the journey would be difficult. Dr Moon had told him that he needed to abstain from alcohol for the rest of his life, and that only after three years without a drink could he begin to consider himself free. Humphries' release from addiction marked the beginning of a new life for him, a life of hard work, single-minded dedication to his career and the development of an increasingly sophisticated range of masks, both public and private.

Remarkably, during the first tumultuous months of recovery, Barry appeared as Edna in a film, appropriately called *The Naked Bunyip*, written and directed by John Murray and produced by Phillip Adams. It was an experimental, semi-fictional documentary subtitled 'A Survey of Sex in Australia', and was a daring but meandering study of the nation's attitudes to sex and sexuality. A young actor, Graeme Blundell, played a shy and gormless market researcher charged with the task of enquiring about the sexual activities of strangers.

The most amusing segment of the film belonged to Humphries. Phillip Adams took Barry and Graeme to his Auntie Con's place in

Balwyn to film the Edna sequence. There were plaster dogs, an iconic green-faced Asian lady on the living-room wall, smoked glass and everything they needed for a convincing setting for Mrs Norm Everage. Graeme Blundell sat dumbly sullen in a chair in 'Mrs Everage's' living room as she attended to the questionnaire, resplendent in pink lipstick and high heels, her glossy bobbed hair flowing out from under a blue pillbox hat. Edna spoke directly to the camera. In answer to the question 'Do you enjoy marital relations?' she swiftly replied, 'No.' Haltingly she read out each question: 'What do you think of lesbianism?' After a short pause she said, 'I don't understand medical terms.' Asked whether she approved of circumcision, Edna responded: 'Well, we had little Kenny done. Norm hasn't been done yet, but we think he should because it's so much cleaner. In fact, the more circumcision the better.' With that she seized a large pair of scissors and with a loud 'thwack' viciously snipped a red gladioli stem in half.

Edna's grimly comic appearance in this short but pungent segment of a successful and provocative film allowed Humphries the space he needed to introduce Edna to a larger audience. The style of the segment was perfect for Barry, as it filmed him in character presenting a monologue. It was just like being on stage.

Despite Barry's bravura performance, Phillip Adams could see that his friend was struggling and sorely needed a full-time manager. He asked the Sydney-based impresario Harry M Miller to take Barry in hand. Fuming after *The Age* cancelled his contract for a column in which he satirised wealthy Melbourne Jews who celebrate Christmas, Humphries took a trip to Sydney. Without invitation he appeared on the doorstep of Miller's house in Woollahra. He walked in past a bewildered housekeeper who watched in horror as Barry took one look at the paintings around him and launched into a crude tirade against Jewish businessmen attempting to buy cultural respectability. The housekeeper assumed Barry was drunk. When he heard about the visit Miller refused any contact with Humphries.

Barry, also wounded by Patrick White's apparent favouring of Ros during their break-up, upset White's secretary on the telephone. Sensing her coolness, he said, 'I'm trying to get in touch with a friend who's become an acquaintance: a Christian writer called Patrick White.' When White invited Humphries to lunch at his home at Centennial Park, Barry arrived an hour late, wearing a 'grazier's hat and monocle'. He declared that he had been 'weaned off one or two toxic breasts', but White was certain he had been imbibing en route to lunch. White reported to Geoffrey Dutton that Humphries 'has flashes of great brilliance, but moments of despair ... He is such an actor one can't decide when acting has stopped.'[6] Concerned for his friend's future, White joined Adams in a request to Miller to reconsider his decision. They explained about Barry's recent hospitalisation, and Miller agreed to see Barry.

During Humphries' visit to Sydney, Margaret Fink visited him at the Gazebo Hotel in Kings Cross. She knocked on Barry's door but he did not answer. She checked the swimming-pool area and then headed for the hotel bar. Fink was shocked to see Barry sitting on a bar stool completely naked. The bemused manager was pouring him a double whisky and urging him to return to his room. Margaret steered Barry away from the bar, packed him up and sent him back to Melbourne.

In December 1970 Humphries was awarded a Commonwealth Literary Fund Fellowship to support his writing. With enviable references from Manning Clark and John Betjeman, he was selected out of 156 applicants. For the first time he had been recognised as a promising writer. It was an opportunity he needed and the generous weekly income the award provided meant he was free to begin in earnest on the script for the film adaptation of the *Barry McKenzie* comic strip.

The fellowship could not have come at a better time for Humphries, as he set about rebuilding his life. Over the next few years he worked much more closely and more happily with others than he ever had before. He was fortunate to have strong and trusted people around him; Bruce Beresford, Phillip Adams and his new friend Ross Fitzgerald helped him through the years of recovery.

Despite Barry's behaviour, Harry M Miller was impressed by his talent and potential, and contributed $10,000 in funding towards his next show, *A Load of Olde Stuffe*. Iris Mason, a dainty, rather winsome professional pianist, was engaged to accompany Barry. Miller also found him a double, enabling him to execute quick costume changes, and a team of technical assistants was hired. Miller's stewardship of Barry's act heralded a new professionalism and seriousness in the performer's career.

A Load of Olde Stuffe was a rambling three-hour show. It opened at the Playbox Theatre in Sydney on 15 April 1971, and featured props 'courtesy of St Vincent de Paul', a cast of familiar characters and a slide sequence of advertisements for Kirk's Ginger Ale, A New Glory Wave, Elma Gossip's Millinery, Vic Bowen's Milk Bar and other items Humphries recalled from his childhood. Suburbia in this show proved to be a source of both innocent delight and nostalgia — only the vicious and the ignorant were singled out for contempt.

To begin, Edna and her dowdy bridesmaid from New Zealand, Madge Allsop, addressed the audience in a film sequence from Stratford-upon-Avon. The intense underground film maker Martin Agrippa; blond, camp business heir Brian Graham; and the pseudo-intellectual Neil Singleton, clad in white trousers and an apron, all appeared again. A new character called Dr Wendy Toole stomped onto the stage in an Afghan coat, blue shorts, an Afro wig and round black glasses. She was undoubtedly a sister of Germaine Greer, an activist, a women's libber and was promoting her book *The Myth of the Vaginal Orgasm*.

With no new inspiration for Sandy Stone, Humphries tried to kill the old man off. But Sandy's end provided one of Barry's most potent monologues. In 'The Land of the Living', Sandy appeared sitting up in an old double bed covered with a pink candlewick bedspread. A cup of Milo in hand, he reads his letters to Beryl, abroad on a *Women's Weekly* World Discovery Tour. He gave Beryl all the news from home, describing the state of her indoor shrubs, recounting the latest events on *Pick-a-Box*, and providing details of neighbour Gweneth Longmire's loin (of lamb). A blackout signalled his demise.

Edna was more strident in this show, in pink hot pants with sequins (and orange chiffon culottes for the finale), spouting outrageous opinions about everyone from the prime minister's wife, Sonia McMahon, to boxer Lionel Rose. She glittered amid all the 'olde stuffe' on stage. Humphries pushed Edna forward in frequent public appearances: Sydney housewives telephoned a radio station and spoke to her as if she was real. Clearly Edna was the future, and Sandy the past. Edna took a new tone with the audience, striking fear into selected targets with her caustic comments and terrorising critics with her insistent command: 'Where is the critic? Stand up!' By the end of the year, after more than two hundred performances, it was Edna, not Barry, who appeared at the Melbourne Cup, referring to her part-time role as a satirist called Barry Humphries.

The reviews were mixed but suggested a new note of respect among the critics for Humphries' comic style. The *Sydney Morning Herald*'s HG Kippax declared the show to be 'expert, infectious entertainment, part hilarious, part savage, part kitsch', and concluded that Humphries 'has done more to create Australian folklore than anybody since the war'.[7] Brian Hoad in the *Bulletin* spoke of the 'flawless and hypnotic' inflection of Barry's Sandy Stone, and the compassion embodied in his monologue.[8] Michael Boddy in the *Sunday Review* referred to Humphries' 'magical understanding and intuition' and his 'meticulous attention to style'.[9] In the *Australian* Katharine Brisbane welcomed the new savagery of Edna as political satirist.[10] Reviewing the show for *The Age* on opening night in Melbourne, Geoff Hutton declared Humphries to be 'the most intelligent, deadly accurate and delicately rude of satirists'. Hutton also remarked that Humphries 'must be funniest in Melbourne', because of the sheer satisfaction of recognition for audiences.[11]

If the 'anthology' format, as Barry liked to call it, of *A Load of Olde Stuffe* reflected some uncertainty on his part about future directions for his one-man show, Humphries' public style was now much smarter and more confident. The dandy of his young adult self returned with new theatricality and verve. In one photograph he posed in a crisp dinner suit and fedora, resembling a more friendly Tristan Tzara. He looked resolute and mischievous, effeminate and glossy. Other photos show him in a monocle, puffing on a cigarette — Noel Coward with long hair. He appeared in public in stylish outfits: two-tone winklepickers, tweed suits and panama hats. He began to woo the audience carefully during press appearances; he penned an educative and mock-admonishing retort to a lukewarm review by Diana Fisher in the *Australian* under the tag line 'The audience, ma'am, was woefully under-rehearsed'. In a witty reference to Oscar Wilde he gallantly thanked the 288 talented bit players who came along to his opening night, but lamented their persistent attempts to upstage the star with their 'offensive laughter and applause'.[12]

Humphries' publicity was innovative, generous and relentless. Between judging the Miss North Shore Competition alongside June Dally-Watkins at Grace Brothers in Chatswood and speaking in the affirmative on the debating topic 'Is Australia Funny?' at the University of Melbourne, Humphries said that he sincerely hoped Australia would become the laughing stock of the world.[13] In extravagant sessions at David Jones' ladies fashion department to select clothing and wigs for his show, he revelled in the plastic gladdies, flying ducks and Victor Sylvester tunes greeting shoppers in the foyer. He performed snippets of the show at suburban shopping centres for 'Mothers' Week' in Melbourne and even arrived at an Old Melburnians reunion in 1971, riding on a camel. It was during the Melbourne run that Barry was touched to receive a volume of *Collected Poems* from his old friend John Betjeman, with the following inscription in the poet's spidery handwriting: 'This enlarged edition is to Barry, Melbourne's mighty genius whose work is poetry, deep, sad, funny & entertainment. From his friends C. Condor, A. Streeton, Tom Roberts, McCubbin, W.B. Griffiths, Horbury Hunt. John Betjeman with admiration and loyal affection.'

Humphries also gave a number of reflective interviews. He confessed to a journalist with the *National Times* that he felt hurt by the silence with which his work had been greeted by critics in Australia, and in a deliberately provocative statement explained to

Jock Veitch of the *Daily Telegraph* the source of his satirical repertoire: 'I suppose one grows up with a desire to murder one's parents, but you can't really go and do that … so I suppose I decided to try and murder them symbolically on stage. I poured out all my hatred of the standards of the little people of their generation.' But he also admitted, that in developing his characters over ten years he found he had 'grown to like them'.[14]

And so had the Australian public. Harry M Miller arranged for a follow-up tour the following year after the filming of *The Adventures of Barry McKenzie*. Humphries was now keen to develop Edna more fully, but fiercely guarded her as his most precious property. In a letter to Miller he vehemently resisted any advertising venture that would devalue the cachet of the character and the integrity of her theatrical presence. He stated emphatically that Edna 'has never before been prostituted in commercials', admitting in the next line, however, that there was one other agency considering Edna's association with the product Coffeetime. He flirted with the idea of a daily radio segment but baulked at the thought of overexposing the character, and thereby cheapening Edna, as well as gobbling up valuable material for 'the boards'. His determination to keep enjoying his creation and his instinct to avoid squandering 'fifteen years of slog' through the hype of 'ultra commercial TV' ventures marked a new determination in Humphries as an artist with a firm grip on the reality of popular entertainment.[15]

The circumstances of Barry's separation and divorce from Ros were messy and protracted and extremely stressful for everyone. Effectively, they had separated at the end of the 1968 Australian tour of *Just A Show*. Ros refused to return to London with Barry after his period of treatment with Dr Moon in 1970, and he accused her of destroying his career. Barry followed Ros to New Zealand, offering her a gold ring embedded with opals and with an inscription of their names inside.

Rosalind eventually found a house in Canterbury in Melbourne, not far from Barry's parents' home, and enrolled the children at a nearby school. Tessa and Emily loved visiting their grandparents in Camberwell. Grandpa Eric, or 'Ekkie' as they liked to call him, would greet them at the door with a cry of welcome, 'Hello possums', perform magic tricks and play jaunty tunes on his ukelele.[16] On his return to Australia, Barry stayed in the house and did a gas advertisement that helped fund heating for the rather damp rooms. After dealing art from her home for a year or so, and fed up with the number of cranks who turned up ostensibly to view the works, Ros opened a gallery in Armadale in July 1971. In October that year Barry came to Australia again and at Ros's request graciously launched an exhibition of small paintings by women artists. Elsa Haas sang a song by Rupert Bunny and Barry recited a poem he had written especially for the launch. As a thank you, Ros gave Barry a Clarice Beckett painting from the girls.

During his visit Ros told Barry that she had entered a relationship with Ian Hollinrake whom she had met through a friend of Barry's called Ed Clarke. Hollinrake had just completed a stint in the Kimberley region surveying mining leases. Barry was furious and said: 'You can't live with him, you're my wife. What do you see in him, he's nothing.' Ros calmly explained that she loved Ian and felt very happy with him. Eventually divorce papers were drawn up. Barry refused to accept them and held up the proceedings for several years.

CHAPTER 19

The Mythical Australian

Although *The Adventures of Barry McKenzie* comic strip was very popular in the United Kingdom, Humphries encountered a series of difficulties in his attempts to introduce Bazza to his countrymen. A collection of the strips had been published in book form in 1968 in London, but Humphries was mystified when he learned that it was banned in Australia because of its supposedly indecent content. By 1971, however, the book was available in all states except Victoria, but only to readers over eighteen, who were 'immune from corruption', as Humphries observed sarcastically.[1]

In a surprisingly favourable article in the *Sunday Review* about Bazza McKenzie, Max Harris identified the squeamishness of Australians when confronted with comedy that reveals the best and worst of the national character. Harris declared the banning of the Bazza book to have been the 'most vile of all the book bannings in the current Customs Department canon'. While Harris initially described Humphries as a self-styled 'febrile ... imaginator of our times' and instructed him to 'hop back to Earls Court where you come from. You'll be safer,' he then retreated, calling for an end to the stoush between them. He declared the Barry McKenzie book, to be 'the most remarkable ... creation that Barry Humphries has produced from his delightful and prestidigitatory bag of cerebral tricks'. He went on to acknowledge the blend of drawings and prose as a 'masterpiece of cultural diagnostics, the most fully rounded and satisfactory realisation we have ever had of the mythic Australian'. Harris praised Humphries for his capacity to hear the Australian vernacular and proclaimed Bazza McKenzie to be the 'direct descendant of Fielding's Joseph Andrews'. Although Harris swore off any further bouts of verbal boxing with Humphries, he could not resist one last punch: he pronounced Barry McKenzie to be a creation who 'leaves the Humphries' stage characterisations for dead'.[2]

Although it had been a struggle to introduce Barry McKenzie to Australian audiences on the page, paradoxically the money to fund the film was offered by the Liberal government. *The Adventures of Barry McKenzie* was fully financed by the Australian Film Development Corporation (AFDC) just two years after the book was banned. Prime Minister John Gorton had established the funding body in 1968 as part of an effort to rejuvenate the dormant Australian film industry after lobbyists, led by Phillip Adams, won over the politicians: 'It is time to see our own landscapes, hear our own voices and dream our own dreams,' they had chorused.[3]

The first chairman of the AFDC was none other than Adams himself, who had led Barry so recently around Melbourne with John Murray to make the ambitious and quirky film *The Naked Bunyip*. Adams was delighted to be working with Barry and Bruce Beresford as producer on *The Adventures of Barry McKenzie*, the AFDC's first film.

Bruce Beresford, still on board as director, was also delighted when he met Barry Crocker, the man Humphries had nominated to play McKenzie, for the first time; he could see immediately that Crocker's boyish charm would allow them to get away with the 'scandalous euphemisms' that filled the script.[4] Crocker had an extraordinary ability to memorise dialogue instantly and was very easy to direct, and Beresford believed that ultimately it was Crocker's comic talent that gave the film its popular appeal.[5]

Beresford, Adams and Humphries were by this time partners in Longford Productions, named after Raymond Longford, who had filmed *The Sentimental Bloke* in 1918. One minor and unforeseen problem was that in England (where Beresford chose to shoot *Barry McKenzie* despite filming in Australia being a condition of funding) many people associated the name with Lord Longford, the pornography czar, and expected the film to be X-rated rather than 'pure Australian sociology', as Humphries described it to journalists.[6]

Humphries, who was beginning to feel much more settled, was calm and alert as he prepared for filming in England. *Barry McKenzie* offered him a creative form of therapy, a writing-out of his hatred of boozy Australians and an opportunity to lampoon public drunkenness now that it was in his past. His parents, both brothers and Barbara farewelled him at the airport. It was rare for the whole family to be together, and Barry was touched. He invited his friend Ross Fitzgerald to appear in the opening scene of the film, farewelling Bazza at Sydney Airport, as he leaves Australia for 'Pommy land'. Both Barry and Ross had so far beaten their devastating drinking habits, and found the release from alcohol energising. Barry looked healthier than he had in years. Returning to London would be a significant milestone for him in numerous ways. He would be leaving his children again, and moving back to the areas he had frequented in his old life with often disastrous consequences for his health. This time he was determined to focus on making a film that would entertain viewers in Britain and Australia, and to enjoy the process of creating his characters.

A cheerful wardrobe manager, Jane Hamilton, took Humphries on a shopping spree for Edna's dresses in High Street, Kensington, causing giggles among the matrons shopping alongside him. With virtually no pre-production time, the film was shot in four weeks in the grubby streets and condemned houses behind Russell Square, during frigid January weather. Humphries was disciplined and attentive, and Crocker bubbly and agreeable in spite of the sleet and having to use the back of a Volkswagen Beetle, shared with a make-up and wardrobe mistress, as his mobile dressing room. Everyone liked Bruce Beresford, who was genial and relaxed with cast and crew.

Apart from Peter Cook arriving on the set for his scene hopelessly drunk, and an attempt by the Technicians Union to replace the Australian cameramen and crew with Britons, the movie was completed without problems. It was easy to find young Australian travellers to act as extras in the pub scenes, but some had to be coached in 'Strine', because they no longer spoke broadly enough for the film. With the two Barrys, Spike Milligan, Peter Cook, a young actor from New Zealand called John Clarke, who played one of Bazza's drinking partners, and the band of pub extras, filming was often interrupted by anarchic behaviour. But the cast and crew enjoyed themselves, and hilarity prevailed.

During filming, Joan Bakewell interviewed Barry for a television program called *Film '72*. Dressed as Edna, Humphries slipped easily into the interview. Bakewell asked him, 'Why is the film set in England?' Without blinking, Barry, referring to the constant strikes and blackouts then bedevilling England, replied, 'The film is set in Calcutta but London looks like Calcutta and is cheaper.' John Clarke, later a noted satirist himself, overheard Humphries' remark and gasped at its audacity. It was 'marketing Dada', he thought to himself.[7] The old Barry was back.

In fact Phillip Adams had wanted to shoot the film in Calcutta 'to give a feeling of inner London poverty' and Humphries wanted to show the Beefeaters at the Tower of London eating out of dustbins.[8] This did not eventuate, but the film depicted England as grey, miserable and mean. Ahead of schedule the cast and crew returned to Sydney to film the last sequences. But cloudy and overcast skies caused a ten-day delay. It would not do to film the return of the golden boy, Bazza, to his homeland under grey skies.

Although the filming was smooth, Humphries encountered difficulties in other areas of work. Before the release of the film in October 1972, relations between Barry Humphries and Harry M Miller became strained. Humphries resented what he interpreted as sloppy treatment of him as a client. Exacerbating Humphries' irritation, his manuscript for a children's book, 'Measles and Mumps', was rejected by Macmillan. He accepted the decision but held on to his desire to write for a young audience.

Although Humphries liked the idea of appearing in a revue-style show involving other performers, he was wary of television after several disappointing experiences with comedy at the BBC. He began to think about doing some television work in Australia, but could not see the point of pouring his energy into what he believed was a 'tenth-rate medium ... expressly designed to make people stay at home'.[9] Yet he was conscious of the threat posed by television to theatre, and worried about the future of live performance. Humphries once found himself eating alone at a dinner party; all the other guests had rushed off to another room to watch him being interviewed on television. He reflected on the strange phenomenon in an introduction to a collection of cartoons by Michael Leunig, lamenting such fascination with 'the alchemical properties of the media', bewildered at the fact that 'the ultimate compliment we can pay reality is to view its simulacrum'.[10]

Humphries' wariness was also based on the memory of the difficulties he had encountered in pleasing the management at BBC Light Entertainment, and the trouble over 'True British Spunk'. With characteristic candour he told Phillip Adams that he feared that a mistake on television might cost him his career, whereas 'if I do a lousy show in the theatre I have only disappointed a few thousand fans'.[11] This wariness and concern for his reputation extended to the details of the credits for the McKenzie film: there were letters backwards and forwards about Humphries' billing, and about the need for Nick Garland to receive his due ('but no more than his due!'). Fed up with negotiating, Barry disguised himself with a short back and sides haircut, planned an escape from 'the treadmill of Melbourne' and set off for a holiday in Prague.[12]

Humphries' anti-hero Bazza McKenzie was a true child of 1960s British satire, in which a key theme was disappointment and disillusionment at the decline of British imperial rule. Fittingly, with the exception of Humphries, Crocker and Clarke, most parts in the film were played by well-known British actors, many of whom had come to prominence throughout the 1960s. Peter Cook played a nasty, camp BBC producer; Dennis Price a depraved and effete ex-public-schoolboy and Avice Landon his spouse; Spike Milligan was a mean landlord in Earls Court; Joan Bakewell played herself and Julie Covington was a folk singer. The expatriate Australian comedian Dick Bentley played the detective. Paul Bertram was Bazza's loyal friend Curly. Paul Hogan, who had been favoured by Phillip Adams for the role of Curly, was passed over. Perhaps he was too genuinely ockerish for Humphries; perhaps Humphries found his confidence threatening. Most likely Bertram's baby face struck Humphries as perfect for the part.

As well as playing 'Auntie Edna', Humphries had two other roles in the film, a mad Viennese psychiatrist, and a hippy singer called Hoot. The casting of English actors saved money as the film was shot in England, but it also signalled that the audience for the film was both British and Australian. With its picaresque tale of a crass but lovable Aussie abroad, the film took up where the British satire boom of the 1960s left off. The energy and charm of Bazza against the backdrop of shabby, grimy London and its perverse and grasping citizenry reinforced some of the themes of the boom from an irreverent colonial perspective. The film cleverly reverses the stock situation of a colonial on the make in one of its funniest sequences, in which a pathetically snobbish English couple who live in a mock-Tudor house in the country attempt to marry off their daughter to Bazza, believing him to be a wealthy station owner.

In reality, Humphries was terrified of the Barry McKenzies of the world. He loathed the Australian ocker figure, and the national obsession with sport. In his bitter experience these were the types of men who did not take kindly to his clever put-downs, or share his sense of comedy; he had suffered several beatings during his alcoholic years, unable to restrain his vitriol towards such people. To many Australians Humphries came across as a pretentious, loud-mouthed intellectual. Ironically the film reversed this image, but Humphries was lambasted by critics for celebrating the vulgarity of Australian society. Once again he caused a massive provocation, this time on a national scale.

Before the film's release, the Commonwealth censor, Richard Prowse, announced his intention of cutting it to shreds, and a director of Roadshow, a distribution company, suggested to Phillip Adams that he should burn the film. Humphries called a press conference, which he opened with the comment that 'Mr Prowse would give his right arm to be here today' — a decidedly provocative statement given that Prowse was an amputee.[13] Adams eventually won an appeal against the censor's decision to cut the film.

But nobody wanted to release *The Adventures of Barry McKenzie*. Having failed to attract a distribution deal, Adams, Beresford and Humphries targeted individual cinemas directly. With help from Clyde Packer, then the designated heir to the family media empire, the world premiere took place on Friday 13 October 1972 at the Capitol in Swanston Street, Melbourne amid a sea of free Foster's Lager and a crowd of exuberant youths. Initially the Carlton and United Brewery had refused to donate beer because it feared the film 'might harm Carlton's image', but was swayed by the prospect that a competitor would be given the opportunity. The initial refusal exemplified the horrified reaction of many Australians to the film's portrayal of 'beer-swilling Australians in London'.[14]

Eric and Louisa Humphries declined their invitation to the premiere of the film. Barry was not surprised that his mother stayed away given the controversy surrounding *The Adventures of Barry McKenzie*, but the disappointment of his father's absence stayed with him; he felt sure that Eric would have enjoyed the event.[15] On a visit to his parents' home just before the premiere, Barry had arrived as Eric's cardiologist, Clive Fitts, was leaving. Barry looked at the eminent specialist and said, 'I hope I don't need a wreath.' When he left the house himself, he gave his father a firm hug.[16] In a matter of weeks Eric was dead. At the age of sixty-seven, Eric Humphries died doing what he loved. He collapsed during a game of golf. His death shocked and saddened Barry, and made Louisa, who grieved with stoic reserve, even more reclusive than she had already been.

CHAPTER 20

Damehood

The critical reception for the film was appalling. Humphries was bewildered by the outrage of the reviewers, and equally startled by his sudden popularity among movie-goers. On the opening night in Adelaide a group of young men formed 'a kind of cavalcade like a military wedding' for his arrival at the cinema.[1] Rather than holding swords aloft they held their tinnies up and sprayed out foaming beer in an archway for Barry, accompanied by Phillip Adams, to run under, the two of them ducking to try to prevent the cascading beer soaking their evening suits. The adulation of the people he both hated and feared, as well as the drenching in beer after almost two years of abstinence, made Barry violently sick. He was shepherded into a box upstairs to recover.

One of the elements of the film that most appealed to the public was the colourful language of Bazza McKenzie. Of all Humphries' characters so far, McKenzie offered the most provocative celebration of Australian English. Some of Bazza's expressions reflected classic features of Australian humour, with its frequent abuse and invective, explicit racism and misogyny, and its focus on men. McKenzie's language also included curious expressions unearthed or made up by Humphries. Bazza insulted people by telling them, 'You smell like an Abo's armpit', 'You're boring the strides off me' or 'Go and stick your head up a dead dingo's bum.' Regardless of his foul mouth, he was a charming, innocent character, rather puritanical, just like many Australians Humphries had encountered.

Bazza's profanities were just exaggerated versions of the actual invective found in Australian English. The expressions invented for him by Humphries revolved around food, drink, sex and elimination. The term 'liquid lunch', meaning a lunch made up mostly of beer or other alcoholic drinks, is one Humphries' expression that has gained currency in Australia. But the expressions for a great thirst — such as 'I'm dry as a nun's nasty', 'I'm that thirsty I could drink out of an Abo's loincloth' and 'I've got a thirst you could flamin' photograph' — for vomiting and for urinating were the ones most movie-goers remembered from Bazza McKenzie. Bazza's term for vomiting — the 'technicolour yawn' — entered the vernacular as did 'big spit' and 'liquid laugh'. One of his terms for urinating, 'siphon the python', also found its way into the idiom.

Most of the expressions for sexual intercourse used by Bazza suggest a battle or a conquest. The f-word was never uttered by the young Australian because of his preference for the euphemistic and the colourful. His choice of words sustained the sexually predatory image of the Australian male, though the hapless Bazza never consummated any of his romantic relationships. His desire to 'park the prawn', 'spear the bearded clam' and 'dip the dagger' did not bring the terms into general usage. However, Humphries helped popularise other terms such as 'go the grope' and 'crack a fat'.

The Adventures of Barry McKenzie was a box-office success in Australia, despite its mauling by critics, who seemed to miss the point of the satire on the cultural cringe. The premiere of David Williamson's *Don's Party* at the Pram Factory, Melbourne, in August 1971 aroused similar reactions. The satirical play exposed the aggressive chauvinism of Australian men at an election night party. Like the McKenzie film, it was a box-office hit, but critics found fault with it in numerous ways. In contrast, Ted Kotcheff's *Wake in Fright*, a dark film portraying the violence and alienation of Australian men in the outback, found favour with the critics but could not attract a sizable audience.

Missing the satire on Australian homosocial excesses, Dennis Altman in his book *Coming Out in the Seventies,* damned *The Adventures of Barry McKenzie* as 'the most vicious anti-homosexual film of all time'.² The Melbourne *Age* critic referred to the film as 'an 8 mm home movie'.³ The *Australian* stated that 'Alongside Bazza, Ned Kelly is a minor abberation', but continued, 'In fairness, the critics are going to hate it and everyone else will fall out of their seats laughing!'⁴ The Melbourne *Observer* concluded that the film was a 'sorry unfunny mess' and Ron Saw's vituperative review in the *Daily Mirror* appeared under the headline 'Bazza McKenzie makes me want to chunder'.⁵

But not all the critics condemned the film. PP McGuinness deemed it both funny and socially relevant. Although he preferred the 'astringency of the comic strip', he thought the 'transmutation' worked and stated that Humphries was 'a superb comedian'.⁶ Keith Dunstan in the *Bulletin* 'adored' the film and commented on the 'oddly lovable' character of Barry McKenzie who is 'utterly unlike any Australian in Earls Court today. He is the mythical Australian seen through the eyes of the *Sunday Times*.' Dunstan predicted great things for the film, assuring readers that it would be 'the biggest success since *The Sentimental Bloke*'.⁷ Indeed the *Bulletin*, with the exception of a lukewarm review by Sandra Hall, championed Humphries' work throughout the early 1970s.

Ironically Senator Hannan, a Liberal from Victoria, questioned the newly elected Labor government in parliament about why federal taxpayers' money had been made available to fund *The Adventures of Barry McKenzie*, a 'ghastly, vulgar film'. In answering, the Minister for the Media, Senator McClelland drew attention to the box-office success of the film, and hastened to add that it was one of the few successes financed by the Film Development Corporation. He went on to remind Hannan that the decision to fund the film had been made by the previous Liberal government.

While the critics panned the film, intellectuals such as Patrick White, Manning Clark and Geoffrey Dutton praised it. Clark wrote to Barry from his office at the Australian National University in euphoric tones. He had no doubt about the importance of the

McKenzie character and the unflattering realism of the film: 'I loved ... your getting those three horrible men to brush up against Bazza in his pilgrimage for booze ... even in a comedy we should be reminded of the sinister ... *Wake in Fright* and Bazza McKenzie are two things we have to accept as being a mirror of what we are — as what is part of us all.'[8] He recognised that Humphries had touched the rawest of raw nerves in the Australian self-image. Barry later told Dutton that the 'confrontation between Bazza and the people who disapproved of him was rather like Caliban viewing his own image'.[9]

Before the release of *Barry McKenzie*, a strange silence had greeted Humphries' work in academic circles. Looking back it seems astounding given his ongoing satirical celebration of Australian society. But there were one or two exceptions to this trend. As early as 1959 Stephen Murray-Smith celebrated Humphries' satirical attacks on philistinism in Australian middle-class life.[10] And in the early 1970s, Geoffrey Serle observed that 'younger-minded Australians revel in Barry Humphries' celebration of our cultural gaucheries'.[11] But even following the film's huge success, John Docker overlooked Humphries in *Australian Cultural Elites*, his study of Australian culture published in 1974. Docker wrote of the national dilemma of reconciling the inheritance of European ideas with the experience of a new country and a new social environment. Yet Humphries, perhaps more than any other artist, had embodied the dilemma and given it comic voice from the very beginning of his career.[12]

The success of *The Adventures of Barry McKenzie*, however, brought about a shift in Barry's comic direction towards a new kind of popular theatre. Of all his roles on stage over the previous ten years, Edna had answered an impulse in Barry's psyche, an impulse to reply to everything that was small-minded and boring in suburban Melbourne. He was becoming partial to this female character. On the set for the film, dressed as Edna, he stayed in character and encouraged the other cast members to address their comments to her, not to him. Edna offered a shield for the newly sober Barry. During the sequences filmed in Hong Kong, Barry walked the streets dressed as Mrs Everage and accosted polite locals who were mystified by the towering and gaudily dressed matron. Just as Barry had terrified the passers-by in his madhouse keeper's costume, sloping along the dark streets of Notting Hill, when he first moved to London, he began to enjoy walking in Edna's shoes. Ray Lawler had pushed him into his first public performance of Edna, and Bruce Beresford first suggested she appear in the film. But with the public's embrace of the film, Humphries was becoming aware that Edna was his 'most valuable property', the character *he* could inhabit to best reach an audience.[13]

Sparring with his critics was also fast becoming an art form for Humphries. Edna's satiric powers provided a vehicle both for defence and attack. Barry used Edna to express anger and irritation when he felt wounded or indignant. In one particularly sharp letter to Harry M Miller, Edna said that she was 'overwhelmed when my friend Mr Humphries told me your friend at the *Australian* newspaper was prepared to pay me nearly fifty dollars for my silly little ode to Adelaide. You see, Mr Miller, I am just an amateur theatrical and housewife bard and not a big-time author and columnist like John Laws, Maggie Tabberer, Dame Zara or Leo Schofield.' She went on to express her gratitude that the newspaper's editor had gone to so much trouble to mention her on the front page, 'particularly after the big spread he gave his drama critic's clever, and justly disparaging review of Mr Humphries' show'.[14]

During the publicity tour for the film Barry suffered from exhaustion so severely that on several occasions he could barely speak. Phillip Adams cajoled him into action with the words that never failed to galvanise him: 'Barry, get Edna. Get Edna'.[15] In radio station after radio station Barry would transform into Edna and spring to life. Edna always revived him; she gave him licence, guaranteed him a reaction, and protected Barry from the insults of the critics.

It was still a difficult time for Humphries as a newly recovered alcoholic. Fortunately people were determined to look out for him. Barry Crocker found himself rushing to Humphries' rescue at a cast party at the Windsor Hotel. He had witnessed a young woman associated with the Melbourne publicity campaign pouring a Scotch and Coke for Barry. Horrified, he marched her off to a corner and made it clear that this kind of behaviour was not on.

With or without alcohol, Barry was a born worrier. He was anxious about what to do next. He worried about his mother and the suffering she endured, missing Eric, and from her severe arthritis. He felt guilty about spending so much time across the other side of the world from her, but he consoled himself with the knowledge that Barbara lived only a few streets away from her. And Louisa was not alone. Michael was still at home, and her sister Elsie, whom she had always been especially close to, moved into the Humphries family home in Christowel Street.

Throughout his life worry and lack of focus seem to have sparked an impulse in Barry to stir. One grey, damp morning back in London, Barry staged one of his old stunts. He had arranged to meet Nick Garland for lunch in the West End. Garland was producing a cartoon every day for the *Daily Telegraph*, as well as working with Humphries on the fortnightly Bazza McKenzie strip for *Private Eye*. The *Telegraph* was then located on Fleet Street in a building featuring expansive glass windows at street level. When Humphries arrived at the offices, he noticed there was an elegant arrangement of Garland's recent cartoons in a display cabinet. Several passers-by gazed intently at the cartoons in the window, some of them smiling to themselves as they scanned the collection.

Garland walked down the stairs, through the busy foyer and onto the crowded street to meet Humphries. On seeing Nick, Barry turned back to the display windows and gave a screech of demonic laughter. His whole body convulsed as he slapped his thighs and pointed at the cartoon display as if it contained something so funny that he could not bear it. He leaned hard against the plate glass, screaming and bellowing with laughter for several minutes. Some of the hurrying pedestrians stared nonplussed at the spectacle, before quickly averting their eyes and walking on, deciding the man was probably unstable. Finally Barry stopped laughing, stood up straight and began to walk beside Garland in the direction of the restaurant where they had booked a table for lunch. Embarrassed, Garland had stood silently to one side throughout the scene.

Within a matter of moments Humphries began to address passing strangers as the two men moved through the crowd. He said to one person after another, in a high-pitched, almost falsetto voice: 'Hello, I'm Barry!' He started to trot and make grotesque faces. People threw Garland sympathetic glances as if to say, 'It's okay. We understand you're taking your nutty brother out. Don't worry.'[16]

Once seated in the elegant wood-panelled restaurant, the friends ordered lunch and drinks and began to chat amicably. They were surrounded by businessmen in white shirts and dark suits. Before long Humphries excused himself from the table. After about five minutes he returned and said in an agitated, loud voice, 'I went to the lavatory but I couldn't do anything because there were other people in there. Last time I was here for lunch I tried to go to the lavatory. I couldn't do anything and I came back and peed all over the table.' A hush came over the other diners as they looked at each other quizzically, carefully averting their gaze from Humphries. There was some muffled laughter. Garland blushed. Consumed by envy and worried about his own work, Humphries was compelled to provoke and embarrass his friend. As usual, his swift return to his regular, charming self meant that Nick and the other people around him easily forgave his outlandish behaviour.

Although they saw him infrequently, the children particularly enjoyed their father's tricks. On car trips and excursions to the country he would become a dribbling, handicapped character called Simon Lacey. He took them to see the film *Don't Look Now* and during the infamous sex scene Barry put on his Simon Lacey voice, shouting, 'What are they doing?' in the crazed tones of a lascivious cretin.[17]

Charles Osborne, the Australian actor Barry met when he first arrived in London in 1959, came to Humphries' rescue, asking him to perform at the Poetry International Festival in the presence of WH Auden and Allen Ginsberg. Barry appeared on stage in London one very warm evening in June 1973. Appearing first as himself in a blue three-piece suit, polka-dot tie and fedora, he read the work of 'innocent versifiers' such as Jack Moses with a broad Australian accent. He also read some not so innocent verse, delighting the sweltering audience with the grimly comic refrain about the dog that shat on the tuckerbox five miles from Gundagai.

A few minutes later, a bejewelled Edna Everage, wearing a full-length dress, white gloves and clutching a large-print edition of Ezra Pound's *Cantos*, interrupted the quietly spoken, urbane Osborne, took over the stage and began to read some 'pomes that mean a lot to me', including one rather sentimental reflection on motherhood by Mrs Tillie Ashton, called 'She Is Your Mother'. When one audience member laughed loudly at a line of doggerel from 'Newsboys' by Joan Torrance, Edna fixed him with a stern look. The audience was delighted. Edna's appearance at the festival marked the first success for Humphries on the stage in the United Kingdom. Edna referred to Charles Osborne as John, and praised him for his plays, before launching into a new hymn to her countrymen with the parodic title 'Terribly Well'. The phrase mocked and celebrated the misuse of 'terribly' that Barry found one of the most endearing yet irritating features of Australian speech. Edna recited numerous jaunty verses.

> *In the world of success or of failure*
> *Have you noticed the genius spark*
> *Seems brightest in folk from Australia*
> *We all leave an incredible mark.*

> *You just have to go to the opera*
> *Or an art show, or glance at your shelves*
> *To see in a trice that Australians*
> *Have done terribly well for themselves.*

> *Joan Sutherland, Rupert Murdoch, Scobie Breasley*
> *Have all pitted themselves 'gainst the Pom*
> *And the cultural race they've won easily*
> *In spite of the land they come from.*

> *Wilfred Thomas, Sidney Nolan, Hammond Innes*
> *To mention a few famous names*
> *Have been taken to Old England's bosom*
> *Along with Skippy and Mr Clive James.*
>
> *Did you know that Rolf Harris was Australian?*
> *Peter Finch, Coral Browne, Keith Michell*
> *All your best dentists come from the land of the gum*
> *And they've all done so terribly well.*

In spite of the inordinate praise from Julian Jebb in *The Times* who claimed that 'since the retirement of Maria Callas, Humphries is the greatest star alive', Humphries was not yet confident enough to return to the English stage with a full show.[18] But the new-found relationship between Humphries and his character Edna Everage was captured by the photographer John Timbers in *Harpers & Queen* magazine.[19] Edna appeared as a gargantuan figure in white lace-up, knee-high boots offering a tiny Barry Humphries, in suit and tie, just one gladiolus from a massive bunch in her arms. In the meantime, Clyde Packer was booking major theatres for Humphries' next Australian show. Compared to the West End, the stages of his homeland held few terrors for Humphries.

But Humphries' home life was difficult. After two years his divorce case came before the court in Melbourne. Just before Christmas 1973 the divorce came through.

The Adventures of Barry McKenzie was the first Australian film to earn over one million dollars at the box office, and the first Australian feature film to make a profit in thirty-five years. Australia's film industry was reborn with a *succès de scandale*. Humphries, Adams and Beresford made considerable fortunes. Crocker, true to the innocent he played, had cautiously opted for a salary, and therefore did not share in the big returns. It was a rather unfortunate outcome for the lead actor whose portrayal of Bazza had made the film a success.

Encouraged by *Barry McKenzie*'s financial returns, the Australian television and film producer Reg Grundy approached Beresford offering to finance a sequel, regretting his decision not to fund the original. Beresford was not keen. He felt the subject was exhausted. But he quickly reversed his decision when Grundy agreed to fund a film version of *The Getting of Wisdom*, the novel Beresford had always dreamed of adapting. Phillip Adams, however, did not want to be involved with a large commercial operation like Grundy's. He was proud of the achievement of Longford, which was the first company in Australian film history to distribute a film outside the major chains, and of the extremely profitable venture *Barry McKenzie* had become. In a long memo to Humphries with the subject 'The Sulks', he attempted to convince Barry of the merits of involving the Australian Film Development Corporation, rather than Grundy's, in the sequel, stating that 'bumbling officialdom may be preferable to hard-nose capitalism'.[20] It was not to be and Grundy Productions furnished the inferior and rather tedious *Barry McKenzie Holds His Own* with ample funding.

There was, however, one unforgettable incident in the sequel. Just two years after the first film was released, yet another prime minister, this time a Labor leader, became involved with the Barry McKenzie carnival. But Gough Whitlam lent a very different and rather dangerous (as it turned out) kind of support. Right at the end of the film, a slightly uncomfortable looking Whitlam, playing himself, conferred a damehood on Bazza's Auntie Edna. In a few short years Humphries' cartoon character Bazza McKenzie had become a controversial symbol of the new nationalism in Australia. Although the second film veered away from the comic strip original, both films celebrated and parodied new nationalism, charming and insulting English and Australian audiences but ultimately challenging the way Australians saw themselves and the way they saw the mother country.

Many Australians viewed the Labor prime minister as the embodiment of home-grown radical nationalism, and his decision to appear in the film alongside Barry Humphries marked a potent moment in Australia's post-imperial history, a moment when the politics of Australian theatre and the theatre of Australian politics directly and hilariously coincided. So receptive were Australians to new expressions of Australian identity at this time, the prime minister could comfortably participate in a strident and farcical attack on British foibles and the cultural cringe. Whitlam, the man who was often said to have lacked the common touch, had capitalised on the popular appeal of both Barry Humphries and Barry McKenzie.

Whitlam's screen debut occurred as Barry Crocker and Barry Humphries, as Bazza and his Auntie Edna, arrived at Sydney airport to cheering crowds, red carpet and government cars. Whitlam and his wife, Margaret, stepped forward to greet them:

> Prime Minister: Welcome, Barry. Australia is proud of you.
> Bazza: Thank you very much sir.
> Prime Minister [to the prostrate Edna]: *Dame* Edna. Arise Dame Edna.
> Edna: [Overcome] Dame Edna. Ohhh!

For Humphries, the bestowal of a damehood on Edna Everage, albeit engineered by himself as script writer, marked a turning point. Edna would now become his signature character. For Australians, too, it was a significant moment. One of Whitlam's first policy changes when he was elected in 1972 was to scrap the imperial honours system. So the Labor prime minister's actions in the film were doubly ironic as he explicitly arrogated the imperial power to himself. It was, as Whitlam noted, the only imperial honour his government ever conferred.[21]

Edna's damehood eventually helped propel the frumpy Moonee Ponds housewife to celebrity status. But when Edna was mistaken for the Queen in the second film and kidnapped, the possibilities of her star-studded future were already apparent, as if Humphries had glimpsed — and was grasping — a new career for the character.

In spite of their different walks of life, Humphries and Whitlam were rather similar figures. Both brilliant verbal performers and erudite Anglophiles, in their separate but overlapping spheres — thanks to Bazza McKenzie — they dramatised the waning British connection felt by Australians. Yet both men still looked chiefly to Britain to define their own sense of nationalism. Despite their interest in defining a new Australian nationalism, both were children of the Empire.

Humphries had not been involved in the 'Artists for Whitlam' activities of the 1972 election campaign. But he felt warmly towards Gough and Margaret Whitlam and told the historian Jim Davidson that they always came to his shows.[22] Early in 1974 he declared support for the Labor government. In fact the Whitlam era provided Humphries with a mass of comic material, and some of Humphries' most potent satire — and characters — appeared in response to events of this period.

In spite of the avalanche of criticism of the McKenzie films, Humphries' preference for comic excess would not be silenced. He hit back with a new record entitled *Barry Humphries at Carnegie Hall*. Photographed in a dinner suit and monocle in front of the squat, flesh-pink Carnegie Hall in Rosstown Road, Carnegie, Melbourne, he parodied the new Australian fixation with self-image, emblazoning the slogan 'Tell Lies — Protect Australia's Image', on the inside cover as if it was an official stamp. He also appeared in the 1974 British sex comedy *Percy's Progress*, a sequel to the successful *Percy*. In another Australian comic film, *The Great McCarthy*, based on a novel by Barry Oakley, Humphries played Colonel Ball-Miller, a rich Melbourne businessman and football identity resembling John Elliot.

By the time the second Barry McKenzie film was playing in cinemas around the nation, it was clear that the two films were a mixed blessing for all parties. For Humphries they highlighted the divisions between popular and high-brow appeal. Bruce Beresford had sensed the possible risks all along, but he could never have predicted the extent of the fall-out. He was shocked by the vehemence of the critical response to the Bazza films, and was being treated as a kind of cinematic lout 'who would never be capable of making any other type of movie'.[23] Ironically he was unable to find work for some time despite the rebirth of the Australian film industry and the profits that flowed from the popular McKenzie movies. The ultimate disappointment for him was that Reg Grundy reneged on the promise to make *The Getting of Wisdom*. By 1975 Beresford was *persona non grata* in Australia and commented sarcastically: 'It certainly came as a surprise to me that the average Australian sees his "image" as that of an elegantly dressed aesthete, standing around coining epigrams, eating croquet sandwiches and playing watercress on the lawn.'[24] In spite of his subsequent success as a film and opera director, he believes he has never fully recovered from the backlash of hostility aroused by the McKenzie films.[25] Barry Crocker did not enjoy the opportunity of any further film roles despite his success as the hero of the film. Phillip Adams who did not participate in the second film walked away unscathed.

Fed up with the response to the Bazza films in Australia, Beresford returned to the UK to make a film about modern-day vaudeville. *Side By Side* was a strange and unremarkable comedy about two clubs that compete for a licence to entertain in a town called Sludgely. Humphries played a rather timid, eccentric pianist called Rodney, the son of two vaudeville performers. It was a musical film with little to recommend it except for some quirky dancing involving Humphries, the appearance of Eric Idle as himself and a few very funny lines. Desperate to get people to come to their club, some characters discuss what 'the people' want. Rodney says to his uncle Max Nuggett, who manages the venue: 'Nostalgia, Uncle, that's what they want.' 'No Rodney,' Max replies, 'they want bingo, booze and bums — they're not interested in art.'

CHAPTER 21

Anarchist

Perhaps it was a reaction to the controversy and the critical drubbing of the two Barry McKenzie films that encouraged Humphries to join the board of the right-wing magazine *Quadrant* in June 1975. Immediately after appearing in a film with the Labor prime minister, he confounded critics with this action. Patrick White, who was then identifying strongly with left-wing elements, was horrified. Ian Britain, writing more than a decade after Humphries' association with the magazine, identified this impulse in the actor as 'artful' and 'mischievous'.[1] Barry took refuge in the safe harbour of the conservative magazine, and remained on its board until 1987, contributing various sketches and articles to its pages. He regarded himself as apolitical, and held a genuine respect for the liberal voices of some of the regular contributors to the magazine. He grew irritated with those on the left who were paralysed by the dismissal of Whitlam and seemed obsessed by 'nostalgia for a non-existent Camelot'. His association with *Quadrant* offered him a vehicle for keeping his name in the public domain under yet another mask: ratbag right-wing establishment figure. Guaranteed to start tongues wagging, Humphries' move provoked criticism and contempt. An anarchist at heart, he continued to revel in the range of labels, such as 'crypto-fascist', applied to him.[2]

Humphries had been honest in his youthful Dada manifesto when he declared, 'We are incapable of treating seriously any subject whatsoever.' A reluctant joiner, he could not resist sending the editor of *Quadrant* these cryptic lines in 1982: 'Long may the radicals of the right bash, baffle and bewilder the poor old pinko conservatives.'[3] A few years later Humphries' friend, the English playwright Peter Nichols, ribbed him as a 'half-arsed political puritan', whose 'game is anarchy'.[4] And Humphries surprised many when he revealed his admiration for the Tasmanian environmentalist Dr Bob Brown during his vigorous protest against the damming of the Franklin River in 1983 and became a life member of the Tasmanian Wilderness Society.

Humphries, however, maintained close ties with the Australian establishment in London after his return following the making of the second Barry McKenzie film. On one occasion he stepped in to open an exhibition of Robert Dickerson's paintings when the Australian High Commissioner was called away urgently. Eloquent and effusive, Humphries announced, 'I have always wanted to be High Commissioner, if only for the pleasure of telling people, "Please don't bother to call me Your Excellency".'

Humphries knew that his refusal to be defined politically or ideologically was essential to his satire. Often those who respond negatively to his act deplore the man himself, concluding that he must hate his satiric targets, his country and his fellow man. But Humphries castigates arrogance and toadyism wherever he finds it, regardless of whether it is expressed by someone on the right or the left, from the middle class, working class or upper echelons of society. Humphries' attitude to his characters is ambivalent and sometimes even admiring. One of the most exhilarating features of his performance is the way in which he revels in the amorality of the characters he puts under the microscope. There is no better example than Humphries' most riotous character, Les Patterson, inspired by the spirit of optimism and change that characterised the Whitlam years.

* * *

Les Patterson first appeared in 1974 at the St George Leagues Club in Sydney. He was, according to his own propaganda, a safari-suit wearing 'survivor' of Whitlam's 'Camelot'. 'I, too, believed that the sun shone out of Gough's freckle,' Les would later reminisce about his rapport with the charismatic Labor prime minister.[5]

Clubs in cities and towns across Australia had become the venues for contemporary variety and vaudeville, and Barry Crocker had talked Humphries into appearing in a double act with him. In the lead-up to the show, Humphries was nearly sick at the prospect of appearing at a club; it was the first time he had played in such a place since a disastrous Sunday morning stand-up gig at the Granville RSL in 1957, where most of the beery punters simply ignored him.

Barry Crocker remembers sitting with Humphries on the beige shag-pile carpet of Crocker's home in Wahroonga, trying to devise material for the show. Crocker regaled Humphries with stories of the lecherous club managers he had met on the circuit, and the character of Les Patterson took shape. The incorrigible Les, then a genial and boorish club functionary, gave Humphries plenty of scope to shock and outrage an audience.[6] Les was also partly inspired by Humphries' Highgate years in London, when he'd become friendly with Barbara Blackman's mother, Mrs Patterson, whom he took care not to offend with his crude tales. Occasionally he would begin one of his stories and then say he could not continue unless he was certain that Mrs Patterson was upstairs in her bed. 'Lest Mrs Patterson hears,' became a kind of mantra for Barry when he launched into something particularly revolting. As he pondered his new character a decade later, the name resounded from the past.[7]

The Two Bazzas ran for four weeks over the summer holiday period. The show hinged on the supposed late arrival of Barry Humphries, who was 'replaced' by the sozzled entertainment officer of the club, Les Patterson, burping and slurping into the microphone, stumbling around muttering 'Time waits for no man,' as he filled in until 'Mr Humphries' arrived to begin the show. On opening night one of the doormen at the club refused to let 'Les

Patterson' into the building, believing him to be a drunken tramp in his sauce-stained tie, crumpled jacket and greasy trousers, and the show nearly collapsed. Dame Edna Everage also appeared, lamenting that her manager, Barry Humphries, could not find a place to park his car outside. Each night Humphries grew more outrageous as Les. Now that he was safely on the wagon Humphries transformed the alcoholic demons of his past into a comic alter ego. He revelled in the excesses of the character. The highlight of the show was a sketch performed by the two Barrys as older versions of themselves, appearing as vaudeville performers in an old people's home of the future. They laughed and ad-libbed about show business personalities as if they were reminiscing, both of them perfectly at home in club land, the vaudeville of their time.

In September 1974, John Romeril's play *The Floating World* premiered at the Pram Factory in Melbourne. The male protagonist, Les, swears, guzzles beer, ridicules his wife and behaves like an ocker. Although the play is not a satire of ocker males in Australia, and the use of the same name is almost certainly a coincidence, Humphries' vision of the crude and patriotic characters in the McKenzie films, together with the newly minted Les Patterson, must have had an influence on the emerging playwright, among many others. The Whitlam government was funding the arts generously, and Australians were beginning to hear their own accents on stage and in film. Typical Australian characters were starting to appear more frequently.[8]

For Humphries, this new-found support for all things Australian was welcome, but its expression provided a continuing source of hilarity. As Barry McKenzie says to Col in *Barry McKenzie Holds His Own*: 'An arty-crafty bloke like you would be laughin' back in Australia right now. The government's shelling out piles of bloody moolah for any bastard who reckons he can paint pictures, write pomes or make fillums.'

By the middle of the decade, however, a spoof of cultural nationalism was no longer satisfactory for those in power, especially in view of the dark clouds on the horizon for the Labor government. By 1975 Gough Whitlam felt impelled to move the debate along,

The Humphries children — Barbara, Michael, Barry and Christopher — sitting on the front wall of the family home at Christowel Street, Camberwell, c. 1950

Eric and Louisa Humphries in the garden at Christowel Street

Barry in fancy dress, c. 1940

Barry Humphries in the garden at home, with Barbara and Louisa Humphries, c. 1954

Barry Humphries as Orsino (third from right) and Zoe Caldwell (seated centre) in Ray Lawler's production of *Twelfth Night*, 1955

Barry Humphries and Peter O'Shaughnessy at The Flask public house, Highgate, 1961

Mrs Norm Everage, in her 'travelling abroad' attire, appearing live on television, 1959

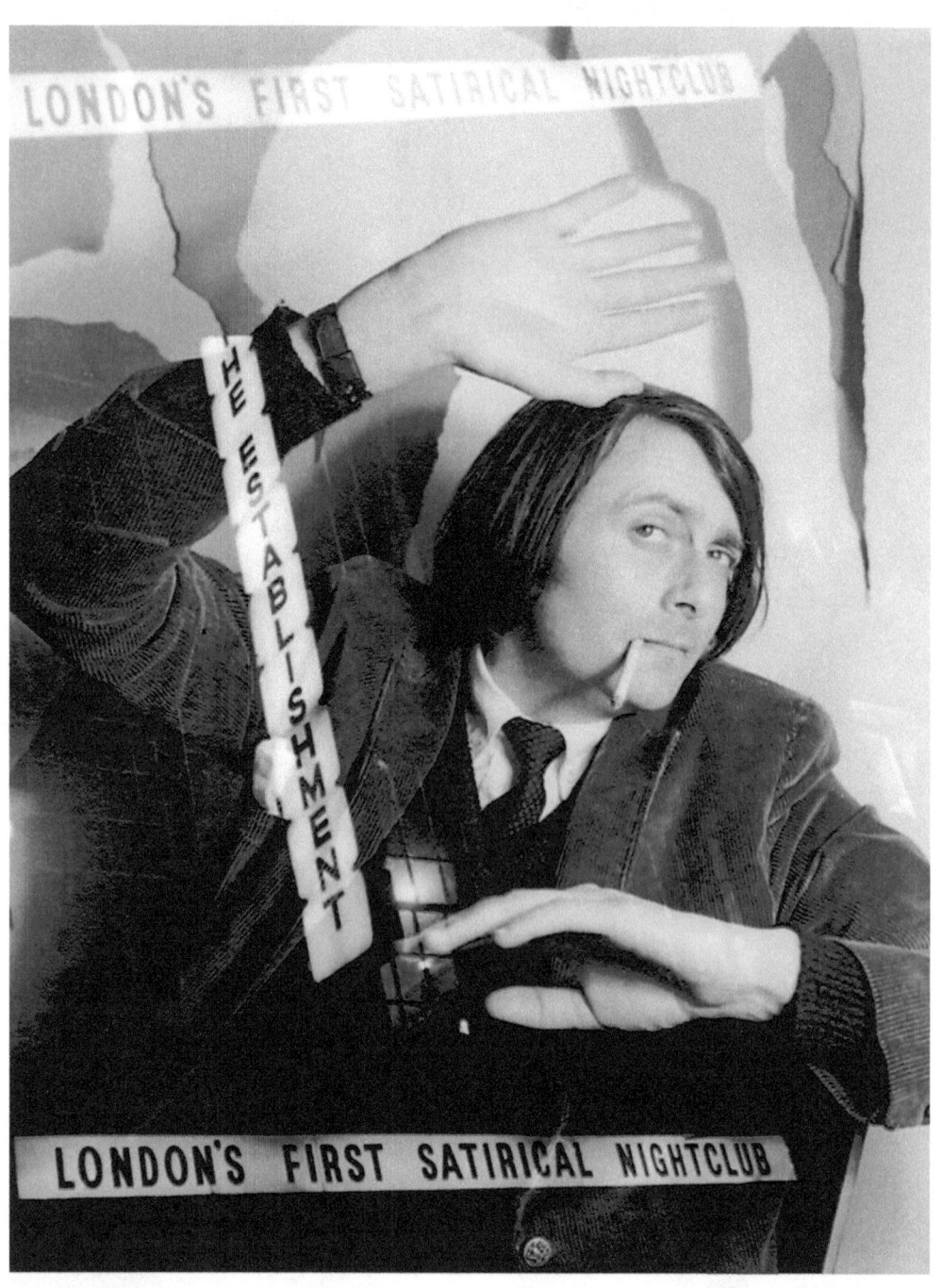

A promotional photograph taken before Humphries' first one-man show in Britain, *A Nice Night's Entertainment*, at the Establishment Club, Soho, 1963

Edna Everage reading out her favourite recipes on the television program *Startime*, 1962

Edna singing in *Excuse I*, 1965

Barry Humphries in Toronto, 1963

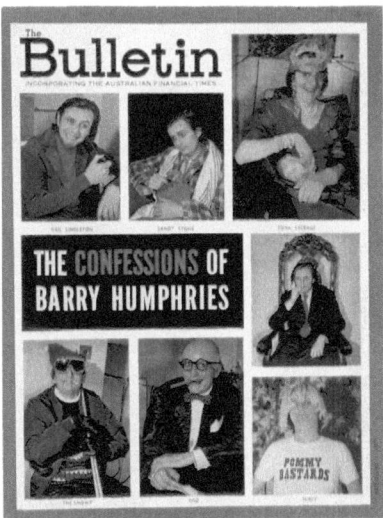

A handbill advertising Humphries' one-man show *Excuse I*, showing Barry dressed in the costumes of his many characters. From top left: the desperate academic Neil Singleton, returned serviceman Sandy Stone, Moonee Ponds housewife Mrs Edna Everage, Barry Humphries, a Melbourne skier, a Collins Street psychiatrist, and a Sydney surfer.

Barry Humphries holding his portrait of Arthur Calwell at the launch of his exhibition at the Bonython Gallery, 1968

Edna Everage in conversation with Bob Rogers, 1968

The Mendicant (Barry Humphries) opening his art exhibition in Sydney, 1968

Barry Humphries arriving at a Melbourne Grammar function with a friend, 1971

Arthur Boyd's drawing of Barry Humphries in hospital, struggling with his addiction to alcohol, with Rosalind beside his bed, c. 1970

Barry Humphries dressed as Dr Wendy Toole, defiantly holding up her latest book, in *A Load of Olde Stuffe*, c. 1971

Barry Humphries with John Betjeman in Radnor Walk, Chelsea, 1973

Barry Humphries playing Dame Edna in *At Least You Can Say You've Seen It*, 1974

Dame Edna on Ladies Day at Royal Ascot, June 1976, wearing her spectacular Opera House hat, designed by Lorraine McKee

Dame Edna enjoying Windsor Great Park with an Australian friend, c. 1976

Humphries playing the trade unionist Lance Boyle in *An Evening's Intercourse with the Widely Liked Barry Humphries*, c. 1981

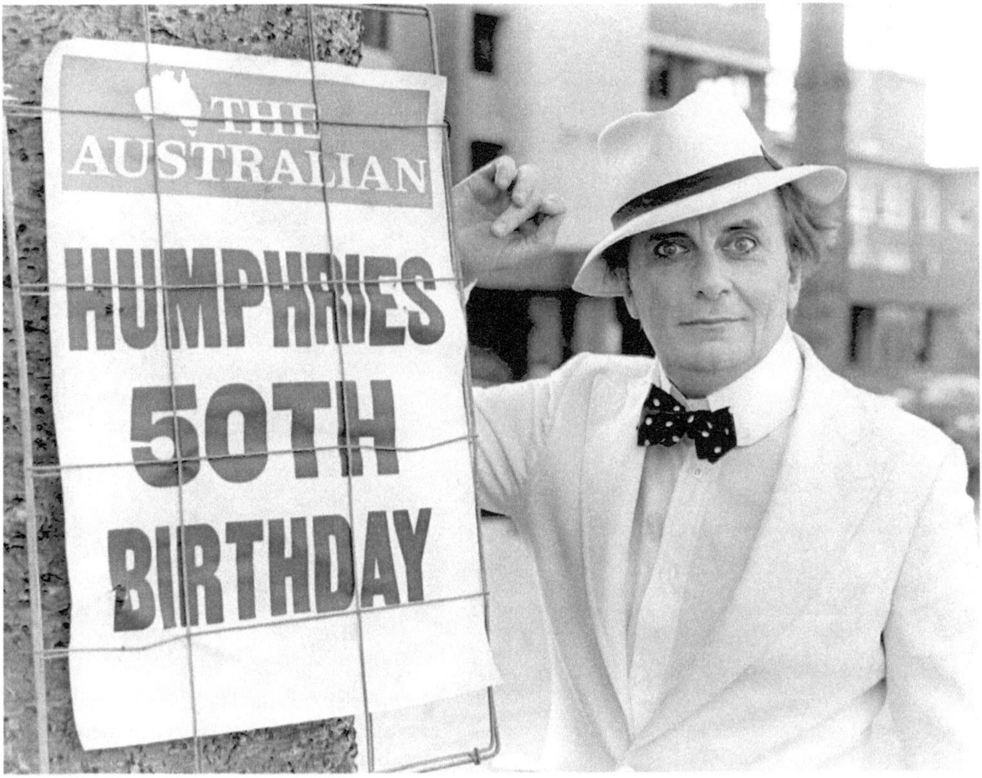

Barry Humphries poses for a photograph to celebrate his half-century, February 1984

Les Patterson relaxing on the beach on Humphries' birthday, 17 February 1984, delighted at the prime minister's designation of the day as a national holiday

The cover of the program for Humphries' show *Tears Before Bedtime*, 1985

Humphries on stage as Dame Edna Everage with a co-operative audience member. Dame Edna is wearing her patriotic gown with its Opera House collar and Union Jack petticoat designed by Bill Goodwin for *The Last Night of the Poms* in 1981.

A handbill for Humphries' show *The Life and Death of Sandy Stone*, 1990–91

Barry's television producer Claudia Rosencrantz on set with Dame Edna during the production of the three-part television series *Dame Edna's Hollywood*, 1990–91

A sketch design for Dame Edna's 'Scream Dress', worn on the television game show *Dame Edna's Neighbourhood Watch*, 1991

Barry Humphries in the garden at Lewis Morley's Sydney home, c. 2008

cautioning Australians: 'We are not a nation of philistines; we should not be content with an image abroad based mainly on Barry McKenzie.'[9] But the influence of Barry McKenzie was pervasive. The lingo of the films had entered the vernacular and Humphries had secured a mainstream audience in Australia. His latest creation, Les Patterson, would do even more to cement what many saw as the regrettable aspects of ocker Australianism in the public consciousness of both the national and international communities.

CHAPTER 22

Housewife Superstar

In the summer of 1974–75, after a three-year break from the theatrical stage, Humphries returned to his preferred mode, the one-man show, and put his mind to creating a parade of new characters. The one-man show suited his personality perfectly. Remembering another of the throwaway lines his aunts used when asked what they thought of a musical they had seen — 'Well, Barry, at least I can say I've seen it' — he called the show *At Least You Can Say You've Seen It,* and gave it the marvellous subtitle *A Tragi-Farce in Two Acts for Those Too Drunk to Dance.* Humphries, of course, was no longer in this category and the newly elevated Dame Edna, resplendent with Glomesh handbag, danced and chatted with the audience. The running order of sketches printed in the program was prefaced with the line 'Subject to Mr Humphries' caprice.'

The first half of the show satirised the brashly affluent and crude new Australian appetite for 'culture' with a character called Morrie O'Connor, an art dealer wearing a light blue suit, who sounded like a used car dealer speaking through a megaphone: 'Hello there, ladies and gentlemen ... a very warm welcome to Morrie O'Connor's Magic Mile of Masterpieces ... it's bonus time out here at Sydney Town's newest big-deal fine art dealership ... special deals on new, used and superseded Nolans, Drysdales and Pro Harts ... I don't have to tell you good people that this is the new currency and it's better than money in the bank because we ... can offer you more money on your art trade-in than anywhere else in town ...' It was anarchic, ridiculous and pointed. Another new character from old Australia appeared but this time there was no visible nostalgia. In a razor-sharp vignette Humphries played Sir Neville Creamer KBE, a retired, cigar-smoking establishment figure, a widower and a closet homosexual. Greed and corruption in Australia were the targets of each of the sketches, with the new hucksters of the arts providing the fresh face of exploitation, but the old silvertails of the boardroom presented an even darker underside to society.

In spite of the cabaret feel to the show, the repartee with audience members and the massive polystyrene model Jaffa rolled out onto unsuspecting heads, Humphries' barbs were savage and topical and most of the sketches tightly written. The program was anything but capricious.

Humphries had decided to keep Sandy on, and solved the problem of the man's demise in the last production ingeniously, with a new monologue. Sandy retold a dream, 'a horrible dream' in which 'I dropped off the twig', and returned in this sketch as a ghost who haunts the marital home in Glen Iris. The sketch included a film directed by Bruce Beresford of Sandy in his dressing gown, walking slowly towards the camera and placing a milk bottle on his doorstep before everything faded to black.

The reviews were favourable, with the *Sydney Morning Herald* praising Humphries for his 'wicked refinements of speech and expression which illuminate 1974-model Australian humbugs with preternatural clarity'.[1] *The Age* reviewer remarked on the 'uproarious' spoof of the art salesman but found the cabaret style of the opening unsuited to the large Comedy Theatre.[2] Brian Hoad in the *Bulletin* prefaced his review with a description of Edna, whom he presumed to have been 'disowned' by Humphries, referring to her as 'a marauding philistine', 'a creature of crude and overbearing images', a 'female chauvinist pig'. Most importantly he identified Humphries as an 'observer, a mirror of Australian life', rather than an inventor of comic figures. Hoad noted a proliferation of savagery in this new show, and concluded that the accurate satirical reflections on the nation 'are really no laughing matter'.[3] By his own estimation, as declared grandiloquently in the third person in the program for the show, Humphries had become one of the 'shining ornaments of the world-famous Australian Theatrical Renaissance'.

The show returned in September 1975 for a new season at Her Majesty's Theatre in Melbourne. It was a leaner offering: Neil Singleton and another character, Brett Grantworthy, were dropped, but there was a brand new character called Craig Steppenwolf, BA Dip Ed, for whom Ross Fitzgerald had helped Barry write the script. Bearded, with fuzzy hair and buck teeth and clad in fatigues, Steppenwolf wandered into a suburban classroom, slumped into a chair and explained to his teenaged charges how to plug into the 'state's new junior adult multimedia sensory input experience apparatus', complete with 'Timothy Leary's *Simple Student's Guide to the Acid Experience*'. If the students 'chose to come to school, and if you don't, that's cool', their options included 'Body Sculpture, Street Poetry, Dysentery and Syphilis Management in the Commune Situation' and much more. Steppenwolf revealed to those 'of you who are still here', that some teachers had dropped out of the optional classes for the afternoon: 'Ms Germaine Cockburn, after a recent abortion, is still transcendentally tripping on the floor of the tuckshop' and 'Aboriginal literature has been temporarily suspended because Hesse Castanada has just OD'd on the roof of the Bertolt Brecht memorial shed'.

Before offering himself up 'for anyone who's into paederasty', every evening in 'the Ho Chi Min Memorial Unisex Toilet Block', he informed the pupils that not so long ago 'illiteracy was a dirty word' in Australia. 'Universities actually barred students from their faculties merely because they were unable to read and write, count and remember. Thank Christ for Labor!'[4] The text of the provocative satire on radical teachers appeared in *Quadrant* with a centrefold of the leering Steppenwolf, complete with a bandolier slung around his chest. It was a particularly extreme and clever caricature, capturing some of the absurd contradictions of the permissive society.

Humphries' mockery of education in Australia did not stop there. A few years later his daughter Emily enrolled at Geelong Grammar, when it first opened its doors to female students. At one point Humphries wrote a stinging, albeit tongue-in-cheek letter to the school, declining the invitation from Council to contribute to a fund for construction of a new tennis court, 'since I am deeply opposed to all forms of sporting activity, which I have always felt receive far too much emphasis in our "better schools"... The dangers of encouraging tennis have been forcibly brought home to me in recent months by the disclosures about the life of the American tennis star Billie Jean King, who has admitted to the press that the game of tennis contributed to her grievous sexual disorder ... I would always be happy to make a generous financial contribution to any proposal which involved the dismantling of Geelong Grammar's sporting facilities.'[5]

When the stage tour of *At Least You Can Say You've Seen It* finished, Humphries took Tessa and Emily for an extended holiday to Mexico and California. His letters and phone calls were sporadic. But he did take the girls on interesting holidays where they met his artistic and influential friends. Sometimes after the excitement and stimulation of the trips they found it hard to settle back into their day-to-day lives in Melbourne.

Back in Australia Barry took up residence with an artist called Diane Millstead. They had known each other for about a year and had met by chance when Barry wandered into an exhibition of her paintings at the Munster Arms Gallery in Little Bourke Street, behind Her Majesty's Theatre, where he was performing. Diane had never seen Humphries on stage, and had dedicated her career so far to set design and the creation of large surrealist paintings and sculpture.

Diane's ethereal paintings of haunted, vulnerable figures set against huge landscapes captured Barry's imagination. And so did their creator. With a heart-shaped, rather angelic face, large blue-grey eyes and long wavy hair, Diane intrigued Barry from the moment he first glimpsed her at the gallery. One night shortly after the exhibition he visited the young artist at her flat in Elwood, hoping to buy a painting. Diane told a reporter from *Woman's Day* a couple of years later that when she opened her front door she found a 'bizarre and romantic' vision of a man, in a broad-brimmed hat, with 'the moon just behind his shoulder'. It was Barry Humphries. There was an instant chemistry between them.[6]

Barry and Diane shared an interest in drawing, painting and sculpture. Diane, like Barry, wrote poetry. She carried a sketchbook around with her, and like Barry, who hated the ending of a show when the sets are bumped out, she found finishing her paintings emotionally very difficult. Mercurial and fiery in temperament, Diane had been known to demand that paintings she had sold be returned to her, and to have taken back her works from people whom she thought unworthy. She was passionate about her work. She described the genre of her paintings to a Sydney reporter as Romantic Surrealism, and stated confidently that her finished works made her happy. 'Whenever I've been away for a long time, I come up and kiss my paintings hello and talk to them. I love them, they're all so beautiful,' she said.[7]

Diane had determination and a fierce sense of independence. Coming from a large, working-class family in Springvale, she had learned early to fight to defend her interests. Her mother had encouraged her to leave school and take a job in a factory when she was fifteen, but she stayed on at high school, and afterwards continued her studies at the Royal Melbourne Institute of Technology. She worked at the Melbourne Theatre Company before extending her skills as a scene painter at the Ulmer Stadt Theatre in Germany. Humphries' blossoming relationship with Diane marked the beginning of a new period of immense happiness and prosperity for him.

A brief television interview changed Humphries' fortunes almost overnight, and propelled him back onto the British stage. Although he had appeared in several sketch comedy shows, Edna, his pre-eminent character, had never succeeded in Britain. She was now a movie star, however, and a Dame, and an appearance on Russell Harty's popular chat show in 1975 changed everything. Edna appeared in an orange and black wool coat purchased from Selfridges, and white knee-high, lace-up boots. Trundling onto the set clutching her handbag, she greeted the host with a cheery 'Hello Simon,' and nodded 'How do you do,' to the studio audience. Edna soon apologised for getting Harty's name wrong and said, 'Haven't you done well? You started from nothing and look at you.' She was outlandish, ridiculous and funny, apologising that Barry Humphries was unable to appear due to jet lag, and because of 'a vasectomy on Diners Card'. Years later Humphries told the broadcaster Melvyn Bragg that it was the first time that he *felt* funny as Edna in the UK.[8] It was twenty years since he had first played Edna in Melbourne as a shy and genteel housewife. He was already well known in Australia; over the next ten years Edna would become a household name in Britain.

Shortly after Humphries' appearance on Russell Harty's program, a producer, Michael White, approached him with a proposal for a new stage show. Humphries was ready to launch himself in the West End again. The orange and black houndstooth coat went into mothballs. It was the last time Humphries bought Edna's costumes off the rack.

A dandyish figure, Michael White had been educated in Switzerland and at the Sorbonne, and gained his stripes as an assistant to Peter Daubeny, the famous impresario and the founder of London's World Theatre Season, an annual festival of foreign plays in their original languages. By 1975 he was regarded as a wunderkind of the West End. Not only was he intelligent and driven, he had an eye for the risqué and the unusual. In Barry Humphries he recognised rare theatrical genius and enormous commercial potential.

Humphries' life moved into an intense and exciting new phase. Thanks to White, he was busily writing scripts for his new stage show. He had also signed a contract for a new television show — *The Barry Humphries Show* — that would screen just before *Housewife Superstar!* was due to open at the Apollo Theatre in Shaftesbury Avenue. His personal life was happy and stable, and he was looking forward to Diane's arrival in London.

Barry had written the three-part comedy series for BBC2 with Ian Davidson, whom he had met when working on *The Late Show*. In Episode One, Edna welcomed viewers to her 'Silver Jubilee'. 'Now don't accuse me of being a copycat,' she said, referring to the Queen's recent milestone. 'Just because a little friend of mine has just had hers and attracted a certain amount of publicity.' The show screened in prime time against *Panorama* on BBC1. One anonymous reviewer in *The Times* declared unequivocally: 'S(he) is exquisite.'[9]

Housewife Superstar! opened on 16 March 1976 at the extraordinary hour of 11 pm so the audiences could catch the show after other West End productions. It was an exciting new beginning for Humphries, with Edna now well and truly the star of the show. This time the title of the show was not one of the phrases tossed off by Barry's aunts, but clearly positioned Edna as a pop idol, borrowing cheekily from the name of the spectacularly successful rock opera launched on Broadway in 1971 and subsequently playing all around the world: *Jesus Christ Superstar*. The show also marked the debut appearance of the character Les Patterson in Britain, elevated by Humphries from entertainment officer at the St George Leagues Club to Australian Cultural Attaché in London.

Seating nearly eight hundred patrons on four levels, the Apollo Theatre had been built during the Edwardian period, and featured sculpted fascia work and a private foyer. With his love of all things Edwardian, it was a fitting venue for Humphries to bring Edna back to London. She regaled the audience with her waspish and arrogant certainties, and her curious revelations about her family. Barry had recently seen Reg Livermore's subversive one-man revue, *Betty Blokk Buster Follies,* in Sydney and felt confident in transforming his own show into a visually spectacular stage event, rather than a show driven primarily by words. Whereas previously the jokes relied on the content of Humphries' sketches and the language, now the show offered a feast for the senses.

Australian flags festooned the theatre as gigantic plastic balls bounced over the front few rows of the audience and across the stage. Les, large-bellied and beery, as if at a great party, described the night's entertainment as Australia's reply to the new 'Pom National Theatre'.[10] This 'reply' included the somnolent Sandy Stone in the second act, nodding off over his *Reader's Digest* in bed.

With a shorter program than usual, and more emphasis on Edna, dolled up with a wisteria rinse, a denim outfit and turquoise tights, Humphries took his performance to new extremes. Edna teased, cajoled and mesmerised the crowd. 'Don't be in awe of me, I'm an ordinary person,' she implored her 'possums', striking up conversations, throwing out barbs and dispensing nicknames: 'Lobes', 'Ashtray', 'Little English Person', 'Virgo' and 'Gargoyles' were a few of her endearments. She chatted about star signs, names and countries of origin. She informed her 'lovely audience' of her psychic powers and ability to read Tetley teabags, mentioning affectionately her sons Brucie, married to Joylene, and Kenny, who sometimes liked to borrow her dresses. Although Edna was manic in this show, she was also affectionate and playful. From time to time she reassured the audience: 'I'm just silly, don't worry.'

The West End critics were enchanted, with Ned Chaillet of *The Times* proclaiming Dame Edna to be a character so exact she was almost real, one who ranked with the creations of George Burns and Jack Benny.[11] At last the critics could see Humphries' vaudeville roots, and appreciated his skill with audiences.

Humphries had given Charles Osborne a ticket for a seat in the front stalls for the show. As the lights went down after interval, Osborne noticed a dishevelled drunk lurching towards the orchestra pit. He wondered whether to alert the ushers who were standing calmly at the end of his row. Unable to catch anyone's attention he watched in horror as the drunk staggered through the pit and clambered onto the stage. Suddenly the spotlight was on the intruder: it was Les Patterson. Les stumbled towards the microphone and slurred, 'Testing ... one, two, three, four ... fuck.' He then vanished, only to reappear with a double Scotch and a cigarette. 'Good evening, ladies and gentlemen ... can I have a little shush up the back?' he began, introducing himself to London's West End patrons. The audience was stunned. Leslie Colin Patterson was the new face of Barry's ocker alter ego, a foul-mouthed, shambolic, yet exuberant political clown. In defiance of the critics of Barry McKenzie and the howls of shame at his destruction of Australia's image in Britain, Humphries unambiguously rubbed salt into the wounds.

His monologue as Les was delivered with perfect nonchalance, despatching the nay-sayers with a mischievous and brilliant spoof of the pious attacks against him. Les confessed to the audience that in his capacity as Cultural Attaché to the Court of St James's and head of the Australian Fine Arts Task Force, he met 'all kinds and I bump into a lot of expatriates, but strangely enough it's the Australian ex-pat that really gives me the toms'. Les explained his antipathy to the 'long-haired, limp-wristed, plum-in-the-mouth elitist variety who come over here and turn a quid by knocking their homeland. You all know the sort who depict their fellow Australians as a bunch of ockers, piss artists and foul-mouthed, beer-swilling Bazza McPhersons.' He reminded the audience that such people are as 'low as the basic wage, as low as snakes' armpits' and that if he ran into one of them 'rubbishing their homeland and knocking our famous finesse and refinement I'll kick his teeth so far down his throat he'll have to stick his toothbrush up his freckle to clean them. Because I am here to tell you we've got culture in Australia, ladies and gentlemen. We've got culture up to our *arseholes*! I'm sorry ladies. I'm a bit full.'

Not only was it razor sharp, Humphries' return of fire towards his critics back in Australia was perfectly judged in its parody. True to Humphries' style it ridiculed the entire episode. The boozy Les Patterson also allowed Barry to revel in the excesses of Australian masculinist humour. In his stained suit and leering at the audience Les came to represent another assault on aspects of Australian masculinity. The vulgar Les is Humphries' most grotesque character; he is boorish and bigoted, but he is not the typical ocker male. Nor is he the larrikin of earlier Australian humour. Les is not archly self-conscious or witty or egalitarian.[12] Nor is he aggressive. He is the ugly public figure who rorts the system for all he is worth, and in Humphries' new cast of characters Les was to become the symbol of the ridiculousness of Australian political life and the excesses of new nationalism. (In the Australia of the 1980s, he became a comic version of Russ Hinze, the corpulent Queensland politician known for his passion for horse racing and sometimes called the 'Minister for Everything'.) Humphries had always relished the opportunity to provocatively reject masculinist culture, ever since he first turned his back on the football at Melbourne Grammar to knit. Now he blended this performance with a parody of the pretensions of Australians fervent for their own 'culcha'.

In 1976 Michael Humphries took his mother to see Barry perform in a short season at the Mandarin Hotel in Hong Kong, staged during a break in the London run. As Louisa and Michael walked out of the lift in the hotel to enter the venue for the show, they were met by a man they didn't recognise who ambled towards them grinning. It was 'Les Patterson'. They had no idea the dishevelled character in front of them was their flesh and blood. Louisa enjoyed the trip to Hong Kong but she never warmed to the drunken diplomat. She would say to Barry with exasperation: 'Do you have to say that?'[13] Barry ignored her protestations and Les became an audience favourite.

It was a particularly hot summer in London and Barry sweated profusely in his polyester Les suit. With no air conditioning at the Apollo or the Globe (where the show had transferred), the four-month season of *Housewife Superstar!* proved to be a gruelling endurance test. But the packed houses filled Humphries with joy. He was thrilled with the warmth of the response to his show. As the horse-racing season approached, Barry asked his wardrobe designer, Jane Hamilton, to arrange a special hat for Dame Edna.[14]

Lorraine McKee created the hat that would launch Edna's image around the world. This headpiece featured a massive model of the Sydney Opera House, the building that had recently replaced the boomerang as the icon of Australia. The upper side of the brim was made of blue and purple satin with turquoise netting. White lace 'wave caps' simulated the waters of Sydney Harbour, complete with six canvas yachts and a shark's head baring diamante-studded teeth. The hat measured 120 centimetres (47 inches) in width and 41 centimetres (16 inches) in height. A sumptuous model of the shell-like buildings in stiffened white satin draped in beige rayon twill resulted in a crowd-stopping racing carnival hat, completing Edna's otherwise demure outfit, a floral dress and white gloves, at Royal Ascot.

In the past, Edna had sometimes failed to attract attention, once throwing herself into the path of Sir Robert Menzies outside the Savoy in London, only to be ignored. But Edna's appearance in her new hat was a triumph, attracting massive publicity. The image of Edna cheekily peeping out from beneath the broderie-anglaise underside of the brim, with its rich purple tinsel braid around the edge, was quirky, kitsch and whimsical. Photographs were splashed across newspapers in the UK and Australia. Edna received more coverage than the Queen and her entourage on that auspicious day.

The Opera House hat was a grand gesture in Humphries' lifelong campaign to bring Australian humour to the world. Dame Edna had appeared in a controversial comedy with the former prime minister, Gough Whitlam, and now wore a model of the most significant public building opened during Whitlam's term in office balanced on her head. It was also a sartorial milestone: the spectacular hat was Edna's first commissioned accessory, and marked the beginning of a new phase in the development of the character. The success of the hat spurred Barry on in his enthusiasm for having Edna's gowns specially designed and made, each one more sumptuous than the last.

By this time Humphries understood the importance of synchronicity in the world of entertainment and commerce. As *Housewife Superstar!* opened in the West End, Humphries released a book entitled *Dame Edna's Coffee Table Book*. It was a slim, large-format, heavily illustrated volume that included the lyrics of a song Edna had crooned on the BBC called 'A Woman's Woman'.

I'm just a woman
Who loves other women.
I'm funny that way.
I adore the caress
Of someone in a dress

A mini
A pinnie
Or a negligee.

If you've had sleepless nights
Because your man demands his 'rights'
Till you think you may be going round the bend
DON'T resort to alcohol like other women have
Gather up your Valium and throw them down the lav,
For there's SOMETHING ELSE on which you
May depend:
When your world is in a muddle
And you crave a nice long cuddle
A woman is a girl's Best Friend!

Barry delighted in announcing that the book was available in 'limp' and 'stiff' formats. It contained commendations from Patrick White, Mia Farrow, James Mason, Dudley Moore, Joan Bakewell, John Cleese, Sidney Nolan, Stephen Sondheim and others. Even the Reverend William P Baddeley, rector of St James's Church Piccadilly and formerly Dean of Brisbane, hailed the work as 'an invaluable guide to gracious living and Higher Thought' from this 'fountain of wisdom and doyenne of Australian womanhood'. Patrick White, the Australian Nobel laureate, praised the book for its useful advice: 'whether beating the daylights into a fluffy sponge or taking a chisel to a plastic doily, whether jollying the timorous male or popping a reluctant blackhead, let Dame Edna be your guide', he wrote.[15] After declaring herself 'the Toast of London', Edna confessed to being a 'teeny bit Left Wing in my views, since my Damehood was bestowed on me by a politician with similar leanings to my good self'.[16]

Humphries had been cautious with the content of the book. He featured saucy photos of Edna on holiday in Paris, ludicrous beauty tips and anatomical drawings of the prostate, but the language was mild in comparison with Edna on stage, and a far cry from the scatological humour of Bazza McKenzie and the provocations of

Bizarre. Edna counsels readers on manners and the right way to use particular phrases, especially for those travelling overseas. 'Why do you think Prince Charles was sent to school in Australia?' she asks, before explaining how to use terms such as 'viable', which she defines as 'something worth doing', unlike the shows by the comic Barry Humphries that are not 'viable' and rather 'irrelevant'. Edna cautions readers that 'when people are having a discussion on the telly or on the stage of one of our smaller subsidised theatres and you cannot understand a word they are talking about, the show is said to be "meaningful"'.

In a section called 'Living and Loving Together', Edna informs readers that 'it is a mother's duty to ensure that her daughter is quietly and firmly instructed before embarking on the Horror of her Honeymoon'. She states that it has been scientifically proven 'that Australians are not very interested in sex. Why should we be interested in the seamy side of life with so many natural wonders to occupy our imagination?' In spite of this she admits that 'due to some glandular abnormality, husbands often overstep the limits of modesty' and that one of her friends from the tennis club had confided to her that whenever the threat of molestation was near, 'five minutes with a needle and cotton on her unsuspecting hubby's pyjama bottoms was time well spent'.[17]

The book is a glorious parody of the standard formula for women's magazines, complete with Edna's cooking ideas for dishes such as Cambodian Camp Pie Surprise, Funnel Web Spider Cake and Moomba Meat Balls, all pictured in grotesque colour spreads, along with instructions for folding a serviette into the shape of the Opera House and an introduction to yoga using the 'Everage Method' — with photographs of the leotard-clad Dame in every pose. Full colour photographs of Edna fill the book, with one spectacular page devoted to a portrait of Edna placing a basket of flowers at the grave of Karl Marx, whom she describes as a 'very wonderful and unassuming little person', whose poems she regrettably has not read. A whimsical drawing of Dame Edna by the theatrical caricaturist Nerman shows her waving a wand-like gladioli stem in the air as she gazes towards the heavens.

Another image shows Edna with the future prime minister, Bob Hawke, reading from a book called *Etiquette*. The caption, 'Me coaching a particularly ambitious little Aussie politician in a few of Life's finer shades', encapsulated Edna's giddy rise since her ennobling at the hands of Hawke's Labor predecessor at the Lodge.[18]

The *Housewife Superstar!* season in London marked Edna's transformation into a recognised West End character. Dame Edna now mixed with 'nobility' and the book featured a photograph of herself drinking tea with Lady Olivier 'at the time we both had runs in the West End'. Humphries parodied Edna's rise but he was ecstatic to have succeeded in London at last.

CHAPTER 23

Hell's Kitchen

In the winter of 1977 Michael White and the American producer Arthur Cantor convinced Humphries to present *Housewife! Superstar!* in New York. It was an ambitious proposal, despite the brilliant London season. Cantor, like White, was a very successful entrepreneur with an especially keen eye for comedy. His instinct for the unusual had paid off for the first time in 1959 when he funded *The Tenth Man*, a strange comedy by Paddy Chayefsky about a young girl possessed by a demon. Tyrone Guthrie directed the play, which was nominated for several awards.

Cantor had not previously seen Humphries perform. The advertisements daringly proclaimed Edna as 'Australia's answer to the Jewish Mother'. *Housewife! Superstar!* opened on 19 October at Theater Four, an off-Broadway venue in Hell's Kitchen on the west side of Manhattan. When Humphries arrived in New York and met Cantor in the flesh, he found him to be a rather lugubrious character and was unnerved when the impresario admitted that he had never seen Humphries perform. Barry learned that *The Boys in the Band*, a bitchy play about a group of homosexual men in Manhattan, had recently played one thousand performances at Theater Four, and was horrified to hear Cantor's expectation that 'another fag show might do well there'.[1]

Ian Davidson helped Barry adapt the London production for an

American audience and Humphries invited Brian Thomson, brother of his friend Ken, to design a whimsical set. Iris Mason, the pianist, was placed atop a 'grassy knoll', complete with fairy lights and small pixies.[2] Humphries appeared on the late-night television comedy show *Saturday Night Live* in the lead-up to his opening, and also on Bill Boggs' midday program. He took tea with journalists at the fashionable Backstage restaurant, where he painstakingly explained his act. An optimist at heart, Humphries was confident that the show would be successful, and the previews went well. The presence of Stephen Sondheim and a group of his friends at one preview gave the production some gravitas. Humphries remembers Charles Addams, the creator of the blackly comical *Addams Family* television series, sitting in the front row laughing uproariously. But Cantor's behaviour worried Humphries. In an effort to reassure him that the show would be a success, Cantor had told Barry that the *New York Times* critic was a friend of his, and that he would drive the critic back to the newspaper office after the show. To Barry, well schooled in British reserve, this was a preposterous idea, guaranteed to tempt fate. But there was no stopping the suave producer.[3]

The show included an overture by Iris Mason at the piano, and 'A Brief Word from Dame Edna Everage'. It lasted nearly two hours, and only one of Barry's other characters appeared. Les Patterson opened the show in his dazzling blue suit and tangerine shirt, introducing himself as Australian Cultural Attaché to the United Nations. It was a huge risk to spring Patterson as well as Edna Everage on an audience who had never set eyes on either character before. Humphries had no idea how Les would go over with Americans. Mustering all his confidence, he clattered onto the stage to explain the rationale for the show: 'Why not present an ordinary woman with no talent whatsoever?' Les said of Edna Everage. Les slurped from a large tumbler of whisky; he was paunchy and toothy, with a clearly padded cock reaching down almost to the knee and seeping ever so slightly — the picture of Australian diplomatic aplomb. Yet only one of the sixteen reviews mentioned Les's priapic appurtenance. 'Australia is the new

America,' croaked Les to his stupefied audience. 'So fast paced is life in the cities down under that Australians love to visit New York for a little bit of peace and quiet.' It was a daring attempt to turn American assumptions and expectations upside-down.

Les described Australia's triumphant defeat of the Japanese in the war, the reason, he said, for the small number of Japanese restaurants in New York. But the focus of the show was squarely on Edna, who flounced on stage in a denim suit and espadrilles, and sat with her legs firmly crossed in a wicker chair as she chatted with the audience, alternately lavishing them with compliments and then insulting them with her gaffes and odd remarks. 'A lot of people think I'm a Red Sea pedestrian,' said Edna, striking a confessional note and taking a risk in a city with the largest Jewish community in the United States. Mentioning a painting at her sister-in-law's place, she quipped: '*The Scream* by Edvard Munch, or is it *The Munch* by Edvard Scream?' It was a revelation to Humphries that New Yorkers seemed to like jokes about art and artists.

Edna hurled gladioli around the theatre, and led the audience in her gutsy gladdie-waving anthem. She chatted to a few 'possums' about their 'homes', and engaged in banter about bathrooms. One audience member announced that she had five bathrooms. It was truly a land of extremes, but the housewifely Edna seemed nowhere near extreme enough to counter the problems of translation. Perhaps the focus on an anecdotal Edna was the problem, without the extravagant dancing and musical interludes that now punctuate the sketches. Barry's accent may also have meant the jokes were not always fully understood. Clearly some of the reviewers found the Australian accent difficult and referred to Les as 'Laz'.

It happened to be a season of one-performer shows on and off Broadway, and so *Housewife! Superstar!* did not immediately stand out. Ultimately the show was a fizzer in the Big Apple but this is not apparent from a survey of the reviews. Don Nelsen of the *Daily News* admired Humphries for his transfiguration into Edna. He remarked that 'No trace of Humphries the man remained.' He *was* Dame Edna. Nelsen praised Humphries' control of the audience and his 'skewering satire' of suburban life. But he found the humour uneven and Edna's voice 'as grating as unoiled gears'.[4] Edmund Newton in the *New York Post* declared the show 'a patently pointless evening with all the redeeming social value of the mumps, yet somehow enjoyable'. Newton found the mix of vaudeville, insult, British wit, farce and surrealism biting, and marvelled at the 'tension between victim and verbal assailant' that sustained the energy of the show.[5] The *Christian Science Monitor* critic found Edna both 'dreadful' and 'dreadfully funny'.[6]

Rex Reed in the *Daily News* praised Edna's 'wonderful, wicked parody of middle-class ignorance', so realistic it was 'downright eerie'. Reed seemed especially attuned to Humphries' satire and theatrical style, delighting in the show as a 'banquet of madness'.[7] Only a few critics warmed entirely to Edna's satiric onslaughts, however. Getting her name wrong, she was by turns Edith and Everedge; they completely missed the satire explicit in the name 'Everage'. And at least a third of the Broadway critics found the prolonged exchanges with the audience dull.

Most frustrating for Humphries was the confusion over whether he was engaging in a drag act. One critic described the show as 'fey and raunchy', and referred to Humphries as a 'female impersonator' who unsurprisingly pelted the audience with gladioli — 'of course, the gayest flower of them all'.[8] Another critic found the 'gay self-mockery' of the act offensive.[9] Others dismissed the blend of low comedy and night-club camp as too undergraduate for their taste.

Howard Kissel of *Women's Wear Daily* announced the show was a 'breakthrough in drag queen class awareness', explaining that many drag queens pretend to stardom but 'Dame Edna knows this is an illusion — she is not afraid to confront the reality of bourgeois life'. He remarked that 'some of Dame Edna's jokes are a bit worn and crude, but the daffiness of it, the inspired silliness of Humphries' character, yes, the endearing middle-class-ness of it all, redeems a lot'.[10] The gossip columnist Earl Wilson proclaimed the show to be 'a smash', the comedian someone 'who rambles on hilariously'.[11]

Some critics did not hold back. Edith Oliver in the *New Yorker* gave Humphries short shrift in a single paragraph reviewing the show. Oliver identified Humphries as a comedian 'in drag without any winking or mincing', who 'impersonates a bitchy middle-aged woman called Dame Edna Everage. The characterization is detailed, but the character is a bore, and most — by no means all — of the jokes are awful. Why the lady is a Dame is never explained, but, God knows, everything else is.' At least Oliver observed Iris enjoying herself in the show, and gave her the last throwaway sentence, declaring that 'Iris Mason cuts up at the piano.'[12] Right at the end of the run, as the audience thinned out, the show received a very positive review in *Variety* as 'hysterically funny', with 'deliciously unmerciful' put-downs of the audience from Edna and the self-appointed master of ceremonies, 'Laz' Patterson, 'who could out-bigot the likes of Archie Bunker'.[13]

It was the *New York Times* review that crushed Humphries and left him bitterly disappointed. In the most damning review of his career, Humphries was slammed by the acidic, newly appointed theatre critic on the major newspaper in the metropolis, under the devastating banner '1-Man Show Is One Too Many'.[14] Richard Eder declared that the show 'gives new depths to the phrase "Down Under". It is abysmal.' Eder was scathing about almost every element of the production. He found it dull, the program 'achingly' slow, with 'no outrage and still less comedy'. For Eder, even the gladioli-waving was laboured; the only bright spot for him was Les Patterson who was 'mildly amusing'.

Not even Iris Mason was spared. Eder was mystified at this woman seated at the piano in her velvet gown, who played briefly and then sat for the rest of the evening 'displaying a fixed grin'. The plaster gnomes that decorated Iris's knoll, thought to be 'humorously decorative' at first, by the end of the show seemed to Eder to represent 'ossified patrons of some earlier Humphries performance'. Speculating that audiences in London might enjoy having their prejudices against loud, beer-swilling Australians nourished, Eder turned the knife, as this was precisely the criticism Humphries encountered from irate Australians who accused him of exploiting his countrymen in order to pander to English audiences. In his review Eder insisted that for New Yorkers this kind of humour was irrelevant and tedious.

For Humphries the vituperative *New York Times* review was not only deflating, it was paralysing, as the word 'Abysmal' appeared beside the notice for the show in every issue of the newspaper, every day for the entire run. Even Cantor, his supposed friend, and White were wounded by the harshness of Eder's review. As the audiences grew thinner Cantor approached Rupert Murdoch pleading for some kind of favour. Gradually they all faced the reality of the situation, and the show closed after four weeks. The truth is that American critics were ill prepared for Edna Everage, and even those who praised aspects of the show regarded it as a lightweight drag act. The only consolation for Humphries was the fact that Diane was with him during the disastrous season. She was a constant source of joy and support as he battled his disappointment.

An Australian reporter rubbed salt into the wounds, describing Edna's reception in New York with humiliating clarity in the national newspaper. Graeme Beaton, the New York correspondent for the *Australian*, turned Barry's Jaffa joke back on its creator: 'Australia's First Lady, Dame Edna Everage, has gone down on Broadway as a Jaffa might descend a lift-well at the Empire State Building.'[15] Beaton summarised the barbs of the Broadway critics, failing to mention all but one of the positive reviews. It was Humphries' worst nightmare and fulfilled all his fears.

Although Humphries' audiences had been small, the considerable praise that he received among the less positive reviews suggested that Americans were not entirely unreceptive to his talents. One reviewer called him Australia's answer to Don Rickles; another mentioned the possibility of the show being intended as a gloss on Strindberg's *The Stronger*. The reception was not nearly as warm as he had hoped for but it was much more favourable than his first appearance in London at the Establishment Club in 1963. It was always unlikely that Humphries would create an overnight success. It took a decade for the Monty Python troupe to attract a following in the United States even with frequent television appearances. But the review in the *New York Times* and the lacerating reports of the response in the Australian press hit Barry hard.

To make matters worse, the most interesting and salutary review appeared after the show had closed. Andy Warhol's magazine, *Interview*, ran a double-page spread on Humphries. A photograph of Barry in a three-piece pinstriped suit and monocle appeared above the caption 'Dame Edna Everage as Barry Humphries'.[16] Ironically the review was written by the waif-like Warhol acolyte Tinkerbelle, who had once had her own rather shocking cable television show. Sometimes called 'Stinkerbelle', she revelled in rude and provocative interview questions, and clearly loved Humphries' stage show, describing Edna as 'versatile' and 'New York's answer to a laughing gas shortage ... anyone itching for a terminal case of the sillies cannot afford to pass up this assault of lunacy.'

If the audiences were not ready for Edna, perhaps Humphries had not been ready for them either. Edna's blatant rudeness and hypocritical excesses were not quite artful enough for New Yorkers, and many of the jokes did not touch the listeners. Visually Edna was not exciting; her sidekick and pianist, the tiny Iris Mason, looked more glamorous in her Mae West wig and feather boa. Edna's hairstyle was understated and her Pegasus-winged glasses were modest by comparison with the spectacles that were to become her signature accessory in the years that followed.

Humphries' critique of society and its deadening domestic rituals was not clearly articulated and therefore not fully apparent to the majority of the reviewers, much less the audience. Americans were confused about whether or not Edna was a drag act, and as John Lahr observed many years later the pantomime dame tradition was not one they understood.[17] It took another two decades for Humphries to summon the courage to perform again on stage in the United States.

CHAPTER 24

Regeneration

Humphries' confidence was shattered. As soon as possible he fled New York for the warmth of Los Angeles and took a suite at the Chateau Marmont on Sunset Boulevard. He was bitter about his reception in New York and uncertain of what to do, and the next few months were difficult. He was disheartened and sometimes behaved recklessly. A warrant for his arrest was issued when he failed to respond to a traffic citation. He was ordered to appear in court on 10 April 1978. When the fines were paid and the mess sorted out, he began to relax a little and stopped brooding about the disaster in New York.

Gradually he regained his energy and started to write sketch material for a new show. He enjoyed the grandeur of the Marmont, and the stories of its glamorous guests. Judy Garland had sung beside the grand piano in the foyer, Greta Garbo retreated to the Chateau for weeks at a time, and Vivien Leigh took comfort in the hotel during her estrangement from Laurence Olivier. Now Humphries was also taking refuge in the infamous, exclusive hotel.

Humphries was pleased to glimpse Edna back on the screen, even if it was in a crowd scene in the bizarre 1978 American musical film flop, *Sergeant Pepper's Lonely Hearts Club Band*, which followed the fortunes of a pop band, played by the Bee Gees and Peter Frampton, with a soundtrack by the Beatles. After the panning of his New York stage show, Humphries' attempt to gain a following in the United States seemed hopeless.

He knew instinctively that the only way to recover from a bruising such as he had experienced in New York was to launch into another show in the relatively safe haven of Australia. In the lead-up to the tour Humphries gave an address at the National Press Club in Canberra. It was not the first time he had addressed the club, but on this occasion his performance was candid and amusing. In a tweed three-piece suit and polka-dot bow tie, his hair combed over from a side part, Humphries appeared to chat amiably about all sorts of topics. In fact the speech was fully scripted and offered journalists a rare glimpse of the man without his usual character masks, reflecting on his work as an 'artiste', as he loved to call himself.

Humphries began with a startling admission: 'I think it surprises members of the public to learn that stage performers, stage artistes and vaudeville personages like myself do suffer from stage fright. But I always do. Quite often in fact I'm physically ill before any public appearance. There's usually a plastic bucket in the wings when I do my stage shows,' he confessed.

He delighted the audience with his revelations about writing the new show and being a 'professional procrastinator'. 'I do not commence writing until the first ticket is bought,' he reported, 'as it is so entertaining to me to think that there's some poor character actually paying for something that doesn't exist.' Humphries charmed his listeners with his remark that audiences come to the theatre, as they do to Press Club luncheons, 'with an immense store of goodwill, which it's very hard to exhaust'. Then he let them in on his technique, explaining that 'an audience always laughs much louder if they're extremely anxious', and so, during the performance, 'I remind them of all the terrible things that could be happening at home. Was the kitchen window firmly locked? What kind of cigarettes is the babysitter smoking? How many friends is she at present entertaining? All of these things, I think, should put them in a very good mood … a very receptive mood.'

Having softened up his audience, Humphries suggested there might be merit in the practice of critics writing 'the reviews first';

typewriters could be provided in the foyer of the theatre so that reviewers could write the review before entering and enjoying the show 'in a relaxed frame of mind'. After more than two decades, a newly philosophical Barry Humphries was attempting to befriend his critics.

The climax of the speech was a droll recollection of an unfortunate reality in show business: 'I have had people die during my shows,' Humphries said calmly. He described one occasion. 'As I left the theatre I noticed some screens had been erected ... until the ambulance arrived. But the usherettes were shaking their heads and alas the customer had caught the last ferry, as they say. But it pleased me to see a seraphic smile on his ashen lips, and in his pale grasp was still clenched a wilting gladioli.'[1]

In May that year Humphries launched his new Australian show, *Isn't It Pathetic at His Age*, at Her Majesty's Theatre in Sydney. Once again he borrowed a familiar refrain from his childhood, recalling his mother's deprecating comments about former matinee idols cavorting on stage in shameful displays of vulgarity, entirely inappropriate for men of their advanced years. He wrote a song with a magnificent chorus for Edna.

> *Wasn't I terrific for my age?*
> *Chockablock with talent and witty persiflage.*
> *Whatever you felt about the show*
> *I'm sure you must agree*
> *That as living legends come and go*
> *There's nothing quite like me ...*

Isn't It Pathetic at His Age defused potential criticism with its subtitle, *The Most Out of Touch Show in Town*. It was four years since Barry had opened a show in Sydney. Ian Davidson directed, there were new stage managers in Ian Tasker and David Murray and a glossy, larger format program with a photo on the cover of a meek and sweet-looking Barry aged four, dressed in a sailor suit. Entirely at odds with this picture of innocence, a haunted adult Barry, dressed as a monk, stared out of a full-page photograph within the program's covers. He was standing beneath a bizarre star-shaped arrangement of human bones affixed to a wall. The image was captured in the Chapel of All Saints at Sedlec, an ossuary near Prague, where Humphries had nourished his interest in funerary customs. Barry's impulse for the strange and grotesque might have been sidelined along with his book *Bizarre*, but it certainly was not extinguished.

Iris Mason, who had worked with Barry for the previous seven years, was no longer part of the show. Iris had been a joyful and colourful pianist and showed affection for Barry's daughters, giving them sweets and biscuits whenever she spotted them visiting the theatre or waiting in the wings for their father. Iris enjoyed a drink, and once Emily Humphries discovered her in her dressing room stabbing at her huge false eyelashes; she had somehow put them on the wrong way. They were clamped shut; Iris could not open her eyes until Emily summoned help for the humiliated woman.

This time Charles Field accompanied Barry on the piano. Once again Les Patterson officiated, describing himself as a 'maverick' and a 'wag', 'a hard-nosed carpet-bagging trouble-shooter … known in diplomatic circles … [as an] Australian Henry Kissinger'. After the disastrous New York show in which Edna dominated, Barry returned to his trusty format of multiple characters, with a firm eye on recognisably Australian caricature. Edna did not appear until after the interval in a long sketch called 'A Glimpse of La Everage'.

One of the two new characters was a homosexual man, bearded and bespectacled, called Roger A Nunn, founder of the First Church of Christ the Motorist, offering the 'good oil' on worship of cars and motorbikes. It was Humphries' third attempt at portraying a queer character. There was also a trade union official — Secretary of the NSW Branch of the AGRO — one Lance Xavier Boyle, on a junket in Hong Kong en route to the Stella B Glickstein Southern Baptist University of Alabama to take up a Churchill Fellowship. In his underwear and short bathrobe and socks, Boyle talked for the entire sketch on his hotel room telephone. He sat on the lounge chatting to a call girl, then to his wife, Maureen, back home, and finally to his secretary, Leonie. On the floor his oversized Samsonite briefcase spilled out its contents of girlie magazines, duty-free cigarettes and gleaming bottles of whisky. Humphries' rapier was pointed at hypocritical left-wing trade union bosses, with their sanctimonious clichés, vulgar expressions and constant trips abroad. Lance's refrain was 'It's hot as buggery up here,' as he ranted to Leonie about his substandard hotel accommodation. 'It's a question of a man's position, isn't it?' he bellowed. 'After all, Halfpenny always stays at the Mandarin, doesn't he? And Bob Hawke is always living it up at the Peninsula with his Jew-boy mates.'

Boyle barked out a press statement for Leonie to take down on the phone: 'Mr Boyle indicated he was sickened and appalled by the conditions suffered by the Chinese ethnic minority in Hong Kong ... Australian businessmen who patronise these sweatshops ... no, no ... Australian elitist multinational fascist businessmen who patronise these sweatshops deserve nothing but —' He stopped dictating as he opened a package of new monogrammed shirts, and looked aghast at the breast pockets. Enraged, he shouted out a stream of abuse. 'Those bastards have got my initials wrong. Those dirty lazy slant-eyed mongrel bastards. Dixon Street will burn for this. I'll slap a green ban on the yellow bastards. They'll pay.'

Boyle's tirade offered one of Humphries' sharpest and funniest portraits of hypocrisy, misogyny and self-righteous greed. It poked fun at the blokey deals that littered Australian political life during this period. It was social criticism of the most biting and excoriating kind.

Immediately after the Lance Boyle sketch, Humphries returned to the stage as Sandy, with his meandering stories and soporific tones. Seated in an armchair, he announced with grim finality: 'I am deceased.' Sandy could be one of Beckett's characters in this monologue, in which he described his own rather meagre funeral. Coming straight after the vehement and repulsive Boyle, Sandy was pathetic and poignant. 'Needless to say there wasn't much of a turn-up at the funeral. My wife must have a bit of Scotch blood in her because she got a few quotes on me first — she put out tenders — but in the end she settled for a very reasonable little firm ... Nice vehicle too — burgundy, power steering ...'

But Sandy also lamented deeds left undone in his life, and all his unfinished business: 'But I suppose that when you catch the ferry you're bound to leave something on the jetty,' he said. Although he remembered waking every morning with good intentions, Sandy never managed to do what he should have done and that was to 'defrost the fridge'. Because of this last failing, a crayfish Sandy had left on the kitchen bench gave off the stench that led the next-door neighbours to his corpse.

The monologue blended innocence and existential pain, its strange mix of the mundane and profound delighting the audience. Sandy's monologue was excruciating as he described the small group of mourners, some of them present by mistake, and Beryl's tepid expressions of grief.

In this monologue, 'Sandy Soldiers On', Humphries established Stone as a character of enduring appeal. He embodies Humphries' most nostalgic portrayal of Australian masculinity, a totally domesticated man who is a ghostly representative of Australia before the social revolution of the 1960s. Sandy is obsessed with the details of domestic life. Unlike Bazza McKenzie and Les Patterson he is a tragic character, a kindly man whose life was exceptionally dull and crushingly conventional. He and Beryl have not been able to have children, but Sandy Stone accepts this just as he accepts everything else. Even his name evokes the dry, the barren and the crumbling. In life Sandy is an emasculated and neglected character, and in death an even more tragic and abandoned figure.

There is no mistaking the critique of Australian masculinity in the depiction of the old man from Glen Iris. In the monologues his voice is croaky and weak, his speech tentative and halting. Yet the descriptions Sandy gives are detailed and vivid. They are full of Australian expressions, many of them obsolete or anachronistic. The expatriate writer and broadcaster Clive James admired the 'satisfying density of texture' of the scripts and the poetic language of this character. For James, Sandy Stone is the only character to whom Humphries is fair.[2]

The show was to be the last one in which Humphries performed male characters so vividly, and with so much variety.

His three best-known male characters offer a picture of continuing alienation from the mother country, with Sandy Stone the most loyal. He is a man who accepts himself as an Austral Briton. Barry McKenzie queried the allegiance to mother England with alternate innocence and contempt. Les Patterson is a travesty of the Austral Briton, exploiting the perks and trappings of his position and mouthing the rhetoric of new nationalism without an iota of real interest in its spirit.

In the second act of the show a rather worldly Dame Edna, 'the thinking man's Eva Peron', appeared in a tennis outfit, showing off a new chestnut perm à la Barbra Streisand. Her barbs were cruel, her put-downs acidic and her smile rather cold. There was no let-up. Even Princess Margaret came in for a drubbing in connection with her much younger lover, Roddy Llewellyn. Edna's vicious attacks both horrified and delighted her Australian audiences.

HG Kippax in the *Sydney Morning Herald* called the show 'dazzling: a performance of astonishing variety, energy and authority by an entertainer (writer and actor) of genius, now at the height of his powers, fooling and (flaying) at the top of his bent'.[3] In *The Age* Neil Jillett compared the experience to a Nuremberg rally, stating that 'Edna is Humphries' supreme and most appalling creation. She *is* Humphries. Compared with her, all his other characters become clever pieces of acting. One is always aware of the creator behind the mask ... Even at the risk of disrespect to history's victims the point has to be made that Edna manipulates her audience the way Hitler manipulated the Germans. She picks out victims in the front stalls; she destroys them with her tongue. They are her Jews, the minority singled out to sustain the majority's frenzied surrender to the performer on stage. And the terrible fact is that she is so funny.'[4] Jillett's comparison of Edna with Hitler was a striking and provocative response to a comic act performed in Sydney three decades after the war. Humphries found the comments amusing and unnerving. It was a hyperbolic and tasteless description, but it found the pulse of Humphries' newly arch comic style, and seized on Edna's menacing hold on a crowd. It also surmised the wafer-thin space between the man and his mask.

When the Australian tour finished, Humphries set about creating a sleek, pared-down version of the show to open in London before Christmas, under the new title *A Night with Dame Edna*. The cover of the program presented a riot of bright purples and reds in a doctored version of Edvard Munch's painting *The Scream*, showing Dame Edna's mouth at full stretch. On the back cover Dame Edna, dressed as Maria von Trapp and brandishing a guitar, leads a band of smiling children over an alpine pass, advertising a new Edna recording, *The Sound of Edna*. The von Trapp children's faces were changed to those of Rolf Harris, Olivia Newton-John and the Bee Gees, with Edna clearly taking charge of Australian expatriate talent.

After a holiday in Madeira with Diane, surrounded by the elderly, Humphries closeted himself at Eastbourne in order to polish the script. He found the conditions in this East Sussex watering place 'ideal for writing', because the seaside town was 'rich and dull'. Humphries bravely answered questions from the English press about the disastrous reviews of his show in New York, declaring boldly, 'I'm going back again ... I have triumphed over fear ... Edna is bigger than Broadway.' It was a prophetic and courageously funny comment, infused with Humphries' gritty determination and magnificent self-belief.

A Night with Dame Edna (And a Handful of Old Cobbers) opened at the Piccadilly Theatre on Wednesday 13 December 1978. It was the second one-man show written by an Australian to attract high praise that year. In the dismal period before Easter when West End audiences are often thin, Gordon Chater had arrived from Australia to star in *The Elocution of Benjamin Franklin* at the Mayfair Theatre. Chater enthralled the critics in the powerful play by the young South Australian Stephen J Spears. The middle-aged paunchy protagonist enters the stage nude. Chater played the flamboyant cross-dresser who dies at the end of the play with sensitivity and energy. Australian drama had changed beyond recognition.

The critics were enraptured with Edna's 'barbed prattle' and Humphries' ability to transform a large theatre into 'a family party'.

The satire of middle-class pretension received high praise from John Barber in the *Daily Telegraph,* who described Humphries as 'a fine actor' whose satire was as aggressive as it was compassionate.[5] At last the London critics seemed to 'get' Humphries. Michael Billington in the *Guardian* praised Humphries' 'talent for grotesquerie, outrage and lewdness', and called him a 'kind of vaudeville Swift'. Billington remarked that he found the anti-Australian jokes 'a bit reflex', but observed that he made up for this 'with a use of language that is cutting as a flint'.[6] The show won the Society of West End Theatres Award for Best Comedy of the Year in 1979.

One night the American theatre critic John Lahr took his seat in the Piccadilly. He was one of 1200 in the audience, waiting for the 44-year-old Humphries to appear on stage dressed up as Dame Edna Everage. It was the first time Lahr had been to a performance by Barry Humphries, and he found himself laughing loudly right from the beginning. Then, after the interval or 'Credibility Gap' as it was called in the program, something happened to Lahr that had never happened to him before, though he had witnessed it happening to others twice in the theatre.[7] After one of Edna's mean and racist jokes Lahr laughed so hard that he lost consciousness and slipped off his chair onto the floor. When he recovered himself he sat spellbound for the rest of the show.

Lahr went back to his flat in Belsize Park and wrote a long review for *New Society*. This was no ordinary review. It was an essay of appreciation that revealed Lahr's insight into 'the delicious precision' of Humphries' satirical art and his stinging character Edna Everage. He was mesmerised by the thrilling spectacle of Edna's mockery of 'every bourgeois value'. 'Her theatre is kinetic, not didactic,' wrote Lahr. 'She corrupts an audience with pleasure … Edna will continue to astonish and knock them dead for a long time. Why? Because she's so nice; and as every mother's child knows, that niceness is a license to kill.'[8]

Lahr's understanding of Humphries as a comedian shone through his response to Edna. Humphries was delighted with the review and wrote to the critic on elegant cream parchment, expressing gratitude for the piece. He admitted that he had read it 'without squirming (I usually do when I read pieces about myself). It is certainly one of the best things of its kind yet done.'[9] It was certainly one of the most affirming and considered reviews Humphries had ever received.

Humphries was already aware of Lahr's particular critical style. Ten years earlier Lahr had published a book about his father, Bert, the comedian who played the lion in *The Wizard of Oz*.[10] Lahr instantly recognised something akin to his own father's personality in Barry Humphries. As he got to know Barry over the next few years, he realised that both his father and the man dressed as Edna Everage seemed to dwell much more happily in the world of imagination than in their real lives. Both revelled in the antics and style of vaudeville and found a kind of peace in the release afforded by the excesses of their performance style. They discovered 'emotional equilibrium' in the act of becoming someone else on stage. Barry confessed to Lahr his love of connecting with an audience in laughter, his motivation for Edna's nightly invitation to her 'possums' to unite in revelry.[11]

Over the next few years Humphries set his sights firmly on establishing himself with British audiences. His influence on Australian playwrights, actors, directors and comedians was already being felt. Later he admitted to feeling infuriated by the fact that Norman Gunston, played by Garry McDonald, and Paul Hogan were becoming national heroes, when he had been pilloried by the critics for his creation of Bazza McKenzie, regarded as a 'national embarrassment'. Gunston's gormless approach to celebrities drew on the innocence of Bazza and ignorance of Edna, and the ocker hero had paved the way for Hogan's successful international comedy career. Humphries' impact had been significant on film and on the stage. When Robyn Nevin brilliantly portrayed Patrick White's garrulous character Miss Docker in the Sydney Theatre Company's popular revival of *A Cheery Soul* at the Opera House Drama Theatre in 1979, there was more than a flash of Edna Everage in her interpretation of the 'tragic clown', as White called his character.[12]

In 1979, in a program about comedy, the television personality Peter Luck called Edna the best of Humphries' comic creations. Australian humour owed a great debt to the vaudevillian tradition and Luck described that heritage, but he was scathing about 'the short-lived cult of ockerism'. Luck questioned Humphries about his own perceptions of the 'deep vein of sardonic humour in Australia'. Appearing rosy-cheeked in a gleaming white suit, bright blue striped shirt and cufflinks, spotted bow tie and newly darkened hair, Humphries declared the custodians of this humour to be 'taxi drivers and homosexuals and homosexual taxi drivers'. He never missed an opportunity to shock an audience, and this interview was no exception. Luck nervously asked him a burning question: how close was the character of Edna to Louisa Humphries? Humphries replied coolly: 'Edna is a synthesis of observations. I presume there is a bit of my mother in Edna. I thought there was a lot of my mother in Edna until I met your mother.'[13]

But it was British television that Humphries wanted to crack. Julian Jebb directed Humphries in a spoof of the increasingly popular genre of profile documentaries, entitled *La Dame aux Gladiolas: The Agony and the Ecstasy of Dame Edna*.[14] The strange program screened on BBC2 during Humphries' long season at the Piccadilly. Lolling on a chaise longue in her suite at the Dorchester Hotel, eating chocolates and dressed in a pale satin gown and pink boa, Edna reflected on her life as a star, answering a string of clichéd and predictable questions from a fawning, invisible interviewer. It was Humphries' first foray into parodic documentary and featured his first real swipe at celebrity culture, now that Edna was a superstar. Edna seemed surprisingly elderly, and slightly otherworldly, offering a parody of Barbara Cartland yet somehow retaining her matronly presence.

Jebb incorporated some television footage of Edna from the beginnings of her career, 'before television came to Europe', as Edna reminded viewers. She described her elevation to damehood by the prime minister, as the extraordinary 'Arise Dame Edna' scene played in the background, explaining that it was at that point 'that I turned socialist'. Edna recited poetry and informed the audience that Sigmund Freud had spent a number of weeks in Melbourne, which she had recently documented in a new pamphlet called 'Sigmund Freud: The Forgotten Weeks'.

Asked about her favourite works of art and artists, Edna replied, 'Scream, I love the work of Edvard Scream. It always makes me laugh, that picture of the woman on the bridge having a nervous breakdown. Scream had a lot of sympathy for women at my age …' She observed that this particular work by the 'Danish expressionist' of a woman who has clearly 'let herself go', was painted during a visit by Scream to Australia and was inspired by a woman he saw on the Sydney Harbour Bridge. In one of several short song sequences, Edna appeared dressed as a kind of Eva Peron figure in dark clothing, performing, 'Don't Cry for Me Australasia'.

There were flickers of the old Humphries of the *Bizarre* days when Edna declared that she would love to be 'a maker of documentaries about things that matter, like death, old age and dwarfs', perhaps a documentary about 'an old, dead dwarf'. Edna then prepared to host a dinner party for her impresario Barry Humphries, Elton John, Esther Williams and Frau Rudolf Hess. It was all faintly creepy by this stage, and the languid style of the program did not portray Edna as dynamic or appealing. Not surprisingly it was a one-off for Humphries, who needed audience interaction to sustain the energy of his own performance. In the 1970s the manic, anarchic Edna still had no regular opportunity to engage with 'her public' on television, and Humphries had a lot to learn about the medium. For now mockumentary seemed the wrong genre for him.

On Saturday 16 June 1979, after the long London run of *A Night with Dame Edna* came to an end, Barry Humphries married Diane Millstead at a ceremony conducted at the grand grey-stone registry office in Marylebone. The newlyweds were to spend the first months of their marriage apart, with Barry travelling to Australia to prepare for a new show. Diane was determined to remain independent and kept her own name. She did not wear a wedding ring and would immediately set about preparing for an exhibition of her work in Paris. They were to reunite later that year in Melbourne. At the ceremony Diane wore an elegant trouser suit with a long jacket in blue and white crepe de chine and a small white hat. Barry looked more conservative than usual in a dark blue suit, white shirt with a tie bearing an image of Santa Claus, and a gold-coloured gladiolus, given to him by the comic Kenny Everett. Ken Thomson was best man. Afterwards the newlyweds were blessed by the Reverend Baddeley in a short ceremony at the fashionable St James's Church in Piccadilly, designed by Sir Christopher Wren three centuries earlier. Nick Garland, Joan Bakewell, John Betjeman, Ian Davidson, John Wells and Madeleine Orr (who played Madge Allsop) were present. Taking off his hat to pose for press photographs afterwards, Barry laughingly declared, 'My career as a drag queen is over.'[15]

PART FOUR
ARRIVISTE

CHAPTER 25

Last Night of the Poms

At the end of the busy West End summer season in 1981 Barry Humphries played Dame Edna in a filmed four-night comedy gala for Amnesty International at the Theatre Royal called *The Secret Policeman's Other Ball*. The middle-aged Humphries outshone the edgy new satire gurus and reigning kings of British comedy. His act was pared down, sharp and original compared with some of the rather pedestrian stand-up acts in the show. As one of eighteen comedians to grace the stage in front of a relatively youthful audience, Humphries demonstrated a new professionalism and a talent for the quick sketch. Ronald Eyre and John Cleese directed the show that included skits by the Monty Python team, Alexei Sayle, Rowan Atkinson, John Bird, John Wells, Tim Brooke-Taylor and Pamela Stephenson, one of only two female performers, as well as musical interludes from the likes of Eric Clapton, Bob Geldof and Sting.

In the opening moments the performers mocked their patrons. John Cleese abused those in the top circle for only paying the price of a prawn cocktail for their seats when people were being tortured all over the world. John Bird ridiculed those in the front stalls with their complimentary tickets and those who would be writing off their tickets against tax. A fresh-faced, curly-haired Rowan Atkinson weighed in against those in the second-cheapest seats who would like to be in the front stalls but were flabby fence-sitters, people who would most likely vote for the Social Democrats. By the end of the five-minute introduction, the thousand-strong audience had all been ridiculed and drawn into the joke. Humphries would later perfect this kind of mass audience put-down.

It was as a rather nervous, besuited Alan Bennett concluded his mutterings on stage about gay encounters in the toilets at Ladbroke Grove that stagehands overheard Edna whisper in the wings: 'He reminds me of my son, Kenny.'[1] A moment later she flounced onto the stage, her pink hair shining, her royal-blue taffeta evening dress sparkling under the spotlight. Before she even opened her mouth, she cut a satirical portrait, with an intricate model of the Sydney Opera House pertly forming part of the collar of her spectacular dress. Humphries was magnetic, polished and meticulously timed. Edna first confessed her reservations about doing a performance for Amnesty rather than her own preferred charity — the Royal Australian Prostate Foundation. She confessed that she was keeping Norm's prostate in the freezer, to the left of the barbie meat, in the hope that some surgeon in the future would be able to repair it. Her only concern with this plan was that her 'marvellous old bridesmaid Madge' might one day mistake it for shish kebab: 'I might come home from one of these wonderful evenings and find my husband's organ down her throat.' She paused, horrified, lips turned down in an expressionistic freeze, before making her exit.

The gala came at a hectic time, with Humphries involved in a multitude of performance activities. But it was a special time too. A few months earlier, on 27 April 1981, with Barry present, Diane had given birth to a baby boy, Oscar Valentine, at King George V Hospital in Sydney. While newspapers joked about the likelihood of the baby being nicknamed 'Aussie', Barry was thrilled by his son's arrival and pleased that Tessa, then aged eighteen, travelled to Sydney to visit her little brother in hospital; Emily was confined to her boarding school in Geelong, and missed the celebrations.

Hot on the heels of his Amnesty triumph, Humphries leaped into another theatrical experiment, playing at the Royal Albert Hall in a televised musical written and conducted by the American-born composer Carl Davis, entitled *The Last Night of the Poms*, with the

London Symphony Orchestra and a full choir. Humphries' friend Ken Thomson had suggested the collaboration, an ambitious enterprise for Humphries. The concert featured a 'profane cantata' by Humphries and Davis — *The Song of Australia* — and an Australian-themed pastiche of Prokofiev's *Peter and the Wolf*, entitled *Peter and the Shark*, narrated by Les Patterson.

The show was a finale to the BBC Proms series of nightly concerts at the South Kensington concert hall, a British tradition since 1895. For Humphries it represented a grand opportunity to become part of an established musical festival while simultaneously presenting a parody of the usual flag-waving 'Last Night of the Proms' that brings the season to a close every year.

In the glossy program for the show Edna appeared on the cover dressed in a mink coat atop the Royal Albert Hall, while inside she was shown prancing in a leopard-skin outfit under the banner 'La Stupedna'. A full-page photo of Humphries, taken by Diane, showed him seated in an old-fashioned parlour, dressed in a cream flannel suit, frowning at the camera, his hair and moustache reminiscent of Adolf Hitler's. Barry was beginning to construct a new persona of middle age, and had started to play an urbane, mysterious, eccentric and at times rather sinister-looking character.

The Last Night of the Poms was a huge risk, demanding everything Humphries had as a performer. It opened with a jaunty, entertaining overture of Australian folk songs, including 'Bound for Botany Bay', 'Click Go the Shears' and 'Waltzing Matilda'. Then Edna appeared in a green silk-chiffon evening gown with batwing sleeves and faux lettuce edging. She boomed her customary 'Hello possums', but looked ghoulish and a little strange. Humphries' make-up had been applied rather haphazardly, and he had failed to cover his neck; on his face the foundation was thickly caked, and the green eye shadow looked sickly. It might not have been a problem except that the show was filmed for television, and the close-ups revealed the mess. Edna chatted with audience members, she waved to a couple she recognised in the front row, and then pointed to a Sikh man: 'Isn't he gorgeous, he might be a chutney czar — I don't mean that in a racist way. I'm proud of Australia, I'm proud of the Commonwealth, what's left of it ... I was playing golf with my tax lawyer this morning. Why are you doing this, you don't have to, he said. I said, I'm sorry, I have to share ... I feel a cantata coming on.' The *Song of Australia*, in nine cantos, proclaimed the creation of the world, of Australia and finally Dame Edna herself.

Edna crashed her way through the song, shrieking uncomfortably and struggling to find the notes. Her music hall style seemed at odds with the magisterial force of the London Symphony Orchestra, massive choir and elaborate score. Although at times the music and lyrics offered an enchanting, whimsical experience and the choir was exceptional, the show was too long and Humphries' voice as Edna was alternately raw and drowned out by the swirling orchestral music. The show was not a success.

It was not until the end of the performance that Edna came into her own, returning to the stage in a magnificent red, white and blue taffeta dress with the Australian flag emblazoned on it. She cajoled the audience into rising to their feet to sing together 'in the standing ovation position'. They obeyed. Instead of 'Rule Britannia' or 'Jerusalem', Edna led the throng in a rousing rendition of one of her most catchy songs, 'Why Do We Love Australia?' A moment before the singing commenced, a gentleman from the audience with plum firmly in mouth interjected, 'What about England?' Edna shrugged and smiled wryly: 'Yes indeed, darling!'

With the end of the show in sight, Humphries, now relaxed and more confident, galvanised the audience of 'Poms' in the comic song of homage to Australia:

Why do we love Australia?
Why does it haunt us still?
There's nobody we know there.
And it costs so much to go there.
And the chances are we never will.
But still we all love Australia.
Whatever Australia may be.

It's the land of milk and honey.
It's so rich and safe and funny.
Australia's the land for me.

Waving their gladdies as they sang, the audience articulated a new affection in the relationship between the two nations, an affection also expressed eloquently by Bazza in his conversation with his 'Auntie Edna' at the end of *The Adventures of Barry McKenzie*. It was a triumphant moment for Humphries if an odd one, with millions of television viewers tuning in to watch the strange spectacle of a man dressed as a woman leading thousands of ordinary Britons in a music hall song of praise for one of their distant former colonies. It was one of the finest performances of patriotic fervour by the confirmed expatriate Barry Humphries.

There was a dark side, however, to this celebration of Australia at the Royal Albert Hall. Britain was in steep economic decline and had even been called the 'sick man of Europe', recalling references to Turkey on the eve of World War I. But this was 1981 and the homeless filled the streets of the West End, sleeping in the Tube stations as they had done fifty years earlier during the Depression. British industry was sinking into ruin and unemployment had reached record levels. As Humphries well knew, hundreds of Britons regularly joined the long queues outside Australia House to investigate their prospects of emigrating.

For Humphries, a one-man performer who is most effective with a minimal support cast, the musical extravaganza was disappointing. Edna is at her best when she is the only one in the spotlight; the act relies on comic monologue, not music. Clearly, Humphries had overreached, perhaps never considering that his voice as Edna simply could not cope with the demands of the singing. He had not fully grasped that audiences want the undiluted Edna, that they love the risk and rudeness of Edna's verbal play.

The English critics were unanimous in their disapproval of Edna's experiments with oratorio in *The Last Night of the Poms*. Irving Wardle recoiled from the 'merciless, parrot-like screech' of Edna's voice 'tearing through the surrounding musical fabric like a rusty carving knife going through velvet'.[2] James Fenton advised Humphries not to repeat his unprecedented comic experiment.[3] Anthony Masters found the televised version funny and sinister but too long.[4] Antony Thorncroft called the venture 'accomplished' but a misuse of Humphries' talents. 'Such an iconoclast as Humphries is really needed on the full-time task of deflating hypocrisy and outraging the bourgeoisie,' counselled the *Financial Times* critic.[5] Humphries was not easily put off by rebuffs from the critics, and continued with his plans to perform the oratorio in Australia.

A week before the extravaganza at the Royal Albert Hall, Barry, dressed up as Dame Edna, had sallied forth to meet a *Times* reporter for lunch at one of Barry's favourite restaurants, L'Escargot in Greek Street, Soho. Done up in a red, white and blue sailor suit, and wearing new glasses with a fan-shaped arrangement of feathers that covered her forehead, Edna chatted to the gracious patronne, Elena Salvoni, who asked discreetly about the Dame's grandchildren as she took down the orders. Moments later, to the astonishment of other diners, Edna slid off her chair and under the table. Later Edna told her lunch partner, Michael Horsnell, that her collapse was due to the shock of hearing that Barry Humphries was trying to upstage her by launching a book of his own scripts, just when the Dame was about to star in *The Last Night of the Poms*. It was not the first stunt Humphries had staged at the restaurant, nor the first time Edna had savaged another person in public, but it was the first time Edna made Humphries the target of her comic attack in the name of publicity. 'It's quite pathetic of him,' she said.

It was a masterstroke on Humphries' part to draw attention to himself through the antics of his garrulous character. This time it was all safe and in-house, unlike Edna's attack on 'her' producer, Michael White, after a quarrel he and Humphries had about money a few years earlier. There was no possible flak this time. It was a brilliant reversal of roles and one that Humphries continued to exploit from that day onwards.

Even at Christmas Barry did not stop performing his alternative selves. He and Diane posed for a black-and-white photograph to be used for Christmas cards. Diane appeared in a dressing gown, puffing on a cigarette and showing off her shapely legs, a packet of Kool tucked into the top of her suspenders. Next to her on an ugly floral couch sat Barry, dressed as Sandy Stone in Homy Ped slippers, and clutching a hot-water bottle and large radio. On the arm of the couch was a massive container of Valium capsules, as big as a biscuit tin. The greeting in large red print said: 'Let yourself go this Christmas … like we have, Barry and Diane 1981'. Humphries was happy.

The following year brought more joy. On 21 October 1982 Diane gave birth to her second son, Rupert Cosmo, a robust baby weighing almost 4.5 kilograms (10 pounds). Barry, who claimed that 'Cosmo' was a reference to Cosimo Medici, was proud to be a father once again. And there was more good news. Humphries was pleased to hear that he would receive the Order of Australia. Typically, an honour like this brought on contrary and provocative behaviour, and when the Australian women's magazine *Cleo* invited Barry to pose nude as their November 1982 centrefold, he couldn't resist. His surprisingly athletic, tanned and mole-strewn body lay across the backs of two scantily clad female models. The pose is strange and dazzling; Barry is laughing heartily, his teeth unnaturally white, a shock of his dark hair obscuring his eyes. Here was yet another side of the actor, lampooning the concept of the centrefold and enjoying the gaze of thousands as he flaunted his body.

Just as audiences gradually warmed to the Barry McKenzie comic strips in the 1960s, Les Patterson began to develop a cult following in Britain during the 1980s. The politics of the Whitlam period continued to provide Humphries with a mass of material as Les reminisced about his role in Australia's 'cultural renaissance', a favourite phrase of the grotesque diplomat, now styling himself 'Sir' Les. Humphries was positioning the character as a mate to everyone in politics, a troubleshooter, and was delighted when his old friend from Melbourne, Don Bennetts, asked him to introduce the Australian Film Institute Awards for 1980 as Sir Les. He arranged for a taxi to take Barry to the BBC in Portland Place to record his views of Australian film-making. Don hung a portrait of the Queen slightly askew behind Les who put his feet up on the desk showing off his two-tone shoes. He did the introduction in just two takes.

Sir Les recounted his contribution to ensuring that Australian 'fillums' reached an international audience. Humphries devised a story of the Bazza McKenzie saga in poetry, making fun of the industry and reminding the audience of the provocations occasioned by the ocker hero:

> *Let me take you back ten years ago*
> *When Gorton and me kicked off the show*
> *And Bazza McKenzie made us a mint*
> *Though now we only mention it in very small print*
> *For them ocker days have been left behind*
> *Now Australia makes movies to prove we're refined*
> *Think of Newsfront Patrick and Max the Maddie*
> *Storm and Stork-boy and the Cars that ate Caddie*
> *Don Blacksmith's Picnic and Jimmy's Party*
> *And the Last Wave in Paris if you like something arty.*
>
> *There's a cultural lesson the world has to copy*
> *The Down Under product has come out on top.*

After the filming Barry stayed in character. He said to Don, 'Let's have a curry. I know a place near here,' as if he was still speaking to the camera, and proceeded to lead Bennetts and Iain Johnston, a journalist friend of Don and Barry, towards Tottenham Court Road. Barry deliberately dropped several paces behind the other two, shouting out insults in Sir Les's slurred and gruff voice. 'Bloody Jews,' he called in the direction of second-hand dealers and bewildered shopkeepers. Don and Iain ate their curries with Sir Les that evening, the Indian staff at the curry house politely ignoring his revolting habits and garrulous manner.[6]

Before Barry left England to perform *Song of Australia* in Melbourne early in 1983, Sir Les travelled to Cambridge on Australia Day for a ceremony in which the diplomat was bestowed with a mock honorary doctorate from the Cambridge Union, in the plush surrounds of the Union Society Debating Chamber. A large crowd of admirers listened as the Choral Scholars of Trinity serenaded Les, who then delivered a special celebratory poem written for the occasion, entitled the 'Cambridge Couplets'. This was Les at his sleazy best and Humphries did not hold back:

> *Tonight you have donned your most solemn regalia*
> *To extol the glory of my homeland, Australia*
> *And I, humble son of that continent brown,*
> *Proudly accept this black cap and gown.*
> *And now I've got it on my back*
> *Let no bastard try to get it back!*
> *But what does the average bloke expect*
> *When he visits this shrine of intellect?*
> *A bunch of poofters and Brideshead blighters*
> *Shirt-lifters and Pommy pillow-biters?*
> *Sure, the girls all love my laid-back Australian style*
> *When I walk past they flash me the vertical smile.*
> *They'd love to join me in a Cambridge punt*
> *For a seminar on Immanuel Kant.*
> *But you're a bonzer bunch of lasses and lads*
> *And I'm real proud to be honoured by youse undergrads,*
> *So, no matter what any bastard sez*
> *When you think of Australia think of old Les*
> *And, with that, gentle ladies, may I now withdraw*
> *And I haven't said THAT to a woman before.*[7]

The undergraduates adored Les. Humphries had found the perfect event for the ribald humour of the drunken diplomat. Of course like so much of Humphries' humour it was risky as some Britons assumed the comedy was tantamount to fact. For Humphries this risk gave him a kind of adrenalin rush as he revelled in burlesquing national stereotypes and comic caricatures of an Australian 'average bloke'.

CHAPTER 26

Intercourse with Millions

In the longer Australian season of *Song of Australia* that played in Sydney and Melbourne in 1983, complete with 130-piece orchestra and the New Antipodean Singers in choral accompaniment, the overture preceded an orchestral fanfare for 'a Doctor of Culture'. Les Patterson, who officiated this time, announced himself as a 'dead ringer' for that 'spag singer Perverotti'. Sir Les welcomed the audience to the show as 'Number One Yartz Supremo' and one of the few 'culturally minded colleagues in the Golden Olden Days of Socialism'. The Sydney season took place during a federal election campaign. After seven years of Liberal rule and high unemployment, the country was ready to welcome into government a whole new Labor machine under the charismatic, self-styled larrikin, Rhodes Scholar and trade union man, Bob Hawke, whom Edna had graciously advised on etiquette some years previously. Les told the concert-goers that the choice of prime minister was between 'a farmer with lockjaw [the Liberal incumbent, Malcolm Fraser] and a dry drunk'.

By the time the Melbourne season got under way, Bob Hawke had been installed as Prime Minister of Australia. Les Patterson's opening speech was possibly the highlight of the Melbourne concerts. He reported that he had been 'as busy as Hazel Hawke's hairdresser'. Even-handed in his swipes at the two sides of politics,

Sir Les revealed that he had the melancholy duty of visiting Malcolm Fraser at his 'country hoam', 'Nareen', to find 'old Tamie [Fraser's wife] haggling with Grace Brothers over the [removalist] quote'. Ushered into the library — 'I knew it was the library. There was a copy of *Reader's Digest* on the table' — Les revealed that 'Mal' had confessed that he had 'spent a bundle on charisma lessons' from Molly Meldrum, a tongue-tied television personality, and others. Les told Fraser that he was just too aloof for the Australian people who could 'only identify with a mug lair as PM'. 'Our ideal politician,' Les explained, 'is evil tempered, foul mouthed and half pissed.' He reassured 'Mal' that the whole of Australia was 'shit scared Hawke was going to give them a job'. Les went on to confirm that Hazel was moving in the teak, and getting rid of Tamie's chintz. He informed the audience that 'she's busy nailing the lamps to the walls and putting a couple of old pairs of pantyhose at the bottom of the bed to make Bob feel at home, making it like a hotel'. He reminded them of his impartiality, however: 'I swing, I'm apolitical', 'I've known them all, ladies and gentlemen. I knew Al Grassby when he was a colour consultant for Darrell Lea. I knew Billy McMahon before they made a fillum about him — *ET* ... are you with me?'

Australian critics were as unimpressed with the musical extravaganza as their English counterparts. Richard Le Moignan in the *Sydney Morning Herald* pointed out that the show lacked the usual intimacy of a Humphries performance, despite the dazzling send-up of the likes of Joan Sutherland and high operatic culture. Leonard Radic regretted that Humphries as a performer was dwarfed by the program; he longed for more of the 'slobbering Sir Les' and Dame Edna in full didactic flight. He disliked the 'kitschy cantata'. The grotesque excesses of Les and Edna were somehow diminished amid the manufactured glitter of the occasion.[1] But the *Australian*'s John Moses pointed to the wit of the music in distinct contrast with the crudeness of Humphries as Les Patterson.[2] Humphries did not attempt a musical extravaganza of this kind again for more than twenty years.

The newly honoured 'Doctor of Culture (Australian Studies)', however, continued his rise to prominence throughout the early

1980s, as the Australian image in London became — conversely — a little more respectable and realistic. Les Patterson became both Humphries' alter ego and a barometer of Australian cultural aspiration in Britain. In Humphries' homeland, too, Les became more interesting to the public. The 'crumpled and dripping' statesman 'who looked as if he had been dragged through a drain', impressed Mike Carlton when he delighted Carlton's radio listeners during a live interview. Carlton proclaimed that after Les, 'Dame Edna was something of an anticlimax.'[3]

However, many Australians disliked the vulgarity of Les Patterson and cringed at the image he projected of themselves. The more Australians railed against the 'damage' done to the reputation of Australia by the likes of Bazza McKenzie and Les Patterson, the more lewd and crass Sir Les became. Just after Sir Les received his doctorate at Cambridge, Humphries seized a golden opportunity for revenge against the nay-sayers and 'straiteners' of his homeland.

Gough Whitlam's government had endowed two chairs in Australian Studies, one at Harvard and one at University College Dublin. Strangely, there was nothing resembling these in the mother country. In 1981 Malcolm Fraser set out to redress this situation and authorised funding for a couple of academic posts at the Institute of Commonwealth Studies, University of London. Before he left Australia the inaugural professor, Geoffrey Bolton, unwisely told a journalist that one of his goals was to overcome 'the influence of Barry Humphries and Rolf Harris'.[4] It was a red rag to Humphries.

In a stunt on the steps of the Georgian house fronting Russell Square, home to the Institute, Les appeared in a mock opening of ARSE, the 'Australian Research and Studies Establishment'. Ironically, the new Australian Studies Centre, based at the Institute, was literally a stone's throw from the derelict buildings in which Bruce Beresford had brought the first Barry McKenzie film into being. Now Les Patterson had taken over from Bazza as the uncouth Australian abroad. The innocent Bazza had metamorphosed into the face of Australian know-how. Les was the perfect man to 'dish out a few flash degrees in Dingo Studies, Possum Pathology and Rogue Wombat Handling'.

By the time the Queen Mother opened the real Centre on a warm June day in 1983, Bob Hawke had become prime minister and presided over the ceremony. Lampooning the ongoing performance of new nationalism, Les announced his vital role in the enterprise as anointed by the new PM. Parroting 'Hawkie', Les declared:

> Australia's international image needs a bit of spit and polish and you're just the man to put his mouth where Australia's money is. Let's face it, Les ... London's chock-a-block with expat knockers making a fat quid selling Australia's credibility short. Smart-aleck galahs like Germaine Greer, Clive James and that old sheila, Dame Edna, who dresses up as a man and tips the bucket on our incomparable cultural attainments in front of the crowned heads of Europe ... We've given this assignment to you, Les, because you're that smart you could sell soap to the Poms.[5]

When Sir Les appeared on the BBC with Humphries' old friend John Betjeman in *Time With Betjeman* soon afterwards, several concerned viewers wrote to the producer commiserating about 'that Australian' who 'had had a bit too much to drink, hadn't he?' One man exclaimed: 'If that's their Cultural Attaché, we should cut off relations at once.'[6] Humphries was ecstatic.

In fact the self-confessed former boozer and ladies' man Bob Hawke gave Humphries almost as much inspiration for material as the previous Labor prime minister Gough Whitlam. In a photograph published in the program for his next show, *Tears Before Bedtime*, Patterson appeared with a young, voluptuous, scantily clad blonde draped over him, and a half-empty whisky bottle in the foreground. Underneath the photograph was a poem by Sir Les entitled 'In Terms of My Natural Life'. It satirised the language of politics, and captured the perverse nature of Australian public life in the 1970s and 1980s when politicians attempted to curry favour with the electorate through occasional outbursts of coarse language and a larrikin style. Patterson seemed to be targeting Talbot Duckmanton, who was head of the ABC, and Senator

Doug McClelland, Minister for the Media, but the words of Bob Hawke also resonated, particularly his comment that any boss who sacked a worker for not turning up after the Australian victory in the America's Cup yacht race in September 1983 was a 'bum'. Later, Paul Keating's choice of epithets for his parliamentary colleagues, Mark Latham's description of John Howard as an 'arse-licker' and Tony Abbott's vulgar comment on national television — 'Shit happens' — are also enactments of larrikinism, and continue to be vividly satirised in the character of Les Patterson.

In the title of Les's poem, Humphries parodied the iconic Australian novel by Marcus Clarke published in 1874.

IN TERMS OF MY NATURAL LIFE

I am an Australian in terms of Nation
And a Public Servant in terms of vocation,
But there's one thing amazes my critics and that's
How many I wear in terms of hats.
I chair the Cheese Board, I front the Yartz;
You could term me a man of many parts.
I'm a Renaissance type, if you know the term,
And I've held long office in terms of term.
Yes, I've long served Australia in terms of years
And in terms of refreshment I like a few beers.
My opponents are mongrels, scum and worms
Who I bucket in no uncertain terms;
And my rich vocabulary always features
Large in terms of my public speeches
My favourite terms in terms of debate
Are: 'broad-based package' and 'orchestrate'.
But one term I never employ is 'failure',
Especially when talking in terms of Australia!
For in terms of lifestyle we've got the germs of
A ripper concept to think in terms of.
Yes, in terms of charisma I've got the game mastered:
In anyone's terms I'm a well-liked bastard.[7]

Although Humphries, via Les Patterson, presented a damning critique of Australian masculinity, his vitality and energy made him an extremely popular character. By his own admission, Sir Les was a figure to be emulated, boasting that he:

> Pioneered the wearing of white shoes for men in Australia ... I also pioneered the long white socks and the shorts which became universal. I've always been at the sharp end of Australian men's fashions ... my biggest triumph in the clothing department was the fashion statement that is the safari suit ... they all copied me — Jim Cairns, Al Grassby, Don Dunstan, Andrew Peacock. They all started strutting out in their safari suits.[8]

As Les's popularity grew, the criticism of Humphries' humour intensified. Various Australian commentators lashed out at Les's creator. The journalist Craig McGregor caught Humphries' show in the New South Wales north coast town Tweed Heads. In a review published in the *National Times* in October 1982 he expressed horror at Humphries' 'deep and abiding contempt for the human race'. In his opinion, Humphries was both misanthropic and anti-Australian, not to mention racist, misogynistic and out of touch.[9]

Humphries' satire is certainly misogynistic at times, but McGregor seemed to misunderstand the targets of the humour and failed to appreciate that Humphries' use of tastelessness and even cruelty to shock and entertain is part of a long tradition of Australian comedy, from Roy Rene to Chris Lilley. A new kind of reactionary blindness to satire seemed to have taken root in Australia.

McGregor prefaced his review with an admission that he admired Barry Humphries and found him 'very, very funny', but appeared to underestimate both Humphries and his audience. As early as 1966 he had observed that Humphries 'had climbed to fame by burlesquing middle-class life' in Australia, but thought that if members of the middle class heard his records they 'probably wouldn't realise they were being sent up'.[10] By 1980 McGregor admitted that the success of the *Barry McKenzie* films signalled the confidence Australians had in themselves to enjoy such parody.¹¹ Paradoxically, he still maintained that the middle classes were unaware that Humphries was 'deadly serious in his attack on them' in his comedy.¹²

Regarding the Tweed Heads show, McGregor acknowledged Humphries was satirising the characters he created, not the target of the characters' jokes. But he disapproved of the sleight of hand that he believed underpinned this kind of comedy. 'Humphries … is somewhere to the right of Ronald Reagan,' he lamented. After all, he observed: 'He's on the editorial board of the conservative *Quadrant* magazine.' McGregor also stated that 'Dame Edna best encapsulates Humphries' hostility towards females; it's surely no accident that his most famous creation is an arrogant, philistine, emasculating bitch who is a bundle of the very worst characteristics of womankind.'¹³

Humphries works in a tradition of male satire that goes right back to the Romans, Horace and Juvenal. Horace is frank in his condemnations of greed, lust and ambition, but ultimately his satire is forgiving of human beings. Juvenal registers his disgust with society at every level. Two thousand years later, Humphries' satire also takes some of these themes and in keeping with the genre it is at times angry, obscene and grotesque.

Edna Everage provides a mask for Humphries to satirise all that is wicked, ignorant, small-minded and hypocritical in people of all sorts. She is also a device that affords comic licence to an audience to laugh at the obscene and the grotesque views she espouses, and for a few hours to escape propriety. Occasionally Humphries' satire takes on the less forgiving, cruel and venomous satirical characteristics associated with Juvenal. Like the Roman, Humphries is a master of invective and uses denunciation, mockery, distortion, exaggeration, sarcasm and wit in order to arouse contempt, fear and mirth in his audience. But in the end there is always the forgiving ritual of the gladdie-waving, and prizes, serenades and accolades for the 'victims' who become part of Edna's cast. That gentleness and celebratory joy of Humphries' performances make him primarily an Horatian satirist, his comedy offering the audience a form of optimism.

Although resilient by nature, Humphries was wounded by the reaction to his work by commentators like McGregor in Australia. He put much of the venom down to his decision to leave his homeland, and included a glossary of Australian words in a volume of his monologues and sketches published in 1981 to deal with this angst among his countrymen. Humphries captured the contempt expressed by critics for those who dared leave Australia by defining the word 'expatriate' as 'a traitor'.

Touring Australia with *Tears Before Bedtime* in 1985, Humphries remarked to the writer Peter Goldsworthy in Adelaide that artists are not in the public relations business and that the obsession with national image is peculiarly Australian. He said, 'No English comedian ever gets asked: "I hope you're painting a favourable picture of us when you perform overseas."'[14] For Humphries, who had always detested 'school spirit', the vitriol of certain critics seemed to deepen his resolve and confirm him in his determination to parody pretence and false national pride wherever he found it.

In the script for a short sketch entitled 'Welcome Back, Mate' that was based on an earlier version from the 1970s, Humphries expressed his exasperation with the interview formula he encountered upon every return visit. A journalist character called Craig Foxcroft babbled:

> Michael, or can I call you Mike? Welcome back to Australia and I mean that most sincerely. Now I know you're going to expect me to ask you the $64,000 question, how do you like Australia again after all these years, but I'm not ... so how do you like Australia, Mike? I guess you've already noticed quite a few radical changes in us after the eleven years you've deserted us. My guess is, correct me if I'm wrong, that we're a good deal more cosmopolitan than we were. We can laugh at ourselves, hopefully, and we can hold our own with the best that overseas has to offer ... My spies told me you had a pretty rough time of it at first when you went overseas. Did you find it a disadvantage having an Australian accent? I notice

you've ditched the old Strine? Not that I'm suggesting for a minute you're ashamed of Australia. After all, let's face it, Australia's been pretty good to you one way or another, but we're not all brown-nose fans either.

Australia may well have become a more 'cosmopolitan' country in the early 1980s but Humphries' focus was firmly on facing new challenges and gathering new audiences in Great Britain.

CHAPTER 27

Chat

In November 1980 the voters of the United States of America elected Ronald Reagan as their new president. The elevation of the elderly former Hollywood actor to the highest office in the land offered the ultimate affirmation of style over substance. Ideology had lost to performance in the television age; exposure was all-important as television made politicians, sporting heroes and entertainers visible to millions all over the world. Barry Humphries found the spectacle compelling, and borrowed the formula for Edna Everage. The Dame proclaimed herself to be a star, and demonstrated on television over the next few years that Britons were just as susceptible to celebrity cant as Americans. Humphries had built Edna's satirical story around the inane domestic rituals of suburbia; in the 1980s he took the cult of celebrity as the centrepiece and target of Edna's satirical world.

Humphries first appeared in his own television program in 1980. It was originally intended to be a one-off show called *An Audience with Dame Edna*. With Diane seated in the second row of a studio audience between Charles Osborne and Ken Thomson, a lavender-haired Edna, wearing a pink and mauve chiffon cocktail gown, asymmetrical earrings and glittering silver stilettos, smiled benevolently at the camera, and sat down in front of the gathering of hand-picked celebrity guests. Joanna Lumley, Suzi Quatro,

Shirley Williams, Hazel O'Connor, Mariel Hemingway, Tessa Wyatt, the Marquis of Bath, Stanley Baxter, Madeline Bell, Ned Sherrin, Frank Ifield, Simon Williams, Lord Longford, Rula Lenska and at least a dozen other well-known figures took turns to ask Dame Edna questions about her life and her lifestyle. Although Humphries used the techniques he had perfected on stage, the format marked a daring departure from his theatrical repertoire.

With Edna's straight-to-camera opening, Humphries established a sense of intimacy with the audience at home, and quickly began drawing out the personalities of individual members of the studio audience. She launched into monologues about her personal life and her world, continuously coming back to specific audience members as though in one-to-one conversation with them, casting witty improvised asides to others and to the broader television audience. On stage Edna talks to those in the first few rows, darting from one to another and back again, remembering names and foibles, and appealing consistently to those who've spoken to her individually. For television, Edna adopted a similar routine, but at a much faster pace. Humphries' sense of daring and quick blindsiding wit, his ingenious ability to improvise and his instinct for redefining the rationale and the art of the 'celebrity audience' resulted in an edgy, spontaneous and anarchic new style of television satire.

As soon as Edna sat down in her chunky beige and chrome-trimmed armchair to chat with her studio guests there was a palpable sense of Humphries' dangerous stage presence. Edna was exuberant; her facial mugging and contorted lips, curled in expressions of exaggerated horror and delight, were perfect for television, with the camera rapidly cutting from her face in close-up to the faces of the celebrity guests.

The carnival atmosphere that infuses Humphries' stage shows became a hallmark of Edna's television *Audiences*. (Following the successful taping of the original show, three more screened during the Christmas holiday season at intervals through the 1980s.) In the first *Audience*, Humphries offered everything that variety shows had featured since the early days of television. The show was a sumptuous spectacle, in front of a studio audience, recreating the atmosphere of a live event. Without an audience Humphries could not perform. But Humphries also offered a parody of the values of 'light entertainment', as it is called in Britain. In doing so he created a whole new genre — the parodic chat show — and subverted the formula of the talk show genre. Chat is held up as the ideal, but monologue is what actually occurred in Edna's first parody. She presented herself as a busy but generous television personality: 'I won't be doing all the talking tonight, 99 per cent of it — I think there should be a little margin for you.' The celebrity guests in the audience, rather than being the focus of the chat, were simply the target of Edna's jokes.

Edna constructed herself as a megastar, crafting her own legend, and Humphries' talent willed it into existence. Incredibly, Edna's rise to stardom was all fiction, assertion and aggrandisement — a fitting reflection of celebrity culture in real life. And the British audience thrilled to Edna's game. Edna mocked and trivialised (rather than celebrated) the achievements and status of her well-known 'guest stars'. Seated in rows like children, they had to raise their hand and wait to be asked to speak by Dame Edna.

The show was a succession of reversals and unmaskings. Just as Humphries' stage shows celebrated the ordinary, the crass and the banal responses of hand-picked members of the audience in order to transform them into 'stars', Edna celebrated the ordinary viewer in her television extravaganza. In answering each question posed by a celebrity, Edna refocused the attention on herself, and put each celebrity firmly back in his or her place. Barely three minutes into the show Edna lampooned the television station and kept up a steady barrage of disparaging remarks about the obsession with ratings, station identification and the rivalry between ITV and BBC, drawing upon a lexicon of magazine jargon, media speak and political shorthand.

Then, after a question about whether she would consider entering politics and raising the tone of public life she compared herself to the prime minister, Mrs Thatcher: 'You've got the Iron Lady in charge in this country — I'm more of an aluminium lady or Formica lady — I see people modelling themselves on me.

Because people follow me so scrupulously I have to keep detached from the political life of Britain. I'm a bit like Margaret Thatcher in that respect, but I could be called upon in an emergency — a sort of Kissinger figure.'

Humphries did not drop the mask at any point in the 45-minute broadcast. In spite of the hilarity aroused by some of Edna's guests, she never let the audience forget who was in charge. In fact Humphries has never dropped the mask of Edna on television or in the theatre. Even when the sultry actress Kim Basinger unexpectedly began to caress Edna's knee in a rather erotic manner during an interview for an American network some years later, Humphries stayed in character, smiling and gently asking Ms Basinger to desist or 'I might forget myself'.

Of course the shows were partly scripted and Humphries spent hours preparing Edna's answers to the prescribed questions, but it was Humphries' talent for improvisation and Edna's anarchic will to provoke the audience that created a kind of manic energy and almost palpable delight. Because Edna is an ignorant woman she felt free to 'discuss any subject'.[1] At the end of the first *Audience*, Dame Edna appeared on set after a break with a new look, sporting purple dreadlocks, a pink tasselled dress and white cowboy boots. Leaning against a white grand piano she sang her witty finale entitled 'That's What My Public Means to Me'. The song captured the grotesque joke of an arrogant megastar feigning sentimental attachment to her 'public' and thanking them for granting her inordinate wealth:

> *The David Hockneys on the wall,*
> *The royal visitors who call*
> *That's what my public means to me.*
> ...
> *But they can keep Roman Polanski and Bianca*
> *It's for the company of nobodies like you I hanker ...*

If anyone was unclear about the vicious and vacuous cult of celebrity in the 1980s, Edna put them straight, crooning:

I may be forced to live in a tax haven
But I know I'm home when I see those gladdies wavin'.

Humphries, too, was becoming a celebrity in the United Kingdom at the time, and a consummate expatriate. While he was circumspect about his personal life in interviews, his innate gift for publicity propelled Edna into the limelight with astonishing frequency. He became a keen student of the chat show. Like his compatriot Clive James, who satirised television on his own regular show, Humphries found himself more and more drawn to the medium.

Initially Humphries did not find the transition to television performance easy. In April 1982 when he appeared as Edna on *Late Night From Two*, a Manchester-based arts discussion program hosted by a prim-looking Susan Brooks, Edna seemed awkward, her conversation stilted and ill judged, leaving the young audience nonplussed.

However, by the time Edna appeared on Michael Aspel's Friday evening live chat program, *The Six O'Clock Show,* in October 1983 she did not seem so gauche. Edna arrived in a vintage Daimler, and stooped to pick up the square of red carpet on the steps, carrying it into the studio to complain about its skimpy size. 'Well, I can take a satirical joke,' she said. Dressed in a Thatcher-inspired navy blue suit, she greeted individual members of the studio audience with hugs and kisses then delighted everyone with her attempt to demonstrate the hula hoop, an Australian invention, as she reminded them.

On television Edna constantly drew attention to the details of her performance and its artifice. She hailed the cameramen loudly on camera, instructed audience members to sit back if they were blocking others, and complained about broadcasters' relentless attempts to build ratings. She appeared on Gloria Hunniford's chat show to promote her book *Dame Edna's Bedside Companion*, and without warning turned the tables on the chat show hostess, asking Gloria how she coped when her husband was away.

Michael Parkinson, the doyen of chat show hosts, gave Barry a spot on his show just before Humphries' stage production, *An*

Evening's Intercourse with the Widely Liked Barry Humphries, opened at the Theatre Royal in Drury Lane in February 1982. Les Patterson presented an adoring 'Ode to Parky' to celebrate the release of a book on the celebrated television interviewer. Taking full advantage of the opportunity offered by Parkinson, Barry also appeared as himself and as Dame Edna. It was the first of only two occasions in his career to date that he has appeared as all three characters in a television show. As himself, Humphries explained to viewers that for a long time 'Australia was a very peculiar and remote place to the British public, and I perhaps flatter myself that I may have been instrumental in towing it, if not as close as the Isle of Wight, almost as close …' He declared his ambition to show people that Australia 'is a funny place'. Humphries' appearance on Parkinson marked the beginning of his immense popularity on television, and he drew on the experience, parodying the popular host's seemingly effortless stream of urbane conversation with celebrity guests during Edna's next *Audience*.

Humphries' impulse to show the British that Australia was a 'funny place' inspired much of his work in the 1980s. In 1982 he produced a curious illustrated book about his homeland, *Barry Humphries' Treasury of Australian Kitsch*. It presented a collage of photographs of streetscapes, sculpture, domestic objects, buildings, suburban interiors and oddly assorted people in outlandish dress against a sardonic commentary by the author. The book allowed Humphries free rein on one of his favourite and enduring interests, developed in childhood, when he would drive around with his father looking at new houses. With his tongue firmly in his cheek, Humphries celebrated and satirised Australian architecture, decor and art. The book, both nostalgic and documentary in style, is devoid of didacticism and exhibitionistic knowledge. Barry dedicated it to the genial vaudeville-style entertainer Smacka Fitzgibbon, who had died just before Christmas in 1979. Fitzgibbon had sung the jaunty Barry McKenzie theme song for the films, and Humphries regarded him as a great jazz musician and a good friend.

The *Treasury* contains colour photographs of the Big Pineapple tourist attraction, labelled 'a typical Queensland home', garish tea towels featuring the Opera House, marsupial moneyboxes and models of Aboriginal men with spears adorning suburban gardens. Humphries diagnosed a 'unique national consciousness' in the extravagant fountains of shopping malls, tile mosaics on the façades of bowling alleys and in the glorious 'escutcheon of Nationhood', the Australian coat of arms with kangaroo and emu in gigantic bronze relief on the front of the Federal Court building in Sydney. Humphries also included Edna's Opera House hat, John Brack's painting of Edna with her cold smile and grotesque hands, Russell Drysdale's *Sunday Evening*, Sydney Long's *The Music Lesson* and the Magpie tram painted by Clifton Pugh. Most arresting are the juxtaposed Archibald-winning portrait of a wizened and austere-looking Dame Mary Gilmore by William Dobell and Albert Tucker's stark and grotesque painting *The Intruder*, in which the emaciated explorer figure designated by Humphries 'The Face of Australia' eerily mirrors Gilmore's attenuated gaze. In spite of the oddities and patterns Humphries explored in Australian visual culture, the book is whimsical and affectionate and offers an overwhelmingly affirmative answer to one of Barry's perennial questions: 'Is Australia funny?'

But Humphries' entertaining book also contained a firm rebuke to the crude and philistine approach to civic design evident in several Australian developments. He pilloried a suburban bank in Melbourne, with its ugly vertical brick towers and oblong protrusions. Under a photo of a public lavatory constructed from exposed aggregate opposite a row of Victorian-era shopfronts, Humphries mischievously warned that 'the Authorities are planning ultimately to re-surface every building in the land with this masculine yet sensitive cladding', and that 'patrons using such a facility must, of course, be prepared to take the rough with the smooth'.[2] His barbs were unforgiving, but softened by unexpectedly hilarious remarks such as 'the Australian is the most insatiably visual' of all races, hence the need for a range of viewing gear in the form of kitsch sunglasses. He contrasted a riot of colour in a butcher's shopfront and a Darrell Lea chocolate outlet with the much more sober bas-relief of an urbane gentleman (complete with cigar) in crisp trousers on the exterior of the Fletcher Jones showrooms in Flinders Street, Melbourne, sculpted in 1948. The book attacks the obsessively utilitarian impulse in Australian civic design and the tawdry and ephemeral character of public space in Australia.

Humphries' survey of kitsch in his home country allowed him to develop an implicit argument in support of the preservation of heritage buildings. For a long time he had lamented the aggressive culture of destruction in Melbourne. Initially, a character he devised called 'Wreckem' captured the wanton vandalism that denuded the city of so many fine Victorian buildings in the 1950s. In *Rock 'n' Reel Revue,* the show he devised and performed with Peter O'Shaughnessy in 1958, the council-sponsored thug spoke proudly of the demolition of many gems of nineteenth-century architecture. The sketch parodied the Australian obsession with new buildings for the sake of new buildings, and with parking space, and the nation's irrational irritation with the architecture of earlier periods. Summing up this insatiable desire for the bland and the new, Wreckem dismissed all of Europe in one remark: 'It's too old.'

As far back as the 1960s Humphries had lent his support to conservation campaigns. In 1968 he helped an appeal to reconstruct the colonial poet Adam Lindsay Gordon's cottage at Brighton, Melbourne. It had been demolished in 1946. In a five-stanza poem he asked for 'a noble resurrection' of the cottage, lamenting the loss of theatres and other 'sacred' buildings in favour of the 'Temples of Mammon': 'Forgive me. It is difficult not to be sarcastic, drowning in a sea of deep mauve plastic.' Eric Humphries had been one of those who prospered from the surge of building in the 1930s. His houses reflected a kind of promiscuity in design with Spanish mission, mock-Tudor, Queen Anne and art-deco styles filling the streetscapes in an almost surreal blend of ersatz features. Fifty years later, the buildings of this period seemed worthy of preservation.

The Humphries family, meanwhile, fittingly began to spend more and more time in one of the most elegant buildings in Sydney, with sweeping views to the north and east, over the

Botanic Gardens, the castle-like crenellations of the Conservatorium of Music, the white sails of the Opera House and the sparkling waters of Farm Cove. Humphries had purchased a flat on the ninth floor of the Astor in Macquarie Street before he married Diane. Built in 1923, the thirteen-storey building is a cream-coloured modernist marvel near the Mitchell Library, with marble steps and a rooftop garden. It had been home to various Sydney personalities including Portia Geach and Dame Eadith Walker. The sophisticated block of apartments even had a song written about it that included the tantalising refrain 'She had to go and lose it at the Astor'. (By the end of the song 'it' is revealed to be her mother's sable cape.) Barry and Diane set about contracting a builder to join two apartments on the eighth and ninth floors. Diane set up a third adjacent flat as an art studio.[3]

Although some of Barry's male friends found Diane frosty, standoffish and rather strange, Barry and Diane entertained extensively in the splendid apartment, inviting their friends to lunches, dinners and to watch fireworks over the harbour. Occasionally they sunbaked on the roof. The Humphries sent their friends a card at Christmas with a photo featuring Edna seated beside Oscar and Rupert, while Diane cuddled up beside Barry on the couch. In a speech balloon Edna says, 'Let's face it, possums, I'm the most normal person these waifs are likely to meet this Chrissie.' Barry says, 'Let's wait a few more Christmases before we tell them she doesn't exist.'

Following his television success, Humphries began to find a new freedom and excitement in his stage shows. Even though the long tours were exhausting he was always happy on stage. In the first months of 1984, the *Tears Before Bedtime* tour filled the largest theatres in cities all around Australia. In Adelaide, one thousand people filled the theatre every night.

In this show, Edna made her entrance to a fanfare of music, careering down a slide supported by a massive Scorched Almonds packet centrestage. Her lips were painted a deep glossy carmine, with pointy edges turning up like wings. Dressed in cerise taffeta shorts with gold ribbons tied above the knee, sparkling strappy high heels and dangling diamante earrings, she waited until the applause began to drop then said quietly, 'I feel a mood here, I feel I'm going to do intimate things tonight, I might say things I've never said before. I love Adelaide. I've always loved country people. I hope you never become sophisticated, possums. Something tells me there's not much chance of that.'

She surveyed the audience, looking closely at the faces of those in the front rows and said pensively, 'I see in front of me a sea of lovely people, women looking up at me, their faces are like flowers ... only the occasional cactus.' Then she seized on her first audience member. 'I'm looking for a woman who intrigues me, and I use that word carefully,' she said. Her voice turned sharp: 'You, third row in. What's your name?' And then in a more gentle voice she responded to the forlorn answer from the stalls: 'Kathleen, K or a C, darling?' Edna's head jerked upwards suddenly: 'Paupers, don't lean forward, we don't want the lemmings syndrome, do we. Where are you from dear?' she continued with Kathleen. And so it went on, with Edna questioning several audience members about their homes and gardens. 'What kind of a home do you have there, darling? An old one? Oh that's lovely. Are there any windows ... or just stone?'

Humphries' masterful control of facial expression moved into overdrive as Edna twitched her mouth and curled her lip downwards. Sniffing in disdain and disbelief she coaxed, wheedled and cajoled selected audience members, to the delight and terror of the rest. 'Are you superstitious, Kath?' she persevered. 'I am. That's a bit of a paradox but I'm a paradoxical old left-wing megastar, you know.' Everything returned to Edna, the egomaniac housewife turned superstar, who reminded the audience that she 'cares'. In Adelaide in 1984 even her appearance was paradoxical: she resembled Margaret Thatcher dressed as Kylie Minogue. But the pantomime dame was present in the swagger and the gestures.

As the lights went down, Edna spooked the audience with a tale about a ghost in the theatre, the ghost of an old lady who died watching a play:

Oft times she sitteth in the stalls
She passed away in the middle of a show
And now she sits in the very first row
She wears old rags ...

Without warning Edna let out a blood-curdling scream. 'I can see the spook,' she shrieked, as she pointed towards Lucy, a matronly white-haired audience member in a floral smock and mustard jacket. Then, as if nothing had happened, Edna returned to her affectionate bantering enquiries.

The Dame then launched into a demonstration of her psychic powers. 'I can read people's character in their shoes,' she declared, thrusting an eight-foot steel pole with a fishing net on the end of it into the stalls towards the victim of her ghost story, demanding her shoe. Louisa Humphries had always claimed that you could tell a lot about people from their shoes. Questions and jokes continued about the audience's footwear. Edna reported, 'I get a very good vibration from this shoe,' as she moved onto the next victim: 'Did you get this in a chemist, darling? No I'm teasing, it's lovely.'

Edna soon launched into a song, complete with maracas, mainly about Adelaide but also canvassing other aspects of Australia that she missed:

I miss my husband Norm, of course I do
The lusts of the flesh have long passed
But that's not the form of intercourse I particularly care for
That's what he's in intensive care for.

The highlight of the show was Edna's barbecue. It became a centrepiece of her act. 'I feel I'm among family here tonight,' she whispered, as she invited her 'special possums' up on stage, offering them a glass of cask wine before assigning tasks to all. She set up her 'senior citizen', Ron, as chef, and then instructed each of the women in the correct way to chop cucumber and tomatoes and butter crusty slices of bread. She left Ron to barbecue chops and sausages on one side of the stage, and joined Lucy, Kathleen and two other female victims at a table on the other side. Edna regaled them with tales about her daughter-in-law, Joylene, who was still breastfeeding her five year old, Yasmine, and obsessively growing alfalfa. With each of the possums busy and quaffing wine, Edna announced, 'I'm off to put on a beautiful frock, get some gladdies and make a few phone calls — I could be gone about an hour.' Casting a casual look in the direction of the audience as she flounced off, she shouted, 'Just amuse them, ducks. If you have to, just eat, or scratch your armpits.'

After intermission Edna returned to the stage in a sparkling royal-blue, sequinned Opera House dress with a large, stand-up collar. She looked like a cross between Aunty Jack and Queen Elizabeth I. Hurling dozens of gladdies into the auditorium, even up towards the paupers, she declared, 'This is the true meaning of Interflora!' Before long an air-raid warning screeched, the stage darkened and Edna's 'exocet gladdie rockets' shot out stems into the audience with a large explosion. When the all-clear resounded through the theatre, Edna's barbecue helpers were assembled into her chorus line, as she taught them a song. They linked arms and performed a triumphant finale, with Edna centrestage. Everyone knew the tune and soon the audience joined in, with rousing voices and loud cheers:

> *I'm forever waving gladdies, pretty gladdies in the air*
> *They fly so high, nearly reach the sky*
> *Then like our dreams they fade away ...*

Edna began to bark instructions to the audience. 'Stand and tremble your gladdie, we want maximum gladdie thrust,' she shouted. Each of the special possums beamed. The ritual was nearly over. But then Edna presented each of her helpers with a gift: a gas lighter — 'You can hang it on a feature wall ... it's a talking point'; a lifetime supply of Nivea; some Perrier water; odour-eating insoles; foot deodorant; Scorched Almonds; Steradent; and a bottle of wine. Lucy was 'knighted' as a 'life-long possum'; as she knelt to be touched by Edna on her shoulders with a gladdie, the band serenaded her and once up on her feet again she danced an impromptu jig. It was a wonderful moment. The warmth and compassion of the show filled the audience with energy and delight. They cheered loudly for those 'lucky possums' on stage.

The audience grew wild with applause as Edna pulled a cord on her huge billowing skirt to reveal an Australian flag in sequins, and launched into her finale, 'That's What My Public Means to Me'. Edna farewelled her audience tenderly, rising through a haze of stage fog on a small elevating platform to the level of her beloved 'paupers', as she continued to sing her farewell song. Returning to terra firma she walked downstage, uttered a final 'Cooee, see you next time,' then dropped to the floor and was suddenly blanketed by the falling curtain. Only her alabaster arm, its white powder visible to those in the first few rows, could be seen reaching out around the bottom of the crimson velvet curtain and its gold tassels. Her huge rings glowed, the blood-coloured, polished nails shone. The disembodied, single hand waved, dropped, quivered as if in a death throe, reached up again, dropped once more and was gone. It was both whimsical and macabre, a magical Dadaist gesture at the end of a night of revelry. The crowd roared in appreciation.

It was a triumphant conclusion to a magnificent show. Humphries was at the peak of his powers and Edna was becoming an all-powerful mask. The critical responses to the show were mixed but reviewers agreed that Edna was 'ferocious', 'devastating' and dangerously realistic.

CHAPTER 28

Formica Lady

In the northern summer of 1984, the Humphries family moved from their English home, a mansion flat in Queen's Gate, Kensington, to a large house in Wedderburn Road, Hampstead. They spent the next six months unpacking hundreds of boxes of paintings and books. At last Barry had somewhere to hang his treasured art, and to display his antique masterpieces, and Diane could have a studio in the house. Humphries had always liked the area, and cherished the memories of his long walks on the heath as he waited for the opportunity to audition when he and Rosalind first moved to Highgate in 1960. Barry was fifty years old, and felt stronger and more at ease than he had for a long time. He was settled, and happy in his new house. It made a pleasant change from the apartment in Sydney, and Barry enjoyed taking his small boys to visit the heath's duckponds, and to roam in the gardens of Kenwood House, with its significant art collection, just up the hill.

Humphries continued his comic assault on celebrity culture with a second *Audience with Dame Edna* that screened on New Year's Eve, 1984. The set, with its magenta lurex curtain and pink grand piano, had the uncanny feel of an RSL club back home in Australia. The show even began as though it was one of Humphries' regular stage shows. A rather Falstaffian Les Patterson did his clubland introduction. He was just like a music hall compere, only more grotesque. But ultimately the focus was on Edna as Les does not work well on television, mainly because of the constraints of the censors.

Edna was resplendent in a silver satin maxi-gown with a split right up to the thigh, and flaunting a large silver peace-sign pendant that dangled to her waist. She was more strident and egotistical than ever: 'I've a reputation as a comedienne but Dame Nature gave me the priceless ability to laugh at the misfortunes of others,' she declared. She continued to construct her own legend: 'I've been accepted by the theatre; I'm basically an amateur but I'm a phenomenon!' She addressed her comments straight to her compatriot Clive James, a noted television commentator, in the studio audience, then moved to jokes about short men. Fixing the grinning James with a knowing look, she confided, 'I rather like shortish men, Clive, men you can look down on ... like Roman Polanski, Lord Snowdon and little Charles Aznavour.' The audience rocked with laughter.

The opera star Dame Kiri Te Kanawa was also in the audience. 'I put you up for that little damehood, I did ... they asked me,' cooed Edna to the diva from New Zealand. Denis Healey, the Labour politician, and his wife, also an Edna, were present too. 'Would you accept a damehood, Edna — you'd be Dame Edna the Second!' declared Edna Everage, as the camera focused on a delighted Mrs Healey. Not to be outdone, Denis Healey put his question to the hostess: 'Have you ever thought of making music with Sir Les Patterson?' 'No, what a facetious question,' she retorted. 'And I think he [Les] is not at all typical of Australia,' she continued curtly. At the end of the show Edna sang, 'I'm shy ... like Paul McCartney I'm almost a recluse.' The rather demure besuited Charles Aznavour appeared unannounced on set with a bunch of gladdies for Edna. He sang along with her: 'I'm shy ... I only wish I was a metre taller,' and they began to waltz. Edna was clumsy, her mannish shoulders dwarfing the fine-boned French singer. It was a ridiculous yet joyful way to farewell the old year and welcome the new.

But behind the good cheer and glitz of the New Year's Eve extravaganza, Humphries was grieving for his mother. Louisa

Humphries had died on 4 October 1984. Barbara had phoned Barry to report that Louisa had been admitted to Box Hill Hospital, but she had said it was not serious. Barry took her at her word, and stayed in London, but phoned to speak to his mother straight away. Barbara telephoned him a few days later and broke the news of their mother's passing. The distance between his home in Melbourne and his home in London had never seemed so great.

In the 1980s, as Barry Humphries achieved celebrity status in the UK, thanks to television, and Edna Everage gradually became a household name, Margaret Thatcher was transforming British politics following the landslide re-election of the Tories in 1983. Humphries was hooked on the Iron Lady's sayings and doings from the moment he read about Mrs Thatcher's embarrassment at a public ceremony, when she arrived to find that the Queen was wearing an almost identical outfit to her own. He was tickled to discover that Mrs Thatcher had sent a memo to Buckingham Palace to find out whether she could be informed beforehand of what the Queen would be wearing. The reply came back: 'Do not worry. The Queen does not notice what other people are wearing.'[1] The incident was a touchstone for the rising tension between the monarch and her prime minister, which was no secret in a nation undergoing rapid social and economic change. For Humphries, however, it was the humiliation inherent in the dress incident that appealed and gave him one of his most enduring jokes.

As the decade of greed and need wore on, Edna could be seen in frequent parody of the indomitable grocer's daughter-cum-housewife leader of the Tories. Humphries had been an eager student of Mrs Thatcher for some years by the time *The Dame Edna Experience*, his most successful show, hit the nation's television screens in 1987. By then Edna Everage had become a potent satirical symbol of the new blend of British conservatism and excess. The disjunction between the mantras of the 'attractive mother of twins', as the prime minister was often described in the early days after she won the seat of Finchley, and the harshness of her policies shocked even hardened conservatives. Margaret Thatcher, with her constant talk of 'honest money' and platitudes of caring and her simultaneous dismantling of the welfare state, found her echo in the barbs of the housewife turned megastar, Dame Edna Everage.

As Thatcher demonstrated the dizzying effects of power on a daily basis, Humphries, in the guise of Edna Everage, also rode on a high, as millions of viewers tuned in to his new prime-time show every Saturday night.[2] *The Dame Edna Experience* was the ultimate chat show. Edna offered the viewing audience a carnival of wish fulfilment as they watched pampered movie stars, Hollywood legends and pop icons treated with a blend of indifference and condescending flattery by the hostess of the show. Undercutting the hype, Edna told viewers in the very first episode as she introduced herself that the show 'is not really a chat show, it's a monologue by a megastar, interrupted by total strangers'.

Like Dame Edna, the prime minister liked to project an image of herself as superhuman. Immediately after an operation on her eye she set out on a tour of Europe. Journalists asked her if a tour might not be a little premature, given that it was only a few days since her surgery. 'It may be too much for a normal person who has had an operation,' replied Mrs Thatcher without irony, 'but, after all, it is me we are talking about.'[3]

Known to need only four or five hours of sleep each night, the prime minister astonished everyone because she never looked tired. Her complexion was milky, smooth and her face unlined. One of her ministers told the *Observer* that he would frequently encounter 'this vision in blue' at 1 am in the corridors of the Commons, looking as if she had just emerged from 'the beauty parlour'. 'Ah,' she would say, 'how are you, dear? Now tell me what you think about these new statistics, and what do you propose to do about them?'[4]

Edna Everage also began to terrify. Her energy and the savagery of her lamentations, always bracketed with 'I mean that in a caring way, I do', clearly satirised the prime minister who would frequently purr, 'Of course I care about the unemployed.' Dame Edna boldly projected a curious affinity with Thatcher. 'She phones me at all hours of the day and night,' Edna reported on national television. Between 1980 and 1989, the ascendancy of the lower middle-class housewife from Moonee Ponds to megastar status stood as a comic corollary of the upwardly mobile fervour of the British prime minister, and the transformations she brought about when she was re-elected in 1983.

It is not surprising that Humphries seemed to understand this powerful woman so completely. Barry Humphries, too, is blessed with enormous energy, never sits still, has rarely visited a doctor and strikes terror into the hearts of many, even those with whom he has worked closely. At the height of his own powers as a performer, Humphries was utterly intoxicated by the popularity of his persona and his burgeoning success on television. Like Thatcher, who came from a lower middle-class background and shredded the world of High Tory politics, Humphries knew what it was like to be treated as an arriviste. He, too, had grown up in a household intent on upward social striving in which both parents had elevated themselves through hard work to the prosperous middle class. He understood aspiration and its Protestant maxims; after all, he had built his career on satirising the almost Victorian social morality of his own class.

Also like Thatcher, Humphries developed an expert repertoire in neutralising criticism. When Angela Thorne portrayed her as a domineering woman with a penchant for the perfect coiffure in *Anyone for Denis?* at the Whitehall Theatre, the prime minister attended a special Sunday performance with all proceeds to be donated to charities of her choice, and hosted the cast for dinner at Downing Street, after the show. She made much of her decision to continue with some of her 'wifely' duties. The Thatchers did not employ a live-in maid or housekeeper and the PM cooked her husband's breakfast every morning, eating only a grapefruit, slice of toast or an apple herself.[5] Of course the cosiness, intimacy and modesty of her life at Number 10 with Denis, her husband, and her preference for chat about housekeeping contrasted powerfully with her contempt for old-school clubby Tory loyalties and consensus politics, her hardline attitude towards the millions of unemployed and her role in the shattering of trade unions. The prime minister's domestic rituals, astounding comments and saccharine public utterances were like manna from heaven for Humphries.

In Edna's portrayal of her own life, from the lavish surrounds of her Thames-side television penthouse, her jokes about paupers, her obsession with her hairstyle, and her tales of Norm's last days, abandoned to his fate in hospital, Edna operated at several removes from the prime minister. But she revelled in some of Mrs Thatcher's homespun homilies. Thatcher's insistence on 'old-fashioned' values inspired Edna: 'Call me old fashioned!' became her signature form of self-congratulatory self-deprecation, as she launched into a tirade of punishing indifference to her 'little' guests. Edna satirised Mrs Thatcher's peculiar style of Tory politics, her appeal to a past era's notion of hard work, sacrifice and saving on the back of her hard-right agenda, her ruthless approach to ordinary people and staggering departure from gender norms. If at times it seemed as though the Tories and their leader were sneering at the unfortunate members of British society, Edna gave this cruelty voice and paraded her own heartlessness.

If the Queen found Mrs Thatcher's regime troubling at times, and the Sex Pistols satirised the national anthem in a punk rock version of 'God Save the Queen', the younger members of the British royal family fell in love with Dame Edna Everage, and became ardent fans of Edna's television appearances. By the end of the decade, Humphries as Edna was a natural on television. His stage presence, spontaneity, his instinct for touching raw nerves, and his mastery of the audience were perfect light entertainment. Edna's voice seemed smoother on television, the songs were rehearsed and more suited to Edna's range than some of her ambitious stage numbers. Occasionally Edna murdered a song deliberately for comic effect, and occasionally it was not so deliberate. But nothing seemed to detract from Edna's growing following.

Edna revelled in the frivolous, the topical, the controversial and the trivial, celebrating the glamour and kitsch of television culture in the 1980s. 'Edna' had learned to transport a television audience in the way that Humphries had perfected in his live theatre shows, presenting a ritual of embarrassment for an audience of millions.

Humphries was rewarded for Edna's first *Audience* when he won a BAFTA for Best Entertainment Program in 1980. More awards followed. At its peak, Humphries' regular chat show, *The Dame Edna Experience*, attracted more than eight million viewers each Saturday night.

Humphries' success on British television in the 1980s is one of the major achievements of his career. More importantly, his success in the prime-time slot with his housewife character from Moonee Ponds was an artistic triumph. In the early 1960s Barry had crashed at the Establishment Club in Soho, in front of an indifferent and bemused nightclub crowd. A quarter of a century later Humphries had not only broken into British television comedy, he had reinvented variety and the chat show. Humphries created his very own theatre of the absurd on television and the me-generation could not get enough.

CHAPTER 29

Mount Edna

Once Edna had climbed the mountain of celebrity and attained the glittering pinnacle of her own weekly chat show, Barry Humphries envisaged a change for his most enduring creation. He decided she should have a wardrobe that reflected her new status, and invited the young costume designer who had been assigned to *The Dame Edna Experience* to come to his home in Hampstead to discuss Edna's new look. A rather nervous Stephen Adnitt arrived at the large, imposing house in Wedderburn Road. Barry outlined for Stephen his ideas for Edna's newly glamorous image. The affable designer had always admired Edna Everage and had never forgotten her hilarious line about the half-timbered car — 'Look! They even have Tudor-style cars here!' — on one of her televised visits to Stratford-upon-Avon in the 1960s as she explored Shakespeare's birthplace. But glamour was not a word he associated with the Dame. Adnitt had envisaged dressing her in Queen Mother-like gowns: staid and dignified, flowing chiffon and pastel hues. But Humphries' vision was very different, leaning towards the bold and ostentatious.

Adnitt embraced the challenge to create a new image for Edna. The budgets for *The Dame Edna Experience* were generous and Barry gave the young designer free rein. Before long Adnitt had transformed the Dame. Adnitt's exceptional eye for colour and texture and his flair for elegance and theatricality marked the end of Edna's matronly days. In dress Edna was now not only glamorous but outrageously glamorous, flaunting full-length fitted evening gowns in velvet and satin embossed with gold and silver. They were regal, highly theatrical and exquisitely made. Like the Queen, Edna always swung a matching handbag over her arm, only relinquishing it for her cabaret numbers that provided the spectacular finale to every show.

Auditions had been held by London Weekend Television to cast a new Madge Allsop. (Madeleine Orr, who had played Madge previously, had died in 1979.) An octogenarian actress, Emily Perry, easily out-performed the other contestants and joined the show. Her impassive face and droopy, diminutive form seemed made for the role of the depressed bridesmaid character. Perry had been a soubrette, playing Susan in *The Desert Song* for twelve years, and had danced in the clubs of Soho in the 1930s. With her experience and love of pantomime, she was perfect for *The Dame Edna Experience*, and it was a thrilling prospect for her to be launching a new chapter of her career at eighty. She arranged to meet Adnitt in the West End one morning to shop for her costumes. Several bemused shop assistants scurried around making helpful suggestions for bright colours and petite styles. Adnitt and Perry blithely ignored them and selected drab grey and fawn sweaters and worsted skirts, all several sizes too large, for the tiny actress to wear as Madge.

The opening sequence of the first series of *The Dame Edna Experience* showed Edna emerging from the entrance of 10 Downing Street with the prime minister, Mrs Thatcher, following her like a dogged assistant. Several frames of Edna in conversation with President Reagan followed, as a voice-over proclaimed that the lady was 'bringing words of comfort to the bewildered'. Next, a few frames of the Dame in polka dots, blowing kisses to a crowd of pilgrims in St Peter's Square beside the Pope, topped off the sequence.

It was not easy to predict how the guests would greet their cross-dressing host. Most opted for a European-style kiss on both cheeks. As each guest took his or her seat opposite the hostess, Edna barked at her dowdy bridesmaid assistant, 'Badge Madge,' then stuck a yellow handwritten name tag on the guest's lapel, explaining that this was a necessity 'in case I forget your name'. The set was grand, with shiny columns, a couch in the shape of Australia, stairs that lit up, a big band in the centre of the stage and the whole performance space crowned by a gigantic pair of Edna spectacles in glittering lights.

Edna loved to point out her guest's embarrassing secrets and took pleasure in raising sensitive issues. In a parody of the tell-all talk show formula, Edna fixed Charlton 'Chuck' Heston with a look of intensity, declaring: 'I want to strip you naked, darling,' before asking him about his early days as an artist's model in New York. But Edna's show was not simply a series of put-downs; that would never have worked. The guests revealed a great deal about themselves. There was chat, wit and badinage. Like Michael Parkinson's interviews or those of Andrew Denton in Australia, they are uneven, with some guests much more forthcoming and relaxed than others. As she kept stating, Edna really does probe. Edna is an excellent interviewer, even if she tends to take over at times. But provocation by a man in a dress drew some spectacular performances from the guests.

Towards the end of the first series of *The Dame Edna Experience*, Humphries requested that a young researcher on the show, Claudia Rosencrantz, take over as producer. His intervention represented an act of faith in Rosencrantz, who had no production experience. But she was young, ambitious and highly articulate, and had an eye on moving into a new role. Before *The Dame Edna Experience* she had worked on other chat shows, researching the histories of guests for Clive James and Russell Harty, and before that as a Fleet Street journalist with the *Sunday Telegraph Magazine*. She was shocked when studio executives approached her with the bald announcement: 'Barry wants you to produce the show.' After some talking she agreed to give it a try.

One of the keys to the successful Humphries–Rosencrantz working relationship was personal. Claudia and Barry got on famously from the beginning, and Rosencrantz immediately put her mark on every aspect of the show. She brought an instinctive understanding of how Humphries performed on stage to work, filming the show in sequence with minimal breaks so as not to interrupt the magic of the live studio event. She was determined to make the filming as tight as possible because she had observed that stopping and starting did not work well for Barry as a performer. Any problems with this form of live recording could be sorted out in the editing suite.

Months before anything was filmed for the second series, Claudia put together a team of researchers with a 'chase list' of celebrities they hoped to persuade to appear on *The Dame Edna Experience*. Claudia knew exactly what she wanted in a perfect Edna guest: someone whose persona was bigger than their talent or chosen field. To be a good or great actor was not enough: Edna needed to build the comedy around the persona, reputation or force-field of the celebrity. If the guest was too intellectual and too knowing, or too retiring, this might spoil the fun of the encounter with Edna. Similarly, she understood Barry's reticence about interviewing other comedians because they might interrupt the rhythm of the comic performance by Humphries as Edna.

Once bookings were made and the mix of guests decided, with a singer always included for the finale, the writing for the show began. Each researcher produced a full biography of the guest to try and tease out the aspects of his or her life that might offer an interesting line of enquiry for Edna. A researcher then visited the guest for a pre-interview. Afterwards the writing continued so that the interview questions and comic material could be built and refined around the guests. Simultaneously the comic monologue for the opening of the show was developed, drafted, revised and rehearsed.

All chat shows have a particular way of prompting the host's memory and reminding them of the interview plan, and Barry was receptive to new techniques for preparing for a performance. When the script was nearly ready, with all the possible questions worked out, Claudia, Barry and Ian Davidson, who had continued to write with Barry over the years, would together work out the 'buzzies'. These were the words that would prompt Barry through his interviews on the autocue, giving him clues as to where to go next with his questioning. It is a technique used by numerous hosts, including Michael Parkinson. Once the buzzies were determined, Claudia and Barry would run through the material again and again until Barry was thoroughly immersed in the script. The more he worked with it the more relaxed he became and the more he ad-libbed. Finally, when he was comfortable, the 'gospel buzzies' were loaded for the autocue. By the time Barry was recording, he knew the words by heart and was thoroughly at home with the material that they signalled.[1]

The paradox of performance in this mode, as Claudia well understood, was that the better prepared the host, the more relaxed he would be with the guest and the more spontaneous the interview. It is no easy feat to hold in your head the map of an interview with each guest. But Barry had already perfected a similar art on stage, of questioning audience members and remembering every detail of their answers, storing them in his head for future retorts and even later scenes in the show. His memory is extraordinary, and though he was able to hold the entire show in his head on stage, with the autocue he could relax a little, knowing that the next buzzword would always anchor his performance.

As well as being a sympathetic producer, Rosencrantz understood Barry's subversive humour. The Edna television chat shows offered quintessential satire, at once celebrating the excesses of the rich and famous and revealing the production and adulation of fame as ludicrous, ritualised, even fetishistic. When Edna described herself as a 'social anthropologist', there was a grain of truth in her words. Humphries' talk show revelled in the baroque vulgarity of the 1980s, as Edna's television world literally brought the celebrity guests down to audience level. The long walk down the staircase as Laurie Holloway's band, the Hollowtones, played Edna's theme music prolonged the suspense, and prepared the guest and the audience for the inevitable and sometimes dazzling comedown of the interview with Edna Everage.

Thanks to Stephen Adnitt's adept eye, Edna's costumes had become a crucial component of the satirical experience. In one episode in the first season, Edna appeared in a swishy black taffeta cocktail dress with a pattern of huge red tongues and lips, in parody of the Rolling Stones signature image. Adnitt in fact designed the magnificent dress for both Edna and her guest Jerry Hall, supermodel and partner of the Rolling Stones' singer Mick Jagger. Normally guests wore whatever they chose on the show, unless they were participating in a song or were part of a joke. The joke in this instance was that Edna was horrified to see Hall appearing in 'her' dress, while Hall, too, was shocked at seeing Edna in 'her' dress.

As part of the joke, Humphries had agreed that Adnitt would copy a costume of Hall's choice for Edna to wear in the finale, when the pair would sing together. Adnitt's jaw dropped when he first saw the garments Hall had selected: a gold lurex cowgirl suit complete with skintight jodhpurs. Adnitt hated to put Edna in trousers; it went against all his aesthetic instincts. He cringed when he first saw Edna dressed up and ready to rehearse the song number. Barry's long skinny legs had not changed much since his days playing Orsino in *Twelfth Night* in country Victoria, even if he'd lost his self-consciousness. But the segment turned out to be one of the most memorable sequences of the series. The sultry and lithe Jerry Hall began crooning Tammy Wynette's country-and-western classic, 'Stand by Your Man'. After about a minute, to the admiring gasps of the audience, Edna appeared beside her, and they sang the rest of the song together.

Edna and Jerry were resplendent in their gleaming gold cowgirl outfits, complete with high-heeled riding boots and diamante-studded Stetson hats. It was a satirical spectacle of high-camp glamour, with both host and guest singing slightly off key.

The sketch relied on audience awareness of Hall's relationship with Mick Jagger, never one to hide his zest for the company of women; not long before Hall's appearance on the show Jagger had been involved in a series of high-profile relationships and a divorce from his wife, Bianca, on the grounds of his adultery with Jerry herself. Hall played along with this ritual of embarrassment, looking innocent, almost gormless and completely in character as she sang. The lyrics took on new layers of comic urgency: 'Sometimes it's hard to be a woman,' Jerry and Edna sang together. 'But if you love him, be proud of him/After all he's just a man,' they whined in true country-and-western fashion. Humphries' comic critique of gender had never been so explicit as in this witty, rather kitsch and magnificently produced number. It also marked a new flirtation, a 'queering' of Edna Everage, who kept her pantomime dame roots but now would not have been out of place at a gay club.

Later in the series, when the actor Michael Gambon, Barry's one-time understudy, told Edna he would really like to play Oscar Wilde's Lady Bracknell, Edna's lips turned down in disapproval as she replied aghast: 'A female role? Are your parents aware of this? Tragic. I suppose Jonathan Miller would think it's a good idea.' It was one of a series of comments in this vein over the period of the show. Several years earlier Edna had appeared on *Aspel and Company*, and pranced onto the set to the jaunty tune of the band, in lime green tights and a pink, lime, yellow and black punk miniskirt, topped off with spectacles featuring large plastic doves on their pointy tips. Michael Aspel, the host, barely got any questions in as Edna took over. 'Isn't it sad about transvestites?' she remarked. 'What sort of homes do those poor people come from?'

As hostess on her own show, Edna talked over any answers that threatened to drag on, and often brought the conversation back to herself. Just as the guest began recounting a life event of some importance to them, she would cut in with a story about herself or her invalid husband, Norm. As Edward Heath spoke about his childhood, Edna enjoyed a quick neck massage from another guest, Dolph Lundgren. Heath was undeterred, but some guests found Edna's manner offputting. Germaine Greer appeared slightly strained when she appeared on the show dressed in a grey sack-like dress and gold lace-up shoes; she seemed nervous, not quite at home with the comic act in which she was participating, but she played along with Edna's story, talking about her brief marriage and recalling the early advice 'Auntie Edna' had given her — that marriage 'was for keeps'. Greer may have found the comic assault by Edna unsettling, but she still managed a few brilliant quips of her own. Deflecting a question about the influence of *The Female Eunuch*, Greer struck out:

> I don't think it's been very influential at all. I think you've been more influential. I mean Mrs Thatcher is someone who's learned every lesson you had to teach. She's going to turn England into Moonee Ponds. That's her stated objective: everybody in their own home, making new surrounds for the fireplace, and mowing the nature strip and polishing the car. It's going to be just like Moonee Ponds.

It was a magnificent moment. Two middle-aged Australians — one a high-profile feminist scholar and social commentator and the other an actor in drag who looked like the prime minister of Great Britain — indulged a prime-time British audience with a camp deconstruction of a talk show, and a discussion of how to make an Australian cake called a lamington. If Humphries had found a way to subvert the cult of celebrity, Greer found an opportunity of her own, lambasting the British prime minister for her suburban narrow-mindedness, and making Dame Edna responsible for the sorry state of the nation.

At other times, Edna's attack could be surprisingly muted, and Humphries' skill as an interviewer would be evident. In the very first episode of *The Dame Edna Experience*, Edna interviewed Mary Whitehouse, the spokeswoman for the pro-censorship brigade in the UK since the early 1960s. Edna introduced Whitehouse as 'a lovely little friend of mine', and the interview was remarkable for its equanimity; the satire was gentle with a parodic subtext. Whitehouse urged Dame Edna to use her megastar status to help fight rampant violence and sex on television. She managed to get her point across. Using her next guest, Cliff Richard, the famously celibate singer, to 'test' her ejection seat (copied by Graham Norton twenty years later), Edna warned Whitehouse to block her ears lest Richard utter something 'uncalled for', as she asked him to 'dredge the sewers of [his] mind, and say something really disgusting'. It was a moment of marvellous incongruity. When Richard said 'blow dry', he was instantly ejected from the set. Whitehouse laughed uproariously.

British audiences revelled in this comic subversion of talk, and Humphries appeared to be at the height of his powers. In the 1970s his *Barry McKenzie* films had embraced populist entertainment, and he perfected his appeal to the people. In *The Dame Edna Experience* the humour reached into what television theorists such as Andrew Tolson called 'post-populist' forms, noting the way such shows presented both 'sincere and insincere talk' with delicious ambiguity.[2]

The guests varied but all of them seemed to enjoy themselves — a hallmark of the genre. Nana Mouskouri giggled defensively as she recalled her childhood in Athens, but relaxed into the interview and offered several interesting recollections of her early life. Slapstick was part of the act, and Charlton Heston was unceremoniously knocked out of his 'wheelchair' by Edna's on-set 'nurse'. No matter who they were, the guests engaged in low comedy with zest and enthusiasm. Zsa Zsa Gabor was welcomed by Edna as 'the best thing to come out of Hungary since goulash', and dressed up like a massive meringue, was at home with the parody, giving a virtuoso comic performance without stealing Edna's thunder. The contrasts between the guests allowed Humphries maximum comic effect.

Product pushing was absent, anathema to the show. Guests were not invited on *The Dame Edna Experience* in order to promote their films or sound recordings. The moment a celebrity launched into a monologue about his or her latest movie Edna cut in. In the second series of the show some celebrity guests were physically removed before they even had a chance to speak. Charlton Heston was literally dropped through a trapdoor.

Though always ready to savage them, Edna was also saccharine and solicitous towards her guests, as though they were infants in need of direction and supervision. She frequently referred to them as 'little', for example calling Charlton Heston 'Little Chuck'. It was a delicious parody of the feigned affection shown by 'real' talk show hosts who fawn over each guest, and later reduce them to tears as the guests are gulled into revealing sad or embarrassing details of their lives. When 'little Kurt Waldheim', who was played by a double, appeared momentarily on *The Dame Edna Experience*, Edna simply 'stroked the console' of her chair, and the floor beneath his feet opened. The real Waldheim, formerly the President of Austria and Secretary-General of the United Nations, had recently made some widely reported racist comments, so was 'despatched back to Vienna' without further explanation. (The Austrian embassy issued a protest immediately after the show screened.) In her Christmas special at the end of the first series of her popular show, Edna explained to viewers that 'niceness is next to holiness'. Humphries via Edna Everage had found his niche on British television and provided an audience of millions with weekly relief from the burden of niceness.

Claudia Rosencrantz devised an ingenious new title sequence for the second series of *The Dame Edna Experience*. Edna was shown in a helicopter flying across London and landing on the roof of her 'penthouse' in order to meet her guests at home for the show. Her luxury apartment block, Everage Towers, was a deliberate parody of Trump Tower in New York. The Queen, Princess Diana and other members of the royal family were among those who waved to Edna as she soared over them in the helicopter. Mrs Thatcher looked up and saluted her affectionately from the doorway of 10 Downing Street, and Mikhail Gorbachev, the Pope, Colonel Gaddafi and a tribe of Kalahari bushmen also all gazed skyward and waved cheerfully to the Dame.

In the first episode of this series Edna informed the audience that she had simply refused to film any more episodes of her show in that 'carbuncle on the South Bank' — the London Weekend Television Studios — and insisted on shooting the show 'in my own home', with its massive portrait of her by Andy Warhol ('I don't much care for it') and a copy of *The Scream* by her old favourite Munch. Humphries was elated when one guest, Liza Minnelli, confessed to believing that the Warhol was genuine. The guests 'stayed' at Edna's penthouse, giving her an opportunity to get to know them and to evaluate them as housemates.

Edna didn't hold back in her assessments — or the insults — in this second series. Speaking to Ron Reagan (son of Ronald and Nancy Reagan) about his dancing career, she remarked that Nureyev, who had appeared on her last show, 'might have passed his sell-by date', and that 'each time he jumped, his little bottom jumped a second later'. Claudia's influence was evident in the show, with each episode tighter and more polished than those of the first series. Edna explained to the audience that she had been inundated with celebrities 'wanting to tell me about their dull little lives. When I say no,' she went on, 'the men in white carry them away and put them on the Wogan show, the next best thing to an intravenous pentathol. I mean that nicely Terry [Wogan], I do.'

There was even a sketch by five acclaimed actors who were treated almost as if they were one whole. Michael Gambon, Tim Pigott-Smith, Antony Sher, David Suchet and Malcolm McDowell marched down the stairs in identical dinner suits and sat squashed together on a bench like schoolboys. Edna informed them that if they wanted an individual appearance they must answer various questions first. In question after question, each actor, when called upon by Edna to respond, gave the same answer as the previous actor. The sketch is one of the funniest sequences of the series, with its witty lampooning of hackneyed talk show questions and the slick, generic answers offered by the same actors who appear over and over again on indistinguishable programs.

In the second series the comic spectacle of Edna's show took on more structure. Douglas Fairbanks Jr and Ted Heath were left waiting in the foyer of Edna's 'penthouse', and spoke to her on a closed-circuit security screen before gaining admission. With a sigh, Edna remarked to the audience that Fairbanks 'looks better in black and white'. Jane Fonda failed to make it through security in the foyer, and 'Imelda Marcos' barely crossed the threshold before being set upon by Edna's guard dogs, with Edna shouting, 'You stole my shoes, you ungrateful klepto,' at the retreating 'first lady of the Philippines'. After a huge build-up for the arrival on set of 'Princess Michael of Kent', there was an explosion as the 'princess' arrived. It set off a booby trap that scooped her up and suspended her upside-down from the ceiling. Edna muttered, 'Had it been any other member of the royal family my career would be over.'

Humphries' nostalgic passion for the music of the big band era, and his enduring obsession with Hollywood glamour infused the show. He favoured guests who had worked as actors in the period of his youth. One of the highlights of the second series occurred in an exchange between Edna and Fairbanks Jr (once he was admitted to Edna's living room). When the elder statesman of Hollywood arrived panting from his 'walk' up the thirty-four flights of stairs to Edna's penthouse, she mopped his brow, making soothing comments as she adjusted his Windsor knot, and then said: 'You old swashbuckler. Your swashing days are over, you're not swashing anymore, you're starting to buckle.' Fairbanks Jr took the insult with a broad good-natured smile. He delighted in Edna's witty remarks and was candid in his responses.

Claudia Rosencrantz was still at the helm for the final instalment of *The Dame Edna Experience*, a special Christmas show, *A Night on Mount Edna*, made the following year, 1990. In this show Edna entertained Mel Gibson, Charlton Heston, Julio Iglesias and Gina Lollobrigida in her 'luxury lodge' in Switzerland. Maggie Howard, the series designer, created a magnificently festive snowy set and Claudia arranged an opening sequence for Edna in which she rather improbably skied down a mountain. Mel Gibson appeared naked to the waist in the sauna with Edna, and Charlton Heston dropped a pot of steaming fondue onto the lap of Julio Iglesias who seemed oblivious to the riotous events around him. The preparations were exhausting and included a manic flight to Los Angeles to film Gibson in the specially manufactured sauna, with Edna's costume still being pinned and sewn together on the aircraft. After introductions were exchanged in the LA studio, Rosencrantz asked Gibson to strip off for the filming, which was completed in a matter of three hours, before the team packed everything up and boarded a plane to fly back to London, in time to record the rest of the show for the next week.

Humphries particularly enjoyed Claudia's company. With her as producer, the series ran smoothly and Humphries allowed her to follow her instincts. It was a dream run for the two of them; they never quarrelled. Barry trusted Claudia and she repaid that trust with vision, energy and talent. She was also a good listener, and Barry hated to be without an audience.

In order to create the opening sequence for the Mount Edna special, Claudia arranged a shoot at an indoor ski slope in Telford. She and Barry organised to travel by train to the venue. During the journey Humphries pulled one of his schoolboyish pranks on her. When Claudia rose from her seat to find the toilet cubicle, as the train waited in a station en route, Barry said: 'You're not meant to use the loo when the train is stopped in a station.' 'Don't be silly,' she said, as he continued to remonstrate with her. Eventually she set off down the aisle with his warnings echoing in her ears. A few moments later there was a loud pounding on the door of the cubicle, and Claudia heard a man's voice; it was a British Rail conductor barking, 'Is there somebody in there? What are you doing in there? I hope you're not having a pee, it's illegal.' His accent was undeniably, perfectly English. She waited a few minutes until the man moved away, then emerged red faced. 'I've just had the most awful experience,' she said to Barry as she returned to her seat. He burst into laughter and Claudia realised it had been Barry at the door.[3]

At its peak *The Dame Edna Experience* drew some 8.3 million viewers, representing 48.7 per cent of the network share. This was about one-seventh of the population of Great Britain. Yet for all his remarkable success in the cut-throat world of television, Barry continued to prefer the stage, relishing the world of the theatre and the freedom it allowed him. For Humphries there is always a feeling of intense nervousness and excitement followed by a rush of adrenalin as the curtain goes up and he walks on stage. In the empty auditorium, before the audience arrives, he performs a series of vocal exercises, making a series of whooping noises, like a whale or dolphin 'singing'. The routine, like sitting for make-up, is comforting. After the shows he enthusiastically talks to the ushers about how the performance went.[4] He once told a London journalist that he had found his 'daily appointment with the public' an enormous help to him during periods of great personal stress and sadness.[5]

By the end of *The Dame Edna Experience*, Humphries' personal life was certainly under pressure. There was considerable tension over Barry's frequent absences and his overwhelming drive to work which meant he did not always have time for his children.

On television, Humphries could not exercise the control he has in a stage show. Paradoxically there are many more variables in the studio. The stage is his and his alone; it is like home for Barry. John Lahr once observed him preparing to perform: after making-up in his dressing room, stepping into his costume and walking onto the stage his anticipation and joy were evident, as if he were thinking 'Alone at last'.[6] It is just Barry, in the guise of his various alter egos, with an audience, who become his supporting cast. On television he needed to please the guests, executives, producers and sponsors, not to mention the millions of viewers. Everything took so much longer to prepare, with script meetings, rehearsals and reshoots. Even the make-up took almost three hours for each television appearance and Humphries had to sit still as it was meticulously applied by a make-up artist. His nails had to be buffed and polished, his arms and legs closely shaved. Worst of all, sometimes he had to stop just as he got into his stride during the recording of a show, and start again.

In television, there were so many factors to consider, and decisions were made by many people. At one stage, Barry waged a campaign to invite guests onto *The Dame Edna Experience* whom he thought would be exciting to interview for their artistic and cultural achievements. He told John Lahr that he suggested inviting the American writer Gore Vidal, but the very firm answer was, 'No one in Bradford has heard of Gore Vidal.' For Humphries, Bradford's ignorance was no impediment as Edna was just as unenlightened: she hadn't heard of Gore Vidal either.[7] He had also hoped to interview the aging German film maker Leni Riefenstahl, and suggested, too, Joan Sutherland, Erica Jong, Jackie Onassis, Paloma Picasso, Jilly Cooper, Edna O'Brien, Margaret Trudeau and Iris Murdoch. He even joked about inviting Mother Teresa, but knew that was absurd. Humphries was usually overruled. Infuriatingly for him, television executives always favoured show business personalities, although Claudia took a broader view.[8] Humphries particularly resisted anyone whom he perceived to be a regular on Johnny Carson's *Tonight Show* or Terry Wogan's chat show. The whole rationale of his show, as he explained to John Lahr, was to puncture the celebrity circus routine, yet ultimately his show became an intrinsic part of that circus.

Although he was kept busy with his television commitments at this time, Barry also toured Australia with his extravagant stage show, *Tears Before Bedtime*. In Melbourne, thousands filled the St Kilda Palais in March 1986 to see Humphries play Sir Les, Sandy and the harping unionist Lance Boyle, now a property developer. The second act was devoted to Edna. Leonard Radic was disappointed with Edna's vanity and monstrous ego and mused that Humphries 'is probably stuck with Edna Everage. He can't retire her.'[9]

And, as on the train with Claudia, he still indulged his love of simple pranks, though they were increasingly benign. In Australia in 1985 he was presented with a 'Wilkie', an award set up by the writer Keith Dunstan and other like-minded opponents of sport to honour the person who has done the least for football in the fairest manner. They called themselves the AFL, or Anti-Football League, and Barry won the award for arranging for a camel to eat a football smothered in cream cake.[10]

Humphries also began planning a film and a book with Sir Les as the main character. *Les Patterson Saves the World* was directed by George Miller, a much fêted director and producer, but the film stands out as one of Humphries' most spectacular failures. Unfortunately it was also the first full collaboration between Barry and Diane, who wrote the screenplay with him. Before it was launched, Diane described the movie rather prematurely as a 'joint triumph of a blue comic and a surrealist artist'.[11] Until this point Diane had pursued her own career as a painter independently, guarding her work and her time fiercely. But the idea of working with Barry on a film appealed to her, although she had never worked on a movie before. Diane was very confident about the film and turned down attractive pre-sale offers from the United States, believing the Australian market would produce better returns.[12] The Queensland stockbrokers Paul Morgan and Co, who had funded Paul Hogan's huge international success *Crocodile Dundee*, underwrote the Les Patterson film to the tune of $6.6 million. There were other backers as well. Diane spent months promoting her husband as an entertainer in the United States in readiness for the launch of the film. It proved to be a gruelling production, with the actors sweltering in unusually warm spring weather in Sydney. Humphries found the stopping and starting and reshooting tedious, and longed to be back on stage, where no one could say 'Cut'. It was hot, noisy and stressful for everyone.

The movie presented a crude spoof of international politics, with Edna becoming a CIA operative called Wisteria One, dressed to resemble Joan Collins and sporting a hairdo like Margaret Thatcher's. Its musical soundtrack, composed by Tim Finn, still holds appeal today, but the script is dull. Humphries was anxious, as always, that the script was not funny and confided to Peter Nichols that he was not sure that it would succeed.[13]

The film was haphazardly put together and convoluted in its plot. Its unnecessarily nihilistic ending was also poorly judged. The beginning of the film is very promising and shows Lady Gwen Patterson at home in Sylvania Waters with her two very strange children, refusing to let Les back into the family home. Joy Grissold, whom Barry had worked with in Melbourne in the 1950s, played Gwen in this darkly comic, surrealistic opening sequence.

But the film revealed the problem Humphries faced in turning his stage caricatures into film characters. His skill and sophistication in presenting anarchic, character-driven sketch did not readily translate into plot-driven feature film work. Humphries is more adept writing and performing monologue than dialogue. If Sir Les was to survive, he needed to remain a vaudevillian stage character.

The Humphries' marriage began to collapse. At the beginning of their relationship Diane had attempted to keep her career going.

She managed to keep painting and exhibiting, and she also appeared at Humphries' side at first nights and other events, smiling for the cameras. She published a book of drawings, designed sets and program covers for at least two of Humphries' stage shows, and willingly entertained his friends at the Astor, and at the grand house in Hampstead. It was not easy travelling across the world with two small children. Oscar and Rupert went wherever Barry and Diane went, including the set of *Les Patterson Saves the World*. But the couple's work partnership suffered a huge blow with the withering reviews of the film. Its failure had crushed Diane's confidence and Barry, too, found it deeply upsetting.

Humphries' misplaced faith in the power of his performance as the boorish diplomat had followed several straight roles in some memorable films. His portrayal of the Reverend Strachey in *The Getting of Wisdom* — Bruce Beresford had eventually realised his dream project in 1977 — had demonstrated his versatility as an actor, and showed that he was capable of serious roles. He also played in the rather bleak satirical film based on a novel by Graham Greene, *Dr Fischer of Geneva,* alongside the acting luminaries James Mason, Alan Bates, Cyril Cusack and Greta Scacchi.

Television, however, remained the main game for Humphries in the 1980s. Although Edna was his primary character, he continued to play Les whenever possible. Les appeared on Joan Rivers' BBC show *Can we Talk?* in March 1986, in a magenta dinner shirt and black bow tie. He recited a poem that included the devilish lines:

> *Congratulations BBC*
> *For introducing Joan and me*
> *She's feminine*
> *I'm butch and macho*
> *We'll stick it up the British chat show.*

Humphries seemed utterly relaxed in his role as the grotesque diplomat, reaching into his grimy suit pocket and pulling out a crushed piece of 'mature Tasmanian brie', which he proceeded to present to Joan. Peter Cook also appeared on the show. He was badly cast as a sort of sidekick to the hostess, but came across as insipid and ineffectual in the shadow of the caustic and tough American Rivers. In one of the worst moments of the series, the provocative comedian Bernard Manning condemned Cook to oblivion with a devastating line: 'You used to be very funny, Peter.' It was a sad and salutary experience for Barry to see the former mogul of British comedy, who had given him some early breaks, brought so low.

In March 1987 Peter Cook joined Les Patterson in opening the Melbourne Comedy Festival. Les described Melbourne as 'a lovely dignified old lady crossing the road in front of a tram,' as Cook sat beside him puffing on a cigarette and smiling. 'A woman leader is what Australia needs right now,' continued Les. 'Let's face it ... poor little Hawkie boy ... he's no longer a hawk, he looks like a grey budgie, doesn't he?' As the two actors cut the red tape and declared the festival open, Les shouted, 'Whacko, no worries!'

It was a triumphant moment for Barry, to be returning to Melbourne to open the comedy festival with one of his heroes beside him. Humphries appeared relaxed and genuinely happy even through his mask of Les. Barry himself had given up alcohol seventeen years earlier, but Cook's drinking had ruined his health and his career. Some years earlier Cook had made a temporary break with alcohol and Barry had helped him celebrate his fortieth birthday at his home in Hampstead; Cook had not touched a drop that day. But the man who had given Humphries his first one-man show in London, and transformed English comedy, now seemed to have diminishing prospects. At forty-nine years of age, Cook had entered a downward spiral of binge drinking and drug taking from which he would never recover. As they opened the festival, it was clear that Humphries was now the star.

CHAPTER 30

Queen of the West End

With Dame Edna now known to millions of television viewers, Humphries opened his new stage show on 17 November 1987 at the Strand Theatre in the West End. *Back with a Vengeance* demonstrated beyond all doubt that Humphries was now king of comedy in Britain. Or more accurately Dame Edna was the queen. To Barry's delight, Ian McKellen, Ronnie Corbett, Cilla Black, Warren Mitchell, Rolf Harris and Antony Armstrong-Jones were among the audience on the first night of the show. The American author Armistead Maupin laughed so much he thought 'some gasket in me might actually burst under the strain of it all'.[1] He felt somehow redeemed by the experience, as if he had been 'washed in the blood of the Dame'.

Humphries also performed a royal gala charity preview of the show in the presence of Prince Charles and Princess Diana before opening night. The striking princess, laughing heartily and clutching her program, posed for a photo standing beside Dame Edna. When it appeared in the newspaper the next day, the caption read: 'The Royals meet Australia's First Lady'. It was Sir Les who spoke to the press, revealing that Prince Philip had told him to 'lay it on pretty thick' for the royal couple. He said that 'Phil' had urged him to go for broke, and had said: '"It won't hurt Old Big Ears and Super Sloane to hear a bit of toilet talk. Look upon it as marriage counselling." So I let it rip.'[2]

Sir Les, now anointed as Minister for Tourism, opened the show to the strains of 'Waltzing Matilda', and crashed around the stage in his Cuban heels, accompanied by four scantily clad dancers called the Lesettes. He was as gross as ever, with his determinedly lewd presentation of his 'broad-based package' for the Australian bicentennial celebrations. Les had suggested they rename the festival the 'hetero-centennial'. He announced that he now represented the 'acceptable face of socialism' and that with these celebrations he would be 'rolling back the foreskin of Anglo-Australian friendship'. He spat as he spoke but reassured the front rows: 'Don't worry, ladies, Les Patterson's saliva is safe,' all the while grabbing his bulging crotch and picking his nose. He declared his acquaintance with everyone in Westminster village — 'I've known Michael Foot since he first stepped out of a flying saucer' — and could not resist an indirect reference to his 'package'. 'I know youse sheilas out there are looking at my penis ... here she is,' he said, winking and gesturing towards the bowing form of his pianist, former singer Victy Silva. It was an old joke but always raised a laugh.

With all three characters — Les, Sandy and Edna — in top form, Humphries exceeded expectations. *Back with a Vengeance* at the Strand was one of his finest seasons, with Sir Les, at his most anarchic, giving way to Sandy, speaking quietly from the afterlife, bemoaning the changes to his former home in Gallipoli Crescent. From sweating, swaggering, fulminating Les to the slow and ghostly form of Sandy Stone, Humphries achieved what one critic called a 'Chekhovian melancholy'.[3] 'The entire bewildered community,' whispered Sandy, 'is much larger than you might think.' Sandy did not want to come back to his old home after his death, he revealed, but was pleased that the Greek couple who had bought the house were calling the spare room the nursery. Of course he and Beryl had not been able to have children. But Sandy accepted this just as he accepted everything. 'I'm glad there'll be a kiddie in "Kia Ora" at last.'

> The house, the street, everything's changed beyond
> recognition since the old days before the war when young

couples like me and Beryl came to live here. Not that we ever had anything against the occasional multicultural ... Italians were a common sight in our neighbourhood too, before the war, and I well remember the Angelo brothers who were terrazzo specialists and did a lot of the front porches in our street ... They were always singing, but when the war broke out, they disappeared, while the terrazzo was still wet. Old Cec Gilchrist had a theory that a lot of dagos who had been Musso sympathisers had been rounded up and interned out near Watsonia. Although Cec was always one for a furphy, we never saw those Eyeties again.

The much slower, quieter pace of Sandy Stone's nostalgic monologue was a risky move for Barry. On the one hand it broke the loud, manic styles of both Les and Edna, and offered a savage attack on the racist excesses of Melbourne suburbia, but its much more sombre quality and the absence of music in the sketch threatened to close off the energy of the show. The audience reaction to Sandy on any given night varied in the UK more than their reaction to the other two characters. Clive James remarked at the time that Humphries expresses 'more complicity than contempt' for Sandy, arguing that he is at his 'most poetic' and 'least satirical' with this character.[4] But Sandy Stone is no benign figure. Humphries punishes Sandy. He is a small-minded bigot whose last days are cruel, and his speeches from the afterlife preside over the final erasure of his entire life.

After the 'comfort stop', as Humphries called the interval in *Back with a Vengeance*, the audience received the shocking news that Norm, Edna's much discussed husband, had died. 'The circumstances,' said the Dame, 'are a little suspicious. We are still looking for his black box, as a matter of fact.' This was a stroke of brilliance in the long-running Edna story, and allowed Edna to confess that she would like to 'talk through' her grief with 'squillions of London possums'. She revealed that there was a moment in which she had thought the show might have to be cancelled because of her bereavement.

But after the funeral, with gorgeous flowers arranged by her son Kenny, the official flower arranger for the Labour Party, Edna decided that she could not let her public down. Peeling off her shiny black widow's weeds to reveal a glittering magenta gown, she offered a manic hour of 'Ednacare', inviting five unknowns from the front rows onto the stage to sit on her lounge and enjoy champagne, taramasalata dip and a chat with their hostess. 'We all need more Vitamin L for Loving,' chirped Edna. 'And I think I secrete more Vitamin L than most people.' The energy of the show was extraordinary, with a thrilling stunt (performed by a professional), in which a 'pauper' plummeted from the dress circle, and Edna's ritual benediction with gladdies culminating in her spectacular, almost saintly levitation up through the auditorium to bless those terrified possums in the gods.

The London critics had never before used so many superlatives in their reviews of a Humphries stage show. Paul Taylor concluded his piece in the *Independent* with this statement: 'In its endless verbal and visual ingenuity, *Back with a Vengeance* confirms Barry Humphries' status as the greatest comic entertainer of our time.'[5] The *Observer*'s Michael Ratcliffe declared that the production was 'breathtaking' and 'by far the funniest new show of the year', marvelling at Humphries' 'explosive' and 'exhilirating' energy.[6] Sheridan Morley in *Punch* announced that 'the almost legendary Barry Humphries has taken possession of the Strand for what could well be forever', describing the evening as 'marathon and exotic … about as long as *King Lear* but with better laughs'.[7] Michael Billington declared that his favourite Humphries creation was Sir Les, and that 'like all great comic creations he makes you laugh before he even opens his mouth'. He added that Les Patterson's 'vulgar ockerisms' remind the audience of 'how plagued we are today by good taste'. Billington proclaimed the humour to be 'pure music hall' and 'liberatingly tasteless'.[8] 'Hugely entertaining' wrote Sue Jameson in *London Broadcasting*, while the *City Limits* critic noted that the audience was weak with laughter as 'Barry Humphries plunges them into Beckett by way of Magritte and Alf Garnett'.[9,10] Michael Coveney declared the Sandy Stone sketch to be the highlight of Humphries' performance; for him it was the 'best written and best prepared of the entire evening'.[11]

There were a few less complimentary reviews. Jack Tinker observed that the 'malodorous Sir Les Patterson, opened the evening 'with a welcome that only the strong of stomach and broad of mind could find irresistible'.[12] Harry Eyres suggested that Sir Les's comic commentary had lost some of its usual sharpness, found Dame Edna's jokes about disabled toilets 'inspirationally tasteless', and suggested that Edna seemed to be 'searching for a target'. He speculated that Humphries had left Melbourne too far behind.[13]

Yet overall the reviews were sensational. Humphries was playing to packed houses, with seven shows a week. Fourteen thousand people streamed into Covent Garden every week to see Edna Everage once the show transferred to the Theatre Royal, Drury Lane. The question of whether he had left Melbourne too far behind did not seem relevant. Humphries' friend, the playwright Peter Nichols, wrote to him to sing his praises: 'There seems to be nothing left for me to do. Offend them? After Les? Woo them with seductive writing? After Sandy? Warm them with the recognition of their own mediocrity after Edna?' Nichols declared that Humphries had 'invented a new kind of play, which is more than Beckett and the rest have done. I don't believe there's a comedian in the world to touch you.'[14]

Back with a Vengeance toured the United Kingdom, with five nights at the Gaiety in Dublin midway through the tour, before returning to London for a second season at the Theatre Royal in Drury Lane more than twelve months later. Billed as Dame Edna's 'Second Coming', the tag line to the show flashed up in lights above the entrance to the venerable old theatre: 'She's back because she cares'. If the words brought to mind those of the Iron Lady running the country, they also mocked the mantra Labour had adopted: 'Labour Cares'. The return show opened on 9 March 1989. The day before the show opened, the box office had taken £600,000 in advance sales.[15] Readers of the *British Theatre Yearbook*, 1990, were informed that 'Those who have not seen Mr Humphries on the stage have missed one of the most vital and disturbing of experiences.' The musical elements of the show were also praised. Humphries' one-man show was not only a witty spectacle but an extravaganza, worthy of comparison with any of the West End musical shows.[16]

Humphries and his team were now a tight operation. Barry kept everyone paying attention. Although he had been performing as a professional actor for more than three decades, he worried about forgetting his lines, missing a cue or finding his place again after a digressive chat with an audience member. The petite, quietly spoken musical director and pianist, Victy Silva, watched Barry like a hawk, and always remembered the cues. In an effort to be fully aware of the action of the show and to enhance the vaudevillian allusion, she committed all the music to memory. During the finale, when Edna rose in the cherry picker high over the auditorium, Victy would play a dramatic sequence of chords on the piano. One night she lifted her hands off the keyboard before the musical climax, and went completely blank. The guitarist and drummer shot her panic-stricken glances. After an awkward minute, she regained her composure and mercifully played the right notes. Terrified as the curtain came down, Victy readied herself for a tongue-lashing from the boss. She rushed across the stage and said to Barry, 'I am so sorry.' Brushing it off, he merely said, 'Don't worry, don't worry.'[17]

Standing beside Barry in the wings a moment before her entrance the next night, Victy was waiting for the spotlight to come down; it was her cue to walk onto the stage ahead of Sir Les. She whispered, 'I hope I don't make the same mistake tonight.' 'Well, you couldn't do any fuckin' worse than you did last night,' replied the figure beside her in the dark. Holding back the tears, Victy made her entrance, stopped centrestage and took her bow, walked to the piano and began to play 'Waltzing Matilda'. Later, during the quiet of the Sandy Stone sketch, she approached the manager Dennis Smith, still upset. 'If Barry has a problem, he should have dealt with it last night when the curtain came down. I did not do it deliberately,' she said in a wounded voice. Dennis looked at her intently and asked, 'How was he dressed?' 'As Les,' she said, 'about to go on.' 'That was Les, that wasn't Barry,' Dennis reassured her, returning to his work.[18]

Everyone learned quickly that when working with Barry they had to use the right mode of address. This idiosyncrasy sometimes puzzled newcomers: everyone from publicist to dresser to stagehand addressed Barry as Edna, for example, once he was in costume, even off the set. There was a certain point at which the change occurred; Barry's voice would suddenly go up several notes. Asked if he'd like a drink in the dressing room, the reply would come in falsetto: 'Coffee please.' The transformation was complete.

At dinner one night on the tour, Victy said to Barry: 'I heard Edna on *Women's Hour* this morning.' Without missing a beat Humphries replied, 'Was she funny?'[19] It is part of a discipline for Barry to separate himself from Edna and to talk about her in the third person, with an assumption of agency, just as novelists may speak about their characters. But in Edna's case it also serves to keep others at a distance. At this time it was especially useful to Humphries as his emotional life was in turmoil. Barry had started a secret affair, one of a number he engaged in over many years, and he felt guilty, wretched and extremely vulnerable. Once more he was haunted by the spectre of a bitter divorce.

The masks of his characters not only offered Humphries refuge from his own emotions, they gave him licence to say things he would not say himself. This freedom proved useful when Humphries, in the guise of Les Patterson, reacted furiously to the art critic Brian Sewell's vituperative remarks about an Australian art exhibition at the Hayward Gallery in 1988. Sewell savaged the 'Angry Penguins' exhibition, deriding the artists, their work and the very notion that Australians may enjoy an intellectual culture and that their response to European artists may be worth considering. He damned the painters as 'fraudulent' and 'muddled', with the 'temperament of ferrets', but did not describe any one work in the exhibition. Sewell frequently penned dismissive art reviews, but this was one of his most insulting, because it denigrated the artists so vociferously. The exhibition had been funded by the Australian Bicentennial Authority and the Australian National

Gallery. Sir Les wrote a hearty private response to Sewell on the mock letterhead of the Australian Cultural Attaché. The letter was obscene and abusive. Patterson concluded his riposte with a warning that the next time he laid eyes on Sewell he would clean his teeth 'by shoving his toothbrush high up' Sewell's arse.[20]

The mask also allowed Humphries to hide his real feelings, which sometimes led to misunderstandings and offence. On one occasion a few years before the triumphant West End season of *Back with a Vengeance*, Edna gave a bubbly address at an exhibition opening. She spotted John Betjeman's friend, Sir John Drummond, in the crowd. At the time Betjeman was critically ill, in hospital. Drummond was invited to meet Barry after the formalities and found him sipping a drink, his stockinged legs resting on a table. Barry and Drummond did not know one another very well but both were fond of Betjeman. Humphries was aware that Betjeman was in hospital and questioned Drummond about his condition. Drummond informed Barry that their friend would probably not last long. To Drummond's horror, Edna — rather than Barry — replied. Drummond was speechless, aghast that Barry would not speak to him about their beloved friend in his own voice.[21] Drummond excused himself and walked out of the gallery. John Betjeman died the following day.

Similarly, a very strange thing happened to Barry's old friend and Barry McKenzie collaborator, Nick Garland, late one night after Humphries' show. Garland and his wife, Caroline, joined a group of Barry's friends in his dressing room. They all complimented Humphries on a fine performance, and after the usual backslapping, he offered everyone a drink. Nick Garland, who requested a vodka, had just returned from a trip to the Soviet Union and had developed a liking for the national drink. He had also observed how the Russians drink their shots. Garland filled his mouth with the whole glassful, swirling it around his palate for a few seconds. Suddenly, Nick stumbled towards the sink and spat out the drink. He was overcome with pain, gagging, coughing and retching. Humphries's assistant stage manager leaned over beside Garland trying to smell the liquid and then exclaimed in horror, 'It's bleach!' She poured some milk into a clean cup for Garland as they waited anxiously for an ambulance to arrive. Nick was rushed to hospital, his mouth seared, his oesophagus burned and his eyes smarting with pain.[22]

Some months later when Garland recovered from the trauma of his injuries, he attempted to get to the bottom of the incident. He asked Humphries directly about it. 'It was strange,' agreed Humphries quite coolly. They never discussed the matter again.

Humphries had begun to repeat the patterns of his earlier life. Once more his marriage was under immense strain. As his first marriage collapsed, Brenda had spent many nights at home in the Bondi flat alone, waiting for her young husband, who was out night after night, to return. Rosalind, too, was left alone as Barry conducted affairs during their ten years together. Diane was so angry when she discovered Barry was having an affair that she sent a T-shirt to the stage door with the contents of an incriminating letter from his lover emblazoned on it. Barry's partnership with Diane Millstead of more than ten years was finished.

CHAPTER 31

Suburbs of the Sacred

In all his years as a performer Humphries' career had never been so hectic. A third *Audience with Dame Edna* went to air on Christmas Day 1988. It was an auspicious year. Australians had celebrated two hundred years of European settlement with parties and special events all through the year. For Humphries the bicentennial festivities on Australia Day 1988 almost outdid Sydney's Gay Mardi Gras 'for sheer overstatement'.[1] He found the preoccupation with presenting Australia as 'sophisticated' rather amusing and marvelled at the choice of activities to mark the bicentenary: fighter jets shattering the skies above Sydney Harbour, thousands of green and yellow balloons floating through the masts of tall ships, beer-drinking competitions and a massive explosion of gunpowder against the dark sky once night fell.

Humphries was not the only high-profile Australian to find the revelry ill judged and excessive. Patrick White, who loathed any expression of 'official patriotism', found the expensive and showy pageantry 'vulgar and embarrassing', a pathetic copy of the American bicentennial extravaganza, 'with cricket and royalty thrown in'.[2]

Indigenous Australians also found the 'invasion day' parties offensive, and organised protest rallies all over the country, with thousands of people of all racial backgrounds marching under the black and red Aboriginal flag with the golden sun in its centre. Many grew weary of the self-congratulatory fervour and empty jingoism. Paul Hogan predicted early in the year that Australians were likely to get sick of all the partying and find themselves wanting to give the country 'back to the Abos'.[3] Humphries summed up the exhausting enthusiasm of his countrymen in a phrase borrowed from Patrick White as the 'overheated fuzz of artificially inseminated patriotism'.[4]

By the end of the bicentennial year Barry Humphries had reached top billing in the mother country. His humour had nurtured a massive audience in the UK, had transformed the chat show and galvanised Australian popular theatre. But like White, Humphries was still enjoying his role as a stirrer. Dame Edna told her British audience on Christmas Day 1988 that the television series *Neighbours* was an 'accurate reflection of Australian life'.

For Australians it was a time of reflection, with novelists and playwrights re-examining the past. At last Humphries' satire was acknowledged by historians, even if their comments were somewhat sceptical. Ross Terrill stated that Humphries 'plays upon nostalgia for a simpler age', and observed that Australians relish demonstrations by the satirist that 'everything in Australia is either flawed or of foreign inspiration', and that the 'devoted audiences' enjoy indulging their ambivalence about the changes in Australia since the Menzies era.[5]

Humphrey McQueen recognised rather grudgingly that Barry Humphries had offered 'one long suburban autobiography' in his stage shows. He pointed out that other dramatists besides Humphries, such as Jack Hibberd of *Dimboola* fame, had sustained an artistic preference for the one-character play or characters who 'create their own history, their own legends and significance'.[6] McQueen not only rejected Humphries' consistent association of suburbia with philistinism as way out of date, he admonished Humphries for abandoning suburbia, failing to disturb our 'collective consciousness' as he did once, and for sneering at the poor. In a stinging and rather bitter strike at Humphries, McQueen proclaimed that Edna's television commercials and Humphries' 'right-wing politics were cause and effect to the dissolution of his childhood realm'.[7]

In spite of his earlier reservations about overexposing Edna, Humphries had appeared as the Dame in several advertisements for Whirlpool products. In one of them she stood beside a gleaming compact washing machine and said, 'We all know that size has nothing to do with performance, don't we possums?'

As Edna created her own legend and became a megastar, she left the confines of suburbia behind for a glamorous life as a television personality. But neither Humphries nor Edna ever abandoned suburbia; suburban life nourishes the Edna act to this day. Suburban taste and bourgeois behaviour have provided the bedrock of Humphries' comic world. Edna's elevation to celebrity status simply provided him with another set of targets. In the 1980s the celebrity guest became the victim of Humphries' satire and allowed an even greater assault on popular culture. In the 1980s and early 1990s, it was English suburbia that preoccupied him, because he spent most of his time in England. McQueen's phrase, 'suburbs of the sacred', referred to the art of Keith Looby and the way in which the ordinary lives of Australians are touched by myth-making and ideas of the sacred. Ironically it captured Humphries' nostalgic celebration of everything he loved and loathed about ordinary life from the 1950s to the present.

It was not an easy time for Barry. His divorce from Diane Millstead was particularly acrimonious. To make matters worse, Diane was making plans to move to Los Angeles with Oscar and Rupert. Humphries had been in this situation once before, and could not believe it was happening again; he was distraught at the idea of living thousands of miles away from his two boys. The large house in tree-lined Wedderburn Road, Hampstead, would have to be sold, and the apartment in the beautiful Astor building in Sydney would also be put on the market. Humphries began the gruelling task of sorting and packing his many books and precious paintings. For Diane it was a lonely and sad end to the marriage. The ex-wife of a celebrity is quickly forgotten and shunned by those who were once warm and friendly. Invitations to glittering parties and first nights dry up. Diane felt she needed to get as far away as she could.

In the midst of the divorce drama, Melvyn Bragg invited Humphries to appear on *The South Bank Show*, a television arts magazine program, in a profile piece. Although the Hampstead house was on the market, Barry, quite unusually for him, agreed to do the interview at his home, inviting Bragg to the house for filming.[8] As Humphries walked down the staircase of the house in the opening sequences of the profile, it was clear that he felt very comfortable and proud of himself in his solid Victorian abode. He was a man of substance, the sequence seemed to suggest. But in his expensive London residence Barry was also very much his mother's son, a polite, well-dressed man whose home displayed his success and his good taste. As always, Barry was perfectly composed for the interview, sitting on a lounge in the conservatory, urbane and debonair. His composure only faltered once, when, with a hint of irritation, he accused Bragg of putting words in his mouth.

After speaking to Humphries at home, Bragg interviewed the Dame. This had not been part of the plan, or not part of Bragg's plan at any rate. In the tiny dressing room at the Theatre Royal, with its gleaming light-bulb mirror, Bragg was forced into a close encounter with Edna — 'knee to knee', as he recalled later.[9] He found it unnerving, but as the interview progressed, Bragg realised Edna was parodying everything Humphries had told him in the earlier sequence shot at his home. In the editing suite, Bragg intercut Barry's measured responses and Edna's vicious put-downs, making a bitingly funny interview. Edna subverted everything Barry said, mouthing the real criticisms Humphries feared:

> Barry: I went to Melbourne Grammar School, a beautiful old stone building. I was unhappy at the school for at least two years because no one recognised me.
> Edna: He has a tendency to brown-nose his way into people's good books.

Barry: I was always immersed in the work of minor artists. It was a form of affectation, a kind of literary snobbery.

Edna: Well, I was always difficult to penetrate in my younger years, but Barry, he takes the prize. Is there anything there? ... He puts up a front.

Barry: I'm interested in periods of history and art history that precede a great catastrophe, pre-cataclysmic art, the art in Europe before the First World War ... the Weimar period ...

Edna: He would put up a front, he parades new knowledge ... 'Know all, know nothing' was a phrase my mother used to use ... I don't mean to sound catty.

Barry: As a child I felt a sense of frustration. I was quite bright. I read a lot.

Edna: He's still trying to find himself ... He's a bit of an old-fashioned person. He describes a world that is no more.

And so it went on. Why did Barry insist on the interview with Edna? He knew it would be funnier than his real interview. He always preferred talking as Edna, and admitted in his memoir some years later that in his own mind he knows it is Edna who people want to see.[10] Edna protects Barry from insult, and neutralises objections with her put-downs. If Edna can dismiss her creator as a pretentious snob, then others are less likely to do so. Inside the 55-year-old man was the young boy whose mother could read him 'like a book', who constantly worried about being cut down to size, who knew people thought he looked ridiculous dancing and running, who longed to be a magician who could make people disappear with a flick of his wrist. Now in middle age, and in the throes of his third divorce, he felt vulnerable again. His brilliant self-parody aroused convulsive laughter of recognition, sympathy and awe.

In February 1989, the *Spectator* — like most British media still keen to emphasise the prime minister's petit bourgeois origins — published a cover featuring a caricature of Margaret Thatcher as

Dame Edna with a menacing grin, drawn by Peter Brookes. The prime minister, resplendent in blazer and pearls, smiled out from a television set, pointing to her star-spangled spectacles. Emblazoned on her lapel are the words 'Housewife Superstar'. In the cover story Noel Malcolm attacked what he perceived to be the 'contradictory populism' of the Tories under the banner headline 'Margaret Thatcher, "Housewife Superstar"', and declared: 'Housewife Superstar may be the formula for success in show business — but it is no way to run a government.'[11] Dame Edna had not only succeeded in satirising the prime minister with flair and dexterity, she had clearly become shorthand for popular entertainment, and had entered the British psyche.

But John Barry Humphries remained elusive. He continued to 'play' Barry. He rarely, if ever, let his guard down in public, even with his friends. He found it difficult to relax and show his true self. He used his characters as a shield. Edna Everage offered a source of enjoyment for himself and for millions of people in two countries. By the end of the 1980s, Edna Everage was almost an institution, and Barry seemed even harder to find.

PART FIVE
BAWD

CHAPTER 32

Mauve-haired Madonna

On the opening page of his memoir *More Please*, published in 1992, Barry Humphries declared that he had suffered all his life from one of the seven deadly sins: greed. 'I have always wanted more,' he confessed: 'More money, holidays, sex, applause, real friends ... unquestioning love.'[1] Humphries' appetite for performance is also insatiable. His stage shows often extend beyond their running time by forty minutes or more. He hates having to end the show, and finds it hard to stop. When the set comes down after a season he always walks back onto the bare stage and stands alone, looking out into the empty auditorium, thinking about the transient and intangible nature of his craft. In the 1990s Humphries lived up to his desire for more, in a dozen different ways. His appetite and his energy as he approached his sixtieth year seemed to be stronger than ever. With Barry, the creative drive is only satisfied by more creative activity. And like another great comic actor of the twentieth century, Charlie Chaplin, Humphries has written not just one memoir but two.

In his second memoir, *My Life As Me*, published in 2002, Humphries reflected at greater length on many of the events of his childhood. Whereas the first book, *More Please*, offered a chronological account of Humphries' life until his marriage to Diane Millstead in 1979, the second book ranged back and forwards in time, filling in the periods of his life not covered in the first book and looking back fondly and with greater objectivity at his parents' lives than his initial portrait did. *My Life As Me* is explicitly and playfully nostalgic, and like *More Please* was received with high praise.

In June 1990 Humphries married for the fourth time. At a ceremony in the Italian town of Spoleto, Barry wed the 39-year-old Lizzie Spender, daughter of the poet Stephen Spender and pianist Natasha Litvin. He had long been an admirer of the poet and his marriage sealed his membership of the English artistic aristocracy. The composer Gian Carlo Menotti gave the bride away. Lizzie was refreshingly beautiful, with her father's high cheekbones and finely shaped nose. She had worked as an actor, a model and a writer, and never married. They had known each other for two years and had met at the Groucho Club in Soho during a period when Lizzie was appearing on British television in a series of Fairy Liquid dishwasher detergent commercials.

Lizzie had grown up in far more bohemian circumstances than Barry, spending her childhood in London, surrounded by her parents' artistic friends, with summer visits to Galway and long sojourns at the home of the film director John Huston and his actor daughter, Anjelica. Her godparents were Elizabeth Bowen and Laurens van der Post. She went to drama school but was told that she was too tall for leading roles. She turned to writing and produced some popular cookbooks and scripts for television drama. She told an Irish reporter some years after her marriage that the sixteen-year age gap between Barry and herself was not a problem. With candour she reflected, 'Well, if you think of all my father figures they all have something different: my actual father, a poet and intellectual; John Huston, who was theatrical, larger than life, in show business and who wore wonderful Irish linen suits; the composer Gian Carlo Menotti. And what's so special is that Barry combines all my father figures, all those images, in one person. Your adult life is greatly formed by your childhood images.'[2]

There *were* some similarities between Stephen Spender and Barry Humphries. Lizzie's father had submerged himself in his writing and was sometimes unreachable, and both men have had their sexuality questioned. Most of all, they both enjoyed recognition to an extraordinary degree. Spender admitted as a younger man to his own 'thirst for publicity', confessing to feeling disgust at reading a newspaper 'in which there is no mention of my name'.[3] Barry entered a new phase of his life with the daughter of Stephen Spender at his side. He fell in love with the whole family and its milieu, captured in his painting of Stephen's house in Provence, with its rosy glow and romantic atmosphere.

When Humphries drafted the closing pages of *More Please*, his mother had been dead for eight years. Yet Barry was still smarting, and smiling, at the memory of a visit he made to the family home in Camberwell to introduce his small son Oscar to his grandmother, Mrs Louisa Humphries. His description of the encounter is one of the most potent moments in the book. Arriving at the back steps of the house in Christowel Street, Barry could see his mother sitting in her usual chair listening to the radio. As he and little Oscar entered the house, his mother raised her hand, indicating to them that she was listening and that she did not want to be disturbed. A talk show host, Patrick Tennyson, was asking listeners whether they agreed with the notion that Barry Humphries was 'selling Australia short overseas'. In call after call women and one or two men expressed their disapproval of Barry's satirical jibes at his homeland. Barry listened as intently as his mother. 'You see, Barry, that's what they think of you,' she said to him at last. Barry walked into his father's study, looked up the phone number for the radio station and dialled. 'This is Dame Edna here,' he said. Immediately he was put through to Tennyson and was on the air. 'Is that you, Pat darling?' he began. 'I adore your show, especially today. How I agree with those wonderful women who are ringing you up. I know Barry Humphries better than anyone, and he is dragging Australia through the mud as often as he can, for base financial gain. The millions who laugh at his shows should be ashamed of themselves, and I HAPPEN TO KNOW THAT HIS MOTHER AGREES WITH ME!'

Barry replaced the receiver. He was shaking. He walked out to the sunroom to his mother. As he entered the room, Louisa switched off the radio and fixed her son with a 'dry smile'. Then, as though nothing had happened, she held out her arms towards Oscar and said, 'Don't just stand there, I want to see my grandson.'[4]

Out of his defensiveness and compelled by his sense of his mother's disapproval, Humphries produced one of the funnier moments on talkback radio in Australia. It was part of a pattern, a response to attack, that he had practised for twenty-five years. It was also a moment of triumph for Barry, suggesting the possibility of reconciliation. He had brought Edna to Louisa in her own sunroom, over the radio waves, and once more turned her disapproving voice into the joke.

Humphries had always been fuelled by a compulsion to redirect negative energy and had the brilliant ability to turn others' doubts and criticisms into comedy. Clearly his retaliatory fervour provided the impetus for many of his works. He looked back at his schooldays at Melbourne Grammar and designated them as a 'getting of ignorance ... the worst education I ever had'.

This impulse for revenge is explicit in a poem he wrote in memory of Patrick White. When White died in 1990 Humphries mourned even though he had been at the receiving end of White's disapproval on several occasions, and their relationship had deteriorated. In Barry's view White had surrounded himself with 'toadies' who were 'quite unworthy of him', while cutting off contact with some of his 'oldest and most devoted friends', especially if they dared to remarry. But he had missed White's company and felt rather cowardly about not attempting to renew their friendship.[5] The year after White's death Barry published a book of his own verse. *Neglected Poems and Other Creatures* included a threnody for his one-time friend. It is both caustic and affectionate, but ultimately rather unforgiving. He referred to White in the first stanza as 'A querulous curmudgeon with a tea-cosy on his head', and registered White's love for and disappointment in his male friends: 'He dropped Sid and Geoff and Lawrence, he dropped Bruce and Brett and me,' wrote Barry. In the final stanza he farewells the man:

Now his writing light is switched off, though his wall-eyed dogs still bark
In that Federation garden beside Centennial Park,
Home of the family picnic and the jogger and the mugger;
Oh I pray God doesn't drop you, you miserable old bugger.[6]

By the 1990s, Humphries had a huge audience in the UK, and so was less anxious about his image in Australia than he had ever been before. *The Dame Edna Experience* television extravaganza and the stage tour that followed in 1989 brought Humphries popularity, recognition and wealth. His achievement had been Herculean. Humphries, true to type, opted for 'more', and decided to try his television act in the United States. Barry would never forget the humiliation and disappointment of his poor showing in New York back in 1977; the vision of Diane or sometimes a stage manager running down the lane beside Theater Four to see if anyone was heading towards the theatre to see the show was etched in his memory.[7]

Humphries had not set foot on stage in the United States since this disappointingly short season in New York in the autumn of 1977. Edna, however, had appeared on Joan Rivers' show in 1986, resplendent in an aqua frock with appliquéd koala and possums. She regaled Rivers, George Clooney and Joan Collins with details of her friendship with the royal family and an account of Norm's rumbling prostate problems. But Humphries was still virtually unknown to American television audiences. After the success of *The Dame Edna Experience* in Britain he sensed that the time was right for another American foray, and that television offered the key. After much negotiation the NBC network contracted Humphries for a short series of Hollywood shows to be screened in 1991.

It suited Barry perfectly to move to the west coast of America as Diane had taken Oscar and Rupert to live in Beverly Hills. Barry and Lizzie settled into a suite at the Beverly Comstock Hotel, fronting elegant Wilshire Boulevard, right next to the Los Angeles Country Club. It was a small, old-fashioned and rather intimate hotel, recommended by Billy Wilder, where Frank Sinatra is rumoured to have conducted his afternoon assignations. The rooms were capacious, with chintz-covered comfortable chairs and a kitchen and dining room, overlooking a leafy central courtyard and swimming pool. For Lizzie, who excelled in all things culinary, it was perfect. Claudia Rosencrantz, who was by then in partnership with Barry in a production company called Megastar Productions, had arrived months earlier to prepare for the shows, and also had rooms in the Comstock.

Humphries worked extremely hard to pave the way for Dame Edna in America, this second time around. He had one important advocate he had been lacking fourteen years earlier. John Lahr, who had been living in the UK for more than ten years and had written the arresting review of Humphries on stage in *New Society* in 1979, published a lengthy feature article in the *New Yorker* in the summer of 1991, explaining Dame Edna to Americans. Lahr had become a friend to Barry after accompanying him on one of his most successful tours of England in 1989 in order to write his backstage romp *Dame Edna and the Rise of Western Civilisation*. He had convinced Humphries that he was just right for the job of educating the transatlantic audience on the subject of Humphries' humour and Edna Everage in particular. Lahr's *New Yorker* essay duly expressed adoration and enchantment for Humphries' characters and performances and compared him to both Chaplin and Baudelaire. The piece, entitled 'Playing Possum', marked Lahr's debut in the esteemed magazine. It was a coup for the critic and offered a moment of promise for Humphries in the United States.[8]

In London, Humphries had initially resisted Lahr's overtures. He believed he had too much to lose. For one thing he hated the idea of a critic hanging around his dressing room learning all about his act. As a master of disguise and one of the more secretive actors around, he loathed the idea of his private life becoming public knowledge. As if this wasn't enough, Humphries had accepted A$430,000 to write his memoirs and feared that Lahr's book might compete with his. But in the end the lure of what Lahr could offer Humphries through his skill as a critic, his tenacity and his charm won Barry over. Unbeknown to Barry, Lahr had recently suffered a terrible bereavement, when his infant twin sons, Nicholas and

James, died. Lahr did not mention this to Barry at the time. Watching Barry's every move during the Drury Lane run somehow helped Lahr confront his loss. He would never forget how Edna's mockery of death made him laugh. When Edna announced that Norm was dead and that her psychiatrist told her that, 'Only time can heal,' she reflected, 'And he was so right. That was four hours ago,' Lahr was flabbergasted. For Lahr, Humphries' 'power to dispel or just suspend grief felt like a blessing'.[9]

Unlike the *New Yorker* profile, Lahr's book was not published in time to help the initial publicity for *Dame Edna's Hollywood*, so Barry could not rely on assistance from that source. Humphries nonetheless was determined to leave nothing to chance in America. He decided to explain his act in Edna's voice so that the purpose of the show would be clear to television critics across the land. One of his new rules was that he never spoke to a journalist as himself. It was always Edna. So Edna invited a host of television columnists to a lunchtime press conference. As they tucked in to their spaghetti and meatballs, Dame Edna confessed to feeling 'a teeny bit nervous' about making her television debut in the United States. She talked about her many friendships, revealing how she had introduced Prince Charles to Lady Di and how she had helped both Margaret Thatcher and Barbara Bush. Of the First Lady she remarked: 'I've helped her out of polyester.' Edna also revealed that 'America has been coming around to the idea of me even though they don't quite know it.'

Most importantly Edna distinguished her style of talk show from the programs familiar to critics. She explained that the stars who appeared on her show would not break down in tears, as they often did with Barbara Walters, for example. 'I'm not interested in catharsis,' she pronounced emphatically, pausing to spell out the word. 'I want people to leave my show happy. Acutely embarrassed, but happy.'[10]

It was one of Humphries' funniest attempts to educate an audience, and captured the essence of his chat show comedy. Edna summed up intention and effect in two short quips. But it was not clear whether American television critics, let alone audiences, would relate to this attack on the excesses of television culture, and whether they would enjoy the unmasking of so many of Hollywood's most popular performers.

The early signs were positive. Lahr's lengthy literary essay of appreciation in the *New Yorker* gave other journalists plenty of background material. Many of them seized on the details of Humphries' life in London and the fact that Prince Charles had been to dinner at the Humphries' house in Hampstead. Around the same time *Vanity Fair* published a photographic portrait by Annie Leibovitz of Edna in a fire-engine red dress, posing on Los Angeles' Muscle Beach, and described her as the 'Mary Poppins of malice'.[11] The English editor, Tina Brown, was a superb interpreter of popular culture: she understood Humphries' humour and knew exactly how to pitch Edna Everage to her American readership. Edna was introduced to readers as a 'superstar whose art form is itself a trenchant analysis of superstardom — sort of like Madonna, only with mauve hair'.[12]

Humphries imagined his audience as mainstream viewers, with plenty of women aged between thirty-five and seventy. Perhaps this was a problem from the outset. American networks were hell-bent on attracting younger viewers. And television was changing. In the week that Dame Edna screened for the first time in America, Carol Burnett called it quits from her struggling variety show on CBS. If the born and bred American icon could not cut it on television anymore, the chances of Edna's success seemed remote at best.

Not surprisingly *Dame Edna's Hollywood* was categorised by NBC as 'entertainment' rather than 'chat'. But the target audience was the same as that of chat shows, because it parodied that genre. Barry and Claudia were shocked by the attitudes of the moguls of television land, though Claudia took the brunt of the exhaustive negotiations. She was stunned when an NBC executive stopped her in the corridor before a meeting and demanded, 'Is Barry gay?' Looking him straight in the eye she said, 'What sort of a question is that?' 'Well is he or not?' the man persisted. Rosencrantz took a deep breath. 'Well, actually he's not, but I don't know what this has to do with the show. He plays different characters. Edna is just one of them,' she said with exasperation rising in her voice. After a few seconds silence, the executive declared imperiously: 'I think it would be helpful for America if Barry would appear in the title sequence having breakfast with his wife and family and then transition into the character of Edna.' With ill-concealed horror Claudia spluttered in reply, 'I think you'll need to try this idea out with Barry.'[13] Not one of the executives dared.

Clearly anxious about the reception for *Dame Edna's Hollywood*, NBC management hounded Rosencrantz on a daily basis during her long stint in Los Angeles arranging the show. At one meeting she faced thirty besuited executives around a massive table. 'Where are the other producers?' queried one of the brigade. 'There aren't any — it's just me,' Claudia responded to the incredulous team around her. Every day she fielded phone calls from most if not all of the thirty producers asking her questions about details of the pilot, until she pleaded with them to delegate one person to keep in touch about progress.

If the pre-production jitters of the network were trying, neither Barry nor Claudia could possibly have predicted the mayhem of the filming of the first show. The one-time boxing champion, and two-metre tall veteran character actor, Jack Palance, staggered onto the set, lurching dangerously towards the tiny and fragile Emily Perry. Claudia recoiled in horror as she heard Palance insulting 'Madge' in the most disgusting manner before he began hurling objects around the studio. Watching Barry's eyes grow bigger and wilder down the camera, Claudia whispered to the cameraman, 'I'm going to get him off.' She set off towards the craggy-faced Hollywood legend who continued trashing the set, ruining the very first American Dame Edna show. Ian Davidson grabbed Claudia's arm and said, 'You explain to him that there's a technical problem and we have to stop filming. I'll invite him to the green room for a drink.' Putting on their bravest expressions, the two nervously approached their guest. Palance stormed off the set and never came back. Claudia spent the next three hours reassuring Emily Perry, restoring the furniture and props of Edna's 'house' and recovering her own equilibrium in order to keep on filming. Later, as she recalled this horror moment with a confidante in Los Angeles, she was told that Palance had a reputation as a 'big sipper'.[14] If she had felt like an ingénue at times during the long and lonely pre-production months, Claudia now felt like a total outsider in the brutal world of Hollywood television.

It was during that most American of holiday seasons, Thanksgiving, that Edna eventually took to the television screens of the United States with *Dame Edna's Hollywood*, a one-hour special, described as a 'modest Christmas party for a few close friends at Edna's Bel Air mansion'. Barry had been a guest at a reception at Zsa Zsa Gabor's Bel Air home and couldn't resist the idea of a party for Edna's guests in Edna's very own 'mansion'. The guests included Cher, Bea Arthur, Mel Gibson, Larry Hagman and Doc Severinsen, collectively called by Dame Edna 'Megastars Anonymous'. Mel Gibson didn't actually make it into the 'house', because Edna mistook him for the swimming pool cleaner.

Americans were not unfamiliar with the style of comedy. Tinkerbelle, who had praised Humphries' New York show in the 1970s and was infamous for being waspish and wild, had made insulting questions her trademark on cable television. She had informed Salvador Dali that Andy Warhol painted 'better and faster' than he; she had recommended that Cher take a long rest because she was doing too much, and she bluntly told Yoko Ono that she was 'looking more like John Lennon every day'.[15]

Humphries had won over millions of British viewers with his subversion of the talk show formula; in Hollywood the narrative of embarrassing the guest was more literal, with a good deal of slapstick and less comic layering in the dialogue. Each celebrity endured insults, put-downs and obstacles. Larry Hagman of *Dallas* fame, holding a flowerpot for Edna as a housewarming present, dropped through a trapdoor into the swimming pool. Then he had to wade out of the pool in his JR Ewing costume in order to reach Edna on the set. He slipped but didn't miss a beat. Edna muttered in her stage whisper: 'Thank heavens for a professional.' It was one of the funniest moments of the show.

Bea Arthur was invited to groom Edna's dog, in retrospect a poor judgment, because it limited the possibilities of a proper exchange with Arthur. Cher was granted the most time with the Dame, appearing in ripped blue jeans with her hair dyed psychedelic orange. The highlight of the show was the duet sung by Edna and Cher: 'I've Got You Babe'. Surely the Americans would warm to the well-established song routine that had kept Britons amused for thirteen episodes. Humphries hit his stride in the next Hollywood special when Edna 'entertained' Robin Williams, Kim Basinger, Chevy Chase, Rue McClanahan, George Hamilton, Burgess Meredith and Ringo Starr. Edna almost flirted with Basinger, and revealed that Ringo had been 'twirling his baton in my vestibule'. The exchange with Basinger was piquant and amusing, but there was an aura of discomfort in Barry in the Hollywood setting, and the show relied too heavily on the physical gags. Chevy Chase seemed utterly dumbfounded by Edna, and was ejected from the sofa out the window as George Hamilton lay trapped in a sunbed.

The finale of the final show created a sparkling television moment, in which Edna, Barry Manilow and Madge hilariously sang 'Can't Smile Without You'. It all seemed to come together. Although Manilow and Sean Young were disappointingly insipid in conversation, Burt Reynolds made up for it. Edna managed a brilliant retort to Young's recounting of an accident that took place during one of her film shoots, remarking, 'Spooky what trivial things we remember, and then bring up on talk shows.' Humphries once more made the lunacy of chat show patter the subject of the humour. In fact this show had been scheduled initially to be screened second but was moved into the third slot because the one with Robin Williams and Kim Basinger was so much funnier.

Overall the reviews were lukewarm. *Dame Edna's Hollywood* was described in *USA Today* as a 'slick but thin talk show spoof'.[16] And as always there were the doubters with their backhanded swipes. *Newsday* declaimed that 'Barry Humphries is flogging a dead koala trying to bring Dame Edna over here like this. He's too intellectual, too biting, too subtle.'[17] Irv Letofsky of the *Hollywood Reporter* described the show as loose and shabby, and thought 'the writing (whatever writing there is) serves her ill', but expressed admiration for the spectacle of 'a fair fight' between Edna and Burt Reynolds.[18]

There was, however, high praise from some reviewers, with Edna hailed as 'one large, astonishingly overdressed woman' who is the answer to your prayers if you are sick of David Letterman laughing at his own jokes and the loud whooping noises from Arsenio Hall's studio audience. Dame Edna, said the Florida-based critic, has 'redefined the art and purpose of the talk show'.[19] 'Are Americans ready for a 6 foot 4 inch Aussie in drag? NBC hopes so, and I do too ... The old gal is hilarious,' enthused one Texan critic.[20] Ray Richmond in California referred to the 'aging transvestite' as 'thoroughly offbeat' and 'clever', declaring the show to be a 'splendid and unique talk show parody'.[21]

Some reviewers expressed disappointment that the show didn't live up to the satirical vigour of the British series on which it was modelled. There were defensive warnings about Edna as well. One Atlanta reviewer complained that Edna's voice 'could shatter Waterford', that the show was 'a drag, but not the kind intended. People who think they like British TV — *Masterpiece Theatre* and all that tony stuff,' moaned the critic, 'should catch a bit of Dame Edna, and see what much of the telly over there is really like'.[22]

One Los Angeles reviewer grudgingly predicted that 'Americans should have no trouble understanding Dame Edna. Insult comedy has thrived here for years. So have talk shows. And so has hype.'[23] Humphries' satire was perceived as 'insult comedy' by some, yet the hallmark of his talk show technique is to insult obliquely and parody the way in which audiences are insulted. This refocuses the satirical humour back on Edna as the apotheosis of the crass, exploitative hostess who tempers any insult with a refrain reminding the guest and the audience of her solicitous intentions: 'That could have sounded rude, but it wasn't meant to be, it was caring.'

Edna even unsettled Phil Donahue when she appeared on his show, revealing the overall uncertainty of the reception for Dame Edna by American television viewers. Edna appeared dressed in a mauve silk dress painted with an image of the Statue of Liberty.

The studio audience laughter was mild and Edna seemed to be reticent. Donahue was not encouraging; although he had been in the business for more than twenty years he did not seem able to handle Edna. He was mannered and stiff, and stopped mid-sentence during a question to read his notes. Perhaps it was Emily Perry's Madge who put him off, as she sat mute throughout the show. As one Australian television critic quipped when the show was screened on Channel 10: 'not since *Waiting for Godot* has a silent role had more impact'.[24]

Dame Edna's Hollywood 10 pm time slot was not ideal. Although it was technically still prime time, it was late at night for most American viewers. Claudia's heart had sunk when she discovered that this was the scheduled time for the show: she knew that if Dame Edna was to gain a foothold she needed a solid prime-time audience. But there was no convincing the American executives: scheduling was not negotiable. In the coveted 6–9 pm time range there were movies, drama, situation comedy shows and documentary, but not 'entertainment'. Entertainment, it was firmly believed, screened in the afternoons or late at night in the slots filled for so long by Johnny Carson and David Letterman. The American executives did not really know where Edna belonged or how to market the show.

In spite of these problems the show gained a small following, the audience share was pleasing and the program earned high praise in some quarters. But none of this was enough for NBC to engage Humphries for a full series. Another Dame Edna program that Barry made for Fox, called *Edna Time*, was shredded at the last minute. Just hours before it was due to screen in February 1993, Claudia took a call instructing her to cut the show by half, to just half an hour. It was heartbreaking. She made one frantic phone call to Humphries' agent to ask if it was worth arguing. 'No,' he said unequivocally. 'Just cut it.'[25]

Once again Humphries was not wanted in the United States. Americans were still not ready for Edna. Looking back at the shows, Humphries' vaudeville style seems strange and slightly forced in the American setting, compared to the breezy, imperious triumphalism Edna displayed in each episode of *The Dame Edna*

Experience series. Nobody in the vast empire of American television was willing to take the risk and offer Humphries a series after the Hollywood specials, and Disney's overtures for an Edna film came to naught after endless meetings with 'studio people'. The extravaganza on the west coast had failed to secure an American television or film audience for Dame Edna. Any idea that a winning formula for a television show in the UK would guarantee success in the United States bit the dust. In fact Humphries' adventure in Los Angeles demonstrated that there is no such thing as a winning formula in television, especially when the great cultural divide of the Atlantic must be crossed.

There are countless examples of the problem of translating British and Australian comedy for Americans. Australians and Britons readily enjoy one another's humour on television without any question of adaptation. But American television audiences usually receive translated 'foreign product'. The adaptation of *Till Death Us Do Part*, *Absolutely Fabulous*, *The Office* and *Kath and Kim* for American television audiences offers evidence of the enduring chasm between the Anglo-Australian comic culture and that of the United States.

Humphries was very disappointed. But he took heart from the fact that Dame Edna had appeared at all on American television with her megastar Hollywood guests, an achievement in itself. Unlike many British and Australian comedy series produced for television, including those referred to above, that end up played by American actors with certain characters dropped and every scene rewritten, Barry Humphries' Edna had appeared in front of a live studio audience, performing 'her' own material in her 'own' voice. Although Humphries was not offered a series, Dame Edna was now known to millions of Americans.

CHAPTER 33

Suburbs of the Mind

Despite his lack of success in the United States, Barry remained in huge demand on British television. In May 1992 London Weekend Television broadcast a new series, *Dame Edna's Neighbourhood Watch*. Edna, dressed in a pink sequinned gown, launched the show at the Savoy Hotel. This series was Claudia Rosencrantz's brainchild, and grew out of Barry's life-long obsession with domestic architecture and decor. Ian Davidson contributed to the writing. From his earliest days driving around the new suburbs of Melbourne to view his father's building projects, Humphries had developed a genuine fascination with houses and their interiors, and especially with the kitsch 'objets' that fill the average suburban home. The perennial questions posed by Edna on stage as she interrogates various audience members relate to the design, colour scheme, style and location of their homes. The television show was a logical extension of Edna's prurient interest in the abodes of the women in the stalls of her stage shows. Edna declared her love of 'homes' in one of the first episodes in delightful parody: 'Homes get my juices going, homes touch my spot, homes turn me on, homes arouse me. You know I once thought I might even be a *homo*sexual!'

Dame Edna's Neighbourhood Watch was a bold experiment in the game show genre. With a jaunty theme song sung by Edna as she walked through a miniature English village, stopping to take the roofs off houses and peep through windows, the program offered a satire on the tabloid obsession with celebrities' living arrangements, and the imperative for ordinary women to aspire to maintain houses like those in *Vogue Living* and *Home Beautiful*. Like *The Dame Edna Experience*, in which Humphries produced and parodied talk simultaneously, the new show both celebrated and parodied the game show format. Initially, however, Barry was sceptical about whether the show would succeed.

It was a whole new genre for Humphries and was aimed at a different audience, though it aired in prime time. Filmed in front of a studio audience of five hundred women, Edna described her new venture as 'seminal, pivotal and mould breaking'; she revealed that it was a women-only event except for the male camera operators 'hand-picked for their effeminacy'. Before the first episode was filmed, Claudia had auditioned a string of young, muscle-bound male body-builders, while Barry made faces at her from around a doorway. Each hunk strutted the stage in the hope of being chosen for the role of warm-up man for the all-female audience. Finally Claudia selected her man, who appeared in scanty shorts to rev up the crowded studio. The laughter and applause were deafening.

The show exaggerated Edna's usual method of involving the audience, with Edna selecting her 'possums' from the rows of seated women with a 'heat-seeking' gladioli stem: she called it her 'purple possum picker'. Edna then took the idea of questioning women about their homes to another level. She sent a film crew to the home of just one audience member unbeknown to that woman herself. Edna let the audience in on the secret of the show, which was that a camera crew would follow Madge on a tour of, say, Dorothy's house in Barnet, or Jackie's place in Farnham, or Margaret's place in Croydon — in front of millions of viewers. Madge led the inspection of the home as Edna barked instructions to her to open this or that drawer, give the furniture the 'finger test' for dust, peer at photographs and check under pillows and bedspreads, as the hapless home owner sat beside Edna in the studio, mortified as the live studio audience and television viewers regarded the nooks and crannies of each room in her house. Edna passed comments on paintings, pets, colour schemes and the nature of looking itself. Humphries vividly satirised the everyday voyeurism in all of us by turning the idea of watching television upside-down. As Edna remarked to her victim Dot on the first show: 'When we watch television we sit in a very ordinary environment looking at another wonderful world, but here we are in a wonderful world looking at a very ordinary environment. It's paradoxical.' Humphries seemed to be looking forward to the horrors of reality television, then in its wretched infancy.

Midway through the show the tension heightened for the targeted 'lady of the house', as the audience chanted after Edna: 'I hope you've said your prayers, because NOW WE'RE GOING UP YOUR STAIRS' and Madge led the camera crew to the bathroom, toilet and bedrooms. 'What's that?' Edna might ask as the camera rested on a tiny oval-shaped image of a small boy weeing. 'Did you get that on a trip to Belgium?' Madge began to take liberties, trying on the contestant's clothes and reclining on her bed. After the tour the two other contestants selected by Edna had to answer questions about what they had seen in order to win enough points for a prize. 'Does Dot's toilet roll unspool clockwise or anti-clockwise?' and 'Where was the stripped pine in this house?' were typical questions.

Dressed in a garish satin tutu with spaghetti straps, Emily Perry as Madge, then in her eighty-sixth year, draped herself across a gleaming red Ferrari and fingered the pointy end of a model of a jet to demonstrate the prizes for the winner. But to 'win', contestants needed hundreds of thousands of points and they only ever acquired five or six. For ten thousand points they might win a box of chocolates 'with all the soft centres removed'.

For double points, contestants were shown three large photographs of men and asked to pick which one was the victim-contestant's husband. Right at the end the real husband appeared beside his embarrassed but happy wife as they received their rewards from Dame Edna, and thunderous applause from the audience. True to the game show formula there was a real prize for the couple of a trip for two to Paris.

Although it had been a success, the show began to feel a little tired in the second series. In order to keep the joke fresh, Claudia ensured that each episode was filmed before any of them were screened, so that none of the guests in the hot seat knew what was in store for them. The genuine surprise and terror on the face of each of the women when they first glimpsed their home on the big screen in the studio provided hilarious television. Then each of them was subjected to Madge's ransacking of their private lives, and the humiliation of Edna's commentary on their wallpaper, carpet and bedroom furniture. Once more Humphries had elevated the ordinary, trivial and mundane to extraordinary heights.

In the fourth episode Edna bounced onto the set in a short 'Scream' dress of orange, purple and green, with matching pantyhose and orange high-heeled shoes. For a long time Humphries had been pestering Stephen Adnitt to make a dress based on one of his favourite paintings, *The Scream* by Edvard Munch. But Adnitt argued that there was no point in Edna wearing a dress with the powerful image on it only to sit down and hide the haunting face of Munch's subject. He recognised that the time was right, however, for a 'Scream' dress when *Neighbourhood Watch* began, because Edna spent the whole show on her feet.

The scenario was perfect for Adnitt's creation in hand-painted silk with its line of screaming latex faces and eyes on stalks that moved ghoulishly in their sockets over Edna's heart. Edna demonstrated the anguish of the screaming woman to wild applause and shrieks of laughter. The dress, with its expressionistic swirls of brilliant colour and the strangely androgynous figure copied from the painting, registered the strangeness and incongruity of hysteria about domestic interiors that drove the humour of this parodic game show.

Edna's costumes soon became even more elaborate. Adnitt and a prop maker built a dress in the shape of a typical English cottage for Edna to wear in the second series, with a model of Madge standing in the doorway in her brown moth-eaten dress. There were cats in the window and smoke coming out of the chimney on Edna's shoulder. At the beginning of each show Edna would bound down the stairs through the audience and dance a little jig when she arrived on the set. At times it was hard to believe that the man inhabiting these extraordinary — and heavy — costumes was nearing his sixtieth birthday.

In one episode Edna galumphed onto the set in a Mary Quant mini-dress in psychedelic orange and lime green, complete with black stripes and a white flower trim. 'Don't you adore my dress?' she trilled. 'Spookily enough I'm the same size now as I was in the sixties. Aren't I a lucky woman! I've had nothing let out, no alterations, my Quant is the same size now as it was then. Let's face it ... that's not something Cilla Black could say.' Cilla Black was the only entertainer besides Humphries who had ventured into the realm of the game show and so the joke had extra resonance.

Apart from quips like that one, the humour in *Dame Edna's Neighbourhood Watch* lost some of Humphries' usual sharpness. It was never malicious; the contestants were treated with the same benevolence as the victims who end up on stage with Edna in a live theatrical performance. Edna may have mocked them but she also attempted to celebrate the lives of these ordinary women. But the joke of looking closely at someone's bathroom cupboard, carpet, make-up bag or the marks on the wall behind the headboard of the marital bed wore thin very quickly. When Edna addressed the audience as hens and made them cluck in one episode, it seemed that the satirical drive of the show had evaporated and Humphries was playing his audience for fools, something he had not done so explicitly or so cheaply before. Until then he had always depended upon wit but *Neighbourhood Watch* depended upon shock, gullibility and predictable routines.

While the series showed that the game show was a fruitful genre for an experiment with variety elements, the contestants did not provide the intrinsic interest or comic potential of the actors, singers and politicians who appeared on *The Dame Edna Experience*. Humphries thrives under the pressure of a contest but the guests on *Neighbourhood Watch* were easy targets, and so the humour never reached the searing satire of the talk show spectacle. The women on this show were unable to fight back, and the humour released little of Humphries' usually blinding wit. An easy conquest for Edna does not stimulate the satirist inside the character; Humphries is a humorist who fires when there is something at stake.

It was all good, cheerful, early evening fun; after all it was a game show. But there was a growing perception that the humour was too harsh on the participants. The notion that Humphries' comedy was cruel and degrading was not a new one. But the idea that it relied on a rather vicious kind of audience exploitation gained traction at this time. A young actor who specialised in impressions, Rory Bremner, impersonated Dame Edna in a short film made in 1993 for Channel 4's *Without Walls: J'Accuse* series.

Bremner accused Humphries of turning Dame Edna into the personification of everything Humphries' early incarnations of Edna satirised. The young actor, one of the best mimics working in Britain, presented a case against Edna's current style of humour with the journalist Anne Karpf, critics Nicholas de Jongh and John Lyttle prosecuting, and Ned Sherrin and Sheridan Morley defending. It was not the first time *Without Walls* had featured a strident attack on an actor. In an earlier episode, Russell Davies had questioned whether Laurence Olivier deserved his status as pre-eminent actor of the British stage. Bremner's performed critique of Humphries for national television picked up on an enduring criticism of Humphries' comedy as vindictive, callous and nasty. It also relied heavily on the assumption that Humphries' characters' views represent Barry's own. It was not an original or a convincing argument, but showed Bremner as a master mimic and clever satirist. The spectacle of the satirist satirised made compelling television.

Humphries found the Bremner program infuriating, but put the young comedian's venomous parody down to envy. He recognised Bremner's talent and has spoken generously about his strength as a comedian in recent years. But it irritated Humphries when people did not understand or respect his vaudeville style. At least he knew that his status as an enemy of political correctness remained firm.

Pleased with the reception of *More Please*, he threw himself into the preparations for his new Australian show, once more named from one of his mother's frequent remonstrations: *Look At Me When I'm Talking to You!* After the artful attack by Bremner, Humphries could not have been more delighted with the comments of various critics. One Adelaide reviewer proclaimed him to be 'the genius of the Australian stage' and 'the last, best music hall artiste'.[1]

Look At Me When I'm Talking to You! opened in Adelaide on 25 October 1993. In the lead-up to the show Humphries worried about how it would be received. As usual he fretted about whether his show was funny right up until he was out on stage and heard the first laugh. 'To be funny is a fugitive gift,' he told the expatriate writer and academic Peter Conrad before the tour to Australia, revealing his chronic anxiety about his ability to make an audience laugh.[2] He consoled himself with the thought that Adelaide was a try-out in a friendly provincial city, and that the audience would most likely be receptive. Besides, he had done it before. But it was his first Australian show for eight years, with the exception of a show exclusively devoted to sketches with Sandy Stone in 1990, and that had been a struggle. The six-week Melbourne season had stretched Barry's patience with the character.

Lizzie toured with Barry and sometimes participated in warm-up exercises on stage at Her Majesty's Theatre with the stage manager and three musicians before Humphries retreated to his dressing room to put on his wig, costume and make-up. Over the speaker system the voices of some of the stars of music hall from the 1930s and 1940s crooned, readying the audience for the show. They included some of Humphries' own favourites, remembered from boyhood when he would listen to the radio in Christowel Street, Camberwell. Rather than risking problems with his voice, Barry now used two radio microphones stuck into place above his temple. It was tedious having the two wires taped to his back and head, but it was a necessity.

Les was the first to appear in this show, in multicoloured platform shoes and a mauve tracksuit, his top bearing the Olympic rings and the slogan 'Sydney 2000'. He bragged that he had been 'as busy as Christopher Skase's chiropractor' in making sure Sydney got the Olympics. He was now a 'fitness fanatic', he announced, drenching the front rows in spit. He told the people of Adelaide, 'I've always had a very hot — sorry, I didn't mean to say hot — very soft, well, hot and soft spot for Adders, as I call it,' confessing to being 'instrumental early on in persuading old Don Dunstan to get the Yartz Festival off the ground'. Les also reminded the citizens of the 'Athens of the south' about a 'television debacle' some fifteen years earlier when he was ejected from Jaye Walton's television show *Touch of Elegance* or '*Crutch of Elephants*, as I called it in those days — for accidentally getting pissed and tangling with a spaghetti-making machine behind a couch'.

When Les disappeared, a new character called Daryl Dalkeith arrived in the theatre; he was a sly business tycoon from Perth (hence the name, taken from the ritzy suburb) who had just finished a term in 'the slammer' for some kind of impropriety in property dealing. But 'corporate bodgie' Dalkeith was proud of his dealings: 'Too close to Hawkie,' Dalkeith explained; it was a 'trumped-up charge' and a 'political vendetta' that landed him in prison for fraud. Dalkeith looked like a jowly Alan Bond. Clad in a suit and dark sunglasses, and clutching a mobile phone, Dalkeith declared, 'I'm just a businessman.' He lamented the changes in Australia, observing that 'in the old days, I would have been knighted for my services to industry'.

Before Act I concluded Sandy appeared, becoming visible after flashes of lightning and smoke, and a tableau of a supermarket under a sign 'ASHWORLD' filled the stage. Sandy sat in his old armchair and gradually moved downstage to meet a standard lamp pushed into place from the wings. Sandy recalled the old grocer's shop in his neighbourhood. This Australia was now just a memory, murmured Sandy, who revealed that the supermarket that was built where his own house once stood in Gallipoli Crescent would soon be demolished to make way for new townhouses. Sandy worked on the anxieties of his aging audience. He mentioned the Regional Geriatric Assessment Authority that might visit at any time to determine whether 'a body should be moved to a Home for the Temporarily Bewildered'. Sandy reported that Beryl, now a widow for the second time, had become a grief counsellor. Sandy's sketch faded to the strains of a Richard Tauber tune on an old 78 rpm record.

Humphries presented a rather grim picture of contemporary Australian life as Sandy conjured up a much more stable time before cities were ravaged by rampant development. Earlier, Les had reported a conversation he'd had recently with the prime minister, Paul Keating, and reminded audiences that Australia had been 'sold' to 'foreign powers'. He tried to suggest schemes to improve the economic situation. 'Sell Tasmania to the Japanese? They own it already. The Simpson Desert to the Arabs? Already spoken for.' Some of the comedy was very close to the bone. It was six years since Keating had warned Australians on John Laws' radio program that Australia was in danger of becoming a 'banana republic' because of the size of its foreign debt, but it was still a raw issue.[3] One critic noted the silence that fell on the Melbourne audience after Sandy's final lines: 'They were better days if you ask me. We had the best of it.'[4]

When Edna made her entrance, sparkling in a sequinned and beaded dropped-waist dress, looking a bit like a gaudy flapper, the energy returned. She picked out several patrons, invited them on stage and dressed them up as members of the royal family, informing the audience that the Queen was preparing to abdicate as Queen of Australia in order to let Edna take over.

The reviews were overwhelmingly positive throughout the country, with Murray Bramwell in Adelaide describing Humphries as 'a burlesque entertainer without equal' and Edna as the 'vortex for all Humphries' miscreant energy'.[5] But Bramwell was lukewarm about Sir Les and denounced the Sandy monologue as 'purple nostalgia'. Leonard Radic noted that Humphries looked a little uneasy in front of his Melbourne audience and he found Edna disappointing, speculating that Humphries was tired of playing her.[6]

Jim Davidson remarked that Humphries, even after running the show in during the Adelaide season, seemed nervous in the role of Dalkeith and that this gave the segment an edge.[7] Davidson found the show striking in the way Humphries played on the anxieties of the audience about the future of Australia, about old age and about changes in society. But he also found Edna's games with the audience dull and 'leached of meaning'. Davidson had been a follower of Humphries, had interviewed him on more than one occasion, and in this review he signalled a new note of disappointment with the satirist whose act, especially in the Edna segment, seemed to lose its charge.

Once the show moved to Sydney, the *Sydney Morning Herald* published a large headshot of Humphries in his panama hat looking straight at the camera with a faint smile on his closed lips. The caption read 'Barry Humphries … eliciting winces of repulsion'. The reviewer, Doug Anderson, wrote that the show 'entertains grandly' but that 'it leaves an aftertaste of repugnance'. Although the critic winced at the banter he maintained that it should not be 'toned down' because 'the flinching reflex is where the social value of such satire derives'. He found it powerful theatre but deceptive in its nostalgia for a lost paradise in the Australian suburbs.[8] There were rave reviews as well. Peter Ward in the *Australian* exclaimed that Humphries' satire is 'devastating. He flushes the national liver. He gives new meaning to cultural cringe. He's the culture; we cringe.'[9]

In February 1994, during the show's Sydney season, Humphries celebrated his sixtieth birthday. Barry's friend Ken Thomson presented him with a privately published, limited-edition hardcover book with recollections, greetings and vignettes written by friends.

Bepraisements included greetings from Gough Whitlam and Joan Sutherland and short prose pieces by numerous friends past and present, including Joan Bakewell, Melvyn Bragg, Geoffrey Dutton, Peter Nichols, John Lahr, Elizabeth Jolley, Germaine Greer, Armistead Maupin and Peter Porter. Stephen Sondheim offered an acrostic and Barry's father-in-law, Stephen Spender, contributed a poem in Barry's honour called 'The Half of Life'. There was one notable omission. Peter O'Shaughnessy's name did not appear in the contents list. He and Barry had never fully repaired their friendship. Nicholas Garland was candid in his piece called 'Topsy-turvy Man', describing his old friend's reckless personality, terrifying addiction to risk and his generous character.

In the back cover portrait of *Bepraisements*, Humphries stands staring unselfconsciously at a camera held by the well-known photographer John Timbers in Dieppe. At a party in a grand house in the harbourside suburb of Darling Point in Sydney, Pat and Lewis Morley lovingly presented Humphries with an Alastair drawing of Salome that he had admired once on their wall. Barry was delighted.

Back in London in October, Barry saw Jonathan Pryce playing his once-coveted role of Fagin in *Oliver!* and arranged to meet the newly appointed Australian Cultural Attaché at Australia House. Her name was Rebecca Hossack and she was nothing like Sir Les. Tall and slender with long flowing hair, she stood opposite Barry in the cavernous foyer on the Strand chatting amicably as she waited for an appointment with her new boss, the Australian High Commissioner. They were off to see an exhibition together. Hossack came from Melbourne and had lived in London for the past fifteen years. She had studied fine art and law before leaving Australia, and had made a name for herself as an art dealer in London. She owned two galleries in the city, one in Fitzrovia and one in St James. As the urbane High Commissioner, Neal Blewett, walked down the stairs and into the dark expanses of the ground floor, he came upon Hossack and Humphries in conversation. It was a little bit like the changing of the guard. Hossack would transform the role carved out by Humphries in the guise of Sir Les. Barry watched somewhat ruefully as Hossack and Blewett stepped into their shiny black car and sped away.

Six months earlier Australia House had launched its search for a cultural development officer, occasioning the usual round of scoffing from the English press. A cartoonist showed Sir Les, Dame Edna and Crocodile Dundee lining up outside 'Keating House' for the job. Hossack was the new face of the Labor government's Creative Nation cultural policy. Humphries sent her a card at Christmas 'from your unworthy predecessor', and enclosed a photograph of Patterson with the greeting 'All the best Becky, love

Sir Les'. The press, including the Australian press, jumped on the bandwagon, crowing about the difficult task awaiting Hossack, whose mammoth job was to reverse the work of the likes of Sir Les and reinvent the image of Australians in Britain. Humphries had heard it all before.[10]

The mythical Australians that Humphries had created were still perceived as a problem by some Australians, but the political landscape had changed, and there was a new commitment to the arts. The Australian government, as Hossack eagerly informed sceptical members of the press in London, was now spending 50 per cent more per citizen per year on the arts than the British government. In addition there was talk that Australia might throw off its imperial past and become a republic. Once Humphries would have supported the cause, but now he wasn't so sure. Whereas once he mocked the royal family, he now held the monarchy in high esteem, and counted himself a friend of Prince Charles.

Regardless of the ambivalence of some of his countrymen, Humphries' influence was increasingly evident in Australian theatre and drama. In a new production of Patrick White's *A Cheery Soul*, directed by Neil Armfield, Robyn Nevin once more brought Miss Docker to life on stage. Nevin's performance was clearly influenced by the ubiquitous Edna Everage. The performance was celebrated by critics, with the *Age* reviewer, Helen Thomson, describing it as brilliant, noting the character's 'grotesquely expressive clown's mouth with its almost constant, blood-red and oversized smile'.[11] Humphries' Edna seemed to infuse this now iconic figure of Australian drama, but it was unclear where Edna and her creator were heading.

CHAPTER 34

Flashbacks

After the Australian tour of *Look At Me When I'm Talking to You!* wound up in Melbourne in December 1995, Humphries took Oscar and Rupert for a holiday at Club Med in Sardinia. There was an intense rivalry between the two teenaged boys who were close in age, and desperate for their father's attention. Barry and Diane discussed sending them to separate schools to try and alleviate the competitiveness and hostility between them.[1] (Eventually, Rupert stayed on at Bryanston in Dorset and Oscar transferred to Stowe in Buckinghamshire.) The New Zealand leg of Barry's tour had been rather disastrous, with pitifully small audiences, and Humphries was in dire need of a break. From Sardinia he headed to his chalet in Gstaad, with the aim of finishing a novel he had been working on, which would be released as *Women in the Background*.

Humphries had struggled with the book for more than a year, attempting to complete the writing in various locations where he hoped to find peace and inspiration. He told Peter Nichols in a letter that he had stayed for a short while in County Wicklow, Ireland, hoping to enter the 'literary force-field' of the tiny nation. But instead, rain and loneliness were his companions and he confessed that sadly 'the spirits of Congreve, Joyce and Beckett failed to come to the party'. Humphries had taken a day trip to Dublin in order to witness the unveiling of a plaque on Oscar

Wilde's family home in Merrion Square. To Barry's delight, it seemed that the ghost of Wilde appeared in front of his very eyes: a tall figure with dyed red hair clad in an Inverness cape emerged from the crowd. 'It was Dorian Gray!' It was in fact the actor Hurd Hatfield who had starred in *The Picture of Dorian Gray* in 1945, a role he would later regret. Hatfield asked Barry if he intended to go to Westminster Abbey for the consecration of the 'Dorian Gray Window'. Humphries was dumbfounded by Hatfield's strange conflation of character and author. Here was a man approaching eighty years of age, who seemed utterly haunted by Oscar Wilde's creation. For Humphries the moment must have offered a glimpse of the madness that seems to dog actors who cannot escape a particular character.[2]

With his usual craving for company, Humphries accepted dinner invitations from his neighbours in the exclusive Swiss alpine resort town, where he was spending significant amounts of time. He marvelled at the extraordinary collections of art in the homes of these mysteriously rich people, and stared enviously at walls 'groaning' with Cezannes, Breughels and Matisses. Lizzie enjoyed the skiing, and Oscar would go out on the slopes with her, on visits from boarding school during his half-term holidays. But Barry missed conversations with his friends, and the familiarity of London. When news reached him of the death of two of his inspirations and colleagues, John Osborne and Peter Cook, from the complications of over-indulgence in alcohol, he was shocked, but not surprised.

Barry entertained his friends in gossipy letters, and rejoiced in his own good health as he ploughed on with his manuscript. In his missives he sounded like one of his early characters, the long-suffering father Colin Cartwright, at times, as he lamented Oscar's propensity for complaining about school where annual fees ran to £15,000. Humphries recognised that he was starting to sound like his own father. He joked sympathetically about his mother-in-law's failing memory, and related his own method of greeting someone he did not recognise. He avoided any embarrassment by saying, 'How nice to see you again!', suffering the depressingly inevitable reply, 'Fancy you remembering!'

Humphries could joke about such failings, and how to cope with them, but he found it difficult to truly laugh at himself. Barry's old friend and Barry McKenzie collaborator Nicholas Garland answered the telephone one day, surprised to hear Humphries' voice. The two men had not seen one another for a few years. Humphries explained that he was in London preparing for the opening of an extravagant new show. The news was out that Nick was to be awarded an OBE. Barry said, 'Let's have lunch together.' When they met Barry put his burning question to Nick: 'There's something I've got to know,' he began. 'Why did they give *you* an OBE?' Garland was mortified and silent as Humphries continued, realising that it was not a joke. 'My question is not without an element of envy,' he said candidly.³ But the damage was done. Garland stared at his old friend in silence. Eventually, as so many times in the past, Garland overlooked Humphries' topsy-turviness and repaired the relationship.

Humphries' novel, *Women in the Background*, was eventually completed and published in 1995, prompting one woman to leap determinedly from the shadows and onto the pages of the tabloids. It was Brenda, Barry's first wife. 'Fame and adulation went to Humphries' head,' she told a reporter. 'There's nothing about Barry Humphries that I want to remember ... I was once very devoted to Barry. I suspected what he was up to, beyond all the drinking. It was doomed. It was not so easy to face divorce in the '50s and I was still a teenager. I was heartbroken.'⁴

In the flagrantly 'incorrect' title of the novel, Humphries mischievously appropriated a phrase from Field Marshal Montgomery talking about the artist Augustus John in 1944: 'Who is this chap? He drinks, he's dirty, and I know there are women in the background!' The book presents the story of the entertainer, a reformed alcoholic called Derek Pettyfer who plays a housewife called Mrs Petty, and thinks of himself as an 'apostate Australian'. It is a bizarre satire on Humphries and his world. Pettyfer tries to evade a hapless journalist in his mission to write Pettyfer's biography. The novel received mixed reviews, and Barry soon turned to a more familiar medium of expression, television.

Humphries was just six years old when Alfred Hitchcock's thriller *Rebecca*, starring Laurence Olivier and Joan Fontaine offered a faithful Hollywood adaptation of the Daphne du Maurier novel. With the intriguing opening scene of the film in mind, and with a nod and a wink to another classic, *The Wizard of Oz*, the writer and director David Mitchell devised a suitably dramatic rendition for Barry as an opener for his new television series about Australian society since the 1950s, *Barry Humphries' Flashbacks*. In an improbable echo of the two Hollywood films, Humphries awoke from a nightmare screaming, then in an enigmatic tone announced: 'Last night I dreamed I went to Melbourne. Dreams of the Australia of my past come in flashes: gaudy, quaint, whimsical flashes of a simple country suffering the same growing pains I suffered. These images swirl around me, disturbing my sleep but reinforcing the childish belief that there's no place like home, there's no place like home, there's no place like home …'

Humphries portrayed himself as an embodiment of the nation, and its journey to maturity, transforming the familiar clichés about Australian history. He mischievously presented the audience with Sandy Stone, Edna Everage and Les Patterson as reliable sources, whose recollections and opinions created a valid version of history. Humphries' characters elevated themselves from comic caricatures into informants. Sir Les, remarkably, was always present at important political events. Humphries' history became Australian history.

David Mitchell trawled through thousands of hours of television tapes for the show. He and Barry had worked together on several programs and had first met when Edna judged a flower-arranging contest on the *Mike Walsh Show* more than twenty years before. Humphries' short and pungent character monologues were filmed in the Ealing studios in London.

In four episodes, *Barry Humphries' Flashbacks* recalled the cosy insularity of the fifties when the radiogram was the centre of family life, the heady sixties when Prime Minister Harold Holt announced that Australia would go 'all the way with LBJ', the seventies when Australia was 'endlessly coming of age' and men wore long sideburns, and the excessive decade of the eighties, with its scam merchants, extravagant parties and mega-mortgages brought to a halt by the recession that changed everything. Sir Les, Sandy Stone and Edna offered their opinions and recollections about the changes that occurred in Australia from the reign of Robert 'Ming' Menzies, right up until the time the party was called off by the stock exchange crash in October 1987. Paul Keating, the working-class prime minister from Bankstown who had a taste for antiques, Humphries recalled portentously, had seen 'bad omens coming out of the endless party mood'. Sir Les condemned Keating as a 'killjoy'. 'We called him the Undertaker,' recalled Les in the documentary. 'Kybosh Keating was another name, because he put the kybosh on all the fun we were having in the golden days of Gough.'

The result was a satirical portrait of Humphries' homeland, as he cast his eye on Australian music, fashion, design, language, ideology and politics in the post-war period. The narrative was unashamedly driven by Humphries' own memories of his childhood in the new suburbs of Melbourne, and the idiosyncrasies of his own family, with Edna providing the detail: 'My mother always used to say "Leave something on your plate at the end of your meal for Mr Manners."' Humphries, who became a 'foodie' in his adult life, took delight ever after in eating everything set before him.

Australian sporting heroes were conspicuously absent from Humphries' account of the fifty-year period. He explained this in a preface to the book that accompanied the series, written by Roger McDonald. Although sport 'is the major preoccupation of many Australians', wrote Humphries, 'I have no knowledge of, or interest in, this topic ...'[5] Reviewing archival footage of advertisements for appliances featuring high-heeled housewives caressing knobs and simpering over gleaming surfaces, Humphries revelled in the insatiable Australian appetite for all things new, and the absurdities of the consumer society. The series lent weight to Edna's anthem to Australia, originally sung at the *Last Night of the Poms*, demonstrating in many ways that the island continent and its inhabitants were indeed 'rich and safe and funny'.

In this essay of affection for the country of his birth, Humphries once again transformed a television genre, positioning himself as social historian and elder statesman of the arts. The comic interludes of Dame Edna, who in one segment appeared in an extravagant black dress with two life-sized stuffed cockatoos on the shoulders, added lacerating comic commentary to the program and a whiff of postmodernist playfulness, as she and the other characters reflected on real figures and real events in a kaleidoscope of colourful vignettes, swirling across Humphries' polished but acerbic narrative.

Edna recalled that she was not really sure why Prime Minister Gough Whitlam 'made me a Dame ... it could have been for my services to Australian culture. After all, I pretty well put Australian women on the map. And my services to conservation are well known.' Pointing to the stuffed birds on her shoulders, and calling them 'lovely marsupials', she said, 'These are not alive, these beautiful sulphur-crested cockatoos; they died a long time ago. But they were friends of mine and I conserved them. Little did they know that they would be turned into a beautiful frock.'

The series also presented a potted history of television in Australia, with advertisements for products, archival news footage of various royal visits and extraordinary sequences from popular television drama and comedy, including *The Mavis Bramston Show*, *Number 96*, *Prisoner* and *Neighbours*. Humphries interspersed this material with the very earliest footage of Edna on television and a clip of Les Patterson's infamous tangling with some spaghetti underneath a table on Jaye Walton's *Touch of Elegance*.

The Whitlam era continued to inform Humphries' satirical repertoire into the 1990s. In the episode about the 1970s, 'On the Map at Last', Humphries offered one of his most nostalgic portraits of the brief Labor government of Gough Whitlam. His portrayal of Whitlam and his 'Camelot' extended the riotous spoof on cultural nationalism that had emerged in the Barry McKenzie films. At the same time it expressed awe, affection and respect for the charismatic Labor prime minister.

Although Humphries had sometimes lamented the way in which Gough Whitlam was sentimentalised by so many, in reflecting on the Whitlam era in *Flashbacks* his tone initially was distinctly nostalgic. Humphries juxtaposed Bazza McKenzie with Whitlam, using the theme song of the film with rewritten words, and retitled 'The Adventures of Edward Gough Whitlam'. Humphries presented Gough as an innocent abroad — 'a very tall lawyer from Cabramatta, eager to walk the world stage' — as footage showed Gough towering over Chinese dignatories, striding youthfully and confidently along a very high section of the Great Wall of China. 'Australia,' exclaimed Humphries in his narration, 'was just glimpsing its own Camelot.' In a brilliant encapsulation of an era, and of Humphries' particular viewpoint, Gough and Margaret Whitlam were shown po-faced in Red Square, being welcomed by crowds of adoring admirers to the tune of the by-then iconic *Barry McKenzie* theme song.

Humphries summed up the period, claiming wearily that Australia in the 1970s was, 'according to our own publicity, endlessly coming of age', and that he himself felt 'partly responsible for this', because of his creation of the crude but lovable McKenzie prior to the election of Whitlam. In merging the two talismans of the era, Humphries depicted Gough as a theatrical character and all but suggested that Whitlam, like McKenzie, had been created by Humphries himself. Humphries' satirical portrait expressed huge regard for the man who, among other achievements, elevated appreciation for the arts in Australia. But it also mocked the strangely innocent zeal of the Labor prime minister 'whose Camelot had its run cut short'.

Sir Les predictably shattered sentiment and nostalgia, improbably associating Whitlam with the rorting and gross impropriety of the imaginary minister. In a stained beige safari suit, gulping whisky from a tumbler, Les explained proudly his relationship with the Labor leader.

> I, Les Patterson, was an integral part of the Whitlam Camelot ... I was Merlin, I was the think tank, the ideas man. And I came to him one day and he locked the door. I said, 'I need money, Gough, for a special project; it's the

disabled black lesbian puppet workshop.' He looked a bit strange when I said that. 'You need big bickies for that, Les?' 'Yes, the black disabled lesbian women's puppet workshop.' As he started to write the cheque, he said, 'Now look, Les, who's this really for?' I said, 'Gough [taking another loud slurp of his drink], it's for me.' 'What are you going to do with it?' I said, 'I'm going to piss it up against the wall.' He said, 'Les, you're an honest man, I'll double it.'

Humphries allowed himself the last word on Whitlam. He declared the facts pompously: 'The Labor government was decisively turfed out, Gough became a self-appointed martyr, canonised by the media, and Sir John Kerr spent the rest of his days in exile and in odium.' Humphries' tone in this summary cut away the nostalgia and affection of the earlier sequence. He brutally consigned Gough Whitlam to history. His judgment of the man revealed a surprising lack of empathy for the leader. It was a stinging portrait and mirrored the searing words in Humphries' threnody for another visionary Australian — Patrick White.

In the spring of 1997 Humphries once again joined the cast of *Oliver!* as Fagin, taking over the starring role from Robert Lindsay. The show was an extravaganza directed by the West End dynamo Sam Mendes, and had been running for three years, making it the most enduring show to be staged at the London Palladium. For Humphries it was the fourth time he had played in this most English of musicals. And it was exactly thirty years since he had last sung the iconic tunes of Lionel Bart, during the heady days of the swinging sixties in London, years before Edna had become a household name in Britain.

Bart had revised and extended the repertoire of numbers for the show, and Barry expressed enthusiasm about revisiting the role.[6] He very deliberately moved away from the exaggerated cockney accent audiences associated with Fagin, as he was only too aware of the character as Dickens' most 'politically incorrect' creation, and did not want to cause offence. Barry had not been impressed with Jonathan Pryce's rather camp version of the villain. Instead he played a 'larky' Fagin, 'more Central European than cockney', barely hinting at a dark side to Fagin's personality.[7] It was a demanding role with backstage climbing and even crawling around the scaffolding. Barry found the role exhilarating, but at sixty-three years of age it was also exhausting. On the other hand, he realised that years of terrifying and delighting audiences as Edna meant that he was at ease in the role of the beguiling rogue.

By the time Humphries finished his contract with *Oliver!*, passing the role to the English comic actor and songwriter Jim Dale, he was in need of a break. He and Lizzie fled to the Algarve in Portugal, hoping for sunshine. But the rain poured down, flooding the countryside and dashing Barry's hopes for basking and bathing under blue skies. However, the break gave him time to think about what he wanted to do next. The newspapers were full of the impending handover of Hong Kong to the Chinese. For Humphries the opportunity seemed obvious for some kind of spoof, perhaps involving Sir Les.

It soon became clear to Humphries that Les Patterson should properly farewell the old colony of the 'Far East'. A young, affable and rather unassuming producer, Clive Tulloh, would produce the program. Tulloh had always admired Humphries and had taken the audacious step of writing to him a few years earlier to suggest a new character for Barry, a kind of failed arts critic. Humphries responded with a witty letter thanking Clive for his idea, and explaining that he thought the arts suffered enough without also being lampooned by him. When they met up to work on the new venture, *Sir Les and the Great Chinese Takeaway*, Clive and Barry got on well. The program they made was the first 'mockumentary' Humphries had appeared in for almost twenty years.

Barry, Lizzie, Oscar, Rupert, Clive and several crew members set off for Hong Kong and began filming. Clive had decided to proceed in an organic and somewhat old-fashioned manner, and make decisions about narrative sequence once a certain amount of footage was available. Les would give the audience an experience of the spectacular city, and reminisce about the old Hong Kong, showing viewers the sights, and telling yarns about his exploits. Barry hoped, for example, to chat with the British troops before they lowered the Union Jack for the last time. For all its frivolity, the program was a nostalgic attempt to preserve the historic moment before the city returned to Chinese control. Like much of Humphries' satire it emerged from an impulse to preserve elements of the past before they disappeared.

Although Barry is fearless on stage, and started his career as a particularly gutsy street performer, he found it difficult to play Sir Les in Hong Kong. Clive noticed as soon as they began filming that it seemed to be hard work for Barry to perform as Les without an audience. At first Barry attempted to stay in character, even when the cameras were not rolling, as he had always done as Edna in his studio shoots. But to stay in character as Les for hours on end with no studio audience was not possible.

It was not the character that presented the problem, but the situation. Humphries had no trouble quickly getting into the spirit of Les: he had recently finished a short season of a show called *Les Patterson Has a Stand Up* at the small, art deco Whitehall Theatre in Westminster, in which Les claimed to have 'put the smile back on the face of Little Di'. But in Hong Kong Humphries found it difficult, for example, to front up as Sir Les on the doorstep of the Chinese Embassy, demanding to speak to the Ambassador, knowing full well that he would be turned away by a humourless guard. Without permission the sequence was a little risky, as the camera was hidden. Barry seemed somewhat cowed by his lack of control in the setting. Sure enough, before he made it to the gate, a guard had unceremoniously farewelled Sir Les. Performing in costume on the street in a country with no interest in Australian comedy made the acting tough. Humphries is no Sacha Baron Cohen, and by then preferred the licensed space of the theatre for his act.

In fact nobody really wanted to know about Sir Les in Hong Kong. The reprobate addressed an Australian business lunch one day, and divided the room. The older men (and they were mainly men) laughed heartily while the younger ones scowled and cringed.

Even the outgoing governor, Sir Christopher Patten, a friend of Barry's, 'respectfully declined' to be interviewed but wished Les and his colleagues all the best with their television program. It was a far cry from the heady days of the Whitlam era, when the curly-haired Bruce Beresford stood in front of the immaculately turned-out Australian prime minister, directing him on how to greet, and anoint, a middle-aged man dressed as a woman in the closing sequences of a film about an imaginary kidnapping of the Queen.

As the date for the handover of the colony approached, the more seriously it seemed to be taken by the British. Prince Charles was scheduled to attend the ceremony on 1 July 1997. *Sir Les and the Great Chinese Takeaway* suddenly seemed too flippant for such an occasion. The British could not afford to be seen to be making fun of the event, or risk offending the Chinese. The BBC buried the mockumentary, screening it very late at night. Millions of people watched the handover ceremony on television around the world, but a far smaller audience in the UK saw Les saying goodbye to the old 'Honkers'.

Humphries, meanwhile, continued to use Sir Les to parade his interest in the priapic with vaudevillian flair. In one particularly daring piece entitled 'Erotic Diplomacy', published in a special issue of the British Erotic Print Society's *Review* devoted to 'Australian Culture', Humphries penned a comical story by Les in which he discussed his adventures with various 'hornbags'. The story hardly rates as erotic, being more of a parody of the erotic. For one thing the language of Sir Les is decidedly unerotic, though he offers several mildly amusing new terms for the male appendage and for the act of sexual intercourse. Humphries had not dared to use the terms on stage, but in print, as Les, he called the penis 'the old blue-veined junket pump' and the 'eight-inch aphrodisiac', and referred to penetration as 'driving the old pigskin bus into Tunatown'.[8] Sir Les declared in the story that during his assignations he usually put a photo of his 'good lady wife, Gwen' on the wall, because 'there is no more steadying or prolonging influence than the face of a beloved spouse staring at you from between the ankles of a compliant research assistant'.

In another work Humphries wrote in Patterson's name, the book *The Traveller's Tool*, he allowed his obsession with Les's voracious sexual behaviour free rein. The book is not as engaging as his short piece in the *Review*, but the glossary of Australian terms at the end of the volume offers a snapshot of Humphries' extreme taste for vulgarity, his understanding of Australian slang and his insatiable wit. Among the terms for a woman's genitalia are 'doughnut — a non-fattening meal'; and 'furry hoop — a doughnut'. There are also numerous expressions for male homosexuals, including 'pillow-biter', 'shirtlifter', 'date packer' and 'kapok kruncher', also defined as 'a South Australian arts administrator'. Humphries lists non-sexual terms too, such as 'bodyline', defined by Les as 'a carefully orchestrated attack on Australian cricket by a bunch of monocled Pommy Pooftahs' and offers some rather pointed invented terms of his own. The term 'pan-handler' is defined scornfully as 'an Australian playwright'.[9]

Barry remained in touch with the Australian vernacular due to the frequent trips he and Lizzie made to Australia. They bought a house in Tasmania that had been built by convicts and had views across the ocean. Humphries had always enjoyed his tours to the island state, and hoped to be able to spend some time painting, reading and travelling around the island. Lizzie's fondness for travel meant that Barry also explored mainland Australia more than he ever had before. He found, to his initial astonishment, that he looked forward to these sojourns, and the opportunities to relax that they provided.

CHAPTER 35

Banishing Edna

After years in television and touring in Australia Humphries longed to return to the stage and to the pleasure of performing in the West End. In Britain, the Labour Party had won an election in a landslide, and was busily shaking things up. Over lunch at the Ivy in Covent Garden with his friend, the lifetime peer Lord Archer, Humphries talked about his plans for a major new show.

Jeffrey Archer, a colourful author of racy, best-selling novels, Conservative MP and no stranger to brushes with the law, had initially been treated with comic contempt by Humphries on *The Dame Edna Experience*, but in the years that followed the two had become friends. Like many successful people from poor backgrounds, Archer was sometimes derided in London as 'common', causing Barry great amusement. He recalled in his second memoir, *My Life As Me*, his impression that in Australia, Archer would be lampooned as 'rather too posh'.[1] Humphries told Archer that he had already begun writing the new show which would portray Edna's whole career and include, unusually for one of Barry's shows, a cast for the first act, with Edna continuing solo in the second act. Barry was determined to include a major musical element in the show, which would require a full orchestra. He explained to Archer that he had already worked up some of the music with the musical theatre writer and comic actor Kit Hesketh-Harvey and the composer James

McConnel. He needed a backer. Archer generously agreed to fund his friend's new venture.

Humphries hoped that *New Edna: The Spectacle* would be the biggest and best show of the Dame's career. It was certainly the most elaborate Barry had ever staged in the West End. If Blair could reinvent Labour under the banner New Labour, so could he reinvent Edna. It was ten years since Barry had played Edna in London. It had been a lengthy break, and in the fast-paced world of entertainment it was a dangerously long hiatus. The show tried out in Guildford, and Barry was cautiously encouraged by the response.

Humphries was excited but still very nervous when *New Edna* finally transferred to the beautiful Theatre Royal in Haymarket for the opening on 21 April 1998. But from the very beginning when he performed the show as a charity benefit in the presence of Princess Alexandra, Barry began to panic. Laughter was muted. The early reviews were extremely disappointing. And they were blunt. 'Has Dame Edna Everage passed her sell-by date?' carped the *Daily Mail*.[2] 'Dame Edna may be a megastar who is just past her glorious comic prime,' hissed the *Daily Telegraph*.[3] Edna had come to prominence during the 1980s. Was she inevitably linked to that era of Margaret Thatcher, and therefore now stale?

The cost of the show had turned out to be more than twice what had been anticipated. The prospect of a failure was suddenly very real. Few critics found anything positive to say about Barry's new style and found the pastiche of musicals tedious. Many were scathing. Humphries faced the prospect of disastrously small houses and the embarrassment of an immense financial loss for his friend Lord Archer.

The show's overture, or 'musical foreplay', presented a medley of popular hits from musicals including *My Fair Lady*, before Sir Les appeared to introduce the various parts of the story of Edna's life that formed the first half of the show. Les reported that Edna had collapsed in a Knightsbridge shop with a frozen chicken stuffed into her pantyhose. As a result she was hospitalised. What followed were Edna's flashbacks of her early life and family history. The audience learned that Edna's grandmother had been transported to the colonies for stealing a bunch of gladioli. Edna's own story began with the Dame as a child, with hair the same wisteria colour as the Dame's mature coiffure, singing a song called 'Why Am I Mauve?' The story went on to portray the young Edna winning a beauty competition for 'Australia's Lovely Mothers' in Moonee Ponds, and eventually showed Edna's arrival in the mother country.

At every stage of Edna's young life a different actress played the role. It was a bold move. Humphries had never before presented anyone else in the role of Edna, unless it was for a stunt or as a costume-change double. Suddenly all of Humphries' mannerisms and mannish galumphing as Edna were gone. And so was the comedy. One critic writing for the *Express* exclaimed: 'The Aussie megastar has done the unthinkable and banished herself from long sections of her own show.'[4]

Humphries, released from his Edna costume, played a young Rupert Murdoch who announced that he was as likely to show a naked lady in the pages of his newspaper as to have a prime minister kissing his arse. Even mute and mousy Madge had moved with the times, sporting a pierced navel and performing a drunken dance. It was raw and ugly comedy. But the finale in which Edna restored the sight of a blind person hit the mark, with its cutting satire of the hideous falseness and arrogance of so many who pretend that they can 'heal' others. Edna the icon rose from the stage, her blue and white gown unfurling from the bottom into yards of white billowing material, as she soared upwards like an angel. Barry pushed a switch and huge white wings appeared.

For *New Edna*, Humphries had recycled elements of earlier shows, further drawing the ire of various critics. Nicholas de Jongh spoke of the 'moth-eaten old material' of Humphries' repartee. Michael Coveney lamented that Dame Edna fans would get nothing much that was new out of the show. Even the costumes, usually one of the failsafe highlights of an Edna extravaganza, aroused the vehement comment that one of Edna's gowns in silver and pink was 'yoked by violence together'.[5] Sheridan Morley, who had revered Humphries in the past and spoke of Edna as 'the greatest drag act' in his lifetime, thought something had 'gone terribly wrong'.[6] Charles Spencer, who had admired Humphries for twenty years, said the show was 'about as entertaining as a Technicolor yawn into a Qantas sickbag during a particularly turbulent flight'.[7] The jokes were 'lazy', the first act laboured and tedious and Humphries seemed to falter.[8]

The *Guardian*'s Phil Daoust was kinder, declaring that Humphries 'was in marvellous spiky form'.[9] And Jeremy Kingston praised the show as a 'mostly jolly evening'.[10] Robert Gore-Langton said that Edna 'still generates an awesome comic voltage'.[11] John Gross in the *Sunday Telegraph* wrote of Les's appearance as 'pure gold'. But the reservations were serious and fully expressed. Gross said the first half was 'thrown together, even amateurish' and the second half dull in patches. He yearned for the old revue style with separate sketches.[12]

New Edna closed on 27 June 1998 after just eight weeks, a far cry from his sell-out nine-month season in 1987 with *Back with a Vengeance*. It had been a dismal and devastating failure. Even now it is hard to explain why Humphries abandoned his comic formula. Perhaps he did not know how to bring Edna back into the limelight after ten years away from the West End. Perhaps he lost faith in the power of his own monologue as the centrepiece of his act. Perhaps he thought that the spoof of the first act would appeal to a new, younger crowd. Clearly Humphries managed to rescue the show with his solo magic in the second act, but the cost of his misjudgment proved to be extreme. The one-man show was his forte and the critics let him know it unambiguously.

If not for the positive review by the Australian expatriate Peter Conrad, who praised the show unreservedly, Humphries may never again have dared to put on another performance in London. Conrad referred to the 'lyrical rapture' of Les Patterson who opened the show, and who represented comedy itself, which, in his opinion, was 'about uncivilised, unsocialised man, refusing to edit his thoughts'. The 'danger of the theatre', Conrad exclaimed, 'its exhibitionism, aggression and improvisatory bravura — is incarnate in the marauding Edna'.[13]

In an intriguing review essay, the King's College London scholar and seasoned theatre critic John Stokes stated that 'the force of Humphries' art lies in the ways in which it obliges us continually to redraw our own lines'.[14] Stokes described a scene at the Black Cap bar, a well-known gay pub in Camden Town, in the small hours of the morning. A drag queen called Jonathan, whose cabaret act went under the title 'The Dame Edna Experience' whipped up a frenzy there each Saturday night on a tiny stage. Clad in a blonde wig, Jonathan belted out versions of 'Delilah' and favourites by Diana Ross, imitating Dame Edna's voice but peppering his speech with the word 'fucking' so frequently that, in Stokes' view, he marked the huge distance between his act and that of its inspiration. Jonathan's act was misogynistic, crude and tawdry. After some time Jonathan would tear off his wig to reveal his short hair and good-looking boyish features. As Stokes observed, drag had come a long way since the beginning of Barry's career some forty years earlier. Through his graphic depiction of the 'cauterising cruelty' of the electronic music of the club, which resembled 'Mykonos in August', Stokes demonstrated the uses for drag in club cabaret and its currency at the end of the millennium. He made a point that was not lost on Humphries: 'the reasons for the perennially changing styles of drag are as varied as the art itself'.[15]

Humphries has never liked Edna to be called a drag act. Technically the performance of Edna is not drag. Edna is a character and Humphries has always described himself as a character actor. The audience for Edna at the Theatre Royal was twenty or thirty years older on average than those who patronised the Black Cap in Camden High Street. Edna may have inspired the young drag actor Jonathan, but Humphries found it difficult to get young people into the theatre to see him perform. The younger generation would have been children during the heyday of *The Dame Edna Experience* on London Weekend Television in the 1980s, and his revue style, particularly the corny musical numbers that filled the first act, would not appeal to this new audience.

The yawning generation gap was only one of Humphries' problems as he contemplated the poor reception for his return to the stage in his beloved West End. Perhaps the more monstrous Edna became, and the further she left 'niceness' behind in her past, the less tolerant her audience was of her outrageous behaviour. Humphries had often been accused of misogyny, with his presentation of women and mothers as grotesque harridans. He had now added crudeness to Edna's repertoire. In the new show Edna talked about 'slots' to be filled, 'secret glands' and 'probing fingers' far too often. The laboured jokes about Norm's prostate were exhausted. In Edna, Humphries had captured the travesty and tragicomedy of a woman's life as it is portrayed in our culture, and turned the cruel banality of this pathology into satire. But now the satire threatened to turn in on itself.

The criticism of Humphries at this time was not universal: the American scholar, Laurence Senelick, lavished praise on Barry's 'masterpiece' character, Edna, and observed the theme of his act to be its searing attack on misogyny. He said that 'for a woman to establish an identity, she has to be as visually lush as one of Dame Edna's gladioli, a paragon of narcissis'.[16]

Humphries was disturbed by the failure of his West End show, but he was not tired of the stage, or of Edna. He agonised about what to do next. As he approached his sixty-fifth birthday, he wondered about where to take his act. Perhaps the time had come for Humphries to embrace drag explicitly, and to seek out a new audience for his glamorous alter ego. He realised that it was time to look once more to America.

PART SIX
SATIRIST

CHAPTER 36

Dragging Up

The failure of *New Edna* was not the first time that Humphries had to pick himself up after a bruising by the critics. But it hadn't happened for a long time. Ever since his West End breakthrough with *Housewife Superstar!* in 1976, he had heaped success upon success on stage and on television throughout Great Britain and Australia. Edna had also been celebrated in Ireland, Germany, Finland and Denmark. Humphries' urge to perform and instinct to write were as strong as ever, but he felt frustrated and bitterly disappointed. He was reluctant to embark on a new show in Australia: the knives seemed to be out again, with Barry's act considered by some to be the ultimate in political incorrectness.

Craig McGregor had denounced Humphries again, describing him as ultra conservative and

> ... on the wrong side on almost any political or social or intellectual issue you'd care to name. There's a weird tonality to his work, and I think it springs from a profound anti-humanism. The stances, biases, extremism and unfairness in his characters, I feel, reveal a ruthlessness against ordinary people and the social and cultural habits and mores that give meaning to a great number of Australians' lives — footie, pop culture, barbecues. He

thinks they're fair game for his arrogant and aristocratic satire.[1]

Charges of snobbery Humphries could handle, and he could swallow accusations of being conservative. He was used to those labels. But to be castigated for a 'ruthlessness' towards Australia and its people cut to the quick, and seemed to him to demonstrate a failure of understanding. Humphries' art is satire, and Australian life his primary subject. His goals as an entertainer throughout his career have been to make people laugh, to bring them joy, and to understand Australia. Sometimes satire is ruthless. Like another great Australian satirist, Christina Stead, who has also been cast as a misanthrope, Humphries' art springs from an interest in people and social life.

Australian critics had become brutally blunt in their assessment of Barry's work. David Marr complained several years earlier that Edna was still using jokes in London that Australians had heard twenty years earlier, and that Edna had lost her early poetry, had 'coarsened', and was now less of a satirist than an 'avenging clown'. 'She and her creator have lived long enough away from home for their Australia to be, more and more, a raw confabulation,' Marr remarked.[2] This sort of criticism rankled with Humphries. Some years earlier he had objected vociferously to the arguments cited in the *Oxford Companion to Australian Literature* — that his absence from Australia had weakened his satire; that 'Dame Edna's megastar status evinces Humphries' megalomania'; and that he was 'deeply suspicious of any progressive movement in Australia'.[3]

During the disastrous run of *New Edna* in London, Humphries revealed his distress in a querulous and reproachful comment piece published in the *Spectator* and the Melbourne *Age*. Humphries was disingenuous, describing himself as 'self-defeatingly circumspect' in his approaches to 'desirable women'. Underneath the anecdotes Humphries seemed to be pleading for recognition of himself as a kind, generous and misunderstood actor.[4] He offered an account of the trouble he always took to arrange free tickets to his shows for all and sundry, only to find that the ingrates had not turned up for the performance. Humphries also lamented the fact that live theatre seemed at risk of becoming a lost art. 'When a person you haven't seen for years rings you up and after a few softening-up pleasantries says, "How do we go about getting tickets for your new show?" you should reply, "I'm afraid we only accept experienced theatre-goers. Have you seen a live show before? *Mousetrap*? *Phantom*? Try a box office, I only work backstage," but you rarely do. Always a craven people-pleaser, you tell them you'll see what you can do.' Despite his dissembling there was some truth in his appeal and the emotional register was decidedly downbeat. Humphries was downcast, disappointed and eager to reconcile with his audience.

Humphries' one-time friend, Phillip Adams, with whom he had worked on *The Naked Bunyip* and the first *Barry McKenzie* film, had also lambasted him in an interview with John Hind as a racist who disparages Aboriginal culture and is given to anti-Semitic comments. Adams criticised Humphries' contemptuous use of the term 'arriviste' about others, 'but that's pretty much what Barry has been'.[5] The rich and influential leader of the Republican movement in Australia, Malcolm Turnbull, also stuck the knife in. Turnbull had created a storm for Margaret Thatcher's government during the *Spycatcher* affair, when Humphries was enjoying his glory days on television in the 1980s. Turnbull condemned Humphries for 'basically making a quid out of denigrating Australia' in order to 'delight the Brits'.[6]

Not only was Humphries' humour criticised for its vulgarity and cruelty, Humphries himself came in for a pasting for what Gerard Henderson described as 'becoming even more sympathetic to the views of the characters he once despised'.[7] Henderson cast Humphries as a man who had lost his touch and abandoned all attempts at political satire. John Lahr's quest in following Humphries around the UK had been, in part, to find out whether an artist can be a genius without being a monster. But many Australian critics had decided that Humphries was monstrous some years earlier, and were sticking to their script. Humphries had tried everything to distance his own image from that of his characters.

His own highly crafted persona was one of his ways of ensuring that he would not be confused with Edna or Les. But this also added a complication: Humphries refused to allow any outsiders to see the man behind the masks. It was not just a case of ensuring his privacy, or maintaining an artist's mystique. Rather it reflected an anxiety about being acceptable to others as himself, an anxiety that had plagued him since he was a boy. He was wounded by the insults and worried about what to do next.

Once more Humphries turned to the United States in a bid to enchant a fresh audience. None of the enduring Australian hostility towards him mattered to Americans. In the US nobody knew or cared about the way Humphries tried out his act on his tours in Australia before returning to London, or any of his clever methods of recycling. He knew he did not have to remake Edna for audiences there. The decision was clear: there was no better time for Barry to head to North America.

Humphries had already turned down a few offers to appear on stage in the US since the debacle in 1977, and relished fan letters from Americans who had seen his chat show on cable television. He had nothing to lose. Joan Rivers, the American comedienne and chat show host, put him in touch with her agent, and in a short time Barry was booked in to the Theatre on the Square in San Francisco for a one-month season.

Dame Edna dined out on the Joan Rivers connection, and Humphries ingeniously built the flop at the Theatre Royal in London into Edna's 'tabloid' story. 'I had overreached myself,' she said. 'There were big sets and chorus dancers, and it was too much. The audience wanted me, not all these extraneous elements.' It was true up to a point, and the ever-resilient Humphries developed the story brilliantly.

'When you're depressed,' Edna reported, 'it's important to call someone more depressed than you. I immediately thought of Joan Rivers. I got her on the phone, and she wanted to talk about her husband's suicide, but I reminded her she'd told me about that many times. Then she wanted to tell me how painful it was to give birth to Melissa. And I agreed that Melissa is painful. But then I asked her advice ... she's a much older woman, a bit like a godmother to me. She told me to go to San Francisco and assured me that the remaining Village People would come to see me, maybe on their walkers, but they might bring their aunties, uncles and grandmothers.'

Before Barry set off for San Francisco, Clive Tulloh asked him how he imagined his audience for his first stage appearance in the United States in twenty-one years. With a wide grin, Barry replied confidently, 'Row upon row of unnaturally healthy men.'[8]

Humphries joked about it, but there was no telling how Edna would be received in San Francisco — by then the gay capital of the world — and whether more mainstream American audiences would warm at last to her eviscerating badinage and manic stage presence. He decided that he would have to tone down some of the vulgarity of his act, and not perform as Les Patterson at all. He felt that he couldn't afford to risk Les's 'pyjama python' jokes in puritanical America. He would only appear as Edna on stage and in the media. And of course it was Edna who would be most likely to appeal in 'Shaky Town', a city that celebrated cross-dressing and welcomed performers in drag.

Since Barry's first performance of Dame Edna off Broadway in 1977, the United States had undergone a cultural revolution. Gay pride events had become an annual ritual all over the country, drawing large crowds. They offered spectacular street theatre. And in the decade after his initial visit, drag had become both more politicised and more mainstream. The costumes and stunts used by activists and performers were artful and glamorous. Cabaret rediscovered its subversive power and took up the fight for gay rights. Drag literally took to the streets.

Americans had also warmed to the comedy of Joan Rivers. Edna's style was not dissimilar to that of the talk show host, with its ranting insults and savage humour. But a grass-roots style of theatre had also affected the professional theatrical landscape. It was a style with a history. In his landmark study of sex, drag and performance in 2000, the American scholar Laurence Senelick described a curious prank practised by US undergraduates in the early 1890s.

College boys of the time liked to dress up and be photographed as nuns, and would then give the photos to the girls they courted. Senelick argued that the provocative Sisters of Perpetual Indulgence had inherited and subverted this tradition almost one hundred years later in the Bay Area of San Francisco.

The Sisters rode motorcycles, attended protest meetings and staged appearances in the black-and-white, Flemish-style habits of the fourteenth century, with rosary beads prominently on display, their faces creased with censorious expressions, accompanied by bare-chested, moustached 'sinners'.[9] Their slogan was 'Give Up the Guilt' and they formed a disciplined theatrical troupe, dedicated to raising consciousness of sexual tolerance and satirising issues of gender and morality through what they called 'gay theatrical maneuvers'. They saw themselves as 'sacred clowns'.[10]

The Sisters fended off criticism of their antics as offensive to women by arguing that in adopting the restrictive clothing historically worn by the brides of Christ, they highlighted the repression of women. The worldwide AIDS pandemic drew attention to and galvanised the troupe, along with many other groups who shared their interests. Their act offered drag performance a whole new lease of life.

In Australia meanwhile, the Sydney Gay Mardi Gras had become one of the social events of the year. It was a spectacle and celebration for thousands of Sydneysiders and visitors from all over the world, especially from the west coast of the United States. The popular film *Priscilla, Queen of the Desert* captured a change in the status of drag, and its new topicality for mainstream audiences. In both Australia and the US drag had become glamorous and exciting. It was not just about dressing up, however. By the mid 1990s the power of performance in drag had never been so politically potent.

Humphries' act had never been political in the sense of offering a precise agenda for social change like the Sisters', but he had made a joke of gender categories for a long time. Like his compatriots, the novelists Christina Stead and David Foster, Barry's satire ridiculed social mores, public figures and human behaviour in a multitude of ways, with no precise program for reform. Since his earliest experiments with Dadaist art, Humphries had been an anarchist and his satire is amoral and subversive.

Yet Humphries' theatrical technique was similar to that of the Sisters of Perpetual Indulgence. Senelick argued that the habits donned by the Sisters both provoked onlookers and protected the actors from violence.[11] Humphries adopted the guise of a middle-aged housewife, thereby defusing attack and deflecting hostility.

When Humphries arrived in San Francisco in 1998, the Sisters of Perpetual Indulgence were preparing to celebrate their twentieth birthday. And the English stand-up comic and 'action transvestite' Eddie Izzard, thirty years Barry's junior, had recently performed in the city, dressing up as a female librarian in matronly clothes and lipstick. The cultural and political stage was therefore well and truly set and the audience primed for the arrival of the Dame. Popular theatre and street theatre had brought new audiences to the proscenium theatres of the Bay Area and beyond. Although Americans had no real tradition of the pantomime dame, this no longer seemed to matter: they 'got' Edna as a latter-day matron of music hall and saw in her a glorious parody of entertainers like Liberace, Dolly Parton, Elton John and Joan Collins. Edna was in good company in the eyes of San Francisco's citizens.

On 7 October 1998 *Dame Edna: The Royal Tour* opened at the Theatre on the Square in Post Street, downtown San Francisco. The stately theatre with its decorated wood panelling, restored tiles and gold frescos built in 1924, offered a relatively intimate theatre space. The show began with a wiggling gladiolus stem thrusting out from behind the closed curtain and some jaunty film clips showing Edna in the arms of Nureyev in a waltz, flirting with Charlton Heston and volunteering to powder Richard Gere's bottom. The chat and audience by-play that followed were interwoven with songs, the accompaniment provided by Billy Philadelphia seated at a white grand piano.

One of the songs offered a centrepiece to the show and celebrated Edna's son Kenny, as yet unmarried, who designed his mother's gowns. Edna called the song 'Ditty of Denial'. It was bound to go down well with the folk of the Bay Area. The chorus presented a rousing hymn of praise to the gay men in the audience, without ever stating anything quite so obvious. Humphries was cultivating this group as never before: 'I never thought that I would see so many Friends of Kenny,' Edna sang:

I never thought I'd see many men
Exactly like my Ken
I always thought his peer group
Was a very slightly queer group
Members of a strange exotic clique
He's a favourite of the women's
Just like Richard Simmons[12]
And if you met him you would think he's unique.

Edna also made some acidic jokes about another Kenny, known to most people as Kenneth Starr, the lawyer who was investigating President Bill Clinton's denial of sexual activity with a 22-year-old intern at the White House, Monica Lewinsky.

A critic from Sacramento declared that 'A mountain of wisteria hair and enough sequins to blind Elton John have become the hallmarks of this drag queen.'[13] Chad Jones of the *Oakland Tribune* proclaimed, 'Dame Edna Everage is the funniest drag diva around.'[14] So there it was: Edna was now a confirmed drag queen.

The critics warmed to the spontaneous elements of the show but were less impressed with the rehearsed stories about Edna's daughter Valmai, now living in East Oakland with her pit bull terrier and female partner, and the game of getting audience members to dress up as members of the royal family. Some critics found the local references overdone and the *Chronicle* rated the show with 'polite applause'.[15] But there was no problem of interpretation and no confusion about the style of humour. One critic said, 'It's the sort of humor that makes you laugh and feel totally mortified at the same time.'[16] Another explained the drill to readers more colourfully. 'Mocking and maligning her beloved audience and trampling the daisies of decorum with her vicious wit and rude barbs, Edna's cruel streak is all the more amusing as it is delivered in her sugar-sweet, couldn't hurt a fly, feigned polite British manner.' There was none of the confusion about the Dame that dogged reviewers of *Housewife! Superstar!* in 1977, though one or two critics in San Francisco felt compelled to explain that Edna is actually Barry Humphries, an elderly Australian actor with a wife and kids.

The energy, costumes, rhinestone-studded glasses, sly wit and audience interaction received full praise. Nobody used the term 'irrelevant'. Houses filled, the Bay Area embraced Edna, and *The Royal Tour* was extended until mid January. The show had even received the San Francisco critics' award for the Bay Area. Barry was elated.

He was also hugely relieved. When he received an invitation to play on Broadway, at the Booth Theater for an open season, he felt a sense of vindication. Barry knew Broadway would not be easy but the success on the west coast gave him confidence, and signalled great possibilities for the Big Apple. Nevertheless he felt extremely nervous. He had persevered with American audiences on various occasions over the previous twenty-two years, but still had to crack it on Broadway or his success in California would not count for all that much.

Barry's friend and champion, John Lahr, was by then the senior drama critic on the *New Yorker* magazine and had suggested that Margo Lion, who had produced the hit musical *Hairspray*, mount a show on Broadway for Barry Humphries. But Lion was wary. 'John, he's funny,' she said, 'but it's never going to play, it's too special.'[17]

As Barry and Lizzie moved their possessions into a penthouse apartment on the upper east side of Manhattan, with views to the elegant Queensboro Bridge and Roosevelt Island, Barry tried to put his vivid memories of *Housewife! Superstar!* and Theater Four out of his mind. He hoped that the *New York Times* theatre critic would be kinder than Richard Eder in 1977. But he knew from bitter experience that the *Times* had an incomparable hold on theatre in the city, and that anything was possible.

Humphries' costume designer, Stephen Adnitt, had accompanied him for the opening of the show to ensure that nothing was amiss with Edna's frocks. As always, Ian Davidson, whom Humphries relied on for jokes, local references and last-minute changes to the routine, was also present. Humphries had even brought Andrew Ross, his trusted pianist, from Sydney for the show, rather than relying on someone he did not know for this very important Broadway season.

Humphries was able to breathe a small sigh of relief when he read a profile by Frank DeCaro in the *New York Times* a fortnight before opening night. The journalist began his long and deferential article with a glorious description of Edna's 'day wear', a sequinned frock with a model of the façade of Radio City Music Hall in appliqué on one shoulder and an image of Broadway embroidered on the other, her glasses decorated with a lady holding a torch 'at one temple and a row of spikes at the other, the glasses make air-kissing an extreme sport', he noted. Both Edna and Barry were quoted exhaustively, with the act summed up brilliantly and breathlessly in Humphries' words as 'a character actor dressed up as an Australian housewife who thinks she's a mixture of Barbra Streisand and Jocelyn Wildenstein, with a little bit of Susan Sontag and Martha Stewart thrown in'.[18]

It had been six years since the Hollywood executive had questioned Humphries' television producer, Claudia Rosencrantz, about whether or not Barry was gay, and had attempted to persuade her that Barry should appear in a sequence as himself with his wife before any shots of Edna were shown, in the lead-up to *Dame Edna's Hollywood*. Humphries had not forgotten the suggestion, and made sure that he referred to his family in his press interviews. DeCaro wrote, 'Although he is gay-friendly and a bit of a dandy, Mr Humphries is not a drag queen', and followed with details of Humphries' life with Lizzie, noting also his four children.[19]

In the publicity blitz that preceded the show, Barry had it both ways. Many of the profile pieces, like the one in the *New York Times*, included a description of him as a married actor with four children. Yet Barry also rejoiced in the glamour of drag and all its associations. Another critic articulated the showbiz truth: 'The performer has discovered there is gold in drag, particularly in England, where this exotic creature has flourished for more than two decades.'[20] Barry did his utmost to ensure that his image would appeal to as many groups as possible, and the early signs were very positive.

Dame Edna: The Royal Tour opened on 17 October 1999 at the Booth Theater on West 45th Street. With seating for almost eight hundred, modest by Broadway standards, the elegant theatre, built in 1913, was the perfect size for an Edna extravaganza. Barry was heartened to learn that Zoe Caldwell would be present at the 'first night revels'. Caldwell was a long-time expatriate just like Humphries, who had made her name as an actor and now lived in Westchester County, to the north of New York City. It was nearly fifty years since she and Barry had played together in *Twelfth Night* on their country tour of Victoria. They had only seen one another once since that uncomfortable perambulation around the small towns of south-eastern Australia. Humphries' first Australian producer Cliff Hocking also attended one of the previews.

The show closely followed the format Barry had used in San Francisco. A video montage that included Dame Edna's exchange with various celebrities introduced New Yorkers to the housewife megastar. Edna was shown chatting with Roseanne Barr, interrogating Sean Connery, crooning with Barry Manilow and teasing her nonagenarian bridesmaid Madge Allsop. Edna then descended a highly decorated staircase to greet her audience, resplendent in her tasselled frock, holding a gladiolus. Barry had convinced his sceptical producer Leonard Soloway to keep two elements in the show that Barry thought had always worked well. In his *Remember You're Out* tour, Australians had loved Edna's invitation to two audience members to come up onto the stage to enjoy a meal in full view of the audience. In England and in San Francisco they had warmed to Edna dressing up a small number of 'victims' in the garb of the royal family in spite of some negative comments by critics. He continued with this element in New York. And each night Edna seized on a couple of unsuspecting

New Yorkers in one of the first few rows, whom she thought looked 'a mite peckish', and hauled them up to eat supper ordered in especially from Barrymore's, a nearby restaurant. Barry's instincts paid off: the Broadway audiences lapped it up.

Edna's purple 'cotton candy' hair, her glittering pink shift dress, diamond-studded eyewear and massive rings on every finger, wowed the audience and impressed the critics. There was scarcely a negative comment in the New York reviews. The show was described as 'mighty entertainment'.[21] With audiences gleefully enjoying Edna's withering attacks on celebrities, Edna cast herself as cult queen of them all. The critics raved about her 'outrageous, funny, bitchy and uninhibited' barbs.[22] In a risky quip Edna shrieked, 'I'm so happy to be back in New York. I feel so at home here. Besides, just like Hillary Clinton, it gives me a chance to rediscover my Jewish roots … it explains a lot about my taste in beautiful jewellery…'

Edna went into overdrive, crowing about how she had mentored Germaine Greer many years earlier. 'When the great feminist was a child, she would come to my house and watch my husband scrubbing the floor. That's when she saw that traditional roles played by the sexes down through the years could be rethought,' she reported. Humphries gave the performance everything he had; Edna talked about acid reflux and joked about the US Attorney-General Janet Reno. Nothing and nobody was sacred. She skewered and she barked. She pranced, stomped and mugged, her astonishing mouth twisting downwards in her signature expression of distaste and disdain. She said that she had advised Hillary Clinton, Margaret Thatcher and, most recently, Nicole Kidman: 'She was a drama student of mine … I was the first person she took her clothes off for. Now she does it for everyone.' Even the Queen herself, reported Edna, 'with all the worries she's had with her family, looks to me for advice'.

There were some tricky moments. One night Edna questioned a couple about their babysitter for the evening. During the exchange Edna gleaned that the child-minder was an immigrant 'without papers' or 'undocumented', as Americans call them. Edna took the bull by the horns and roared: 'One of the great things about democracy is that you can have a slave class without calling it that.' The audience gasped and then broke into squalls of laughter. It was a close call; Philip Olander reported that the audience 'almost turned'.[23] The audience reaction, as always, was integral to the momentum of the show. As Edna often scoffs to her possums, they pay to see her in a show, but then as various members tiptoe onto the stage, they '*are* the show'. In the glossy pages of the *New York* magazine with its cover story on Dame Edna, the question was put: 'Can a rude, clueless, provincial Australian woman who's actually a man conquer Broadway and win a place in the American cultural pantheon?' The answer? Barry Humphries' Dame Edna is on the verge.'[24]

Edna's style was captured in succinct phrases by the award-winning drama critic Jack Kroll, who called her 'the patron saint of the politically incorrect', and 'an insult comic who made Don Rickles sound like a Hallmark card'.[25] This kind of comment was more than Humphries could have hoped for. Rickles is a celebrated American comedian, who has made insult an art form over the past fifty years. The *New York Post* declared *The Royal Tour* to be 'by far the funniest and cleverest show in town'.[26] *Newsday* ran a short piece urging readers to go to the show: 'You'll have the time of your life,' wrote the rather breathless, folksy reporter, because 'such hilarity hasn't reigned since *Hellzapoppin*'.'[27] John Lahr observed that the show was 'generous and gallant', and that Humphries 'is almost single-handedly bringing the vaudeville tradition into the twenty-first century'.[28] The *Wall Street Journal* critic sounded one of the few negative notes. She said that 'the whole campy endeavor feels a bit shopworn'.[29] And *Newsday*'s theatre critic stated that the act was a 'cross-cultural acquired taste'.

It seemed as if Humphries had outdone Joan Rivers, outshone David Letterman and trumped Jackie Mason. He had read the audience and although he did not change Edna's style, he dropped references to Moonee Ponds and worked in tricks and gags that were familiar to New Yorkers. He had 'dragged up' just enough. His local references were perfect. In Australia during Paul Keating's term of office as prime minister, Edna dropped the 'Dame', having discovered that she was Catholic and therefore, in her twisted logic, naturally sympathetic to the Australian Republican Movement. In New York, Edna 'discovered' her Jewish personal history, and that she was distantly related to the US Secretary of State, Madeleine Albright, who had been brought up as a Roman Catholic but in 1997 learned of her Jewish background.

The sweetest victory for Humphries was waking up to the *New York Times* review of *The Royal Tour*, written by the newspaper's chief theatre critic Ben Brantley, who recognised Dame Edna's attack on the monstrous behaviour of celebrities and praised Humphries as a 'great instinctive physical comic'.[30] Brantley identified exactly what it is about Edna that enraptures an audience. It is not so much the content of the jokes, but the 'overwhelming presence of the narcissistic creature making them', he said. 'The Dame lifts an audience' with her 'reality-warping rhapsody', he continued.[31] Brantley understood the power of Edna over a live audience, and Humphries' monumental stage presence. At last Humphries had found the universal in his comic repertoire. No longer tied to jokes about Australia, his appearance at the Booth Theater was more liberating than any show he had ever launched. Humphries demonstrated his essential power as a performer, his understanding of the dupe, his wizardry in improvisation and his mastery of aggressive sport with his audience. At sixty-five, Humphries had charmed Broadway. He was ecstatic.

Humphries' success was reported in the British and Australian press. To Barry's delight the newspapers ran reports of the standing ovations the show received in its first week playing on Broadway. It was music to his ears. *The Royal Tour* commanded huge audiences, and the show ran on for another month, then another, and ultimately for ten months. It captured the imagination of the city and impressed the Broadway cognoscenti. John Lahr's friend Margo Lion, who had felt that Broadway audiences would not respond to Humphries, was one of them. She was furious with herself because Barry was huge and she had not seen the power or the potential in spite of all Lahr had said, until the night she was part of the enthusiastic audience at the Booth Theater.

If Edna was born again as a Broadway star, Humphries was too. He was overjoyed with his success on the Great White Way. Suddenly he had a new career, a planned tour around the United States and thousands of new fans. In the first year of the new millennium he had achieved his heart's desire. On 8 May 2000 *The Royal Tour* was nominated for a Tony Award by the American Theatre Wing and the League of American Theatres and Producers.

On 4 June Humphries attended the lavish award ceremony at the newly renovated Radio City Music Hall. He beamed when he heard that *Dame Edna: The Royal Tour* had won a Special Tony Award for a Live Theatrical Event. In the program Dame Edna was quoted, explaining the nature of the show, as 'a meditation on gender, the nature of perception and the politics of gladioli'. Humphries' Dadaist impulse was unmistakable. An Australian journalist asked him what it was like to win a Tony and he replied triumphantly that 'it was like winning one thousand Gold Logies at the same time'.[32]

Humphries embarked on his tour of the United States with seasons in Minneapolis, Fort Lauderdale, Boston, Detroit, Chicago, Phoenix, Los Angeles and Denver. He even ventured across the border to Toronto for a season at the Royal Alexandra Theatre. It brought back vivid memories of his first visit with *Oliver!* in 1963 when he railed about the frozen and wowserish city in letters to his friend Peter O'Shaughnessy. He found himself staying at the same hotel he'd stayed in thirty-six years earlier, the elegant Fairmont Royal York built in the 1920s, opposite the railway station. This time he installed himself at the front of the building in a large suite. Barry enjoyed every stop on his momentous tour except for Atlantic City, with its enormous casinos and vast car parks on the edge of town for the workers. Barry recalled acidly in his memoir that 'the once romantic lido of New Jersey', with its run-down buildings and busloads of tourists, now resembled a 'Chernobyl-sur-Mer'.[33]

During the tour Barry fielded numerous phone calls regarding his possible appearance as Dame Edna on stage at the closing ceremony of the Olympic Games in Sydney on 1 October 2000. He had already met with the director of ceremonies, Ric Birch, several times. With an audience of millions across the globe, the ceremony would be an extravaganza for Edna beyond anything she had achieved before. Birch wanted Edna to close the Games with a speech and a song. The actor and director Robyn Archer stated her public support for Edna to 'strut the stage' at the Australia Stadium in Homebush Bay. Archer, who was also director of the Adelaide Arts Festival, told a reporter that 'I can't think of a more endearing drag queen farewelling the world from this most important event.'[34] But the Committee wavered and Edna did not appear.

Humphries made up for the disappointment with a stunning appearance at another major event — the Queen's Jubilee Concert at Buckingham Palace in June 2002. Twelve thousand Britons assembled in the palace grounds, with more than a million filling the Mall and London's parks to enjoy a pop concert to celebrate the monarch's fifty-year reign. Some 200 million viewers throughout Great Britain and the Commonwealth watched the 'Party at the Palace' on television. Edna joined Lenny Henry, Elton John, Eric Clapton, Paul McCartney, Tom Jones, the Beach Boys, Shirley Bassey and others to entertain the massive crowds. Brian May played *God Save the Queen* from the roof of the palace. Sir Les also enjoyed a cameo role: he appeared on screen in a drunken and futile attempt to gatecrash the party. But Dame Edna outdid every other celebrity when she introduced the Queen with the words: 'The Jubilee girl is here, possums!' The laughter of thousands rang out across London. Edna Everage had dared to make a joke about the Queen, and got away with it.

As Humphries focused on his new career in the United States, his elder son, Oscar, who suffered from depression, was experiencing serious difficulties. Oscar had struggled with alcohol since leaving school three years earlier. Humphries had been horrified to hear that Oscar had been interviewed by the Suffolk police, who had been summoned to a guesthouse because of Oscar's behaviour. There were complaints that the young Mr Humphries had urinated on a bed and inscribed a large cross on the wall with purple nail polish. On Christmas Day 2002 his psychological state deteriorated further: Oscar was admitted to hospital after taking a large number of paracetamol tablets and drinking a bottle of gin, while staying with the parents of his friend Chloe King in Hampshire. Diane, who was also staying with the King family, had accompanied Oscar to the hospital.

Humphries was in Gstaad with Lizzie for Christmas when he received the disturbing news. The press went into overdrive, revelling in the details of Oscar's hedonistic lifestyle and lost-boy image, as well as the latest dramatic episode that was allegedly related to a break-up with the socialite Octavia Khashoggi the year before. On Boxing Day, at Barry's insistence, Oscar checked in to the Priory Clinic in South London to deal with his alcohol and cocaine addictions.

Over the next twelve months Oscar's condition improved; he began to write and to paint. He stayed with Diane, taking a job at a garden centre in London, in an attempt to establish a routine to his daily life, and exhibited some of his paintings at the Firehouse in South Kensington in the summer. Barry told him firmly, 'At twenty-one my alcoholism was in front of me. Yours is behind you.'[35] But Humphries' problems with alcohol never made the headlines in quite the manner of his son. The world had changed, and the children of celebrities and their lifestyles were now the bread and butter of the tabloid press. By the end of the year, Oscar seemed to have settled into his new and more wholesome life. Barry, Lizzie and Oscar spent Christmas together in Australia, where Oscar planned to settle.[36]

In the autumn, during another visit to Australia, Humphries could not resist a daring stunt as Sir Les outside Government House in Canberra. When the Queen's representative, Governor-General Peter Hollingworth stepped down on 11 May 2003, Les Patterson seized the opportunity to put himself forward for the job. Dr Hollingworth, formerly Archbishop of Brisbane, had been forced to resign as pressure mounted on him in the wake of a church enquiry that found he had failed to take action against a paedophile minister. Sir Les appeared on national television standing outside the gates of the official residence of the Governor-General, waiting to accept the position as Queen's representative in Australia. It was a devilish display by the 69-year-old comedian who was undaunted by the serious and sensitive circumstances surrounding Hollingworth's fall from grace. He also understood Australians' ambivalence about their ties to the mother country better than many politicians and cultural commentators.

Humphries was now devoting a lot of time and energy to touring in the United States. In order to keep Edna on the public radar, he appeared in the long-running American television series *Ally McBeal* in which Calista Flockhart played a young lawyer in search of love. Barry played a Dame Edna-ish character called Claire Otoms. It was a low-key role in the fifth season of the series, but it gained Humphries much-needed publicity. The task of keeping Edna's name 'up' in the US was gargantuan. With this in mind, Humphries agreed to write a regular advice column for *Vanity Fair* in the guise of Dame Edna. In February 2003, one of Edna's barbed throwaway comments in her column, 'Ask Dame Edna', caused a storm of controversy. A reader remarked on the fact that so many people speak Spanish and requested advice from Edna as to whether she should take lessons in the language. Edna responded with this swipe:

> Forget Spanish. There's nothing in that language worth reading except *Don Quixote*, and a quick listen to the CD of *Man of La Mancha* will take care of that. There was a poet named Garcia Lorca, but I'd leave him on the intellectual back burner, if I were you. As for everyone's speaking it, what twaddle! Who speaks it that you are really desperate to talk to? The help? Your leaf blower? Study French or German, where there are at least a few books worth reading, or, if you're American, try English.

Beside the column an illustration appeared of a tourist wearing an oversized sombrero asking an armadillo, '*Habla Español?*' A furore erupted. Hispanics all over the United States expressed their outrage and offence at the 'ignorant' and 'callous' remarks made by the fictional agony aunt. The cover of the magazine had featured a photograph of Salma Hayek, the Hollywood actress born in Mexico, and producer and star of the celebrated film *Frida* about the revered Mexican artist Frida Kahlo. The actress wrote a bitter letter to the magazine complaining about Edna's advice.

Graydon Carter, the editor of the magazine, was inundated with protest letters and the National Council of La Raza, the largest Latino advocacy organisation in the US, called for a boycott of Humphries' show *A Night with Dame Edna*, as did the National Association of Hispanic Journalists and *Latina* magazine. Humphries even received death threats. *Vanity Fair* released a statement of regret immediately, promptly cancelled Edna's column and ran a full-page apology to the Hispanic community in the April issue of the magazine. The editors laboured to describe the satirical intent of Edna's words. 'Clearly, this advice column should not be taken seriously ... Edna is the last person on Earth that anyone would go to for sound advice ... We are asking those who feel offended by this piece to forgive us for our insensitivity. We also ask them to consider the context — the fact that these statements were meant to be read ironically ...' They added, 'Humphries practices a long comedic tradition of making statements that are tasteless, wrongheaded, or taboo, with an eye toward exposing hypocrisies or prejudices. Anyone who has seen Dame Edna's over-the-top performances ... knows that she is an equal-opportunity distributor of insults ...'[37]

But all the editors could hope to achieve was to limit the damage. Throughout the country commentators and outraged citizens condemned Edna Everage and *Vanity Fair*.[38] The *Los Angeles Times* defended satire in theory, but insisted that Humphries' column did not constitute 'successful satire' because it was 'hurtful, bound to be misunderstood and, quite obviously, lacked literary value'. Humphries lamented the episode some months later with world-weary disdain: 'If you have to explain satire to someone, you might as well give up.' Perhaps his brief period of success in the United States had led him to forget his copious explanations of his own work to American television critics and New York columnists in recent years, and the way he had found himself trying to clarify his satirical method. Unrepentant, Edna revealed that

Hayek's protests were due to 'professional jealousy', as the role of Frida Kahlo had first been offered to Edna: 'I turned it down, and she was the second choice,' said Edna. She made it clear why she had turned down the role: 'I'm not playing ... a woman with a moustache and a monobrow, and I'm not having same-sex relations on the screen. I'm not racist. I love all races, particularly white people. You know, I even like Roman Catholics.'

Australian critics often yearn for and admire the freedom of expression in the US, where journalists and comedians do not have to concern themselves with restrictive libel laws.[39] But American interest groups exercise control in a manner that is equally prohibitive, and just as devastating for satirists. Humphries was staggered by the reaction to his mockery of American bigotry, and by the fact that many who complained seemed to think the satire was directed at Latinos, when in fact it was directed at those who denigrate the group. He tried to ignore the vitriolic reaction to Edna's satirical stab at wealthy, ignorant, monolingual Americans who are oblivious to the culture of members of a substantial number of people in their country.

Humphries did not give up on the United States, and has toured the country three times since the *Vanity Fair* uproar, receiving one of the most positive reviews of his career in 2009 from a *Los Angeles Times* critic.[40] He has established a niche following for his one-man stage show, with a strong gay contingent among Edna's fan base. But Edna is not a household name in the United States, as she is in Australia and Great Britain, and most Americans do not recognise the name of her creator. Humphries has not managed to crack American television. The sheer velocity of the reaction to Edna's comments in *Vanity Fair* in February 2003 demonstrated that Humphries could not get away with his typical Edna barbs in the United States of America, and that identity politics was more potent there than ever, and more powerful than Humphries could have imagined. Undoubtedly television producers have become wary. Edna had turned out to be wrong when she barked at her New York audience in 1999: '*You* can't be politically incorrect. But I can.' In the land of extremes Edna proved to be an acquired taste.

CHAPTER 37

Recognition

Barry Humphries had achieved one of his major goals as an entertainer, and successfully brought a peculiarly Australian type of humour to the United States. But the incident with *Vanity Fair* seemed to Humphries to prove another point. There are limits around humour in every culture, and the repercussions of transgression can be extreme. In spite of the fall-out he still enjoyed performing Edna. For him the attraction of live performance is almost like going to church: 'I rather like the communal experience,' he declared a couple of years after the debacle.[1]

Another of Humphries' life-long desires — to offer grand spectacle — was fulfilled in Melbourne in 2005. His stage shows in the 1990s had featured a triumphant and spectacular climax in which Edna levitated skyward like a saint. Even more triumphantly, Edna appeared at the Australian Football League Grand Final match at one of the sites of his first transgressions: the Melbourne Cricket Ground. It was the first time Humphries had attended a football game since high school, and it was an apotheosis for the actor. Fifty years earlier, Humphries had turned his back on the football-playing performers in front of all his peers and begun to knit. The story had become legend, and in retrospect the bold knitting incident might be seen as an early rehearsal.[2]

On Saturday 24 September 2005, in front of a crowd of 92,000 screaming, chanting fans, Edna arrived in a limousine, climbed onto a stage and belted out the Peter Allen classic, 'I Still Call Australia Home', in a duet with the boyish cabaret singer Michael Bublé. It was awesome and rather strange to see the man who loathed sport singing to a crowd of football fans.

The citizens' reaction to Humphries' next spectacular appearance was not quite so universally sanguine. On a mild autumn night in Melbourne in 2006, the crowd at the Commonwealth Games closing ceremony hushed to hear the words of the Australian swimmer Michael Klim, as he offered a speech of thanks on behalf of all the athletes. It was 10.08 pm and Klim addressed an audience of 80,000 spectators in the stadium, and millions on television. Halfway through his speech, Klim was interrupted by the high-pitched voice of Dame Edna Everage whose gleaming visage could be seen on a gigantic screen above the Melbourne Cricket Ground via satellite link. It was fifty-one years since Humphries had introduced Edna to his hometown in Ray Lawler's Christmas revue, with his satire on the housing crisis for visiting Olympic athletes.

Edna was beamed in from Los Angeles, where Humphries was about to open his show at the massive Ahmanson Theatre. As she sang her tribute to the city, 'We've Made the Most of Melbourne,' one thousand 'Commonwealth Dames', women dressed up as Edna Everage and carrying gladioli stems, danced for the crowd, before finishing in a human formation in the shape of Edna's signature butterfly glasses. The applause was deafening as Edna crooned, 'It's not as small as Adelaide, compared to Canberra it's bliss/And if you've been to Melbourne, you can give Sydney a miss.' Edna declared that it was definitely an historic event 'because only ten minutes ago Melbourne finished paying off the 1956 Olympic Games, which really introduced Melbourne as one of the world's most hospitable cities'. If the crowds in the stadium enjoyed the thrill of Edna and the 'mini-Ednas' cavorting in front of them, clearly some television viewers found Humphries' appearance irritating. One viewer from Shepparton complained: '… why, in a celebration of Melbourne, did we have a tribute to an expat?'[3] The television critic Ross Warneke found Edna's act 'unfunny' and 'her anthem to Melbourne ... as lame and excruciatingly old hat as the rest of her act these days'.[4]

Humphries returned to Britain and faced similarly weary attitudes from television producers. It was three years since he had performed on television for a British audience, and he had fallen out of favour with commissioning editors. Many of them felt that Edna Everage was a product of the 1980s, and now well out of date. Clive Tulloh, then at Tiger Aspect, an independent production company, produced a one-off special in which Edna appeared at Buckingham Palace in a rather uneven Christmas show for BBC1 in 2003, during a break in Barry's tour of the United States. One of the funniest moments of the show was when Edna discovered Madge Allsop in bed beside rock star Ozzy Osbourne. Later, the 96-year-old Perry said to Barry: 'Who was that funny man? He seemed very nervous.'[5]

Two years passed before Tulloh telephoned Barry again to pass on the message that ITV was nibbling once more; this time they would like a new chat show with Edna. Without hesitation Barry replied, 'Tell them that you've found Barry Humphries in a home on the South Coast and he feels there's another series in him.'[6]

Humphries and Tulloh set out to make another program along the lines of *The Dame Edna Experience*, with the guests entering Edna's care for therapy of one kind or another. Humphries insisted that everyone in the studio audience wear a white dressing gown; this time, instead of Madge, Edna's daughter Valmai would appear as a kind of spa helper. *The Dame Edna Treatment* was a rather risky venture, and there was very little time to produce the show.

To make things more difficult Humphries was not in the UK to develop the series. He was enjoying a successful tour of Australia with a long season in Melbourne at the Performing Arts Centre on St Kilda Road. In a small gallery in the theatre building several rooms were decorated in the style of Mrs Everage's home, circa 1956, attracting throngs of visitors. Melbourne was celebrating the return of a highly successful son. Before the tour commenced, John

So, the Lord Mayor, presented Dame Edna with the keys to the city. Australia Post released a set of stamps bearing Edna's visage. The 'arriviste' had arrived, and had fulfilled yet another of Humphries' dreams of being celebrated on a postage stamp.

Throughout the holiday season thousands filled the theatre every night for *Barry Humphries and Friends Back with a Vengeance*. Many of the audience members had seen Barry perform on numerous occasions in Melbourne, and the average age of the patrons on any given night was close to fifty. In the show, Les Patterson confessed to having seen the ghost of Kerry Packer by his bed. He revealed that 'KP' pleaded with him to 'get Channel 9 out of the toilet'. Flanked by two athletic dancing girls he sang a delightful music hall ditty and two-stepped off the stage, crooning, 'Life is Just a Show'.

But Humphries' performance of Sandy Stone was the highlight of this show. His demeanour, his Parkinson's shake and his repeated phrases perfectly captured an old man. This time the revenant character discussed Beryl's old people's home. A couple of young actors opened the scene with a mime. They wheeled in plaster models of an old man and an old woman stuffed into wheelchairs, set up a television set, sneaked a cigarette at the back of the gloomy TV room and began to kiss in full view of their elderly charges. 'Beryl got a call from a lady in India called Rhonda offering her a time-share in Dubai,' reported Sandy. 'Beryl thought that Dubai was probably on the Sunshine Coast ... Rhonda didn't know that Beryl did not have much time to share ...'

In his digressive and languid manner, Sandy continued. 'Dubai is like Dubbo ... that's an Abo word for "meeting of the waters" ... all Abo words mean "meeting of the waters" ... except Woy Woy, it means "deep water". Which Woy means "deep"? I think the Abos have been pulling our leg for a long time ... perhaps it's time for them to say "Sorry".' The sketch was one of the cleverest Humphries had performed as the old man. The prime minister, John Howard, had refused to make a formal apology to the indigenous people of Australia for past wrongs. It was a burning issue, and Humphries allowed everyone to laugh at the 'Sorry' debate.

Sandy reported that a dance would be held at Beryl's old people's home that night. 'Beryl is getting her hair done,' he said. 'Women all over Australia in facilities like these have their hair done, as if they are going somewhere. And if you think about it, they are.' At the end of the sketch Stone stood up and hobbled over to the centre of the stage where a young woman appeared, fresh faced and smiling, with her arms outstretched. Sandy took the young woman in his arms, enfolding her lovingly, and began a very slow waltz around the stage. The lights went down.

At the end of the three-hour show, Dame Edna came out dressed in a candy-striped creation with an enormous tiered skirt in the shape of a birthday cake, a '50' in fairy lights glittering on it. There was a collective gasp in the auditorium, when the final curtain fell, and Edna disappeared from the stage. The audience could see her on a massive screen, locked in her dressing room, and shrieking to be let out. A few minutes later Humphries appeared on stage in a black dinner suit and gleaming white shirt, as the triumphant strains of the iconic theme from *The Magnificent Seven* filled the auditorium. The applause was deafening as Humphries stood under a single spotlight and greeted his beloved Melbourne fans. He had rarely taken a curtain call as himself before, and looked completely relaxed, smiling broadly. This departure from the usual fuelled all sorts of speculation. Was this to be the last tour?

Because of time constraints and the huge demands of developing the new television chat show series, Clive Tulloh travelled to Melbourne to work on the concept with Barry while Barry was on tour. ITV lavished the show with a full prime-time budget. It did not match the extraordinary budgets of the 1980s but it was healthy, with enough money to fly guests in and out of London for their interviews. Clive, like everyone else, was anxious to bring Edna into the new millennium and to distance the program from the glitzy chat show of the Thatcher years. Every morning he walked with Barry through Fitzroy Gardens to toss around ideas, and every morning Barry would lecture his polite English producer on the history of the gardens. When the Australia Day long weekend arrived Barry took a break. The city seemed deserted, as so many of its residents escaped to the Mornington Peninsula, or to beaches further afield. Each day during their walk through the gardens, Barry began the same lecture. Clive felt a knot in the pit of his stomach as he listened again and again to the same stories. He feared the worst, that Barry was exhibiting the early signs of dementia. On the fourth day as they traipsed across the parched grass past the reconstructed Captain Cook Cottage, Clive jumped in first, determined to prevent a repeat performance: 'Now Barry, what about these elms?' he asked decisively. Barry laughed, and in a flash was off again with his history lesson: 'Well, funny you should mention them,' he said with a wide grin. Clive realised it was all a joke. Barry was about to celebrate his seventy-third birthday and still could not resist playing a trick on a companion.

The Dame Edna Treatment premiered on ITV in March 2007. The title song, performed by Robin Gibb of the Bee Gees, was magical. It had been written by his brother Barry especially for Humphries' extravagant new show. As Gibb's sweet and distinctive voice rang out, Edna pranced and posed against a gaudy animation of storks and Edna-style glasses that flew off as butterflies. It was whimsical and kitsch. Edna sat at a white grand piano and then lolled on a garden lounge in her lollipop-pink dressing gown, her face caked with a thick white cosmetic mask, circles of orange over her eyes as she sipped a blood-red cocktail. A rainbow hovered over her antebellum mansion. The song was catchy and dripping with irony: 'She's a gem, she's a jewel, an icon, she's an angel of light from above/She is poetry in motion, she's a rock in an ocean of love/So give us the Edna Treatment — a world exclusive mega-spa.' Just as the song reached its highpoint, Edna stood up and snapped a rubber glove onto her right hand.

As always the executives were desperate to secure a younger demographic for the show, and therefore wanted Edna to interview young stars. The fact that Edna wanted to subject gleaming, youthful actresses such as Mischa Barton to a make-over in her spa gave the joke considerable mileage. But it was an uphill battle as

Edna's dominance of the chat show parody was a distant memory for viewers. Since her heyday the genre had been well and truly conquered by Mrs Merton, Alan Partridge and Keith Barret. In the 1980s there were only four channels for British viewers to choose from; in 2007 the television choices seemed endless.

Humphries had returned to London to shoot the seven shows in a break between seasons of his Australian tour, so he was also trying to catch up on sleep. The Australian tour had opened in Perth in November 2006 and he was weary. As soon as shooting finished for the television show, in April 2007, Humphries packed up and made the long return journey to Australia to open *Barry Humphries and Friends* in Sydney.

At times throughout the series Humphries looked tired and awkward and the interviews were occasionally halting and repetitive. Edna appeared uneasy with some of the guests. Mischa Barton seemed oblivious to the comedy and Michael Bolton was so serious that Edna could not make much headway with him. Humphries was far more relaxed with Engelbert Humperdinck, Deborah Harry, Martin Sheen and Shirley Bassey. Sigourney Weaver initially seemed genuinely affronted by Edna but recovered quickly. Edna's interview with *Little Britain* duo Matt Lucas and David Walliams was one of the highlights of what turned out to be a rather uneven and disappointing series. The Valmai character did not work nearly as well as Emily Perry's Madge in the glory days, and the jokes about colonic irrigation and other bodily functions were laboured and crude. For the first time in years Ian Davidson did not write for the show. Instead two younger writers were engaged to assist Barry with material. Davidson had worked with Humphries on almost every show for forty years, but the directive came down that this Edna needed to be distinct from the old Edna and that a new style was imperative.

Humphries' ingenuity as a performer derives from his instinct for improvisation and even the highly produced and researched interviews with guests are unpredictable. Some of them fail — that is the nature of the genre. But when Humphries is at his best and the guest plays along or says something unexpected, the audience is treated to exceptional satirical theatre. In Episode Seven of *The Dame Edna Treatment*, Edna interviewed k.d. lang, as Ivana Trump sat beside her. The inscrutable singer sat stiffly for the first few minutes. Dressed in a man's black suit and steel-rimmed glasses, lang was wary and clipped in her initial replies. Edna, resplendent in a ruffled silver and black full-length evening gown, began, as usual, with a virtual monologue. She railed about the 'gender games' so talked about in the media:

> Edna: I wonder if I should play gender games. What do I have to do, stand up at the toilet, or something …
> k.d. lang: (begins to laugh)
> Edna: (fixing lang with a stern look) I don't think I'd make a very convincing man, k.d.
> k.d. lang: No, no.
> Edna: No way. I think there's too much fuss about this gender business … women's magazines are full of it. It's a sort of fad really. I think women might be too liberated.
> k.d. lang: You do?
> Edna: Well, do you get that feeling?
> k.d. lang: (with certainty) Yes.
> Edna: I think so, it's all overdone. I think we are liberated. Look at us.
> k.d. lang: Yes, I don't think we need to liberate any further.
> Edna: Here we are, three very liberated women chatting away like this.
>
> *The camera crosses to Ivana Trump in her plunging, skin-tight red cocktail dress and four-inch stilettos. She laughs tentatively and folds her arms.*
>
> Edna: I'm going to be a bit liberated now, I'm going to talk about something personal. This could offend people. (k.d. does not react, Trump looks anxious.)

> I'm never one to run away from confrontation. My son Kenny, who designed this beautiful dress — he made some decisions, k.d., and I embraced them, as far as it was possible for me to do so.
>
> k.d. lang: You're a liberal, loving woman.
>
> Edna: (laughs a little) I am darling, I surrendered to the love in my heart. And I don't think there's anything that two intelligent women cannot discuss — there's no taboo — I make no apologies for the words, the terminology, perhaps the coarse terminology that I'm going to use now. (Edna's lips curl down as she pauses.)

The camera crosses to lang and shows her bow her head, smiling, as if to hide embarrassment.

> Edna: (holding her hand up to hush the audience.) When (takes a deep breath) did you first know you were ... Canadian?

lang bursts into laughter and rocks forward. Loud laughter fills the studio.

The warmth and hilarity of the interview demonstrated beyond doubt that Humphries' power as a performer was as strong as ever, and that in the guise of what Lahr calls the 'harpie of happiness' he could elicit laughter from the least likely targets.[7] Edna whittled away at lang's laconic persona. And suddenly it all cracked. The serious singer burst into fits of laughter, and so did the audience. The interview and its artful critique of gender, wittily played out by a 73-year-old man in an evening dress, a young crop-haired woman in a man's suit and a peroxide blonde of indeterminate age poured into a sheath dress, offered a breathtaking sartorial and satirical spectacle.

It was the most enchanting interview of the series, and one of the funniest encounters of Humphries' television career. For timing, suspense and surprise it offered several textbook comic moments.

With the audience breaking up again in laughter, Edna and k.d. lang brought the show and the series to a climax with the cabaret duet that followed: 'I'm Every Woman'. Edna flounced around the set with several purple-haired dancers as lang's sonorous voice belted out the 1970s hit song. The segment reminded viewers of Humphries' ingenious satirical energy and wit as well as his strength as a physical comic.

In spite of this triumphant moment, the all-important viewing figures in Britain were disappointing. Only an estimated 2.5 million viewers in prime time tuned in to *The Dame Edna Treatment*. This represented less than one-third of the number of viewers for *The Dame Edna Experience* during the 1980s. *The Treatment* ran in a latish Saturday night time slot and was up against *The X Factor* and other popular programs. Humphries had not performed live in the UK for almost ten years. The ratings did not warrant a second series. Barry was disappointed but not concerned.

Back in Australia, Humphries was delighted to hear, in June, that he had been made a Commander of the British Empire in the Queen's Birthday Honours list, receiving the news just after coming off stage in Brisbane. He was moved by the honour. He had lampooned Australians and Britons for the past fifty years, and had made a special point of lampooning imperial honours. In reality he held the royal family in high esteem, but he joked about the award: 'At last I can address Sir Les Patterson and Dame Edna Everage on an improved footing.'

Since boyhood Humphries had hungered for recognition and acknowledgment of his talent. His award for services to entertainment meant that he would receive a medal at Buckingham Palace at a ceremony in October 2007. On the day, Lizzie, Oscar and Rupert Humphries proudly spoke to a throng of journalists. Lizzie was reminded of her father and attempted to explain the significance of the award to her as an Englishwoman: 'It's wonderful that he [Barry] got the CBE. I'm English, my father got the CBE and KBE, so for Barry to get it as well — it's just fantastic.'[8] Strangely, Barry didn't say all that much. He chatted for a few minutes with the Queen, and then outside in the courtyard he posed in his soft grey suit for the cameras. Smiling proudly he held his delicate blue and gold medal aloft with one hand, his other hand on his hip. He looked completely relaxed, slightly dandyish and very happy. Humphries had met the Queen before, but as Edna. This was altogether different. On that autumn day in London, at the age of seventy-three, Humphries was received and recognised by the reigning monarch as himself.

POSTSCRIPT

Life is Just a Show

Barry and Lizzie were relieved to be back in Sydney a couple of weeks before Christmas in 2007. They were looking forward to meeting up with old friends, and Lizzie invited a large group to their apartment in The Rocks overlooking the Harbour Bridge to celebrate New Year's Eve. Barry wanted to see his friends before he left Australia for a US tour, which would keep him away for several months. But two days before the party Barry complained of severe stomach pain. He was suffering from a burst appendix, and the following day he was admitted to hospital for an appendectomy. Lizzie decided not to cancel the party. So a jolly crowd watched the fireworks over Sydney Harbour from Barry's place without their host.

Barry had never had surgery. He rarely suffered from anything more serious than tiredness and jet lag. The last time he was hospitalised was in 1970, when he sought treatment for his depression and alcohol addiction. After the operation his doctors administered a massive quantity of antibiotics to combat possible infection resulting from the burst appendix. But he did not recover as expected; within days his surgeon performed another operation to treat peritonitis, a potential killer. The next few weeks were hellish, as Humphries fought for his life.

As soon as Barry was out of danger, his doctor ordered him to take six months off work. With a groan of resignation, he instructed his agent to cancel his appearance at the Glasgow Comedy Festival and all of his American tour. He had never cancelled a tour before. As soon as he felt stronger he travelled to Byron Bay for a few weeks rest near the sea. As he began to feel more like himself, his mood changed to glum irritation and grumpy frustration. Just after his seventy-fourth birthday in February 2008 he heard that Emily Perry had died at 100 years of age. When he travelled to Melbourne a few days later, Humphries spoke to journalists about Perry and her long career in theatre. He recalled the wispy magic of the actress who had played the mute Madge Allsop beside him for more than fifteen years. Reminiscing about many hilarious moments with Perry lifted his spirit.

Later in the year when Humphries returned to his home in Greencroft Gardens in London, he recalled his 'tap on the shoulder'. As many reminded him, Harry Houdini had died of a burst appendix leading to peritonitis. Humphries confessed in the *Spectator* that in hospital he had sensed that he had suddenly turned into Sandy Stone.[1]

Relieved to have regained his strength, Humphries threw himself into the national search for new talent to play in a West End revival of the musical *Oliver!*. Every week on BBC1 television for three months Barry, with Denise van Outen, John Barrowman and Andrew Lloyd Webber, sat in judgment upon hundreds of hopefuls for the main roles, in a series called *I'd Do Anything* (drawing on the name of one of the famous songs from *Oliver!*). As a chorus of little Olivers began to intone those all-too-familiar notes of 'Food, Glorious Food', Barry wondered how he had allowed himself to be swept up in Bart's musical all over again.[2] He seemed destined to hear those songs innumerable times until his dying day. Humphries was rather restrained for most of the series, but told one contestant from Ireland that 'You've got a touch of guttersnipe about you,' which passed as a compliment given that she was hoping to play Nancy. When another contestant performed Aretha Franklin's popular song 'Respect', wearing a tight red dress, Barry suggested that she would be good in a comic role. But he was essentially kind to all of the hopefuls. He understood the terror of auditioning for a part, and recalled his own nervous excitement all those years ago when he arrived at a draughty old hall in Soho, his heart set on playing Fagin. The casting of a West End production had become a respectable form of reality television, and Barry gleefully played himself.

Humphries eventually honoured his commitment to tour the United States and performed in short seasons in San Francisco, Fort Lauderdale, Boston, San Diego and Los Angeles in a show called *Dame Edna: My First Last Tour*. One of the sketches included a series of jokes about the former president George W Bush. Some audience members walked out of the theatre, clearly offended by the critique of the Republican from Texas. The show followed Humphries' trusted formula, and the barbs still stung.

Early in 2009 Humphries announced a follow-up tour of the UK and Ireland. At seventy-five years of age he scorned any suggestion of retiring. He told his brother Michael that he found it hard to understand how little most people of his age do in their day-to-day lives. The Dadaist boy from Camberwell felt fitter than ever and could not imagine a life without performance. As Sir Les Patterson put it in one of his recent song and dance routines in Melbourne, 'Life is Just a Show'.

Notes

Introduction
1. J.M Cooper, 'Conception, Conversation and Comparison' in *Writing Biography*, p. 87.
2. Manning Clark quoted by John Rickard in 'Manning Clark and Patrick White: A Reflection', *Australian Historical Studies*, vol. 25, no 98, April 1992, p. 120.
3. Peter Conrad, 'Humphries on the Couch' in *Feasting with Panthers, or the Importance of Being Famous*, p. 281. John Rickard referred to the 'kingdom of nothingness', *AHS*, p. 120.
4. John Lahr, *Dame Edna and the Rise of Western Civilisation*, p. 240.

PART ONE DADA BOY
Chapter 1 Suburban Eden
1. Urban Conservation Committee, National Trust of Australia, *Golf Links Estate City of Camberwell*, p. 10.
2. ibid., p. 19.
3. Barry Humphries, *More Please*, pp. 26–7.
4. Mrs Ray Brown quoted in the film by Alex West, *The Man Inside Dame Edna*.
5. Barry Humphries, *My Life As Me*, p. 21.
6. Barbara Johnson to author, 5 November 2007.
7. Humphries says this in *More Please*, p. 76 and also said it in *The Man Inside Dame Edna*.
8. Barry Humphries, *More Please*, p. 83.
9. Barbara Johnson to author, 5 November 2007.
10. Chester Eagle, *Play Together Dark Blue Twenty*, p. 35.
11. Ian Donaldson, *Barry Humphries: Bepraisements*, p. 25.
12. Humphries explains this in *More Please*, p. 103.
13. Papers of Barry Humphries, diary fragment, Performing Arts Collection, Melbourne.

Chapter 2 The Wubbos
1. Barry Humphries, *My Life As Me*, p. 130.
2. John Perry to author, 18 December 2007.
3. Barry Humphries, *My Life As Me*, p. 129.
4. *ibid.*, p. 123.
5. Keith Dunstan, *No Brains at All*, p. 253.
6. Dunstan quotes Humphries, *ibid.* p. 253.
7. Barry Humphries, 'Wubbo Manifesto' Papers of Barry Humphries, Performing Arts Collection, Melbourne.
8. Melbourne Dada Group, 'Wubbo Music', 1952, on CD 'Artefacts of Australian Experimental Music 1930–1973', compiled by Clinton Green and released 2007; held in the National Film and Sound Archives, Canberra.
9. Peter O'Shaughnessy, 'How Edna Everage took to the stage', *The Age*, 26 January 1985, p. 9. O'Shaughnessy cites the joke about 'Her Royal Magotty Queen Lizard'.
10. Don Bennetts to author, 31 October 2007.
11. In 1948 *Rusty Bugles* premiered in Sydney but was initially banned because of its strong language; it played in Melbourne in 1949, and toured Australia and New Zealand in 1952.
12. 'Hello Jim', written by John Perry and Barry Humphries. A copy of the script is held in the Papers of John Lahr, Howard Gotlieb Archival Research Center, Boston University.

Chapter 3 A Perfectly Timed Spectacle
1. Zoe Caldwell, *I Will Be Cleopatra*, p. 51.
2. John Sumner to author, 14 August 2006.
3. John Sumner to author, 14 August 2006; John Sumner, *Recollections at Play*, p. 38.
4. Brian Westmore and Joy Grissold to author, 21 December 2007.
5. Barry Humphries to author, 26 June 2010.
6. *The Age*, 27 December 1993, p. 11.
7. John Sumner to author, 14 August 2006.
8. John Sumner to author, 14 August 2006; Peter O'Shaughnessy, 'How Edna Everage took to the stage', *The Age*, 26 January 1985, p. 9.
9. *ibid.*
10. *ibid.*
11. *ibid.*
12. *ibid.*
13. *ibid.*
14. Stephen Spender, *World Within World*, p. 103.
15. John Sumner to author, 14 August 2006.
16. Barry Humphries, *More Please*, p. 121.
17. Freddy Parslow quoted Barry Humphries to author, 2 February 2007.
18. Barry Humphries, *More Please*, p. 133; Parslow to author, 2 February 2007.
19. Peter O'Shaughnessy, 'How Edna Everage took to the stage', *The Age*, 26 January 1985, p. 9.

20 Peter O'Shaughnessy to author, 7 August 2006.
21 Peter O'Shaughnessy, How Edna Everage took to the stage', *The Age*, 26 January 1985, p. 9.
22 Peter O'Shaughnessy to author, 7 August 2006.

Chapter 4 Orsino and the Monster
1   Ray Lawler to author, 1 February 2007.
2   Barry Humphries, *More Please*, p. 142.
3   Peter Batey to author, 6 May 2008.
4   Freddy Parslow to author, 2 February 2007.
5   Zoe Caldwell, *I Will Be Cleopatra*, p. 59.
6   Peter Batey to author, 6 May 2008.
7   Barry Humphries, *More Please*, p. 143.
8   Peter O'Shaughnessy to author, 7 August 2006.
9   Ray Lawler to author, 1 February 2007.
10 John Cargher, *Luck Was My Lady*, p. 77.
11 Robin Boyd, *Australia's Home*, p. 12.
12 Craig McGregor used the term 'matriduxy' in 1966, stating that 'The most surprising feature of family life in Australia, for such an overtly masculine nation, is the way the family group is dominated by the mother … Australian families could well be called a form of "matriduxy" – the mother does not rule, but she certainly leads.', *Profile of Australia*, p. 342.
13 The *Listener-In* review of *Return Fare*, 24–30 December 1955.
14 Ray Lawler to author, 1 February 2007.
15 Barry Humphries, *More Please*, p. 139.
16 *ibid.*, pp.146–7.

Chapter 5 Waiting for Barry
1   John West, *Theatre in Australia*, p. 205.
2   Bud Tingwell, *Bud*, p. 70.
3   Gordon Chater, *[The Almost Late] Gordon Chater*, p. 80.
4   *ibid.* p. 76.
5   *ibid.* p. 83.
6   Barry Humphries to Peter O'Shaughnessy, undated letter.
7   Bud Tingwell, *Bud*, p. 70.
8   Barry Humphries discusses Max Oldaker in a foreword to Charles Osborne's book, *Max Oldaker: Last of the Matinee Idols*, p. x.
9   Philip Jones, *Art and Life*, p. 138.
10 Bud Tingwell, *Bud*, p. 71.
11 Reg Livermore, *Chapters and Changes*, p. 17. Livermore was Gordon Chater's understudy. In Humphries' foreword to *Last of the Matinee Idols*, he recalls the comment as one of Chater's teasing lines: '"Isn't it funny, Max," panted Gordon one night as he dashed down the rickety wooden stairs to execute a lightning costume change, "in a few years time, Barry will be 30, I'll be 40 and you'll be dead."', p. xi.
12 Barry Humphries, Foreword to *Max Oldaker*, p. xi.

13 Wendy Blacklock to author, 8 June 2006.
14 Barry Humphries to Peter O'Shaughnessy, undated letter.
15 John Cargher, *Luck Was My Lady*, p. 78.
16 Gordon Chater, *[The Almost Late] Gordon Chater*, pp. 76, 84.
17 Barry Humphries to Peter O'Shaughnessy, undated letter.
18 Barry Humphries to Peter O'Shaughnessy, undated letter.
19 Barry Humphries to Peter O'Shaughnessy, undated letter.
20 John Sumner, 'The Doll in London', *Australian Theatre Year Book*, 1958, p. 18.
21 Patrick White to Keith Michell, 9 October 1957, in Marr, David (ed.), *Patrick White: Letters*, p. 124.
22 Barry Humphries to Peter O'Shaughnessy, undated letter.
23 Barry Humphries to Peter O'Shaughnessy, undated letter.
24 Barry Humphries, *More Please*, p. 171.
25 Margaret Fink to author, 24 October 2007.
26 Barry Humphries to Peter O'Shaughnessy, undated letter.
27 Barry Humphries to Peter O'Shaughnessy, undated letter.
28 Barry Humphries in Geoffrey Dutton, *The Innovators*, pp. 199–200.
29 Barry Humphries to Peter O'Shaughnessy, undated letter.
30 Barry Humphries, *More Please*, p. 171.
31 Barry Humphries to Peter O'Shaughnessy, undated letter.
32 Barry Humphries to Peter O'Shaughnessy, undated letter.
33 Peter O'Shaughnessy, unpublished essay, 'Portrait of the artist as a young man'.
34 Peter O'Shaughnessy, 'How Edna Everage took to the stage', *The Age*, 26 January 1985, p. 9.
35 Barry Humphries to Peter O'Shaughnessy, undated letter.

Chapter 6 Eucalypso Nights
1 Peter O'Shaughnessy, unpublished essay, 'Portrait of the artist as a young man'.
2 *ibid*.
3 Don Bennetts to author, 31 October 2007.
4 Peter O'Shaughnessy, unpublished lecture, Papers of Peter O'Shaughnessy, National Library of Australia.
5 *Herald*, 7 September 1957.
6 *The Age*, 7 September 1957, p.57.
7 Margaret Fink is quoted by Christine Wallace, *Greer*, p. 70, and Margaret Fink to author, 24 October, 2007.
8 Clifton Pugh, 'Barry Humphries: A Portrait in Words', unpublished essay.
9 *The Age*, 30 September 1957, p. 6.
10 Clifton Pugh, 'Barry Humphries: A Portrait in Words', unpublished essay.
11 Clifton Pugh, 'Barry Humphries: A Portrait in Words', unpublished essay.
12 Peter O'Shaughnessy, 'How Edna Everage took to the stage', *The Age*, 26 January 1985, p. 9.
13 *The Age*, 31 December 1957.

14 Barry Humphries to author, 20 October 2007.
15 Rosalind Hollinrake to author, 15 June 2009.
16 Don Bennetts to author, 31 October 2007.
17 Don Bennetts to author, 31 October 2007.
18 Some 5000 television sets had been sold by the time the Olympic Games began in November 1956, as noted by Elizabeth Jacka and Lesley Johnson, 'Australia', in *Television: An International History*, p. 335.
19 Don Bennetts to author, 31 October 2007.
20 Peter O'Shaughnessy quotes the newspaper in his unpublished essay 'Portrait of the artist as a young man'.
21 Rosalind Hollinrake to author, 15 June 2009.
22 *Sydney Morning Herald*, 9 May 1958, p. 5.
23 *Bulletin*, 14 May 1958, p. 24.
24 *Daily Telegraph*, 9 May 1958, p. 16.
25 Keith Dunstan quotes Barry Humphries, *A Nice Night's Entertainment*, in *Moonee Ponds to Broadway*, p. 40.
26 Peter Conrad, *At Home in Australia*, National Gallery of Australia, Canberra, 2003, p. 216.

Chapter 7 E-Scape
1 Clifton Pugh, 'Barry Humphries: A Portrait in Words', unpublished essay.
2 Barry Humphries quoted in the *Australian Women's Weekly*, 10 September 1958, p.7.
3 Clifton Pugh, 'Barry Humphries: A Portrait in Words' unpublished essay.
4 Phillip Adams to author, 6 August 2007.
5 'Sandy Stone' scripts from *Rock ' n' Reel Revue*, Private Collection of Peter O'Shaughnessy, p. A2.
6 Rosalind Hollinrake to author, 15 June 2009.
7 *Rock n' Reel Revue* program.
8 Peter O'Shaughnessy, unpublished essay, 'Portrait of the artist as a young man'.
9 Chris Wallace-Crabbe to author, 17 December 2007.
10 Rosalind Hollinrake to author, 15 June 2009.
11 Barry Humphries to Peter O'Shaughnessy, 15 January 1959.
12 Rosalind Hollinrake to author, 15 June 2009.
13 *Testimonial Performance* program.
14 Barry Humphries to Peter O'Shaughnessy, undated letter.
15 Rosalind Hollinrake to author, 15 June 2009.
16 Denison Deasey, *Australian Letters*, vol 2, no 1, June 1959, p.25.

PART TWO ACTOR
Chapter 8 A City for Performance
1 Charles Osborne, *Giving it Away: Memoirs of an Uncivil Servant*, p. 189.
2 Peter Porter, Address to the Academy of Humanities Symposium, 14 Nov 2008, Sydney.

3   Barry Humphries to Peter O'Shaughnessy, 11 August 1959.
4   Barry Humphries to Peter O'Shaughnessy, 9 March 1960.
5   Barry Humphries to Peter O'Shaughnessy, undated.
6   Stephen Alomes discusses the expatriation of Australian writers and performers in *When London Calls*, pp. 18–38.
7   Rosalind Humphries (now Hollinrake) to Shirley Smith, 14 February 1960.
8   Barry Humphries to Peter O'Shaughnessy, 1 December 1959.
9   *ibid*.
10 Barry Humphries to Peter O'Shaughnessy, undated.
11 Barry Humphries to Peter O'Shaughnessy, 14 February 1960.
12 Barry Humphries to Peter O'Shaughnessy, 3 February 1960.
13 Barry Humphries to Peter O'Shaughnessy, 14 February 1960.
14 Darlene Bungey, *Arthur Boyd: A Life*, p. 311.
15 Bryan Robertson in the *Recent Australian Painting* Catalogue, 1961.
16 Barbara Blackman, *Glass after Glass*, p. 257.
17 Anne Pender, *Christina Stead: Satirist*, pp. 5, 204.
18 Rosalind Hollinrake to author, 15 June 2009.
19 Barry Humphries to Peter O'Shaughnessy, 28 April 1960.
20 *ibid*.

Chapter 9 The Expatriate Game
1   Charles Dickens, *Oliver Twist*, (ed.) Kathleen Tillotson, Oxford University Press, 1966, p.50.
2   Barry Humphries to Peter O'Shaughnessy, 9 March 1960.
3   Barry Humphries reflects on his various performances in *Oliver!* in the London *Daily Telegraph*, 12 June 1997, p. 27.
4   John Hind quotes Lionel Bart in an article, 'With friends like these', the *Independent*, 26 April 1997.
5   Barry Humphries to Peter O'Shaughnessy, 16 May 1960.
6   Charles Dickens, *Oliver Twist*, (ed.) Kathleen Tillotson, Oxford University Press, 1966, p.20.
7   Barry Humphries to Peter O'Shaughnessy, 28 April 1960.
8   Rosalind Hollinrake to author, 15 June 2009.
9   Barry Humphries to Peter O'Shaughnessy, 6 October 1960.
10 Barry Humphries to Peter O'Shaughnessy, 13 January 1960.
11 Barry Humphries to Peter O'Shaughnessy, 16 May 1960.
12 Barry Humphries, Papers of Barry Humphries, Performing Arts Collection.
13 Barry Humphries, 'Australians in London', *Salient*, vol 1, no 4, Spring 1960, pp. 10–13.
14 Barbara Blackman to Judith Wright, 5 March 1961, in *Portrait of a Friendship*, p.78.
15 Barbara Blackman to author, 27 October 2007.
16   Barbara Blackman to author, 27 October 2007.
17 Darlene Bungey, *Arthur Boyd: A Life*, p. 363.
18 Charles Osborne to author, 28 August 2006.
19 Barbara Blackman, *Glass After Glass*, p. 258.

20 Barbara Blackman to author, 27 October 2007.
21 Rosalind Hollinrake to author, 15 June 2009.
22 John Betjeman is quoted in the program for *A Nice Night's Entertainment*.
23 Bevis Hillier, *Betjeman: the Bonus of Laughter*, p. 206.
24 Barbara Blackman quotes Humphries in a letter to Judith Wright, 16 Aug 1961, *Portrait of a Friendship*, p. 89.
25 Rosalind Hollinrake to author, 15 June 2009.

Chapter 10 Homecoming
1 Rosalind Hollinrake to author, 15 June 2009.
2 Barry Humphries, Performing Arts Collection manuscript.
3 Peter Coleman quotes Max Harris in *The Real Barry Humphries*, p. 62.
4 Barry Humphries to Peter O'Shaughnessy, 31 August 1962.
5 *Sydney Morning Herald*, 16 August 1962, p.7.
6 Jock Veitch, *Sun-Herald*, 19 August 1962, p. 80.
7 *Daily Telegraph*, 19 August 1962.
8 *Startime*, Episode 10, 1962, held in the National Film and Sound Archives, Canberra.
9 See cover of *Wildlife in Suburbia* compact disc.
10 Barry Humphries to Peter O'Shaughnessy, 31 August 1962.
11 Clifton Pugh, 'Barry Humphries: A Portrait in Words', unpublished essay.
12 Barry Humphries to author, 26 June 2010.

Chapter 11 Soho Nights
1 Barry Humphries to Peter O'Shaughnessy, undated.
2 *ibid*.
3 Barry Humphries to Peter O'Shaughnessy, undated.
4 Interview with Peter Cook by John Lahr, transcript held in the Howard Gotlieb Center, Boston University.
5 Barry Humphries, *More Please*, p. 214.
6 Stuart Ward offers an extended discussion of Cook and the other satirists in '"No nation could be broker": the satire boom and the demise of Britain's world role' in Ward (ed.) *British Culture and the End of Empire*, pp. 91–110.
7 Barry Humphries, *More Please*, p. 218.
8 Barry Humphries, the *Australian*, 28 May 1966, p. 27.
9 *Startime '63*, Episodes 18 and 27, held at the National Film and Sound Archives, Canberra.

Chapter 12 Highgate Babies
1 Barbara Blackman to author, 27 October 2006.
2 Jane Goodall discussed these images of Madonna in a talk at the University of New England in April 2009.
3 Barry Humphries quotes Oscar Wilde's letter to Harris, in *Bizarre*, p. 71.
4 Jerry Seinfeld said 'comedy is socialised aggression'. He was quoted by Richard Stengel in *Time*, 30 October 2002, www.time.com/time/magazine/article/.

5   Carl Stead, 'Barry Humphries – Contemporary', in *The Writer at Work*, 2000, p. 132.
6   Darlene Bungey, *Arthur Boyd: A Life*, p. 343.
7   Michael Humphries to author, 15 June 2009.
8   Quoted by John Hind in 'With friends like these', the *Independent*, 26 April 1997.
9   Ros Hollinrake to author, 16 June 2009.
10 Manning Clark's diary entry of 22 March 1964, quoted by Brian Matthews in his biography of Clark, *Manning Clark: A Life*, p. 245.
11 Barry Humphries (ed.), *Barry Humphries' Book of Innocent Austral Verse*, 'The Old Actors', pp. 55–7, p. 56.
12 Barry Humphries, *More Please*, p. 225.

Chapter 13 Bazza
1   Barry Humphries, *More Please*, p. 229.
2   Nick Garland to author, 25 June 2002.
3   Rosalind Hollinrake to author, 21 September 2009.
4   Barry Humphries wrote about his attitude to English humour in his column in the *Australian* on 6 February 1967, p. 12.
5   Nick Garland to author, 25 June 2002.
6   Harry Thompson, *Richard Ingrams: Lord of the Gnomes*, p. 164.

Chapter 14 My Favourite Things
1   Clifton Pugh, 'Barry Humphries: A Portrait in Words', unpublished essay.
2   'Ming' was the nickname given to Robert Menzies, then the prime minister of Australia.
3   *Sydney Morning Herald*, 18 October 1965, p. 18.
4   Some lines of the sketch were included in Humphries' column in the *Australian*, 7 May 1966, p. 22.
5   Barbara Blackman to author, 27 October 2007.
6   FR Blanks, *Sydney Morning Herald*, 12 October 1965, p. 17.
7   *Sun-Herald*, 17 October 1965, p. 88.

Chapter 15 Suitor to the Devil
1   Humphries recalls this in an article he wrote about his performances in the musical, published in the London *Daily Telegraph*, 12 June 1997.
2   Barry Humphries, the *Australian*, 4 June 1966, p. 22.
3   Martin Collins, the *Australian*, 6 August 1966, p. 24.
4   Barry Humphries to Max Oldaker, 25 July 1968.
5   Barry Humphries to Harold Holt, 14 June 1967, National Archives of Australia, File M2684/84.
6   Harold Holt to Barry Humphries, 15 June 1967, National Archives of Australia, File M2684/84.
7   Papers of Barry Humphries, Performing Arts Collection.
8   Peter Coleman quotes Humphries in his book, *The Real Barry Humphries*, p. 78.

NOTES

Chapter 16 On a Tightrope
1   The song is recorded on *Barry Humphries Moonee Ponds Muse* vol 1, Raven Records compact disc, 1991.
2   Susan McKernan offers a useful discussion of the way in which playwrights, especially Hibberd, followed Humphries, in her book *A Question of Commitment*, pp.189–208.
3   Bruce Beresford to author, 29 May 2007.
4   Barry Crocker to author, 30 May 2007.
5   *Sun-Herald*, 25 Aug 1968, p. 116.
6   *Sydney Morning Herald*, 21 August 1968, p. 18.
7   *Sydney Morning Herald*, 24 August 1968, p. 22.
8   Clifton Pugh, 'Barry Humphries: A Portrait in Words', unpublished essay.
9   *ibid*.
10 Mandy Sayer quotes Humphries requesting Brack paint Edna Everage in 'Satirists of Suburbia: Mrs Edna Everage Paints John Brack', *Art & Australia*, Spring 2007, pp. 126–7, p. 126.
11 Helen Brack on ABC TV's *7.30 Report*, 22 April 2009; Christopher Allen quoted John Brack in the *Weekend Australian*, Review Section, p. 9: 'I was saying in effect ... look at these people, with their boredom and their dull lives. I should have known ... that their lives were just as complex as mine.'
12 John Reed to Barry Humphries, 2 August 1968, in *Letters of John Reed*, p. 710.
13 Margaret Fink to author, 24 October 2007.
14 Gordon Chater reflected on this phenomenon from his own point of view in his book, *[The Almost Late] Gordon Chater*, p. 199, and on what he learned from Elizabeth Ashley's book *Postcards from the Road* and Ashley's view that this is the truth about being an actor.
15 John Lahr quotes Humphries in a newspaper interview from 1982, recalling his behaviour towards Rosalind, in *Honky Tonk Parade*, p. 160.

Chapter 17 True British Spunk
1   Robert Waterhouse, *Plays and Players*, vol 16, no 8, May 1969, p. 27.
2   Irving Wardle, *The Times*, 18 March 1969, p. 15.
3   Lewis Morley to author, 14 January 2009.
4   Barry Humphries, *Moonee Ponds Muse* vol 1, Raven Records compact disc, 1991. Humphries recorded an edited version of this rousing song for Philips Records, but he reports that they cut two extra verses of the song; see *More Please*, p. 284.
5   Bevis Hillier, *Betjeman: the Bonus of Laughter*, p. 218.
6   *Union Recorder*, 22 April 1971, pp.8–9.

PART THREE DAME
Chapter 18 Sobriety
1   Ross Fitzgerald to author, 5 May 2008.
2   Ross Fitzgerald to author, 5 May 2008.

3   Ross Fitzgerald to author, 5 May 2008. In 2009, Fitzgerald co-authored *Under the Influence: A History of Alcohol in Australia* for ABC Books, Sydney. In 2010 his memoir, *My Name is Ross: An Alcoholic's Journey*, was published by New South Books, Sydney.
4   Ross Fitzgerald to author, 5 May 2008.
5   Phillip Adams to author, 6 August 2007.
6   Humphries and White are quoted by David Marr in *Patrick White: A Life*, p. 500–01.
7   *Sydney Morning Herald*, 17 April 1971, p. 17.
8   *Bulletin*, 24 April 1971, p. 52.
9   *Sunday Review*, 2 May 1971.
10 The *Australian*, 21 April 1971.
11 *The Age*, 7 Aug 1971, p. 2.
12 Barry Humphries, *Sunday Review*, 18 April 1971, p. 34B.
13 Humphries quoted in *News* (Adelaide), 12 Oct 1971.
14 Kevon Kemp, *National Times*, 19–24 April 1971, p 21; Humphries quoted in the *Melbourne Herald*, 31 August 1971. Humphries quoted by Jock Veitch, Sydney *Daily Telegraph*, 21 March 1971.
15 Barry Humphries to Harry M Miller, 13 March 1971, *Oxford Book of Australian Letters*, p. 275.
16 Emily Humphries to author, 11 February 2010.

Chapter 19 The Mythical Australian
1   Barry Humphries quoted in *Sunday Review*, 24 January 1971.
2   Max Harris, *Sunday Review*, 25 Oct 1970, p. 13.
3   Phillip Adams to author, 6 August 2007.
4   Bruce Beresford, *Bazza Comes Into His Own*, p. 4.
5   Bruce Beresford interview with Hazel de Berg, Oral History Papers, National Library of Australia.
6   Barry Humphries quoted in the *Bulletin*, 5 February 1972, p. 30.
7   John Clarke to author, 29 April 2008.
8   Phillip Adams, the *Australian Weekend Review* 12–13 Sept 1992, p. 3.
9   Barry Humphries to Phillip Adams, 2 June 1972, Papers of Harry M Miller, National Library of Australia.
10 Barry Humphries' Introduction to the *Penguin Leunig*, 1974, para. 2.
11 Barry Humphries to Phillip Adams, 2 June 1972, Papers of Harry M Miller, National Library of Australia.
12 Barry Humphries to Harry M Miller, 2 June 1972.
13 Phillip Adams to author, 6 August 2007.
14 Melbourne *Observer*, 8 October 1972, p. 5.
15 Barry Humphries, *More Please*, p. 301.
16 Michael Humphries to author, 15 June 2009; Barry Humphries, *More Please*, p. 301.

Chapter 20 Damehood
1   Phillip Adams to author, 6 August 2007.

2   Dennis Altman, 'Bazza McKenzie: The Anti Homosexual Film', *Coming Out in the Seventies*, p. 36.
3   *The Age*, quoted by Phillip Adams, *Nation Review*, 28 October–3 November, 1972, p. 53.
4   Barrie Watts, the *Australian*, 13 October 1972, p. 3.
5   *Observer,* quoted by Phillip Adams, *Nation Review*, 28 October–3 November, 1972, p. 53; Ron Saw, *Daily Mirror*, 12 Oct 1972, p. 4.
6   *National Times*, October 1972.
7   *Bulletin*, 19 August 1972, p. 6.
8   Manning Clark to Barry Humphries, letter reproduced in *Bazza Comes Into His Own*, p. 73.
9   Geoffrey Dutton, Australian National University Public Lecture Series, Lecture 3, 1978.
10 Stephen Murray-Smith, 'A New Satirist', *Overland*, 14, 1959, p. 39.
11 Geoffrey Serle, *From Deserts the Prophets Come*, pp. 216, 217.
12 Susan McKernan explores this point in *A Question of Commitment*, p. 202.
13 Barry Humphries to Harry M Miller, 2 June 1972, Papers of Harry M Miller, National Library of Australia.
14 Barry Humphries to Harry M Miller, 6 April 1972, Papers of Harry M Miller, National Library of Australia.
15 Phillip Adams to author, 6 August 2007.
16 Nick Garland to author, 25 June 2002.
17 Emily Humphries to author, 11 February 2010.
18 Julian Jebb, *The Times*, reproduced in the program notes for *Isn't It Pathetic At His Age*.
19 Reproduced with the obituary for John Timbers in the *Guardian*, 15 December 2006.
20 Phillip Adams to Barry Humphries, 24 May 1973, Papers of Barry Humphries, Performing Arts Collection.
21 Gough Whitlam, *The Whitlam Government 1972–1975*, p.141. Mr Whitlam observed in a personal letter to the author, of 25 May 2004, that his appearance in the film was his 'only significant contact with Barry Humphries'.
22 Jim Davidson, 'A Fugitive Art: An Interview with Barry Humphries', *Meanjin*, 2, 1986, p. 155.
23 Bruce Beresford to Hazel de Berg, Oral History Unit Transcript, National Library of Australia.
24 Quoted by Peter Coleman, *Bruce Beresford: Instincts of the Heart*, p. 60.
25 Bruce Beresford to author, 29 May 2007.

Chapter 21 Anarchist
1   Ian Britain, *Once An Australian*, p. 60.
2   Barry Humphries cited terms others used to describe him on ABC Television, December 1973.
3   *Quadrant,* vol. xxvi, no 10, October 1982, p. 3.
4   Peter Nichols to Barry Humphries, 23 October 1987, Papers of Peter Nichols, British Library, London.

5   Humphries first used the term 'freckle' in 1968 as Barry McKenzie, and again in relation to the former Labor Prime Minister in 1978 as Les Patterson: 'I too believed that the sun shone out of Gough's freckle'; *The Australian National Dictionary*, p. 259.
6   Barry Crocker to author, 30 May 2007; see also Crocker's book, *The Adventures of Barry Crocker*, p. 380.
7   Barbara Blackman, *Glass After Glass*, p. 267.
8   Julian Meyrick discusses this in 'Loved Every Minute of It: Nimrod, Enright's *The Venetian Twins* and the Invention of Popular Theatre' in Anne Pender and Susan Lever (eds) *Nick Enright: An Actor's Playwright*, pp. 157–72.
9   *Commonwealth Parliamentary Debates*, Reps, vol. 93, 11 February 1975, p. 66.

Chapter 22 Housewife Superstar
1   Romola Costantino, *Sydney Morning Herald*, 3 July 1974, p. 7.
2   *The Age*, 22 August 1974, p. 2.
3   *Bulletin*, 6 July 1974, pp. 42–4.
4   The text appeared in *Quadrant*, vol. 19, November 1975, pp. 47–52.
5   Barry Humphries to Richard Allen, 4 December 1981, *The Oxford Book of Australian Letters*, p. 276.
6   Quoted by Heather Kennedy, *Woman's Day*, 14 July 1978, pp. 3, 9.
7   Diane Millstead quoted by Margaret Rice in the *SMH Good Weekend Magazine*, 27 September 1986, p. 11.
8   Barry Humphries interview with Melvyn Bragg, *The South Bank Show*, 19 November 1989, London Weekend Television.
9   *The Times*, 5 Dec 1977, p. 25.
10 The National Theatre building in London opened in 1976.
11 *The Times*, 18 March 1976, p.12.
12 John Rickard discusses definitions of the larrikin in his essay 'Lovable Larrikins and Awful Ockers', *Journal of Australian Studies*, 56, 1998, pp. 78–85, p. 81.
13 Michael Humphries to author, 15 June 2009.
14 The Opera House hat is now held in the Victoria and Albert Museum, London.
15 Patrick White's commendation appears in *Dame Edna's Coffee Table Book*, p. 2.
16 Dame Edna in *Dame Edna's Coffee Table Book*, pp.19–20.
17 ibid. p. 32.
18 ibid. p. 23.

Chapter 23 Hell's Kitchen
1   Barry Humphries quoted Cantor's comment in an interview with John Lahr; transcript held in the Howard Gotlieb Center Collection, Boston University.
2   Barry Humphries, *My Life As Me*, p. 197.
3   Barry Humphries interview with John Lahr; transcript held in the Howard Gottlieb Center.

4 *Daily News*, 20 October 1977, p. 85.
5 *New York Post*, 20 October 1977, p. 45.
6 *Christian Science Monitor*, 28 October 1977, p. 27.
7 *Daily News,* 28 October 1977, Friday section p. 3.
8 *Our Town*, 4 November 1977, p. 11.
9 *Village Voice*, 7 November 1977, p. 83.
10 *Women's Wear Daily*, 20 October 1977, p. 14.
11 *New York Post*, 20 October 1977, p. 24.
12 *New Yorker*, 7 November 1977, p. 106.
13 *Variety*, 16 November 1977, p. 92.
14 *New York Times*, 20 October 1977, C20.
15 *Weekend Australian*, 22–23 October 1977, p.6.
16 *Interview*, December 1977, pp. 26–7.
17 John Lahr to author, 19 September 2006.

Chapter 24 Regeneration
1 Barry Humphries' 27 April 1978 National Press Club speech is reproduced in *The Power of Speech: 25 Years of the National Press Club*, (ed.) Tony Maniaty, pp. 144–52.
2 Clive James, *Snakecharmers in Texas*, p. 35.
3 *Sydney Morning Herald*, 26 May 1978, p.8.
4 *The Age*, 26 July 1978, p. 2.
5 *Daily Telegraph* (London), 14 December 1978, p. 15.
6 The *Guardian*, 15 December 1978.
7 John Lahr told the author in an interview that he saw this happen to someone watching his father and once to someone watching Spike Milligan (19 September 2006).
8 *New Society*, 11 January 1979, pp. 86–7.
9 Barry Humphries to John Lahr, 22 February 1979, Papers of John Lahr, Howard Gotlieb Collection.
10 John Lahr's book about his father is *Notes on a Cowardly Lion*, published in 1967.
11 John Lahr to author, 19 September 2006.
12 White's description of Miss Docker is in the program notes for *A Cheery Soul*, 1979.
13 *This Fabulous Century,* produced and directed by David Salter and Peter Luck (1979); held in the National Film and Sound Archives, Canberra.
14 Screened on 19 March 1979 on BBC2, and on 17 February 1984 in recognition of Barry Humphries' fiftieth birthday.
15 The *Australian*, 18 June 1979, p. 1.

PART FOUR ARRIVISTE
Chapter 25 Last Night of the Poms
1 *Sunday Times* 13 September 1981, p. 32.
2 *The Times*, 15 September 1981, p. 10.
3 *Sunday Times*, 20 September 1981, p. 41.

4 *The Times*, 4 January 1981, p. 9.
5 *Financial Times*, 15 September 1981, p. 17.
6 Don Bennetts to author, 31 October 2007.
7 Barry Humphries, *Neglected Poems and Other Creatures*, p. 75.

Chapter 26 Intercourse with Millions
1 Richard Le Moignan, *Sydney Morning Herald*, 11 February 1983; Leonard Radic, *The Age*, 4 March 1983, p. 14.
2 The *Australian*, 11 February 1983, p. 12.
3 *Sun-Herald*, 6 February 1983, p. 119.
4 The *Australian*, 21 August 1982; Bolton explains the incident in 'The Shoals of Celebrity', *Meanjin* 2004, 3, p.144–8.
5 Humphries, Barry, 'Professor Patterson's Christmas Package for the Poms', *Quadrant*, Jan–Feb 1983, p. 36–7.
6 Quote from *The Times* in Margaret Jones, *Thatcher's Kingdom*, p. 232.
7 Barry Humphries, *Neglected Poems and Other Creatures*, p.83.
8 *Barry Humphries' Flashbacks*, ABC Television, and Roger McDonald, *Barry Humphries' Flashbacks*, p. 134.
9 *National Times*, 3–9 October 1982, p. 12, pp. 12–13.
10 Craig McGregor, *Profile of Australia*, p.99.
11 Craig McGregor, *The Australian People*, p. 70.
12 ibid.
13 Craig McGregor, *National Times*, 3–9 Oct 1982, p. 12, pp. 12–13.
14 *Adelaide Review*, September 1985, pp. 4–5.

Chapter 27 Chat
1 Barry Humphries in the film *The Man Inside Dame Edna*.
2 *Barry Humphries' Treasury of Australian Kitsch*, p. 80.
3 See Jan Roberts, *The Astor: the Biography of a Macquarie Street Icon*, Ruskin Rowe Press, Avalon, 2003.

Chapter 28 Formica Lady
1 Marianne Sinclair and Sarah Litvinoff (eds), *The Wit and Wisdom of the Royal Family*, p. 51.
2 Margaret Jones wrote: 'Power obviously acts on Thatcher like an intoxicant. She is permanently high on it.' *Thatcher's Kingdom*, p. 33.
3 ibid.
4 ibid. p. 32.
5 ibid. p. 31 and Nicholas Wapshott and George Brock, *Thatcher*, p. 8.

Chapter 29 Mount Edna
1 Claudia Rosencrantz to author, 16 December 2008.
2 Andrew Tolson discusses *The Dame Edna Experience* and the way it is 'totally ambiguous about its ability to differentiate between sincere and insincere talk', p. 198, 'Televised Chat and the Synthetic Personality' in P Scannell (ed.), *Broadcast Talk*, Sage, 1991 London, p. 198.

3   Claudia Rosencrantz to author, 28 August 2008.
4   As told to John Lahr and published in *Automatic Vaudeville*, p. 57.
5   Quoted by Andrew Billen in the *Evening Standard*, 4 March 1998, pp. 25–6.
6   John Lahr in author's interview with him (19 September 2006), paraphrasing a comment made by Humphries on an ITV *Great Comedians* television show.
7   Barry Humphries to John Lahr, Papers of John Lahr, Howard Gotlieb Center.
8   Barry Humphries to John Lahr, Papers of John Lahr, Howard Gotlieb Center.
9   Leonard Radic, *The Age*, 24 March 1986, p. 12.
10 Keith Dunstan, *No Brains at All*, p. 201.
11 Leonard Radic, *The Age*, 24 March 1986, p. 12.
12 *Womans's Day*, 25 June 1986, pp. 6–7.
13 Barry Humphries to Peter Nichols, 19 August 1986, Papers of Peter Nichols, British Library, London.

Chapter 30 Queen of the West End
1   Armistead Maupin, 'Laughter as a Health Hazard' in Ken Thomson (ed.), *Barry Humphries: Bepraisements on his Birthday*, pp. 52–3, p. 52.
2   The caption read: '… the Royals meet Australia's First Lady', the *Daily Mirror*, 17 November 1987.
3   Francis King, London *Sunday Telegraph*, 22 November 1987.
4   Clive James, *Snakecharmers in Texas*, p. 35.
5   Paul Taylor, *Independent*, 19 November 1987.
6   *Observer*, 22 November 1987.
7   *Punch*, 25 November 1987.
8   *Guardian*, 19 November 1987.
9   *London Broadcasting*, 18 November 1987.
10 *City Limits*, 26 November 1987.
11 *Financial Times*, 18 November 1987.
12 *Daily Mail*, 18 November 1987.
13 *The Times*, 18 November 1987.
14 Peter Nichols to Barry Humphries, 23 October 1987, Papers of Peter Nichols, British Library, London.
15 John Lahr, *Dame Edna and the Rise of Western Civilisation*, p. 2.
16 *British Theatre Yearbook* 1990, (ed.) D. Lemmon, Christopher Helm, London, p. 15.
17 Victy Silva to author, 22 September 2006.
18 Victy Silva to author, 22 September 2006.
19 Victy Silva to author, 22 September 2006.
20 Brian Sewell's review, 'Angry penguins and realist painting in the 1940s', appeared in the *Evening Standard*, 23 June 1988, p. 29, and Sewell quoted the letter from Sir Les in John Hind's 'With friends like these', the *Independent* (London), 26 April 1997.
21 John Drummond, *Tainted by Experience*, p. 31–4.
22 Nick Garland to author, 25 June 2002.

Chapter 31 Suburbs of the Sacred
1. *Barry Humphries' Flashbacks,* 'The Party of a Lifetime – the 1980s', Episode 4, screened on ABC Television, 1998.
2. David Marr, *Patrick White: A Life,* p. 633.
3. *Barry Humphries' Flashbacks,* Episode 4.
4. Barry Humphries quotes White in *Barry Humphries' Flashbacks*, Episode 4, 'The Party of a Lifetime – the 1980s'; Patrick White's comment was originally noted in the Special Supplement, 'Patriotism in Australia', *Sydney Morning Herald,* 26 January 1984.
5. Ross Terrill, *The Australians,* 1987, p. 324.
6. Humphrey McQueen, *Suburbs of the Sacred,* p. 49.
7. *ibid.* p. 6, pp. 36–7.
8. Melvyn Bragg, 'The Power and the Spookiness', in Thomson, *Barry Humphries: Bepraisements on his Birthday,* p. 21–3, p. 21.
9. *ibid.* p. 22.
10. Barry Humphries, *My Life As Me,* p. 336.
11. Noel Malcolm, 'Margaret Thatcher, Housewife Superstar', *Spectator,* 25 February 1989, pp.8, 10.

PART FIVE BAWD
Chapter 32 Mauve-haired Madonna
1. Barry Humphries, *More Please,* p. xiii.
2. Quoted by Donal Lynch, the *Sunday Independent,* 25 September 2005.
3. Stephen Spender, *World Within World,* p. 91.
4. Barry Humphries, *More Please,* p. 314-15.
5. Barry Humphries to James Stern, 20 April 1986, Papers of James Stern, British Library, London, and interview with Jill Kitson, ABC Radio, 14 January 1993.
6. Barry Humphries, *Neglected Poems and Other Creatures,* pp. 43–4.
7. Humphries, *My Life As Me,* p.30.
8. John Lahr, 'Playing Possum', *New Yorker,* 1 July 1991, pp. 38–65.
9. John Lahr to author, 19 September 2006.
10. *San Diego Union-Tribune,* 24 November 1991.
11. *Vanity Fair,* December 1991.
12. *ibid.*
13. Claudia Rosencrantz to author, 28 August 2008.
14. Claudia Rosencrantz to author, 28 August 2008.
15. Steve Gaines, *Vanity Fair,* January 1987, pp. 85–8.
16. Matt Rouch in *USA Today,* 29 November 1991.
17. Quoted in *The Times,* 10 December 1991, p. 7.
18. *Hollywood Reporter,* 30 December 1992.
19. Tim Smith, *Fort Lauderdale Sun-Sentinel,* 31 December 1992.
20. Diane Holloway, *Austin American-Statesman,* 29 November 1991.
21. *Orange County Register,* 30 November 1991.
22. *Atlanta Journal and Constitution,* 29 November 1991.
23. *Los Angeles Daily News,* 8 May 1992.

24 Philippa Hawker, *The Age*, 31 August 1993.
25 Claudia Rosencrantz to author, 28 August 2008.

Chapter 33 Suburbs of the Mind
1 Peter Goers, *Daily Mail*, 7 November 1993.
2 Quoted by Peter Conrad in *Feasting with Panthers*, p. 284.
3 Paul Keating said this to John Laws on 14 May 1986.
4 John Larkin, *Sunday Age*, 19 December 1993.
5 *Adelaide Review*, November 1993.
6 *The Age*, 17 December 1993.
7 *Independent Monthly*, March 1994, p. 84, pp. 84–5.
8 *Sydney Morning Herald*, 2 December 1993, p. 22.
9 The *Australian*, 1 November 1993.
10 Karen Noack reported on the meeting between Sir Les and Rebecca Hossack and the appointment of Hossack as Cultural Attaché in London; *Sydney Morning Herald*, 19 January 1995, p. 17.
11 *The Age*, 9 May 1996, p. 17.

Chapter 34 Flashbacks
1 Oscar Humphries stated in the *Spectator* that his parents put them in separate schools so 'that they don't kill one another', 14 February 2009, p. v.
2 Barry Humphries to Peter Nichols, 21 February 1995.
3 Nick Garland to author, 25 June 2002.
4 *Mail on Sunday*, quoted in the *Canberra Times*, 18 January 1996, p. 5.
5 Barry Humphries' preface to McDonald, *Barry Humphries' Flashbacks*, p. viii.
6 *Observer*, 16 March 1997.
7 Barry Humphries quoted in the London *Daily Telegraph*, 12 June 1997, p. 27.
8 Barry Humphries, 'Erotic Diplomacy', the Erotic Print Society *Review*, Winter 1995, no 2, pp. 9–10.
9 Les Patterson, *The Traveller's Tool*, pp. 145–51.

Chapter 35 Banishing Edna
1 Barry Humphries, *My Life as Me*, p. 319.
2 *Daily Mail*, 22 April 1998.
3 *Daily Telegraph* (London), 22 April 1998.
4 Robert Gore-Langton, the *Express*, 22 April 1998.
5 *Evening Standard*, 22 April 1998.
6 *Spectator*, 2 May 1998.
7 *Daily Telegraph* (London), 22 April 1998.
8 John Peter, *Sunday Times* 26 April 1998; Will Buckley, *Independent on Sunday*, 26 April 1998.
9 *Guardian*, 23 April 1998.
10 *The Times*, 26 April 1998.
11 *Express*, 22 April 1998.
12 *Sunday Telegraph*, 26 April 1998.

13 *Observer*, 26 April 1998.
14 John Stokes, 'Why am I mauve?' *Times Literary Supplement*, 15 May 1998, pp.9–10.
15 *ibid*.
16 Laurence Senelick, *The Changing Room*, p. 474.

PART SIX SATIRIST
Chapter 36 Dragging Up
1 Quoted by John Hind, 'With friends like these', the *Independent*, 26 April 1997.
2 *Washington Post*, 22 November 1992.
3 The entry in the *Companion* listed a number of criticisms of Humphries at the end of the short essay on Barry Humphries' career; William H. Wilde, Joy Hooton and Barry Andrews (eds), *Oxford Companion to Australian Literature*, pp. 358–60, p. 359.
4 *Sunday Age*, 3 May 1998.
5 John Hind, *Independent*, 26 April 1997.
6 Turnbull was interviewed by Roy and HG on *The Channel Nine Show*, ABC TV, 18 April 1998.
7 *The Age*, 16 March 1999.
8 Clive Tulloh to author, 2 September 2008.
9 Laurence Senelick, *The Changing Room*, p. 466.
10 *ibid*. p. 467.
11 *ibid*. p. 468.
12 Simmons was the host of a television fitness show.
13 *Sacramento Bee*, 10 October 1998.
14 *Oakland Tribune*, 10 October 1998.
15 *San Francisco Chronicle*, 9 October 1998; *Press Democrat Santa Rosa*, 11 October 1998.
16 *Sacramento Bee*, 10 October 1998.
17 John Lahr to author, 19 September 2006.
18 *New York Times*, 3 October 1999.
19 *ibid*.
20 Michael Kuchwara, AP Online, 17 October 1999.
21 *ibid*.
22 *New York Daily News*, 17 October 1999.
23 Philip Olander, *Meanjin* 2002, vol 61, no 2, p. 181.
24 *New York* magazine review quoted by Andrew Rule, *Sunday Age*, 19 December 1999.
25 *Newsweek*, 18 January 1999.
26 *New York Post*, 18 October 1999.
27 *Newsday*, 21 October 1999.
28 *New Yorker*, 1 November 1999, p. 120.
29 Debra Jo Immergut, *Wall Street Journal*, 20 October 1999.
30 *New York Times*, 18 October 1999.
31 *ibid*.

32 *Spectator*, 30 September 2000.
33 Barry Humphries, *My Life as Me*, p 334.
34 *Australian*, 10 March 2000.
35 *Daily Telegraph* (London), 1 July 2003.
36 Oscar Humphries served as the editor of *The Spectator Australia* in 2008–09 and was appointed editor of the British art magazine *Apollo* in February 2010. He also works as an art dealer in the contemporary gallery of Timothy Taylor in London.
37 *Los Angeles Times*, 8 February 2003.
38 *Houston Chronicle*, 21 February 2003; *Hartford Courant*, 14 February 2003; *Seattle Post*, 19 February 2003; *San Diego Tribune*, 17 February 2003.
39 Imre Salusinzsky, 9–10 May 2009, *Weekend Australian, Review* p. 36.
40 Reed Johnson review of *Dame Edna: My First Last Tour, Los Angeles Times*, 11 June 2009.

Chapter 37 Recognition
1 Humphries quoted in the *Sydney Morning Herald Good Weekend*, 27 August 2005, p. 47.
2 Don Bennetts to author, 31 October 2007.
3 *The Age*, 28 March 2006.
4 *ibid*.
5 Barry Humphries recalled Perry's comment on *BBC News*, 20 February 2008.
6 Clive Tulloh to author, 2 September 2008.
7 John Lahr, *New Yorker*, 1 November 1999, p. 118.
8 *ABC News*, 11 October 2007.

Postscript
1 *Spectator*, 7 May 2008.
2 Barry Humphries to author, 4 June 2008.

Select Bibliography

Manuscripts and Papers
Papers of R.F. Brissenden, National Library of Australia, MS 8162
Papers of John Lahr, Howard Gotlieb Archival Center, Boston University
Papers of Harry M Miller, National Library of Australia, MS 7981
Papers of Peter Nichols, British Library
Papers of Peter O'Shaughnessy, National Library of Australia, MS 2272
Papers of James Stern, British Library

Books and Articles by Barry Humphries
'Australians in London', *Salient*, vol. 1, no 4, Spring 1960, pp. 10–13
Bizarre, Elek Books, London, 1965
The Barry Humphries Book of Innocent Austral Verse, Sun Books, Melbourne, 1968
Dame Edna's Coffee Table Book, Harrap, London, 1976
Bazza Comes Into His Own, Sun Books, Melbourne, 1979
Treasury of Australian Kitsch, Macmillan, Melbourne, 1980
A Nice Night's Entertainment: Sketches and Monologues 1956–1981, Granada, London, 1981
Dame Edna's Bedside Companion, Corgi Books, Sydney, 1982
Dame Edna Everage: My Gorgeous Life, Macmillan, Melbourne, 1989
The Humour of Barry Humphries, Currency Press, Sydney, 1984
Les Patterson: The Traveller's Tool, Michael O'Mara Books, London, 1985
The Life and Death of Sandy Stone, Pan Macmillan, Sydney, 1990
Neglected Poems and Other Creatures, Angus & Robertson, Sydney, 1991
More Please, Penguin, Ringwood, 1992
Women in the Background, Reed Books, Melbourne, 1995
My Life As Me, Penguin, Camberwell, 2003
Handling Edna, Hachette, Sydney, 2009

Other Books

Allen, John, *The Humour of Barry Humphries*, Currency Press, Sydney, 1984
Altman, Dennis, *Coming Out in the Seventies*, Wild & Woolley, Sydney, 1979
Alomes, Stephen, *When London Calls: the Expatriation of Australian Creative Artists to Britain*, Cambridge University Press, Melbourne, 1999
Appignanesi, Lisa, *Cabaret*, Methuen, London, 1984
Arkley, Howard, *Not Just a Suburban Boy*, Duffy & Snellgrove, Sydney, 2002
Auslander, Philip, *Liveness*, Routledge, London, 1999
Australian National Dictionary: a Dictionary of Australianisms on Historical Principles, (ed.) WS Ramson, Oxford University Press, Melbourne, 1988
Baker, Roger, *Drag*, Cassell, London 1994
Beck, Chris, *On the Couch with Chris Beck*, HarperCollins, Sydney, 1996
Bergan, Ronald, *Beyond the Fringe and Beyond*, Virgin, London, 1989
Blackman, Barbara, *Portrait of a Friendship: the Letters of Barbara Blackman and Judith Wright 1950–2000*, Cosgrove, Briony (ed.), Miegunyah Press, Melbourne, 2007
—— *Glass After Glass*, Penguin, Ringwood, 1997
Boyd, Robin, *Australia's Home*, Melbourne University Press, Melbourne, 1952
Britain, Ian, *Once An Australian*, Oxford University Press, Melbourne, 1997
Bungey, Darleen, *Arthur Boyd: A Life*, Allen & Unwin, Sydney, 2007
Caldwell, Zoe, *I Will Be Cleopatra: An Actress's Journey*, WW Norton, New York, 2001
Campbell, John, *Margaret Thatcher: The Iron Lady*, vol. 2, Jonathan Cape, London, 2003
Cargher, John, *Luck Was My Lady: Memoirs of a Workaholic*, Brolga Publishers, Victoria, Australia, 1996
Chater, Gordon, *[The Almost Late] Gordon Chater*, Bantam Books, Sydney, 1996
Coleman, Peter, *Obscenity, Blasphemy, Sedition: 100 years of Censorship in Australia*, Angus & Robertson, Sydney, 1961
—— *The Real Barry Humphries*, Robson Books, London, 1990
—— *Bruce Beresford: Instincts of the Heart*, Angus & Robertson, Sydney, 1992
Conrad, Peter, *Feasting With Panthers, or the Importance of Being Famous*, Thames & Hudson, London, 1994
—— *At Home in Australia*, National Gallery of Australia, Canberra, 2003
Cook, Judy, *Loving Peter*, Piatkus, London, 2008
Coombs, Anne, *Sex and Anarchy*, Penguin, Melbourne, 1996

Cooper, JM, 'Conception, Conversation and Comparison' in Lloyd E. Ambrosius (ed.), *Writing Biography*, University of Nebraska Press, London, 2004, pp. 79–102
Crocker, Barry, *The Adventures of Barry Crocker*, Pan Macmillan, Sydney, 2003
Curran, James, *The Power of Speech*, Melbourne University Press, Melbourne, 2004
Curran, James and Stuart Ward, *The Unknown Nation: Australia After Empire*, Melbourne University Press, Melbourne, 2010
Dickens, Charles, *Oliver Twist*, Kathleen Tillotson (ed.), Oxford University Press, Oxford, 1966
Docker, John, *Australian Cultural Elites*, Angus & Robertson, Sydney, 1974
Drummond, John, *Tainted by Experience,* Faber, London, 2000
Dunstan, Keith, *No Brains at All: An Autobiography*, Penguin, Ringwood, 1990
——*Moonee Ponds to Broadway: The Legendary Barry Humphries*, Australia Post Corporation, Melbourne, 2006
Dutton, Geoffrey, *The Innovators*, Macmillan, South Melbourne, 1986
Eagle, Chester, *Play Together Dark Blue Twenty*, McPhee Gribble, Melbourne, 1986
Ferrier, Noel, *There Goes Whatsisname: the Memoirs of Noel Ferrier*, Macmillan, South Melbourne, 1985
Fitzpatrick, Kate, *Name Dropping: An Incomplete Memoir*, John Wiley & Sons, Milton, Qld, 2005
Goodall, Jane, *Stage Presence*, Routledge, London, 2008
Gordon, Mel (ed.), *Dada Performance*, PAJ Publications, New York, 1987
Henderson, John, *Writing Down Rome*, Clarendon Press, Oxford, 1999
Hillier, Bevis, *Betjeman: The Bonus of Laughter*, John Murray, London, 2004
Hirst, John, *The Australians*, Black Inc, Melbourne, 2007
Holmes, Richard, 'Biography: Inventing the Truth' in John Batchelor (ed.), *The Art of Literary Biography*, Clarendon Press, Oxford, 1995, pp. 15–25
Horne, Donald, *The Australian People*, Angus & Robertson, Sydney, 1972
Jacka, Elizabeth and Lesley Johnson, 'Australia' in Anthony Smith (ed.), *Television: An International History,* Oxford University Press, New York, 1995, pp. 331–57
James, Clive, *Snakecharmers in Texas,* Jonathan Cape, London, 1988
—— *North Face of Soho*, Picador, London, 2006
Jones, Margaret, *Thatcher's Kingdom*, Collins, Sydney, 1984
Jones, Philip, *Art and Life*, Allen & Unwin, Sydney, 2004
Kiernander, Adrian, Jonathan Bollen and Bruce Parr (eds), *What a Man's Gotta Do? Masculinities in Performance,* CALLTS, Armidale NSW, 2006

Kippax, HG, *A Leader of His Craft*, Currency House, Sydney, 2004
Kirkpatrick, Peter and Fran de Groen (eds), *Serious Frolic: Essays in Australian Humour*, St Lucia, University of Queensland Press, 2009
Lahr, John, *Automatic Vaudeville*, Methuen, London, 1984
—— *Dame Edna and the Rise of Western Civilisation*, HarperCollins Publishers, London, 1992
—— *Light Fantastic: Adventures in Theatre*, Bloomsbury, London, 1996
—— *Honky Tonk Parade: New Yorker Profiles of Show People*, Duckworth, London, 2006
Lemmon, D (ed.), *British Theatre Year Book*, Christopher Helm, London, 1990
Leser, David, *Twenty-one Remarkable Women*, Park Street Press, Sydney, 2006
Livermore, Reg, *Chapters and Changes*, Hardie Grant Books, South Yarra, 2003
Leunig, Michael, *The Penguin Leunig*, Penguin, Ringwood, 1974
Lury, Karen, *Interpreting Television*, Hodder Arnold, London, 2005
Macintyre, Stuart, *A Concise History of Australia*, Cambridge University Press, Cambridge, 1999
Maniaty, Tony (ed.), *The Power of Speech: 25 Years of the National Press Club*, Bantam, Sydney, 1989
Marr, David, *Patrick White: A Life*, Vintage, Sydney, 1992
—— *Patrick White: Letters*, Random House, Sydney, 1994
Matthews, Brian, *Manning Clark: A Life*, Allen & Unwin, Sydney, 2008
McCallum, John, *Belonging: Australian Playwriting in the 20th Century*, Currency Press, Sydney, 2009
McDonald, Roger, *Barry Humphries' Flashbacks*, HarperCollins, Sydney, 1999
McGregor, Craig, *Profile of Australia*, Hodder & Stoughton, London, 1966
—— *People, Politics and Pop*, Ure Smith, Sydney, 1968
—— *The Australian People*, Hodder & Stoughton, Sydney, 1980
McGregor, Craig (ed.), *Life in Australia*, Southern Cross International, Sydney, 1968
McInnes, Graham, *Humping My Bluey*, Hogarth Press, London, 1986
McKernan, Susan, *A Question of Commitment*, Allen & Unwin, Sydney, 1989
McQueen, Humphrey, *A New Britannia*, Penguin, Middlesex, England, 1970
—— *Suburbs of the Sacred*, Penguin, Ringwood, 1988
Meyrick, Julian, 'Loved Every Minute of It: Nimrod, Enright's *The Venetian Twins* and the Invention of Popular Theatre', in Anne

Pender and Susan Lever (eds), *Nick Enright: An Actor's Playwright*, Rodopi, Amsterdam, 2008, pp. 157–72

Milne, Geoffrey, *Theatre Australia Unlimited*, Amsterdam, Rodopi, 2004

Morrison, Andrew, *Shame: The Underside of Narcissism*, The Analytic Press, Hilldale NJ, 1989

National Trust of Australia Urban Conservation Committee, *Golf Links Estate, City of Camberwell*, Melbourne, 1989

Osborne, Charles, *Max Oldaker: Last of the Matinee Idols*, Michael O'Mara, London, 1988

—— *Giving it Away: Memoirs of an Uncivil Servant*, Secker & Warburg, London, 1986

Oxford Companion to Australian Literature, William H. Wilde (ed.), Oxford University Press, Melbourne, 1995

Oxford Book of Australian Letters, Brenda Niall and John Thompson (eds), Oxford University Press, Melbourne, 1998

Parr, Bruce (ed.), *Australian Gay and Lesbian Plays*, Currency Press, Sydney, 1996

Pearson, Hesketh, *The Life of Oscar Wilde*, Methuen, London, 1946

Pender, Anne, *Christina Stead: Satirist*, Common Ground, Melbourne, 2002

Porter, Hal, *Stars of Australian Stage and Screen*, Rigby, Adelaide, 1965

Reid, Barrett and Nancy Underhill (eds), *Letters of John Reed*, Viking, Melbourne, 2001

Rickard, John, *Australia: A Cultural History*, Addison Wesley Longman, Harlow UK, 1996

Roberts, Jan, *The Astor: The Biography of a Macquarie Street Icon*, Ruskin Rowe Press, Avalon NSW, 2003

Robertson, Bryan, *Recent Australian Painting* (catalogue), Whitechapel Gallery, London, 1961

Roper, David, *Bart! The Unauthorised Life and Times, Ins and Outs, Up and Downs of Lionel Bart*, Pavilion Books, London, 1994

Senelick, Laurence, *The Changing Room: Sex, Drag and Theatre*, Routledge, London, 2000

Serle, Geoffrey, *From Deserts the Prophets Come*, Heinemann, Melbourne, 1973

Sharkey, Michael (ed.) *The Illustrated Treasury of Australian Humour*, Oxford University Press, Melbourne, 1988

Sinclair, Marian and Sarah Litvinoff (eds), *The Wit and Wisdom of the Royal Family*, Plexus Publishing, London, 1990

Smith, Anthony (ed.), *Television: An International History*, Oxford University Press, New York, 1995

Smith, Russell and Chris Ackerley, 'Samuel Beckett's Reception in Australia and New Zealand' in Mark Nixon and Matthew Feldman (eds), *The International Reception of Samuel Beckett*, Continuum, London, 2009, pp. 108–128

Spender, Stephen, *World Within World*, Hamish Hamilton, London, 1951

Stead, Carl, 'Barry Humphries — Contemporary' in *The Writer at Work*, University of Otago Press, Dunedin, 2000

Sumner, John, 'The Doll in London', *Australian Theatre Year Book 1957*, Australian Elizabethan Trust, Cheshire, Melbourne, 1958

—— *Recollections At Play: A Life in Australian Theatre*, Melbourne University Press, Carlton, 1993

Terrill, Ross, *The Australians*, Bantam, Sydney 1987

Thomson, Ken, *Barry Humphries: Bepraisements On His Birthday*, Enitharmon Press, London, 1994

Thompson, Harry, *Richard Ingrams: Lord of the Gnomes,* Heinemann, London, 1994

—— *Peter Cook: A Biography*, Hodder & Stoughton, London, 1997

Tingwell, Bud and Peter Wilmoth, *Bud: A Life*, Pan Macmillan, Sydney, 2004

Tolson, Andrew, 'Televised Chat and the Synthetic Personality' in P Scannell (ed.), *Broadcast Talk*, Sage, London, 1991

Van Straten, Frank, *Tivoli*, Lothian, South Melbourne, 2003

Wallace, Christine, *Greer: Untamed Shrew*, Picador, Sydney, 1997

Wapshott, Nicholas and George Brock, *Thatcher*, Macdonald, London, 1983

Ward Russel, *The Australian Legend*, Oxford University Press, Melbourne, 1958

Ward, Stuart (ed.), *British Culture and the End of Empire*, Manchester, Manchester University Press, 2001

West, John, *Theatre in Australia*, Cassell, Stanmore NSW, 1978

Whitlam, Gough, *The Whitlam Government 1972–1975*, Viking, Ringwood, 1985

Williamson, Kristin, *David Williamson: Behind the Scenes*, Viking, Ringwood, 2009

Articles

Britain, Ian, 'Bazzamatz', *ABC Radio 24 Hours*, August 1996, pp. 36–41

—— 'Barry Humphries and the Feeble Fifties', *Australian Historical Studies*, vol. 27, 109, 1997, pp. 6–20

Curran, James, 'The "Thin Dividing Line": Prime Ministers and the Problem of Australian Nationalism, 1972–1976', *Australian Journal of Politics and History*, vol. 48, no 4, 2002, pp. 469–86

Davidson, Jim, 'The Babe Among the Gladdies is Perambulating Nicely, Thankyou', *Meanjin Quarterly*, vol. 33, no 4, Summer 1974, pp. 443–5
—— 'The De-dominionisation of Australia', *Meanjin*, vol. 38, July 1979, pp. 139–53
—— 'A Fugitive Art: An Interview with Barry Humphries', *Meanjin*, vol. 45, no 2, 1986, pp. 149–68
—— 'Mr Whitlam's Cultural Revolution', *Journal of Australian Studies*, no 20, May 1987, pp. 83–91
Deasey, Desmond, 'Barry Humphries', *Australian Letters*, vol. 2, no 1, G Dutton, B Davies and Max Harris (eds), June 1959, pp. 24–5
Hughes, Graeme, 'A Memoir of Barry Humphries', *Melbourne University Magazine*, 1961, pp. 42–4
Lahr, John, Review in *New Society*, 11 January 1979, pp. 86–7
—— 'Playing Possum', *New Yorker*, 1 July 1991, pp. 38–66
Murray-Smith, Stephen, 'A New Satirist', *Overland*, 14, 1959, p. 39
Olander, Philip, 'The Shtick's the Thing', *Meanjin*, vol. 61, no 4, 2002, pp. 180–83
Pender, Anne, 'No More Please: Barry Humphries and Australian English', *Journal of Australian Studies*, no 68, 2001, pp. 160–66
—— 'Lethal Humour: Nick Garland, Barry Humphries and *The Adventures of Barry McKenzie*', *London Papers in Australian Studies*, no 7, 2003
—— 'The Mythical Australian: Barry Humphries, Gough Whitlam and "New Nationalism"', *Australian Journal of Politics and History*, vol. 51, no 1, March 2005, pp. 67–78
Pierse, Simon, 'Australian Artists in London in 1961', *Art & Australia*, pp. 227–34
Rickard, John, 'Manning Clark and Patrick White: A Reflection', *Australian Historical Studies*, vol. 25, no 98, April 1992, pp. 116–22
—— 'Lovable Larrikins and Awful Ockers', *Journal of Australian Studies*, 56, 1998, pp. 78–85
Sayer, Mandy, 'Satirists of Suburbia: Mrs Edna Everage Paints John Brack', *Art & Australia*, Spring 2007, pp.126–7
Ward, Stuart, '"Culture Up to Our Arseholes": Projecting Post-Imperial Australia', *Australian Journal of Politics and History*, vol. 51, no 1, March 2005, pp. 53–66

Index

BH = Barry Humphries

AA, 172, 173
Abbott, Tony, 256
ABC, 91, 152
Abicair, Shirley, 112
Absolutely Fabulous (television show), 330
Actors' Equity (US), 117
Adams, Phillip
   chairs AFDC, 182
   declines to produce film sequel, 197, 200
   helps in BH's recovery, 175
   lambasts BH in interview, 365
   produces *Adventures of Barry McKenzie*, 184–5, 186–7, 188, 192
   produces *The Naked Bunyip*, 173–4
   profits from *Adventures of Barry McKenzie*, 196
   puts music to *Battleship Potemkin*, 79
   relieved to see BH's recovery, 173
Addams, Charles, 221
Addams Family (television series), 221
Adelphi Theatre, London, 130
Adnitt, Stephen, 281–2, 286, 334, 372
The Adventures of Barry McKenzie (book), 181
The Adventures of Barry McKenzie (film), 179, 182–92, 196–7, 199–200, 247
The Age, 68, 72, 112, 174, 177, 190, 207, 233, 342, 364
Ahmanson Theatre, Los Angeles, 384
Alastair (Baron Hans Henning Voigt), 341
Albery, Donald, 98
Albright, Madeleine, 376
Alexandra, Princess, 356

Alice in Wonderland (stage play), 60
Allsop, Madge
   abused by Jack Palance, 327
   appears on *Phil Donahue Show*, 329
   in *A Load of Olde Stuffe*, 176
   in Amnesty International gala, 244
   in Buckingham Palace show, 385
   in *New Edna: The Spectacle*, 357
   in *The Dame Edna Experience*, 325
   leads house inspections, 332–3
   Perry shops for skirts for, 283
   played by Emily Perry, 282, 395
   played by Madeleine Orr, 239
   teased by BH, 373
Ally McBeal (television show), 380
ALP Club, 27, 29
Altman, Dennis, 190
American Theatre Wing, 377
Amnesty International, 243–4
Anatomical Anomalies and Medical Freaks (book), 127
Anderson, Doug, 340
Anderson, John, 69
Angry Penguins exhibition, 305–6
'Antique Harry', 172
Antrobus, John, 126, 146
Anyone for Denis? (revue), 278
Apollo Theatre, London, 211, 212
Ararat, 46
Archer, Jeffrey, 355–6
Archer, Robyn, 378
Armfield, Neil, 342

Armstrong, David, 63, 69
Armstrong-Jones, Antony, 301
Around the Loop (revue), 56, 58, 65
Arrow Theatre, Melbourne, 66, 101
art classes, Malvern, 20
Arthur, Bea, 326, 327
Artists for Whitlam campaign, 199
Arts Council of Great Britain, 87
Arts Society, 47
Ashcroft, Peggy, 95
Ashton, Tillie, 195
Aspel and Company (television show), 287
Aspel, Michael, 265, 287
Assembly Hall, Melbourne, 36–7, 82, 109
Assembly Hotel, Sydney, 62
Astley, Thea, 94
Astor building, Sydney, 268–9
At Least You Can Say You've Seen It (revue), 206–9
Atkinson, Rowan, 243
Atlantic City, 377
Auckland Light Opera Company, 70
Auden, WH, 194
An Audience with Dame Edna (television show), 261–4, 274–5, 280, 308
Austen, Tony, 144
Australia House, 102, 247, 341
Australia Post, 386
Australian, 147, 177, 190, 192, 225, 253, 340
Australian Bicentennial, 305, 308–9
Australian Bicentennial Authority, 305
Australian Cultural Elites (book), 190, 191
Australian Film Development Corporation, 182, 190, 197
Australian Film Institute Awards, 249–50
Australian Galleries, 93
The Australian Legend (book), 76
Australian Letters, 84
Australian National Gallery, 305–6
Australian Republican Movement, 376
The Australian Ugliness (book), 147
Australian Women's Weekly, 78, 106
Aznavour, Charles, 275

Back with a Vengeance (revue), 299–305, 358
Backstage restaurant, 221
Bacon, Francis, 132
Baddeley, William P, 217, 239
Bakewell, Joan, 184, 185–6, 217, 239, 340

Barber, John, 235
Barr, Roseanne, 373
Barret, Keith, 389
The Barry Crocker Show (television show), 156
Barry Humphries and Friends Back with a Vengeance (revue), 386–7, 389
Barry Humphries at Carnegie Hall (recording), 199
Barry Humphries' Book of Innocent Austral Verse, 131
Barry Humphries' Flashbacks (television show), 346–8
The Barry Humphries Scandals (television show), 163–7
The Barry Humphries Show (television show), 211–12
Barry Humphries' Treasury of Australian Kitsch (book), 266–8
Barry McKenzie Holds His Own (film), 197, 199–200
Bart, Lionel, 97–8, 106, 129, 137, 350
Barton, Mischa, 388, 389
Basinger, Kim, 264, 327
Bassey, Shirley, 378, 389
Bates, Alan, 297
Batey, Peter, 42, 45, 49, 52
Bath, Marquis of, 262
Baxter, Stanley, 262
Bazza McKenzie comic strip, 134–8, 150
BBC, 90, 150, 165–6, 216, 353
BBC Light Entertainment, 185
BBC Proms, 245
BBC Television, 163
BBC2, 212, 237
Beach Boys, 378
Beardsley, Aubrey, 19, 127
Beatles, 227
Beaton, Cecil, 132
Beaton, Graeme, 225
Beaumont, Hugh, 31
Beaverbrook, Lord, 136–7
Becker, Sue, 153
Beckett, Clarice, 180
Beckett, Samuel, 65, 67, 75, 101
Bedazzled (film), 150–1
The Bedsitting Room (play), 126, 132
Bee Gees, 227, 234, 388
Bell, George, 20
Bell, Madeleine, 262

INDEX

Bennett, Alan, 120, 244
Bennetts, Don, 72, 73–4, 249, 250
Bentley, Dick, 112, 186
Bepraisements (book), 340–1
Beresford, Bruce
   agrees to film sequel, 197
   BH phones re Bazza character, 156
   directs *Adventures of Barry McKenzie*, 182–3, 187, 192, 254
   directs film on Sandy Stone, 207
   directs prime minister, 353
   friendship with BH, 175
   makes *The Getting of Wisdom*, 297
   meets BH, 149–50
   profits from *Adventures of Barry McKenzie*, 196
   provides inspiration for Martin Agrippa, 155
   returns to UK to make film, 200
   shocked by response to Bazza films, 199–200
   suggests Bazza film to BH, 150
Bergner, Ruth, 94
Bergner, Yosl, 94
Berlin, Irving, 27
Berry, Alex, 17
Bertram, Paul, 186
Best, Elizabeth, 54
Betjeman, Sir John
   attends BH's wedding, 239
   BH dedicates anthology to, 131
   death, 306
   hosts *Time with Betjeman*, 255
   inscribes book to BH, 178
   invites BH to lunch, 105–6
   laughs at BH's song, 166
   love of Australia, 143
   on Sandy Stone, 111
   praises BH's work, 105
   provides reference for BH, 175
Betty Blokk Buster Follies (revue), 212
Beverly Comstock Hotel, 321–2
Beyond The Fringe (revue), 118, 119–20
Billington, Michael, 235, 302
Birch, Ric, 377–8
Bird, John, 120, 163, 243
Bird, Mrs (bookshop proprietor), 16
Bizarre (book), 127–9, 131, 218, 230
Bizarre (magazine), 126–7
Black Cap bar, Camden Town, 359
Black, Cilla, 301, 335

Blacklock, Wendy, 55, 56
Blackman, Barbara
   amused by Tony Austen character, 144
   BH gives recordings to, 102–3
   BH keen not to offend mother of, 203
   friendship with BH, 94
   gives birth to third child, 125
   member of the London Drift, 103–4
   returns to Australia, 166
   worries lest mother finds BH's book, 128
   writes poems for *Bizarre*, 127
Blackman, Barnaby, 125
Blackman, Charles
   BH gives recordings to, 102–3
   contributes to *Bizarre*, 127
   frequents Swanston Family Hotel, 68
   friendship with BH, 94
   gives BH copy of *Bizarre*, 126
   helps BH out after theft, 119
   member of the London Drift, 103–4
   mentioned in BH's sketch, 112
   moves to Highgate, 125
   returns to Australia, 166
   wins Helena Rubinstein scholarship, 93
Blewett, Neal, 341
Blundell, Graeme, 173–4
Boddy, Michael, 177
Boggs, Bill, 221
Bolton, Geoffrey, 254
Bolton, Michael, 389
Bonython Art Gallery, Sydney, 148
Booker, Christopher, 137
Booth Theatre, New York, 371, 373, 376
Boston, 377, 396
Bourke, Tony, 172
Bowen, Elizabeth, 318
Bowler, Anton, 73
Box Hill Hospital, 276
Boyd, Arthur
   competitiveness of, 93
   frequents Swanston Family Hotel, 68
   friendship with BH, 94
   marches in anti-nuclear protest, 99
   member of the London Drift, 103–4
   mentioned in BH's sketch, 112
   paints backdrop for *Love's Labour's Lost*, 74
   removes pubic hair from backdrop, 128
   signs anti-war petition, 148

Boyd, David, 68, 69
Boyd, Hermia, 68, 69
Boyd, Martin, 83
Boyd, Robin, 50, 147, 159
Boyd, Yvonne, 94, 103
The Boys in the Band (play), 220
BP Hit Parade (television show), 73
Brack, John, 39, 158–9, 267
Bradley, Dorothy, 80
Bragg, Melvyn, 211, 311, 340
Bramwell, Murray, 339
Brantley, Ben, 376
Braybrook, Margot, 161
Bremner, Rory, 336–7
Bridge, Peter, 162
Brisbane, Katherine, 177
Bristol Old Vic, 105
Britain, Ian, 201
British Erotic Print Society, 353
British Film Institute, 149
British Theatre Yearbook, 303
Bron, Eleanor, 120, 151
Brook, Peter, 31
Brooke-Taylor, Tim, 243
Brookes, Peter, 313
Brooks, Susan, 265
Brown, Bob, 202
Brown, Breckston, 4
Brown, Dorothy (Billie), 4, 11, 107
Brown, Elsie, 4, 12, 48, 193
Brown, Georgia, 98
Brown, Louisa *see* Humphries, Louisa
Brown, Tina, 324
Brown, Walter, 94
Bruce, Lenny, 120
Brunell, June, 52
Bublé, Michael, 384
Bulletin, 74, 177, 190, 207
Bunny, Rupert, 180
The Bunyip and the Satellite (pantomime), 71–5, 103
Burnett, Carol, 324
Burroughs, William, 78
Burstall, Betty, 69, 156
Burstall, Tim, 69, 143
bush ethos, 76
Bush, George W, 396
bush realism, 51

Cabaret (revue), 146
Cairns, Jim, 257
Caldwell, Zoe, 32, 33, 40, 44, 50, 101, 373
Call Me Madam (musical), 27
Call Me Madman! (revue), 27–30
Calwell, Arthur, 148
Camberwell Grammar School, 8, 14
Camberwell, Melbourne, 4–5
Camberwell South State School, 7
Campaign for Nuclear Disarmament, 99
Can We Talk? (television show), 297–8
Canberra Theatre, 159
Cantor, Arthur, 220, 225
Cantos (poems), 195
Capitol Theatre, Melbourne, 187
The Caretaker (play), 95
Carew, Elsie, 131
Cargher, John, 49, 58
Carlton and United Brewery, 187
Carlton, Mike, 254
Carnegie Hall, Melbourne, 199
Carson, Johnny, 295, 329
Carter, Graydon, 381
cartooning, 134–8
Casey, Richard, 29
The Caucasian Chalk Circle (play), 106
Cavendish, Lady Elizabeth, 106
Chaillet, Ned, 213
The Chairs (play), 82
Chapel of All Saints, Sedlec, 230
Chaplin, Charlie, 317
Charles, Prince of Wales, 143, 299, 324, 342, 353
Chase, Chevy, 327
Chateau Marmont, Los Angeles, 227
Chater, Gordon, 55, 56, 58, 60, 234
Chayefsky, Paddy, 220
A Cheery Soul (play), 124, 236, 342
Cher, 326, 327
Chetwode, Penelope, 106
Chicago, 377
Chifley, Ben, 148
The Children of the Dark People (Davison), 71
Christian Science Monitor, 223
Christie, Campbell, 36
Christie, Dorothy, 36
Christowel Street, Camberwell, 5
Chronicle, 370
Churchill, Winston, 130

INDEX

City Limits, 302
Clapton, Eric, 243, 378
Clark, David, 157
Clark, Manning, 130, 175, 190–1
Clarke, Ed, 180
Clarke, John, 184
Clarke, Marcus, 256
Cleese, John, 217, 243
Cleo, 249
Clinton, Bill, 370
Clinton, Hillary, 374
Clooney, George, 321
Cold War, 41
Coleman, Peter, 63, 111, 112
Collins, Joan, 296, 321, 369
Collins, Philip, 146
Collins St. 5 p.m. (painting), 39
Colony Club, London, 100, 118, 132
Comedy Theatre, London, 126, 132
Comedy Theatre, Melbourne, 207
Coming Out in the Seventies (book), 190
Commonwealth Games, 384–5
Commonwealth Literary Fund, 94, 175
Conder, Charles, 99, 149
Connery, Sean, 373
Conrad, Peter, 76, 337, 358
Cook, Peter
   acquires *Private Eye*, 134
   appears on *Can We Talk?*, 298
   death, 344
   drinking problem, 298
   in *Adventures of Barry McKenzie*, 183, 184, 185
   in *Bedazzled*, 150–1
   in *Beyond the Fringe*, 118, 120
   invites BH to write comic strip, 137
   listens to recordings of Sandy and Edna, 119
   offers BH season at The Establishment, 120–1
   offers BH stint in Soho club, 106
   opens Melbourne Comedy Festival, 298
   recommends BH for film role, 150
Cook, Wendy, 118
Cooper, Jilly, 295
Corbett, Ronnie, 301
Cornwall, 106–7
Corvo, Baron, 127
Council of Adult Education, 44
Counihan, Noel, 18

Country Women's Association, 47
Covell, Roger, 112–13
Coveney, Michael, 302–3, 357
Covington, Julie, 186
Coward, Noel, 31, 52
Cracknell, Ruth, 54
Creative Nation policy, 341
Crocker, Barry
   asks BH to appear in double act, 203–5
   difficulty in finding film roles, 200
   in *Adventures of Barry McKenzie*, 156–7, 182–3, 192–3, 196, 198
Crocodile Dundee (film), 296
cult of celebrity, 261, 264–5
Cusack, Cyril, 297
Cymbeline (play), 104

Dadaism, 18, 22, 24, 28, 77–8, 127, 369
Daily Mail, 122, 356
Daily Mirror, 190
Daily News, 222, 223
Daily Telegraph, 113, 179, 193, 235, 356
Dale, Jim, 351
Dali, Salvador, 22, 118, 326
Dally-Watkins, June, 178
Dame Edna and the Rise of Civilisation (book), 322–3
The Dame Edna Experience (television show), 276–7, 279–94, 321, 355, 359, 392
Dame Edna: My First Last Tour (revue), 396
Dame Edna: The Royal Tour (revue), 366–77
The Dame Edna Treatment (television show), 385–92
Dame Edna's Bedside Companion (book), 265
Dame Edna's Coffee Table Book, 216–19
Dame Edna's Hollywood (television show), 321–30, 372
Dame Edna's Neighbourhood Watch (television show), 331–6
Daoust, Phil, 358
Daubeny, Peter, 211
d'Aurevilly, Barbey, 127
David Jones, 178
Davidson, Ian
   accompanies BH to New York, 372
   attempts to locate BH, 163
   attends BH's wedding, 239
   co-writes scripts with BH, 164, 212
   directs *Isn't It Pathetic At His Age*, 229

helps BH adapt show for US, 220
Davidson, Ian (*continued*)
  on set for *Dame Edna's Hollywood*, 325
  replaced by new writers, 389
  writes for *Dame Edna Experience*, 284
  writes for *Neighbourhood Watch*, 331
Davidson, Jim, 199, 339–40
Davidson, Rodney, 26
Davies, Russell, 336
Davis, Carl, 244, 245
Davison, Frank Dalby, 71
Daws, Lawrence, 83, 89, 93
de Jongh, Nicholas, 336, 357
de Sade, Marquis, 127
de Valois, Dame Ninette, 128
Deasey, Denison, 84
DeCaro, Frank, 372
Dekyvere, Nola, 54
Delmont Private Hospital, 172
The Demon Barber (musical), 90–1, 92
Denver, 377
Denzil (pianist), 104
The Desert Song (operetta), 56–7, 282
Design for Living (play), 52
Detroit, 377
Detroit Motors, 17
Diana, Princess of Wales, 299
Dickens, Charles, 97
Dickerson, Robert, 202
Dimboola (play), 156, 309
Disney (film studio), 330
Dobell, William, 267
Docker, John, 190, 191
Dominique (au pair), 141
Donahue, Phil, 328–9
Donaldson, Ian, 90, 96
Donen, Stanley, 150–1
Donovan, Gerry, 54
Don's Party (play), 189
Don't Look Now (film), 194
Douglas, Lord Alfred, 164
Dr Fischer of Geneva (film), 297
drag acts, 359, 367–8, 372–3
the Drift, 69–70
Drummond, Sir John, 306
Drysdale, Russell, 267
du Maurier, Daphne, 346
Duchamp, Marcel, 118
Duckmanton, Talbot, 255

Duckworth, Eric, 54
Duke of Wellington hotel, 104
'Dunmoochin' (house), 71, 114, 158
Dunstan, Don, 257, 338
Dunstan, Keith, 24, 190, 295
Dutton, Geoffrey, 175, 190, 191, 340

Eastern Hill Theatre, 70
Eder, Richard, 224–5, 371
Edinburgh Fringe Festival, 119
Edna (mother's help), 3, 7, 12
Edna Time (television show), 329
Elek, Paul, 127
Elektra (ballet), 128
Eliot, TS, 61
Elizabeth II, 276, 290, 374, 393
Elizabethan Theatre Trust, 44
Elliott, Margaret *see* Fink, Margaret
Ellis, Jacqueline, 126
The Elocution of Benjamin Franklin (play), 155, 234
Eltham, Victoria, 71, 158
Embers Supper Club, Melbourne, 157
EMI Records, 36–7
Encounter, 36
The Establishment Club, 120–2, 126, 137, 225, 280
An Evening's Intercourse with the Widely Liked Barry Humphries (revue), 265–6
Everage, Edna
  appears at Buckingham Palace, 385
  appears at Commonwealth Games, 384–5
  appears at football grand final, 383–4
  appears at Wangaratta Festival, 74
  appears in advertisements, 310
  appears in *Ally McBeal*, 380
  appears in *Harpers & Queen*, 196
  appears in Queen's Jubilee Concert, 378
  appears on *Can We Talk?*, 321
  appears on inaugural HSV7 broadcast, 60
  appears on *Late Night From Two*, 265
  appears on Michael Parkinson's show, 266
  appears on *Phil Donahue Show*, 328–9
  appears on postage stamp, 386
  appears on *Startime*, 113–14
  appears on *The Six O'Clock Show*, 265
  appears on *Women's Hour*, 305
  appears with Independent Theatre, 64–5
  as an interviewer, 283, 288–90, 390–2

INDEX

attends Melbourne Cup, 177
attends Royal Ascot races, 216
BH and Batey develop character, 49
BH guards closely, 179
BH makes short episodes for ABC, 91
BH on, 237
BH plans to mothball, 90
blueprint for, 37–8
celebrity status, 261, 263, 310
compares herself to Margaret Thatcher, 263–4
conducts audience sing-alongs, 145, 272
costumes become more elaborate, 334–5
criticises BH at L'Escargot, 248
discovers Jewish roots, 376
enjoys success in UK, 210–11
finds new Madge Allsop, 282
first clothes, 51
first performances, 49–52
gains following in Australia, 123
has gowns designed, 216, 281–2, 286
holds barbecue on stage, 271–2
holds press conference in Hollywood, 323
humour of, 258–9
impersonated by Rory Bremner, 336–7
in *A Load of Olde Stuffe*, 177
in *A Nice Night's Entertainment*, 109–10
in *A Night With Dame Edna*, 234–6
in America, 220–6, 321–30, 366–77
in *An Audience with Dame Edna*, 261–4, 274–5, 280, 308
in *At Least You Can Say You've Seen It*, 206, 207
in *Back with a Vengeance*, 301–4
in *Barry Humphries and Friends Back with a Vengeance*, 387
in *Barry Humphries' Flashbacks*, 346–8
in BH's Christmas card, 269
in *Dame Edna: My First Last Tour*, 396
in *Dame Edna: The Royal Tour*, 366, 369–77
in *Dame Edna's Hollywood*, 321–30, 372
in *Dame Edna's Neighbourhood Watch*, 331–6
in *Excuse I*, 143, 144
in *Housewife Superstar!*, 211–13, 215–16, 219, 220–6, 363, 371
in *Isn't It Pathetic At His Age*, 230, 233
in *Just a Show*, 153–4, 157
in *La Dame aux Gladiolas*, 237–8
in *Last Night of the Poms*, 245–8

in *Look At Me When I'm Talking To You*, 339–40
in *New Edna: The Spectacle*, 353–8, 360
in *Remember You're Out*, 373
in *Sergeant Pepper's Lonely Hearts Club Band*, 227
in *Tears Before Bedtime*, 269–73, 295
in *The Adventures of Barry McKenzie*, 186, 191–2, 247
in *The Barry Humphries Scandals*, 164
in *The Dame Edna Experience*, 276–7, 280, 281–94
in *The Dame Edna Treatment*, 385–92
in *The Naked Bunyip* (film), 173–4
in *The Secret Policeman's Other Ball*, 243–4
in *The Two Bazzas*, 204
interviewed by Melvyn Bragg, 311–12
Jane Hamilton designs hat for, 215–16
muted reception at The Establishment, 121–2, 225
opens art exhibition, 306
opinion of *Neighbours*, 309
opinion of Sydney Opera House, 64
parodies Margaret Thatcher, 276–9
passes out gladioli, 144–5, 272
performs in royal gala charity preview, 299
performs *Song of Australia*, 245, 246, 250, 252–3
portrait of by Brack, 158–9
publishes *Coffee Table Book*, 216–19
reads at poetry festival, 194–5
receives damehood from Whitlam, 197–8
receives keys to city of Melbourne, 386
rings talk show host, 319
scrupulous about staying in character, 305, 306
seen as a drag act in US, 223
shops for dresses, 183
skill at improvising, 80
subverts BH, 311–12
Thatcher caricatured as, 312–13
upsets Hispanic community, 380–2
Vanity Fair publishes photo of, 324
visits Stratford-upon-Avon, 281
writes for *Vanity Fair*, 380–2
writes sharp letter to Harry Miller, 192
Everett, Kenny, 239
Excuse I: Another Nice Night's Entertainment (revue), 138, 140–5

Eyre, Ronald, 243
Eyres, Harry, 303

Fadden, Arthur, 148
Fairbanks, Douglas Jr, 291, 292
Fairmont Royal York Hotel, Toronto, 377
Fantoni, Barry, 137
Farrow, Mia, 217
Faust, Beatrice, 69
The Female Eunuch (book), 288
Fennessey, Desmond, 138–9
Fenton, James, 248
Ferguson, Mrs ('Fergie'), 12
Ferrier, Noel, 37, 49–52
Festival Ballet, 100
Field, Charles, 230
Film '72, 184
Financial Times, 248
Finch, Peter, 112
Fings Ain't Wot They Used T'Be (musical), 92–3, 97
Fink, Leon, 160
Fink, Margaret (née Elliott)
  affair with BH, 62–3, 65, 68, 81
  BH visits in Toorak, 160
  visits BH at Gazebo Hotel, 175
Finn, Tim, 296
Firbank, Ronald, 127
Firehouse Gallery, London, 379
Fisher, Diana, 178
Fitton, Doris, 64
Fitts, Clive, 187
Fitzgerald, F. Scott, 33
Fitzgerald, Ross, 172–3, 175, 183, 208
Fitzgibbon, Smacka, 266
Fitzpatrick, Brian, 69
Fitzroy Gardens, Melbourne, 387–8
Fitzroy, Melbourne, 19
Flint, Mrs (teacher), 3, 7
The Floating World (play), 204
Flockhart, Calista, 380
Fonda, Jane, 291
Foot, Michael, 300
Fort Lauderdale, 377, 396
Fortune, John, 120
Fortune Theatre, London, 162
Foster, David, 368
Fox (broadcasting company), 329
Frampton, Peter, 227

Franklin, Aretha, 395
Franklin River, 202
Fraser, Malcolm, 252–3
Fraser, Tamie, 253
free love, 69
French, Leonard, 68, 103, 166
Froome, Alan, 96

Gabor, Zsa Zsa, 289, 326
Gaddafi, Colonel, 290
Gaiety Theatre, Dublin, 303
Gambon, Michael, 126, 287, 291
Garbo, Greta, 227
Garland, Caroline, 306
Garland, Judy, 227
Garland, Nicholas
  acknowledged in film credits, 185
  attends BH's wedding, 239
  draws *Adventures of Barry McKenzie*, 134–5, 137–8
  draws BH, 136
  drinks bleach unwittingly, 306–7
  embarrassed by BH at lunch, 193–4
  pays tribute to BH, 340–1
  receives OBE, 345
Garrett, Ian, 37
Gascoigne, Bamber, 122
Gatliff, Violet (née Brown), 10
Gatliff, Wilfred, 10–11
Gay Mardi Gras, Sydney, 308, 368
Gazebo Hotel, Sydney, 175
Geach, Portia, 269
Geelong Grammar, 143, 209
Geidt, Jeremy, 120
Geldof, Bob, 243
Genesis (band), 146
Gere, Richard, 369
The Getting of Wisdom (book), 150
The Getting of Wisdom (film), 197, 200, 297
Gibb, Barry, 388
Gibb, Robin, 388
Gibson, Mel, 292, 326
Gielgud, Sir John, 31
Gilmore, Dame Mary, 267
Ginsberg, Allen, 194
Glasgow Comedy Festival, 395
Globe Theatre, London, 215
Gnatt, Paul, 70
Goldsworthy, Peter, 259
Golf Links Estate, Camberwell, 4, 5

INDEX

The Goon Show (radio show), 164
Goossens, Sir Eugene, 57–8, 64
Gorbachev, Mikhail, 290
Gordon, Adam Lindsay, 268
Gore-Langton, Robert, 358
Gorham, Kathleen, 60
Gorton, John, 148, 182
Gotham Book Mart, 118
Graham, Colin, 90
Grant, Bruce, 68, 72
Grant, Mr (Whizzer), 18
Grassby, Al, 253, 257
Gray, Dulcie, 58
The Great McCarthy (film), 199
Greed, Albert, 18
Greene, Graham, 297
Greenway, Francis, 55
Greer, Germaine
    appears on *Dame Edna Experience*, 287–8
    BH models character on, 176
    contributes to BH tribute, 340
    Edna Everage as mentor of, 374
    helps BH mount exhibition, 77, 78
    Les Patterson on, 255
    member of the Drift, 69
Grissold, Joy, 92, 296
Gross, John, 358
Groucho Club, London, 318
Groves, Murray, 110
Grundy, Reg, 196–7, 200
Gstaad, 343, 379
Guardian, 235, 358
Guthrie, Tyrone, 220

Haas, Elsa, 180
Hagman, Larry, 326
Hairspray (musical), 371
Hall, Arsenio, 328
Hall, Jerry, 286–7
Hall, Sir Peter, 104
Hall, Sandra, 190
Hamilton, George, 327
Hamilton, Jane, 183, 215
Hannan, Senator, 190
Hardwicke, Elizabeth, 131
Harpers & Queen, 196
Harris, Donald, 152
Harris, Frank, 127
Harris, Max, 111, 112, 181–2

Harris, Rolf, 234, 254, 301
Harrison, Rex, 130
Harry, Deborah, 389
Harty, Russell, 210–11, 283
Hatfield, Hurd, 344
Hawke, Bob, 219, 252–3, 255–6, 298
Hawke, Hazel, 253
Hayek, Salma, 381, 382
Hayward Gallery, London, 305–6
Healesville, 10
Healey, Denis, 275
Healey, Edna, 275
Hearn, Lafcadio, 127
Heath, Edward, 287, 291
Hemingway, Mariel, 262
Henderson, Gerard, 365
Henry, Lenny, 378
Her Majesty's Theatre, Melbourne, 56, 208
Her Majesty's Theatre, Sydney, 229
Herald, 67–8
Herald and Weekly Times, 141
Hesketh-Harvey, Kit, 355
Heston, Charlton, 283, 289, 292, 369
Hibberd, Jack, 156, 309
Hind, John, 365
Hindemith, Paul, 17
Hinze, Russ, 215
His Excellency (play), 35–6
Hitchcock, Alfred, 346
HM Tennent group, 31
Hoad, Brian, 177, 207–8
Hocking, Cliff
    asks BH to do one-man show, 105
    attends BH's Broadway preview, 373
    BH breaks with, 162
    BH meets Bill Walker through, 129
    BH paranoid about, 151
    books theatres for BH's show, 112
    caricatured by BH, 154
    faith in BH, 138
    organises Australian tour, 138
    refuses to cancel show, 159
Hogan, Paul, 186, 236, 296, 309
Holland, John, 122
Hollingworth, Peter, 379
Hollinrake, Ian, 180
Holloway, Laurie, 285
The Hollowtones (band), 285
Hollywood, 321–30

Hollywood Reporter, 327–8
Holt, Harold, 80, 149, 346
Holy Trinity Church, Thornbury, 4
homosexuality, 155
Hone, Mr (principal), 21
Hong Kong, 215, 351–3
Hooton, Harry, 62, 63, 68, 69
Horace, 258
Horsey, Martin, 97
Horsnell, Michael, 248
Hossack, Rebecca, 341–2
The Hostage (play), 92
Hotel Australia, Sydney, 58
Hotter, Hans, 64
Houdini, Harry, 395
Housewife Superstar! (revue), 211–16, 220–6, 363, 371
Howard, John, 386
Howard, Maggie, 292
Howerd, Frankie, 120
HSV7, 60
Hughes, Billy, 148
Hughes, Graeme, 25, 28, 112
Hughes, Meryl, 113
Humperdinck, Engelbert, 389
Humphries, Barbara Helen (BH's sister)
  attends BH's school play, 19
  attends BH's wedding, 48
  birth, 7
  closeness to BH as a child, 10
  distressed by uncle's death, 11
  enjoys holidays at Healesville, 10
  farewells BH on trip to England, 183
  finds mother in distressed state, 12
  greets BH in London, 87
  intrigued by BH's performances, 26
  lives close to mother, 193
  tells BH of mother's illness, 276
  travels to Europe, 81
Humphries, Barry
  as a performer (*see also* Everage, Edna; Patterson, Les; Stone, Sandy)
    accused of misanthropy and racism, 257–8, 381–2
    accused of misogyny, 360
    accused of ruthlessness, 363–4
    acts in O'Shaughnessy's productions, 36–8
    American tours, 220–6, 321–30, 366–77, 380–2, 396
    appears in first feature film, 150–1
    appears in own television program, 261–4
    appears in Queen's Jubilee Concert, 378
    appears on inaugural HSV7 broadcast, 60
    appears on *Startime*, 113, 123
    appears on *Time with Betjeman*, 255
    appoints Rosencrantz as producer, 283–5, 290–3
    audience member dies during show, 229
    auditions for Royal Shakespeare Company, 104–5
    Australian tours, 108–14, 138, 140–5, 152–9, 176–9, 202–9, 228–33, 250, 259–60, 269–73, 295, 336–41, 385–7, 389
    chastised by O'Shaughnessy, 88
    comparison of characters, 232–3
    creates Basil Clissold, 56
    creates Brian Graham, 154–5, 157, 176
    creates Craig Foxcroft, 259–60
    creates Craig Steppenwolf, 208
    creates Daryl Dalkeith, 338
    creates Dr Aaron Azimuth, 23
    creates Dr Wendy Toole, 176
    creates Edna Everage, 49–52
    creates furore with 'True British Spunk', 164–6, 185
    creates Lance Boyle, 230–1, 295
    creates Les Patterson, 202–5
    creates Lionel Hunter, 155
    creates Martin Agrippa, 155, 162, 176
    creates Morrie O'Connor, 206–7
    creates Neil Singleton, 143–4
    creates Neville Creamer, 207
    creates Rex Lear, 156, 157, 162
    creates Roger A Nunn, 230
    creates Sandy Stone, 75–6
    creates Tid, 59
    creates Wreckem, 268
    critical acclaim in London, 234–6, 302–4
    critical acclaim in New York, 374–6
    difficulty finding work in London, 89–90, 93–4, 95–6
    difficulty in stopping performance, 317
    disappointed by London reception, 363
    early performances, 8, 10

establishes himself with British
    audiences, 236–8
experiments with recording, 19–20
first television appearances, 72–3
forced to cancel engagements, 395
gives interviews in Australia, 178–9
helped by Charles Osborne, 87
hones cabaret skills, 60
impromptu performance in pub, 46–7
improvises at parties, 69
in *A Kayf Up West*, 132–3
in *A Load of Olde Stuffe*, 176–7
in *A Nice Night's Entertainment*, 108–14, 120–2
in *A Night With Dame Edna*, 234–6
in *An Audience with Dame Edna*, 261–4, 274–5, 280, 308
in *An Evening's Intercourse with the Widely Liked Barry Humphries*, 265–6
in *At Least You Can Say You've Seen It*, 206–9
in *Back with a Vengeance*, 299–305
in *Barry Humphries and Friends Back with a Vengeance*, 386–7, 389
in *Barry Humphries' Flashbacks*, 346–50
in cast of *The Late Show*, 163
in *Dame Edna: My First Last Tour*, 396
in *Dame Edna: The Royal Tour*, 366–77
in *Dame Edna's Hollywood*, 321–30, 372
in *Dame Edna's Neighbourhood Watch*, 331–6
in *Excuse I*, 138, 140–5
in *Housewife Superstar!*, 211–16, 220–6, 363, 371
in *Isn't It Pathetic At His Age*, 229–33
in *Just a Show*, 148, 152–9, 162
in *La Dame aux Gladiolas*, 237–8
in *Last Night of the Poms*, 244–8
in *Les Patterson Saves the World*, 295–6
in *Look At Me When I'm Talking To You*, 336–41, 343
in *Maggie May*, 129
in *New Edna: The Spectacle*, 353–8, 360
in *Oliver!*, 97–100, 104, 106, 107, 146, 350–1, 377
in *Percy's Progress*, 199
in *Pygmalion*, 70
in *Remember You're Out*, 373
in *Rock 'n' Reel Revue*, 78–80, 268

in *Side By Side*, 200
in *Sir Les and the Great Chinese Takeaway*, 351–3
in *Tears Before Bedtime*, 255–7, 259–60, 269–73, 295
in *Terra Australis*, 32–3
in *Testimonial Performance*, 82–3
in *The Adventures of Barry McKenzie*, 182–7, 190–2
in *The Barry Humphries Scandals*, 163–7
in *The Barry Humphries Show*, 211–12
in *The Bedsitting Room*, 126, 132
in *The Bunyip and the Satellite*, 71–5
in *The Dame Edna Experience*, 276–7, 279, 280, 281–94, 321, 355, 392
in *The Dame Edna Treatment*, 385–92
in *The Demon Barber*, 90–1, 92
in *The Merry Roosters Panto*, 132
in *The Olympic Follies*, 60
in *The Secret Policeman's Other Ball*, 243–4
in *Treasure Island*, 146
in *Waiting for Godot*, 65, 66–8, 74
interviewed by Melvyn Bragg, 311
invited to perform on Broadway, 371
judge on audition panel for *I'd Do Anything*, 395–6
lack of training, 38
Lahr writes book on, 322–3, 365
lambasted by Australian critics, 363–6
makes *Edna Time*, 329
North American tour of *Oliver!*, 116–19
performs at fundraiser in Holt residence, 80
performs at The Establishment, 120–2, 126, 225, 280
performs in school drama, 19
performs *Song of Australia*, 245, 246, 250, 252–3
Pravda's advice to, 52
pre-performance nerves, 98, 116, 121, 152, 228, 293
profits from *Adventures of Barry McKenzie*, 196
reception in US, 222–6, 327–8, 329–30
records at Carnegie Hall, 199
satire of, 92–3, 257–8, 364, 368–9, 380–1
savaged by Cyril Pearl, 157
savaged by London critics, 162, 356–8

Humphries, Barry
  as a performer (*see also* Everage, Edna; Patterson, Les; Stone, Sandy) (*continued*)
    shocked by NBC executives, 324
    stage versus television, 293–5
    stages *Call Me Madman!*, 27–30
    strained relations with Harry Miller, 184
    street performances, 25–7, 28, 38–40
    takes Edna to Hollywood, 321–30
    teasing of the audience, 47, 270–3
    tours UK and Ireland, 396
    transition to television, 261–6
    tries new genre, 331–2
    unsure about one-man show, 105
    upsets Hispanic community, 380–2
    wins BAFTA award, 280
    wins comedy award, 235
    wins Tony Award, 377
    with Phillip Street Theatre, 53, 54–61, 64–5
    with Union Theatre Repertory Company, 31–7, 44–53
    works up cabaret act, 100
    wounded by criticism, 259
  as a songwriter
    adapts 'All Things Bright and Beautiful', 153–4
    adapts 'My Favourite Things', 142
    co-writes *Song of Australia*, 245, 246, 250
    writes 'A Woman's Woman', 216–17
    writes 'Ditty of Denial', 369–70
    writes 'Don't Cry for Me Australasia', 238
    writes 'Drop the Bomb', 108
    writes song for *Isn't It Pathetic*, 229
    writes 'Terribly Well', 195–6
    writes 'That's What My Public Means To Me', 264–5
    writes 'Too Drunk To Dance', 163–4
    writes 'True British Spunk', 164–6
    writes 'War Saving Street Song', 109
    writes 'Why Do We Love Australia?', 246–7
  as a writer
    addresses National Press Club, 228
    begins script for Bazza musical, 150
    contract with *The Age* cancelled, 174
    correspondence from Switzerland, 344
    early skill with language, 8
    joins board of *Quadrant*, 201
    knowledge of the vernacular, 354
    language of Bazza McKenzie, 188–9
    launches book of verse, 160
    produces radio programs, 11
    receives Literary Fund Fellowship, 175
    takes break to write in Cornwall, 106–7
    works on script for *Barry McKenzie*, 175
    writes *A Night With Dame Edna*, 234
    writes about London, 102
    writes 'Australians in London', 102
    writes *Bizarre*, 127–9, 131, 218, 230
    writes *Book of Innocent Austral Verse*, 131–2
    writes children's book, 184
    writes comic strip in *Private Eye*, 134–8, 150
    writes *Dame Edna's Bedside Companion*, 265
    writes *Dame Edna's Coffee Table Book*, 216–19
    writes 'Dear Beryl' monologue, 82
    writes for the *Australian*, 147
    writes for *Vanity Fair*, 380–2
    writes for *Vogue*, 102
    writes 'In Terms of My Natural Life', 256
    writes 'Lizard of Oz', 168
    writes *More Please*, 317, 318, 319, 322, 336
    writes *My Life As Me*, 317–18, 355
    writes *Neglected Poems and Other Creatures*, 320–1
    writes poem for undergraduates, 251
    writes 'Sandy Agonistes' monologue, 92
    writes 'Sandy Soldiers On', 231–2
    writes scripts for *Just A Show*, 152
    writes sketches with O'Shaughnessy, 82
    writes 'The Stranger in the Princess Louise', 102
    writes *The Traveller's Tool*, 354
    writes threnody for Patrick White, 320–1, 350
    writes *Treasury of Australian Kitsch*, 266–8
    writes 'Welcome Back, Mate', 259–60
    writes *Women in the Background*, 343, 345–6

INDEX

as an artist
 collects Conder paintings, 149
 early skill at drawing, 8
 exhibits at school, 18
 exhibits at university, 24, 25
 exhibits at Victorian Artists' Society, 77–8
 exhibits in Myer Mural Hall, 148
 frequents galleries in London, 95
 interest in Dadaism, 18, 22, 24, 77–8, 127, 369
 invites artists to school, 18
 makes film *Le Bain Vorace*, 26
 opens Dickerson exhibition, 202
 opens exhibition of women artists, 180
 paints at Mornington, 13
 paints caricatures of politicians, 148
 paints watercolours, 17

opinions and beliefs
 on Australia, 114
 on Australians in London, 102–3
 on Canada, 116
 on critics, 228–9
 on his schooldays, 320
 on New York, 117–18
 on ockers, 186
 on Sydney, 57, 59
 on television, 185
 on treatment of artists, 58

personal life
 ability to redirect negative energy, 319–20
 anarchic driving, 132
 appearance, 19, 23, 38, 61, 99, 152, 163, 178
 becomes a father, 125
 becomes part of the Drift, 69–70
 belief in Father Christmas, 35
 birth, 6
 black sense of humour, 55, 56–7, 61, 128
 buys flat in the Astor, 268–9
 celebrates 60th birthday, 340–1
 competition between friends in London, 93
 cringes at expatriate Australians, 91, 100–1
 cultivates the influential and famous, 149
 decides to move to England, 80
 defends length of hair, 16
 desire for fame, 8
 disturbed by mother's illness, 12
 early love of theatre, 12
 expelled from Old Melburnians, 26
 explores London, 95
 extra-marital affairs, 62–4, 305, 307
 falls out with Clifton Pugh, 158
 fascination with the grotesque, 127–8, 131, 230
 fear of physical aggression, 61
 finds a flat in London, 87
 finds bicentennial celebrations excessive, 308, 309
 friendship with John Betjeman, 105–6
 friendship with Peter Cook, 118
 friendship with Peter O'Shaughnessy, 34–5, 88–9, 104–5
 friendship with the Blackmans, 103
 friendships at school, 15
 grieves over mother's death, 275–6
 has appendectomy, 394–5
 has contents of car stolen, 119
 has face dipped in sauce, 13
 holidays at Mornington, 13
 implores wife to refuse ballet role, 100
 insists son check into clinic, 378
 invites Prince Charles to dinner, 324
 judge in Miss North Shore competition, 178
 knits at football games, 16–17
 lives at Rembrandt Hotel, 57
 lives in Lang Road, 57
 loathing for sport, 8, 15–16, 209, 347
 London residences, 91, 99–100, 125, 140, 274, 310
 loses university scholarship, 36
 love for Healesville house, 11
 love of music, 17, 20, 27, 34, 64
 love of objets d'art, 140
 love of reading, 13, 19, 20
 lunches with Dulcie Gray, 58
 marches in anti-nuclear protest, 99
 meets Bruce Beresford, 149–50
 military service, 41–3
 mortgages flat to buy painting, 160
 moves out of parental home briefly, 37
 moves to Hollywood, 321–2

435

Humphries, Barry
  personal life (*continued*)
    musical soireés at parental home, 20, 37
    nicknames, 8
    opens 'Barry's Shoppe', 9
    particularity with food, 13
    perambulations around Fitzroy, 19
    personal insecurities, 311–12
    plays pranks on the unsuspecting, 22–6, 38–40, 42–3, 46, 52, 92, 104, 128, 129–30, 193–4, 248, 293, 306–7, 388
    political affiliations, 148, 199, 201–2
    poses nude for *Cleo*, 249
    pre-school years, 6–7
    receives CBE, 392
    receives Order of Australia, 249
    recuperates at Byron Bay, 395
    relationship with Brenda Wright, 48–9, 60, 81, 307, 345
    relationship with Diane Millstead, 209–10, 238–9, 296–7, 307, 310–11, 317
    relationship with Lizzie Spender, 36, 318
    relationship with parents, 13–14
    relationship with Rosalind Tong, 70–1, 74–5, 81–2, 95, 99–100, 103, 122, 136, 138, 147, 149, 159, 161, 166–7, 171, 179–80, 196, 307
    remains neutral on the Vietnam War, 148
    returns home to Greencroft Gardens, 395
    robbed and bashed in Richmond, 171
    school days, 3–4, 7–8, 14–21, 320
    self-doubts, 20–1, 337
    sells Hampstead home, 310
    skill as a debater, 17
    spends New Year 2007 in Sydney, 394
    stays with the Pughs in Eltham, 158
    struggles with alcoholism, 96, 100, 103, 129–30, 138, 147–9, 151, 159–61, 171–3, 175, 192–3, 298
    suffers from greed, 317
    supports conservation campaigns, 268
    takes son to visit his mother, 319–20
    taunts people at parties, 61
    teaches at Sunday school, 11
    undergoes hypnotism, 147
    unhappy in Sydney, 57–9, 61–2
    university days, 22–31, 35–6
    visits Earls Court, 101
    wins anti-sport award, 295
    work precludes time for family, 294
    works at EMI, 36–7
    works at ice cream factory, 89
    worries about his mother, 193
  travels
    accident in Cornwall, 107
    American tours, 220–6, 321–30, 366–77, 380–2, 396
    Australian tours, 108–14, 138, 140–5, 152–9, 176–9, 202–9, 228–33, 250, 259–60, 269–73, 295, 336–41, 385–7, 389
    California, 209
    Cyprus, 163
    England (1959), 83–4
    England via Turkey, 146
    Hong Kong, 351–3
    Ireland, 343–4
    Los Angeles, 227
    Madeira, 234
    Melbourne to Sydney, 66
    Mexico, 152, 209
    New York, 119, 371
    New Zealand, 82
    Portugal, 351
    Prague, 185
    Sardinia, 343
    Snowdonia, 96
    Switzerland, 343, 344
    Vienna, 103
Humphries, Brenda (née Wright) (BH's first wife)
  divorces BH, 81
  gets black eye trying to help BH, 61
  invited to join Phillip Street Theatre, 53
  lives in Bondi with BH, 64
  meets and marries BH, 48–9
  on BH in retrospect, 345
  relationship with BH, 60, 307
  stays in Sydney after BH's departure, 66
Humphries, Christopher Charles (BH's brother), 9, 183
Humphries, Dick (BH's uncle), 10, 49
Humphries, Emily Sarah (BH's daughter), 140–1, 180, 209, 230, 244
Humphries, Jack (BH's grandfather), 4

INDEX

Humphries, John (BH's cousin), 10–11
Humphries, John Albert Eric (BH's father)
  as a builder, 4–5, 6–7, 268
  attends BH's school performances, 19
  attends BH's wedding, 48
  BH recalls in memoir, 318
  builds beach house at Mornington, 12–13
  builds BH a play shop, 9
  builds holiday shack at Healesville, 10, 11
  buys BH a cape, 8–9
  buys BH boxing gloves, 14
  buys tickets for BH's Melbourne show, 109
  collects BH for lunch each day, 7
  death, 187
  declines to see *Adventures of Barry McKenzie*, 187
  farewells BH on trip to England, 83, 183
  fetches BH home, 37
  gives BH six acres of land, 81
  lives in Christowel Street, 5–6
  love of nicknames, 9
  marries Louisa Brown, 4
  sends BH to Melbourne Grammar, 14
  shocked by BH's book, 129
  takes over cooking for family, 9
  tries to buy protrait of BH, 158
  unhappy about BH's wedding, 48
  unimpressed by BH's Dada performances, 26
  visited by grandchildren, 180
  worries about BH, 8, 21, 26, 36, 171, 173
Humphries, Lewis (BH's uncle), 83
Humphries, Louisa (née Brown) (BH's mother)
  attends BH's school performances, 19
  attends BH's second wedding, 81
  becomes reclusive, 187
  BH recalls in memoir, 318
  BH worries about, 193
  death, 275–6
  declines to see *Adventures of Barry McKenzie*, 187
  dips BH's face in sauce, 13
  farewells BH on trip to England, 83, 183
  gives birth to BH, 6
  gives birth to daughter, 7
  gives birth to second son, 9
  gives birth to third son, 12
  in family performances, 8
  marries Eric Humphries, 4
  nicknames, 9
  on shoes as an indicator of character, 271
  penchant for decorating, 6
  relationship with BH, 14
  relays conversations to BH, 11–12
  sees BH perform in Hong Kong, 215
  skill as a cook, 9
  suffers breakdown, 12
  takes children to theatre, 12
  unhappy about BH's wedding, 48
  unimpressed by BH's Dada performances, 26
  visited by grandson, 319–20
  worries about BH, 21, 26, 36, 171
Humphries, Michael Eric (BH's brother), 12, 48, 67, 183, 193, 215, 396
Humphries, Oscar Valentine (BH's son)
  attends BH's award of CBE, 392
  birth, 244
  complains about school, 344
  exhibits at Firehouse, 379
  holidays in Sardinia, 343
  in BH's Christmas card, 269
  lives in Los Angeles, 310, 321
  plans to settle in Australia, 379
  rivalry with brother, 343
  school days, 343
  skis in Switzerland, 344
  struggles with depression and alcohol, 378–9
  travels to Hong Kong, 351
  travels with parents, 297
  visits grandmother, 319–20
Humphries, Rosalind (née Tong) (BH's second wife)
  advises BH against using Edna, 121
  attempts reconciliation with BH, 166–7
  becomes an art dealer, 180
  begins dance lessons in London, 91
  BH plays trick on, 129–30
  co-writes scripts with BH, 72, 108, 141, 152
  colludes in BH's prank, 92
  decides to leave BH, 161
  decides to move to England, 80
  divorces BH, 179–80, 196
  endures BH's absences, 136, 138, 307

Humphries, Barry
 travels (*continued*)
  explores London with BH, 95
  finds work in London, 87, 89
  first pregnancy, 115
  gives birth to daughter, 125
  gives birth to second daughter, 140–1
  has accident in Cornwall, 107
  has difficulty getting US visa, 116–17
  helps BH mount exhibition, 77, 78
  holidays at Palm Beach, 75
  illness, 90, 140, 141, 161
  in *Rock 'n' Reel Revue*, 78–9
  marries BH, 81
  meets BH, 70–1
  moves to Highgate with BH, 99–100
  performs in lunch-hour revues, 74
  reassures BH after failure of show, 122
  returns to Australia with BH, 108–9
  second pregnancy, 138
  settles in Melbourne, 179–80
  shops in New York, 119
  stage manages *Excuse I*, 141
  stays with the Pughs in Eltham, 158
  suggests one-man show to BH, 105
  terrorised by louts, 118
  thinks BH hams it up, 98
  tires of noisy parties, 104
  travels to England (1959), 83–4
  travels to New Zealand with BH, 82
  trip to Snowdonia, 96
  turns down Festival Ballet role, 100
  worries about BH's drinking, 103, 147, 149, 159
Humphries, Rupert Cosmo (BH's son)
 attends BH's award of CBE, 392
 birth, 249
 holidays in Sardinia, 343
 in BH's Christmas card, 269
 lives in Los Angeles, 310, 321
 rivalry with brother, 343
 school days, 343
 travels to Hong Kong, 351
 travels with parents, 297
Humphries, Tessa Louise (BH's daughter), 125, 180, 244
Hunniford, Gloria, 265
Huston, Anjelica, 318
Huston, John, 318

Hutton, Geoff, 112, 177
Huysmans, Joris-Karl, 40, 127

Ibsen, Henrik, 95
I'd Do Anything (television show), 395
Idle, Eric, 200
Ifield, Frank, 262
Iglesias, Julio, 292
Imperial Theater, New York, 117
Independent (newspaper), 302
Independent Theatre, Sydney, 64, 74
Ingrams, Richard, 136–7
Institute of Commonwealth Studies, University of London, 254
Interview (magazine), 226
The Intruder (painting), 267
Ionesco, Eugene, 82, 95
Isherwood, Christopher, 35
Isn't It Pathetic At His Age (revue), 229–33
ITV, 90, 385, 387
Izzard, Eddie, 369

Jagger, Bianca, 286
Jagger, Mick, 286
Jago, June, 51
James, Clive, 232, 255, 265, 275, 283, 301
Jameson, Sue, 302
JC Williamson Ltd, 138
Jebb, Julian, 196, 237
Jensen, Mrs (teacher), 8
Jesus Christ Superstar (musical), 212
Jillett, Neil, 233
John, Augustus, 345
John, Elton, 369, 378
Johnston, Iain, 250
Johnston, Roma, 51
Jolley, Elizabeth, 340
Jones, Chad, 370
Jones, Tom, 378
Jong, Erica, 295
Jonson, Ben, 127
Joy Boys, 113
Just A Show (revue), 148, 152–9, 162
Juvenal, 258

Kahlo, Frida, 381, 382
Karpf, Anne, 336
Kath and Kim (television show), 330
Kauffmann, Bettine, 80

INDEX

A Kayf Up West (play), 132, 150
Keating, Paul, 256, 339, 347, 375
Keeler, Christine, 122
Kerouac, Jack, 118–19
Kerr, Graham, 164
Kerr, Sir John, 54, 350
Khashoggi, Octavia, 379
Kidman, Nicole, 374
King, Billie Jean, 209
King, Chloe, 379
King George V Hospital, Sydney, 244
King Lear (play), 104–5
King, Truby, 6
Kingston, Jeremy, 358
Kippax, HG, 157, 177, 233
Kissel, Howard, 223
Klim, Michael, 384
Kotcheff, Ted, 189
Krapp's Last Tape (play), 67
Kroll, Jack, 375

La Dame aux Gladiolas: The Agony and the Ecstasy of Dame Edna (television show), 237–8
La Mama collective, 156
La Sonnambula (opera), 95
Lahr, Bert, 236, 295
Lahr, James, 323
Lahr, John
  BH explains rationale of show to, 295
  contributes to BH tribute, 340
  Cook gives opinion of BH to, 118
  observes BH perform, 294
  on BH's humour, 391
  on why Edna confused Americans, 226
  reviews *The Royal Tour*, 375
  suffers loss of two sons, 322–3
  suggests BH to producer, 371
  writes book on BH, 322–3, 365
  writes essay on BH in *New Yorker*, 322–3, 324
  writes review of BH in *New Society*, 235–6
Lahr, Nicholas, 322–3
Landon, Avice, 185
lang, k.d., 390–2
The Last Night of the Poms (musical), 244–8, 347
Late Night From Two (television show), 265
The Late Show (television show), 163

Latham, Mark, 256
Latina (magazine), 381
Lawler, Ray, 44–53, 112, 192, 384
Laws, John, 113, 123, 339
Lawson, Henry, 74, 82–3
Le Bain Vorace (film), 26
Le Malade Imaginaire (play), 36–7
Le Moignan, Richard, 253
League of American Theatres and Producers, 377
Lee, Margo, 55
Leibovitz, Annie, 324
Leigh, Vivien, 31, 227
Lenska, Rula, 262
Les Patterson Has a Stand Up (revue), 352
Les Patterson Saves the World (film), 295–6
L'Escargot restaurant, 248
Letofsky, Irv, 327–8
Letterman, David, 328, 329, 375
Leunig, Michael, 185
Levi, John, 15, 19, 20
Lewinsky, Monica, 370
Lewis, Peter, 162
Liberace, 369
Liddle, JE, 131
Lilley, Chris, 257
Lindsay, Robert, 350
Lion, Margo, 371, 376
Listener-In (magazine), 51
Little Britain (television show), 389
Littlewood, Joan, 90, 92, 96, 132–3
Litvin, Natasha, 318
Livermore, Reg, 212
Llewellyn, Roddy, 233
Lloyd Webber, Andrew, 395
A Load of Olde Stuffe (revue), 176–7
Lola Montez (musical), 70
Lollobrigida, Gina, 292
London Broadcasting (magazine), 302
London Drift, 103–4
London Magazine, 87
London Palladium, 350
London Symphony Orchestra, 245, 246
London Weekend Television, 282, 290, 331, 359
Long, Sydney, 267
Longford, Lord, 182, 262
Longford Productions, 182, 197
Longford, Raymond, 182

Looby, Keith, 310
Look At Me When I'm Talking To You (revue), 336–41, 343
Los Angeles, 377, 396
Los Angeles Times, 381
Love's Labour's Lost (play), 48
Luard, Nick, 120, 122
Lucas, Matt, 389
Luck, Peter, 237
Lucky Jim (novel), 61
Lumley, Joanna, 261
Luna Park, 19, 23
Lundgren, Dolph, 287
Lygon Street, Carlton, 69
Lymburner, Francis, 91
Lynn, Vera, 164
Lyric Theatre, Hammersmith, 90
Lyttle, John, 336

Machen, Arthur, 127
Maclellan, Robert, 17
Macmillan, 184
Mad (magazine), 134
Madeira, 234
Maggie May (musical), 129
The Magic Forest (television show), 72
Malcolm, Noel, 313
'The Malouf Concerto', 24
Malouf, Mr (shop proprietor), 24
Mandarin Hotel, Hong Kong, 215
Manilow, Barry, 327, 373
Mann, Peter, 75, 82
Manning, Bernard, 298
Marcos, Imelda, 291–2
Margaret, Princess, 233
Marr, David, 364
Marshall, Alan, 94
Marx, Karl, 218
Mason, Iris, 176, 221, 224, 226, 230
Mason, Jackie, 375
Mason, James, 217, 297
Masters, Anthony, 248
Mathews, Race, 17
'matriduxy', 51
Matthew, Ray, 112
Maupin, Armistead, 301, 340
The Mavis Bramston Show (television show), 156, 348
May, Brian, 378

Mayfair Theatre, London, 234
McCartney, Paul, 275, 378
McClanahan, Rue, 327
McClellan, Dora, 81
McClelland, Doug, 256
McClelland, Robert, 190
McConnel, James, 355–6
McDonald, Garry, 236
McDonald, Roger, 347
McDowell, Malcolm, 291
MCG, 16, 383–4
McGrath, Mr (barber), 6
McGregor, Craig, 51, 129, 257–8, 363–4
McGuiness, PP, 190
McKellar, John, 54, 60
McKellen, Ian, 301
McMahon, Billy, 253
McMahon, Sonia, 177
McQueen, Humphrey, 309–10
Megastar Productions, 322
Melba Hall, Melbourne, 112, 141
Melba, Nellie, 145
Melbourne Comedy Festival, 298
Melbourne Cricket Ground, 16, 383–4
Melbourne Grammar School, 14–21, 320
Melbourne Theatre Company, 32, 210
Melbourne University, 22–31, 35–6
Meldrum, Max, 18
Meldrum, Molly, 253
Mendes, Sam, 350
Mendoza, Dot, 55
Menotti, Gian Carlo, 318
Menzies, Sir Robert, 110, 148, 216, 347
Meredith, Burgess, 327
Mermaid Theatre, London, 126
Merman, Ethel, 27
Merrick, David, 117
The Merry Roosters Panto, 132
Michael, Princess of Kent, 292
Michell, Keith, 59
Mike Walsh Show (television show), 346
Millais, John Everett, 160
Miller, George, 295
Miller, Harry M
   arranges follow-up tour for BH, 179
   contributes to BH's show, 175–6
   Edna writes sharp letter to, 192
   manages BH, 176

refuses to be BH's manager, 174
strained relations with BH, 184
Miller, Jonathan, 120, 287
Milligan, Spike, 126, 136–7, 142, 146, 184, 185
Millstead, Diane (BH's third wife)
accompanies son to hospital, 379
attends BH's television show, 261
birth of first son, 244
birth of second son, 249
collaborates with BH, 295–6
divorces BH, 310–11
entertains in Astor apartment, 269
exhibits in Paris, 238–9
holidays with BH in Madeira, 234
in BH's Christmas card, 248–9, 269
joins BH in New York, 225, 321
marriage to BH collapses, 296–7, 307
marries BH, 238–9, 317
meets BH, 209–10
moves to Hampstead with BH, 274
settles in Beverly Hills, 321
Minneapolis, 377
Minnelli, Liza, 290
Mirbeau, Octave, 127
Mitchell, David, 346
Mitchell, Warren, 301
Molière (Jean-Baptiste Poquelin), 36
Moncrieff, Gladys, 56
Montgomery, Field Marshal, 345
Monty Python (troupe), 225, 243
Moody, Ron, 97, 104, 107
Moon, Dr John, 172, 179
Moore, Dudley, 120, 151, 217
Moore, Gerald, 64
More Please (memoir), 317, 318, 319, 322, 336
More Pricks Than Kicks (short stories), 65
Morison, Elsie, 112
Morley, Lewis, 121, 163, 341
Morley, Pat, 341
Morley, Sheridan, 162, 302, 336, 357–8
Mornington, 12–13
Morven, Myrette, 89
Moses, Jack, 195
Moses, John, 253
Mouskouri, Nana, 289
Mr and Mrs (revue), 53, 55
Mrs Merton Show (television show), 389

Mulcahy, Lance, 54
Munch, Edvard, 222, 234, 290, 334
Munro, Colin, 25, 26, 76, 96
Munster Arms Gallery, Melbourne, 209
Murdoch, Iris, 295
Murdoch, Rupert, 225, 357
Murray, David, 229
Murray, John, 173, 182
Murray-Smith, Stephen, 190, 191
The Music Lesson (painting), 267
My Life As Me (memoir), 317–18, 355
Myer Emporium, 4, 33, 40
Myer Mural Hall, Melbourne, 148
Myers, Stanley, 150

The Naked Bunyip (film), 173–4, 182
Nathan, Robert, 20, 23
National Association of Hispanic Journalists, 381
National Council of La Raza, 381
National Press Club, Canberra, 228
National Times, 178, 257–8
NBC (television network), 321, 324–5
Neglected Poems and Other Creatures (poems), 320
Neighbours (television show), 309, 348
Nelsen, Don, 222–3
Nerman, Einar, 218
Nevin, Robyn, 236, 342
New Antipodean Singers, 252
New Edna: The Spectacle (revue), 353–8, 360, 364
New Society, 235, 322
New Theatre, Melbourne, 78
New York, 116–18, 119, 220, 222, 227, 371–6
New York (magazine), 375
New York Post, 223, 375
New York Times, 221, 224–5, 371, 372, 376
New Yorker, 223–4, 322, 324, 371
New Zealand Ballet Company, 152
Newell, Alannah, 127
Newell, John, 127
Newman Society, 29
Newsday, 327, 375
Newton, Edmund, 223
Newton-John, Olivia, 234
A Nice Night's Entertainment (revue), 108–14, 121–2

Nichols, Joy, 112
Nichols, Peter, 202, 296, 303, 340, 343
A Night on Mount Edna (television show), 292–3
A Night with Dame Edna (revue), 234–6, 381
Ninth Circle (bar), 118
Nolan, Sidney, 93, 112, 217
Norman, Frank, 132–3
Norton, Graham, 288
Norton, Rosaleen, 57
Number 96 (television show), 348
Nureyev, Rudolf, 291, 369

Oakland Tribune, 370
Oakley, Barry, 199
O'Brien, Edna, 295
Observer (newspaper), 190, 277, 302
ockerism, 236–7
O'Connor, Hazel, 262
The Office (television show), 330
Oh, What a Lovely War! (play), 133
Olander, Philip, 375
Old Melburnians, 26, 178
Oldaker, Max, 54, 56, 61, 87, 148
Oliver, Edith, 223–4
Oliver! (musical), 97–100, 104, 106–7, 116–19, 146, 341, 350–1, 377, 395–6
Olivier, Dame Joan Ann, 219
Olivier, Laurence Kerr, Baron Olivier, 12, 31, 95, 227, 336, 346
The Olympic Follies (television show), 60
Olympic Games, Melbourne (1956), 49, 60, 73
Olympic Games, Sydney (2000), 337–8, 377–8
Onassis, Jackie, 295
Ono, Yoko, 326
Orr, Bill, 53, 54, 55
Orr, Madeleine, 239, 282; *see also* Allsop, Madge
Osborne, Charles, 194, 213, 261
Osborne, John, 142, 344
Osbourne, Ozzy, 385
O'Shaughnessy, Brian, 68, 94, 99, 103
O'Shaughnessy, Caitlin, 64, 103
O'Shaughnessy, Peter
  appears in court for BH, 81
  attends BH's wedding, 48
  auditions for Royal Shakespeare Company, 104–5
  BH laments lack of satire to, 55
  BH misses, 58
  BH on Australia to, 114
  BH requests advice of, 121
  BH writes to, 57, 61, 63, 94–5, 98, 101, 117, 377
  chastises BH, 88
  criticises BH after show, 122
  decides to move to England, 80
  directs BH in *Le Malade Imaginaire*, 36–7
  directs BH in *Love's Labour's Lost*, 37
  directs BH in *Waiting for Godot*, 65–8
  encourages BH with Sandy Stone, 75
  joins Bristol Old Vic, 105
  moves to London, 103
  performs in *Pygmalion*, 70
  presents *Pygmalion*, 68
  presents *Waiting for Godot* in Sydney, 74
  produces lunch-hour revues, 74
  produces *Rock 'n' Reel Revue*, 78–80, 268
  produces *Testimonial Performance*, 82–3
  produces *The Bunyip and the Satellite*, 71–2
  recognises BH's talent for comedy, 52
  relationship with BH, 88–9, 105, 340
  tries to persuade BH to invest in show, 115
  works at Independent Theatre, 64
O'Shaughnessy, Red, 103
O'Shaughnessy, Sally, 103
O'Shaughnessy, Shirley, 48, 58, 64, 80, 103
Oxford Companion to Australian Literature, 364

Packer, Clyde, 187, 196
Packer, Kerry, 386
Page, Stanley, 46
Pakie's nightclub, Sydney, 62–3
Palance, Jack, 325–6
Parkinson, Michael, 265–6, 285
Parslow, Freddy, 36
Parslow, Joan, 39
Parton, Dolly, 369
Partridge, Alan, 389
Paton, George, 31
Patten, Sir Christopher, 353
Patterson, Les
  addresses Cambridge undergraduates, 250–1
  appears in Queen's Jubilee Concert, 378
  appears on *Can We Talk?*, 297–8

appears on Michael Parkinson's show, 266
appears on *Time with Betjeman*, 255
appears on *Touch of Elegance*, 348
becomes Sir Les, 249
character of, 233
created by BH, 202–5
debut in London, 212–15
develops cult following, 249
dines out at curry house, 250
in America, 221–2, 224
in *An Audience with Dame Edna*, 274–5
in *Back with a Vengeance*, 299–300, 302–3, 304
in *Barry Humphries and Friends Back with a Vengeance*, 386
in *Barry Humphries' Flashbacks*, 346, 347, 349–50
in 'Erotic Diplomacy', 353
in *Isn't It Pathetic At His Age*, 230
in *Les Patterson Has a Stand Up*, 352
in *Les Patterson Saves the World*, 295–6
in *Look At Me When I'm Talking To You*, 337–8, 339
in *New Edna: The Spectacle*, 356, 358
in royal gala charity preview, 299
in *Sir Les and the Great Chinese Takeaway*, 351–3
in *Song of Australia*, 252–4
in *Tears Before Bedtime*, 255–7, 295
introduces Australian Film Institute Awards, 249–50
narrates *Peter and the Shark*, 245
offers himself as Governor-General, 379–80
on Australia's international image, 255
opens ARSE, 254–5
opens Melbourne Comedy Festival, 298
presents 'Ode to Parky', 266
reacts to criticism of art exhibition, 305–6
receives doctorate from Cambridge, 250–1, 254
rises to prominence, 253–4, 257
writes *The Traveller's Tool*, 354
Patterson, Mrs (mother of Barbara Blackman), 203
Paul Morgan and Co, 296
Peacock, Andrew, 257
Pearl, Cyril, 112, 157

Perceval, John, 68, 103
Perceval, Mary, 103
Percy's Progress (film), 199
performance art, 27
Performing Arts Centre, Melbourne, 385
Perry, Emily, 282, 325, 389, 395; *see also* Allsop, Madge
Perry, John
   BH uses name of family business, 17
   exhibits with BH, 18, 77
   forms the Wubbos with BH, 24
   meets BH at school, 15
   performs with BH, 25, 28
   records skits with BH, 20
   visits BH at home, 20
Peter and the Shark, 245
Petrov Affair, 55
Philip, Prince, 299
Phillip Street Theatre, 53, 54–61, 64–5
Phillips, Stephen, 127
Phoenix, Arizona, 377
Phoenix Pub, Melbourne, 161
Picabia, Francis, 22
Picasso, Paloma, 295
Piccadilly Theatre, London, 234–5
The Picture of Dorian Gray (film), 344
Pigott-Smith, Tim, 291
Pinnell, Ron, 79–80
Pinter, Harold, 95
Playbox Theatre, Sydney, 176
Plowright, Joan, 219
Poetry International Festival, 194–5
Polanksi, Roman, 275
political satire, 55
Porter, Cole, 54
Porter, Peter, 88, 340
Portofino, Italy, 108
Pound, Ezra, 195
Pram Factory, Melbourne, 189, 204
Pravda, George, 52
Price, Dennis, 185
Princess Theatre, Melbourne, 167
Priscilla, Queen of the Desert (film), 368
Prisoner (television show), 348
Private Eye, 134, 136–8, 150, 193
Profumo, John, 122
Prowse, Richard, 186–7
Pryce, Jonathan, 341, 351
Puckapunyal army camp, 41–3

Pugh, Clifton
   BH takes Rosalind to house of, 71
   features in BH's book, 267
   helps BH mount exhibition, 77
   impressed with Rosalind Humphries, 141
   launched by Bryan Robertson, 93
   meets BH, 68
   member of the Drift, 69
   paints portrait of BH and Rosalind, 115
   paints portraits of BH, 78, 81, 84, 158
   sees change in BH, 158
   travels to Mexico, 141
   visited by BH at 'Dunmoochin', 114–15
   wedding present to BH, 81
Pugh, Marlene, 83, 114, 141
Punch, 302
Pygmalion (play), 68, 70

Quadrant (magazine), 201, 208, 258
Quatro, Suzi, 261
Queen's Jubilee Concert (2002), 378

Radic, Leonard, 253, 295, 339
Radio City Music Hall, 371, 372, 377
Ratcliffe, Michael, 302
Rattigan, Terence, 31
Ray, Man, 22
Reagan, Ron (son of Ronald), 291
Reagan, Ronald, 261, 282
Rebecca (film), 346
Record Mirror (magazine), 99
Reed, John, 80, 160
Reed, Rex, 223
Reed, Sunday, 80
Rembrandt Hotel, Kings Cross, 57
Remember You're Out (revue), 373
Rene, Roy, 257
Reno, Janet, 374
repertory theatre, 31, 33–4, 44–8
Return Fare (revue), 49, 51–2, 55, 58
Review (British Erotic Print Society), 353
Revill, Clive, 117
revues *see names of specific revues*; Phillip Street Theatre
Reynolds, Burt, 327, 328
Rhinoceros (play), 95
Richard, Cliff, 288–9
Richardson, Henry Handel, 150
Richmond, Ray, 328

Rickles, Don, 225, 375
Riddell, Alan, 61, 99
Riefenstahl, Leni, 294
Rivers, Joan, 297–8, 321, 366, 367, 375
Roadshow, 186
Robertson, Bryan, 93
Robinson, Canon, 14
Rock 'n' Reel Revue (revue), 77, 78–9, 268
Romeril, John, 204
Rook, Jean, 136–7
Rose, Lionel, 177
Rosencrantz, Claudia
   co-writes material with BH, 284
   devises *Dame Edna's Neighbourhood Watch*, 331, 334
   forms production company with BH, 322
   negotiates with NBC executives, 324–6, 329
   produces *Dame Edna Experience*, 283–4, 285, 290–3
   relationship with BH, 283–4, 293
Rosmersholm (play), 95
Ross, Andrew, 372
Roundabout (television program), 91
Rowell, Kenneth, 112
Royal Albert Hall, London, 244–5, 247
Royal Alexandra Theatre, Toronto, 377
Royal Ballet, 128
Royal Court Theatre Club, 100
Royal Melbourne Institute of Technology, 210
Royal Shakespeare Company, 104–5
Rushton, William, 137
Rusty Bugles (play), 28
Ryland, John, 136

Salter, June, 54, 56
Salvoni, Elena, 248
San Diego, 396
San Francisco, 366–7, 396
Sanders, Tom, 83, 92, 99, 166
Saroyan, William, 47
Saturday Night Live (television show), 221
Saw, Ron, 190
Sayle, Alexei, 243
Scacchi, Greta, 297
Scarfe, Gerald, 137
The Scream (painting), 222, 234, 238, 290, 334
The Secret Policeman's Other Ball (comedy gala), 243

INDEX

Senelick, Laurence, 360, 367–8, 369
The Sentimental Bloke (film), 182
Sergeant Pepper's Lonely Hearts Club Band (film), 227
Serle, Geoffrey, 190, 191
Severinsen, Doc, 326
Sewell, Brian, 305–6
Sex Pistols, 279
Sheen, Martin, 389
Sher, Anthony, 291
Sherrin, Ned, 262, 336
Shiel, MP, 127
Shores, Mrs (housekeeper), 12
Side By Side (film), 200
Silva, Victy, 300, 304–5
Sir Les and the Great Chinese Takeaway (television show), 351–3
Sisters of Perpetual Indulgence, 368–9
Sitwell, Dame Edith, 143
Six Day War, 146
The Six O'Clock Show (television show), 265
66 and All That (revue), 156
Skipper, Matcham, 68, 81
Slessor, Kenneth, 61
Smilde, Roelof, 62
Smith, Alex Bernard, 24
Smith, Dennis, 304–5
Snowdon, Lord, 275
So, John, 385–6
Society of West End Theatres Award for Best Comedy of the Year, 235
Soloway, Leonard, 373
Sondheim, Stephen, 217, 221, 340
'Sorry' debate, 386
The Sound of Edna (recording), 234
The Sound of Music (musical), 142
The South Bank Show (television show), 311
Spears, Steven J, 155, 234
Spectator, 122, 134, 311, 364, 395
Spencer, Charles, 358
Spender, Lizzie (BH's fourth wife)
 attends BH's award of CBE, 392
 does warm-up exercises with BH, 337
 life before BH, 318
 marries BH, 36, 318
 travels with BH, 321–2, 344, 351, 371
Spender, Stephen, 36, 318–19, 340
Spoleto, Italy, 318
Spycatcher affair, 365

St George Leagues Club, Sydney, 203
St James' Church, London, 239
St James' Church, Sydney, 55
St Kilda Palais, Melbourne, 295
St Regis Hotel, New York, 118
St Vincent's Hospital, Melbourne, 171–2
Stainton, Betsy, 66
Stainton, Philip, 66, 67
Standish, HA, 67–8
Stark, Graham, 126
Starr, Kenneth, 370
Starr, Ringo, 327
Startime (television show), 113
Stead, Carl, 128
Stead, Christina, 364, 368
Stephenson, Pamela, 243
Sting, 243
Stokes, John, 359
Stone, Sandy
 appreciation of by Peter Cook, 119–20
 BH plans to mothball, 90
 'Dear Beryl' monologue, 82
 emergence of as a character, 75–6
 features in BH's Christmas card, 249
 Harris pans 'Sandy Agonistes' recording, 112
 in *A Load of Olde Stuffe*, 176, 177
 in *A Nice Night's Entertainment*, 110
 in *At Least You Can Say You've Seen It*, 207
 in *Back with a Vengeance*, 300–1, 302–3
 in *Barry Humphries and Friends Back with a Vengeance*, 386–7
 in *Barry Humphries' Flashbacks*, 346, 347
 in *Excuse I*, 143, 144
 in *Housewife Superstar!*, 213
 in *Isn't It Pathetic At His Age*, 231–3
 in *Just a Show*, 154, 157
 in *Look At Me When I'm Talking To You*, 338–9
 in *Tears Before Bedtime*, 295
 'Sandy Agonistes' monologue, 92
 stage debut, 79
Strand Theatre, London, 301
Strasser, Eve, 33
Strindberg, August, 225
The Stronger (play), 225
The Stuffed Owl (anthology), 131
suburbia, 50, 176, 309–10
Suchet, David, 291

Summer of the Seventeenth Doll (play), 45, 51–2, 59
Sumner, John, 31–2, 44, 52, 130
Sun, 67
Sun-Herald, 113, 144, 157
Sunday Evening (painting), 267
Sunday Mirror, 122
Sunday Review, 177, 181
Sunday Telegraph, 358
Sunday Telegraph Magazine, 283
Sunday Times, 101, 190
Sutcliffe, Mr (principal), 14–15, 17
Sutherland, Joan, 95, 111–12, 145, 295, 340
Swanston Family Hotel, 68
Sydney Morning Herald, 74, 112–13, 144, 157, 177, 207, 233, 253, 340
Sydney Opera House, 64, 74, 215, 236, 269
Sydney Push, 62, 63, 68, 144
Sydney Theatre Company, 236
Sylvania (ship), 119

Takapuna, 82
Tasker, Ian, 229
Tasmanian Wilderness Society, 202
A Taste of Honey (play), 92
Taylor, Paul, 302
Taylor Sisters, 113
Te Kanawa, Dame Kiri, 275
Tea and Sympathy (play), 58
Tears Before Bedtime (revue), 255–7, 259–60, 269–73, 295
television, 73
temperance laws, 5
'Ten Little Australians' (exhibition), 148
Tennyson, Patrick, 319
The Tenth Man (play), 220
Teresa, Mother, 295
Terra Australis (revue), 32
Terrill, Ross, 309
Testimonial Performance (revue), 82–3
Thatcher, Margaret
   appears on *The Dame Edna Experience*, 282, 290
   BH parodies, 276–7, 278–9, 296
   caricatured by the *Spectator*, 311–12
   Edna as advisor to, 374
   Edna compares herself to, 263–4
   embarrassed at public ceremony, 276
   Germaine Greer on, 288

   personal style, 276–7, 279
   similarities with BH, 278
   Spycatcher affair, 365
Theatre Four, New York, 220, 321
Theatre on the Square, San Francisco, 366, 369
Theatre Royal, London, 243, 266, 303, 311, 356, 366
Theatre Royal, Sydney, 58, 142
Theatre Workshop, 132–3
Thomas, Wilfred, 112
Thoms, Albie, 155
Thomson, Brian, 221
Thomson, Helen, 342
Thomson, Ken, 221, 239, 245, 261, 340
Thomson, Lord, 136–7
Thorncroft, Antony, 248
Thorne, Angela, 278
Three Old Friends (play), 156
Thring, Frank, 49, 51, 66
Tiger Aspect, 385
Tighe, Edith, 125–6, 152
Till Death Do Us Part (television show), 330
Timbers, John, 196, 341
The Time of Your Life (play), 47
Time with Betjeman (television show), 255
The Times, 162, 196, 212, 213, 248
Tingwell, Bud, 54, 55
Tinker, Jack, 303
Tinkerbelle (writer), 226, 326
Tivoli Theatre, Melbourne, 60
Tivoli Theatre, Sydney, 62, 152
Tolson, Andrew, 289
Tomasetti, Glen, 69
Tong, Angela, 82
Tong, Jim, 82
Tong, Rosalind *see* Humphries, Rosalind
Tonight Show (television show), 295
Toronto, 377
Toronto Art Gallery, 116
Toronto, Canada, 116
Torrance, Joan, 131, 195
The Torture Garden (book), 127
Toscana (ship), 83
Touch of Elegance (television show), 338, 348
The Traveller's Tool (book), 354
Treasure Island (play), 146
Trudeau, Margaret, 295
Trump, Ivana, 390
Truth, 19, 26, 128

Tucker, Albert, 267
Tucker, Bert, 111
Tulloh, Clive, 351–2, 367, 385, 387–8
Turnbull, Malcolm, 365
TV Listener (magazine), 157
'The TV Showman' sketch, 49, 58
Twelfth Night (play), 44–7, 373
The Two Bazzas (revue), 203–4
Tycho, Tommy, 113
Tzara, Tristan, 132, 178

Ulmer Stadt Theatre, Germany, 210
Underhill, Jeffrey, 71
Union Theatre, Melbourne, 27, 30, 31
Union Theatre Repertory Company, 31–2, 33–4, 44
USA Today, 327
Utopian anarchism, 69
Utzon, Joern, 64

van der Post, Laurens, 318
van Outen, Denise, 395
Van Vechten, Carl, 22
Vanity Fair, 324, 380–2
Variety, 224
Veitch, Jock, 144, 179
Victorian Artists' Society, 77–8
Vidal, Gore, 294
Vietnam War, 148

Waiting for Godot (play), 65, 66–8, 82, 101
Wake in Fright (film), 189, 191
Waldheim, Kurt, 290
Walker, Bill, 129, 138
Walker, Dame Eadith, 269
Wall Street Journal, 375
Wallace-Crabbe, Chris, 69
Walters, Barbara, 323
Walton, Jaye, 338, 348
Wangaratta Festival, 74
Ward, Peter, 340
Ward, Russel, 76
Wardle, Irving, 162, 247–8
Warhol, Andy, 226, 326
Warneke, Ross, 385
Warrandyte, 73
Warsaw Ghetto, 10
Waterhouse, Robert, 162
Weaver, Sigourney, 389

Webb, Marty, 146
Weill, Kurt, 37
Welch, Raquel, 151
Wells, John, 137, 163, 239, 243
Werther, Frank, 71
Wesley Church, Lonsdale Street, 48
West, Morris, 54
Westmore, Brian, 33, 70, 92
Whelan the Wrecker, 80
White, Michael, 211, 220, 225, 248
White, Patrick
  BH writes threnody for, 320–1, 350
  commends BH's book, 217
  explores suburbia in writing, 124
  finds bicentennial celebrations excessive, 308, 309
  horrified when BH joins *Quadrant* board, 201
  introduces BH to Beresford, 149
  invites BH for lunch, 175
  on Australian dialogue, 59
  praises *Adventures of Barry McKenzie*, 190
  productions of *A Cheery Soul*, 236, 342
  savaged by Cyril Pearl, 157
  upsets BH, 174
Whitechapel Art Gallery, London, 93
Whitehall Theatre, London, 278, 352
Whitehouse, Mary, 288–9
Whiteley, Brett, 93
Whitelock, Don, 71
Whitlam, Gough, 197–9, 204–5, 216, 254, 340, 348–50
Whitlam, Margaret, 199, 349
Wild Life in Suburbia (recording), 105
Wilde, Oscar, 127, 164, 178, 287, 343–4
Wilder, Billy, 321
Williams, David, 389
Williams, Robin, 327
Williams, Shirley, 262
Williams, Simon, 262
Williamson, David, 189
Wilson, Dennis Main, 164
Wilson, Earl, 223
Without Walls: J'Accuse (television series), 336
The Wizard of Oz (musical), 236, 346
Wogan, Terry, 291, 295
Woman's Day, 210
Women in the Background (book), 343, 345–6
Women's Wear Daily, 223

World Student Relief, 27
World Theatre Season, 211
World War II, 10
Wren, Sir Christopher, 239
Wright, Brenda *see* Humphries, Brenda
Wright, Judith, 82
Wubbophonic Chamber Ensemble, 24
The Wubbos, 24
Wyatt, Tessa, 262
Wyndham Theatre, London, 132
Wynette, Tammy, 286

Xavier College, 34–5

The Young Elizabeth (play), 33–4
Young, Sean, 327

Picture Credits

Humphries family photographs: Michael Humphries

Barry Humphries as Orsino in *Twelfth Night*: the Arts Centre, Melbourne, Performing Arts Collection, Margaret Braybrook Collection

Barry Humphries and Peter O'Shaughnessy (photograph by Rhonda Small): the Arts Centre, Melbourne, Performing Arts Collection, Peter O'Shaughnessy Collection

Mrs Norm Everage appearing live on television: the Arts Centre, Melbourne, Performing Arts Collection, Barry Humphries Collection

Promotional photograph taken before *A Nice Night's Entertainment* opened at the Establishment Club, Soho: Lewis Morley

Edna Everage reading out her favourite recipes on the television program *Startime*: the Arts Centre, Melbourne, Performing Arts Collection, Barry Humphries Collection

Edna singing in *Excuse I*: the Arts Centre, Melbourne, Performing Arts Collection, Barry Humphries Collection

Portrait of Barry Humphries in 1963 (photographer unknown): the Arts Centre, Melbourne, Performing Arts Collection, Barry Humphries Collection

Handbill advertising Barry Humphries' one-man show *Excuse I* 1965, showing Humphries dressed in the costume of his many characters: the Arts Centre, Melbourne, Performing Arts Collection; the *Bulletin*, 6 November 1965

Barry Humphries with his portrait of Arthur Calwell: the Arts Centre, Melbourne, Performing Arts Collection, Barry Humphries Collection

Edna in conversation with Bob Rogers: the Arts Centre, Melbourne, Performing Arts Collection, Barry Humphries Collection

The Mendicant (Barry Humphries): the Arts Centre, Melbourne, Performing Arts Collection, Barry Humphries Collection

Barry Humphries arriving at a Melbourne Grammar function with friend (Herald and Weekly Times): the Arts Centre, Melbourne, Performing Arts Collection, JC Williamson Archive

Arthur Boyd, *Rosalind Humphries in a hospital bed with Barry Humphries* c. 1970 (National Gallery of Australia, Canberra, The Arthur Boyd gift, 1975): Reproduced with permission of Bundanon Trust

Barry Humphries dressed as Dr Wendy Toole (Peter Carrette, Icon Images): the Arts Centre, Melbourne, Performing Arts Collection, Barry Humphries Collection (George Fairfax Collection)

Barry Humphries with John Betjeman: Don Bennetts

Barry Humphries playing Dame Edna in *At Least You Can Say You've Seen It*: the Arts Centre, Melbourne, Performing Arts Collection, Barry Humphries Collection

Dame Edna at Royal Ascot wearing her Opera House hat (photograph by John Timbers): the Arts Centre, Melbourne, Performing Arts Collection, John Timbers Photographic Archive. The John Timbers Photographic Archive was donated by The Sidney Myer Fund in honour of Geoffrey Cohen, Trustee 1992–2003.

Dame Edna enjoying the grounds of Windsor Great Park with an Australian friend: the Arts Centre, Melbourne, Performing Arts Collection, John Timbers Photographic Archive. The John Timbers Photographic Archive was donated by The Sidney Myer Fund in honour of Geoffrey Cohen, Trustee 1992 – 2003.

Humphries playing the trade unionist Lance Xavier Boyle in *Isn't It Pathetic at His Age?* (photograph by D. B. Simmonds): the Arts Centre, Melbourne, Performing Arts Collection, Barry Humphries Collection

Barry Humphries poses for a photograph to celebrate his half- century: Newspix

Les Patterson relaxing on the beach: Newspix

Cover of the program for Humphries' show *Tears Before Bedtime*, featuring artwork by Diane Millstead: the Arts Centre, Melbourne, Performing Arts Collection, Barry Humphries Collection

Humphries on stage as Dame Edna Everage with a co-operative audience member at the end of *Tears Before Bedtime*: the Arts Centre, Melbourne, Performing Arts Collection, Barry Humphries Collection

Handbill for Humphries' show *The Life and Death of Sandy Stone*: the Arts Centre, Melbourne, Performing Arts Collection, Barry Humphries Collection

Claudia Rosencrantz on set with Dame Edna: Claudia Rosencrantz

Costume design for Dame Edna's 'Scream Dress': Costumes for Dame Edna designed by Stephen Adnitt

Barry Humphries in the garden at Lewis Morley's Sydney home: Lewis Morley

Acknowledgements

I would like to acknowledge the support of the Australian Research Council for a Discovery Grant that made the research for a large-scale project on Barry Humphries possible.

I acknowledge Barry Humphries for all his help with the research for this study. I would also like to acknowledge the very generous support of Michael Humphries, Barbara Johnson, Emily Humphries and Dorothy White.

I especially acknowledge the generosity of Rosalind Hollinrake in sharing her memories with me on many occasions. Special thanks are also due to Nick Garland who gave up hours of his time to talk to me and to show me his cartoon archive.

I particularly thank Angelo Loukakis for his encouragement and direction of the publishing project in the beginning. I thank Wendy James for her patience, insight and thorough work as research assistant throughout the process of researching and writing the book, and for her help on the work for the Discovery Grant project. I am very grateful to Amanda O'Connell for her sensitive and talented editing of the manuscript and for her gracious care of every aspect of the development of this book. I thank Lana Cooper and Elizabeth McClelland for their transcription of many interviews.

In particular I thank the staff of the Dixon Library at the

University of New England for their help with locating sources, particularly Meredith Duncan, Allison Hall and Kathy McMaugh. I thank the staff of the Performing Arts Centre Collection in Melbourne for the use of so many resources, and access to costumes for study. I especially thank Patricia Convery, Margot Anderson and Elyse White. I acknowledge the staff of the Petherick Room and of the Manuscripts Collection at the National Library of Australia. I am very grateful to Kate Dorney at the Victoria and Albert Museum, London, for taking the trouble to show me the Opera House hat and other costumes held there. I thank the staff of the National Film and Sound Archives, the Australian Broadcasting Corporation and British Film Institute for access to their archival materials.

The Menzies Centre for Australian Studies at King's College London hosted me during an Australian Bicentennial Fellowship devoted to this project. I thank Carl Bridge, Ian Henderson, Kath Kevin and Kirsten McIntyre for their generous support and help to me during my stay.

I am very grateful to John Lahr for his generosity in allowing me to read his papers in the Howard Gotlieb Archival Research Centre at Boston University, and for taking the time to share his knowledge with me. I thank Rosemary Brissenden for permission to read the papers of R. F. Brissenden held in the National Library of Australia. Special thanks are due to Harry M Miller for allowing me access to his papers with their detailed records of Humphries' shows in the 1970s. I acknowledge the generosity of Peter O'Shaughnessy for allowing me to read his personal papers held in Winchester in the UK, as well as the ones held in the National Library of Australia.

I am indebted to the following people for giving up their time to share recollections, information and resources for this project: Phillip Adams, Stephen Adnitt, Philip Bacon, Peter Batey, Don Bennetts, John Bird, Bruce Beresford, Wendy Blacklock, Barbara Blackman, Margo Braybrook, Zoe Caldwell, John Clarke, Barry Crocker, Ian Donaldson, Margaret Fink, Ross Fitzgerald, Jane Hamilton, Alan Hopgood, Jill Kitson, Don Laird, Ray Lawler,

ACKNOWLEDGEMENTS

John Levi, Joshua Blanchard Lewis, Roger McDonald, David Mitchell, Lewis Morley, Patricia Morley, Collin O'Brien, Philippa O'Brien, Charles Osborne, Fred Parslow, John Perry, Peter Porter, Nicholas Pounder, Claudia Rosencrantz, Elena Salvoni, Victy Silva, Barry Smith, Ken Stewart, John Sumner, Ken Thomson, John Timbers, Clive Tulloh, Frank Van Straten, Chris Wallace-Crabbe, Brian Westmore and Joy Westmore (Grissold).

Thanks are also due to Diane Millstead for allowing me to use her artwork, to Lewis Morley for allowing me to reproduce photographs and to Peter Carrette, Stephen Adnitt, Michael Humphries and Claudia Rosencrantz for permission to reproduce photographs and artwork.

I am particularly grateful for the ongoing support of friends and colleagues whose unflagging interest in, and willingness to share sources, made the project so enjoyable: Lizette Amorsen, Steven Amorsen, Lil Baad, Barbara Banks, David Banks, Bruce Bennett, Trish Bennett, Dean Biron, Frank Bongiorno, Leon Braun, Julian Croft, Sue Fell, Jane Ford, Rebecca Forge, Suzie Gibson, Lisa Gardiner, Glen Gardiner, Jane Goodall, John Gordon, Elizabeth Hale, Penelope Hanley, David Harman, Steve Harris, Monica Henman, Dorothy Jauncey, Adrian Kiernander, Susan Lever, Vicki McLean, Bruce Moore, Louise Noble, Peter O'Donoghue, Jane O'Sullivan, Felicity Plunkett, Julia Robinson, Pauline Richards, Richard Richards, Michael Sharkey, Russell Smith, Nicola Speden, Ruth Thompson, Fiona Utley, Stuart Ward and Michael Wilding.

Thanks also to Meredith Allen, Patricia Evans and Nicola Pedlingham of Barry Humphries' office for their assistance during the research and writing of this book.

Last but not least I thank the members of my family: Howard and Robyn Pender, Michael Pender and Connie Contis, Suzanne, David and Penelope Richardson, Sheila and Michael Morris, and Lex and Bob Duncan for their unstinting support and hospitality. In particular I thank my husband, Peter Quiddington, and daughters, Grace and Louisa, for putting up with me over so many months of hard work. To them I owe a great debt.

In 2002–03, Canberra-born Anne Pender was living in England, teaching Australian Literature at King's College London. She started work on a small project on Barry Humphries that grew and grew to become this full-scale biography. Anne holds degrees from the Australian National University, Harvard University and the University of New South Wales and now lectures in English and Theatre Studies at the University of New England. Her other books are *Christina Stead: Satirist* (2002) and Nick Enright: *An Actor's Playwright* (2008), an edited set of essays. Anne is married, has two daughters, and lives in Armidale in northern New South Wales.